THE SONS OF BELIAL

David Walsh

The Sons of Belial

*Protest and Community Change
in the North-West, 1740-1770*

The Growth of Capitalism on the
Eve of Industrialisation, Volume I

BREVIARY STUFF PUBLICATIONS
2018

First published in 2018 by Breviary Stuff Publications,
BCM Breviary Stuff, London WC1N 3XX
www.breviarystuff.org.uk
Copyright © David Walsh, 2018
The centipede device copyright © Breviary Stuff Publications

All rights reserved. No part of this publication may be reproduced, stored in a retrieval system, or transmitted, in any form or by any means, electronic, mechanical, photocopying, scanning, recording, or otherwise, without the prior permission of Breviary Stuff Publications

A CIP record for this book is available from
The British Library

ISBN: 978-0-9929466-9-2

Contents

Introduction	1
1. The Economic System in 1750s Britain	9
2. The Spread of Alternative Views of Trade and Commerce	17
3. The Seven Years War and the Onset of Modern Imperialism	35
4. Employer and Worker: Agency and Class	45
5. The Moral Economy in Theory and Practice	63
6. The Development of Cotton Manufacturing in Lancashire	77
7. The Changing Nature of Work Practices	87
8. Social Protest in Lancashire in the 1750s: Provisions	107
9. The Legal Death of the Industrial Moral Economy	127
10. Mass Protest in the 1760s: The Provisioning Sector	143
11. Mass Protest in the 1760s: The Industrial Sector	171
12. The Political Dimension: The Heightened State of Politics in the 1760s	183
13. The Political Dimension: The Preston Election of 1768	201
Conclusions	217
Bibliography	231
Appendices	249
Index	257

About the author

Dr David Walsh was formerly a Research Fellow of the Institute of Historical Research, University of London, Senior Research Associate, University of Liverpool and Lecturer in History at the Department of History and Economic History, Manchester Metropolitan University.

By the same author
Making Angels in Marble: The Conservatives, the Early Industrial Working Class and Attempts at Political Incorporation.

And in the fourth year of the dearth when George the son of George, had ruled the land thirty and one years; when the famine was sore in the land; there arose certain men the sons of Belial; and they took counsel together, and said There is corn in the land of Chester; go to let us buy all the corn in the land of Chester: for it will come to pass that the Lord will continue the famine yet three years. And when there is no bread in all the land, and that the people faint for the lack of bread, we will sell unto the people bread for their money at our own price: and when their money doth fail, we will sell unto them for their cattle; and we will give them bread in exchange for their horses; for their flocks and for their herds both of great and small cattle. And it shall be, when we have bought with our corn, and our bread, all their cattle, small and great, that they will sell unto us their houses their orchards, and gardens; their corn-fields, their meadows, and pastures; their woods, yea, all their land, and themselves also: and we will buy them and their land, and they, and their seed after them, all the servants unto us for when the sons of Belial did as they had counselled, and they bought all the corn in the land of Chester, and the sum was exceeding great: but the cry of the people for want of bread did reach the ears of the king and the Mug's counsellors; who took counsel together how they might preserve the lives of the people: for they wish not of the deeds of the sons of Belial, and that the sons of Belial had added by their counsels unto the sufferings of the people. So the king and his councils did order that corn should be brought from foreign lands to nourish the people.

And when the sons of Belial saw that by the wisdom of the law the king and his counsel had made that corn was plentiful in the land; and that their counsels were brought to nought like the counsels of Akithrophd, they went unto the merchants of the city even to several rulers of the city and said unto them: You know how the time of plenty maketh the people to be idle and that you can have no more work done for two-pence in times of plenty than ye can have done for one penny in times of dearth and famine. Now therefore as it is not good for you nor for us that bread be plentiful in the land; lend unto him upon usury to many talents in gold, and talents of silver as may be necessary; and we will buy also all the corn that is brought into the land and will sell unto the people for two talents, what we buy for one talent: and when we have sold unto them till their money fail we will sell unto them, for their cattle yea, we will buy their cattle, and their land, and themselves also, to be our servants, and we will divide the people, and their land, and their cattle between you and us; and the people, and their sons and daughters, yea even the great men and the rulers of the neighbouring cities shall serve us and you; as men servants, and maid servants, as hewers of wood, and drawers of water, forever. Now the chief men of the city did hearken the words of the sons of Belial, and did take a covenant between themselves and the sons of Belial and delivered unto the sons of Belial sixteen hundred talents of gold and twenty thousand talents of silver; and the sons of Belial did therewith buy all the corn which the merchants of the cities of the sea had brought into the land; and they did cause that the famine did increase. Yet was there found among the chief men of the city, some that did not worship Belial, or go astray after the manna of un-righteousness, or hearken unto the words of the sons of Belial.

The Truth in a Mask or the Shude-Hill Fight, John Collier (Tim Bobbin). (Manchester, 1758) pp. 1-3. Belial was originally a Hebrew term of several usages, but came to be indicative of an opponent of God, whose sons are suggestive of a lawless, evil force, focused on self-gratification and greed.

Introduction

The primary focus of discussion in the following study is the impact and effects of the introduction of new methods of industrial production in the cotton sector in the North-West of England between 1740 and 1770. It attempts to specify quite distinctly the point at which the traditional system of this branch of textile manufacturing underwent such significant change as to justify the onset of an Industrial Revolution. However, in order to give context to the impact of this change a range of related topics and areas have to be investigated including just where the ideas for the transformation of the practical application of economic processes came from and the effects these had on the labouring population of the region. Also the cultural and political *milieu* within which this transformation was occurring will also have to be considered, as will related aspects of the provisioning of essential foodstuffs which were an ever-present concern to the working population as this time and which itself was undergoing a process of an alteration from marketing practices which attempted to protect the most vulnerable consumers dating back centuries, to a more open system based on the principles of political economy.

The causes and origins of the Industrial Revolution has been mulled over since the nineteenth century and it continues to be the subject of intense debate, indeed over the last twenty years or so even the term itself has been called into question.[1] In fact originally it was not used in the British context at all, but from the early nineteenth century in relation to change taking place within French industry.[2] Yet it was Britain that Marx had in mind when he developed his theory of the consequences of the rise of modern capitalism in *Das Kapital: Critique of Political Economy* in 1867. Before him and an undoubted influence on Marx was Friedrich Engels' *The Condition of the Working Classes in England* first published in 1845 but not into English for another forty years. However, among the British themselves the term 'Revolution' was rarely if ever used to describe the momentous and transformative effects of what had been happening during the previous hundred years or so. What early writers tended to focus on were either the changes in economic organisation concentrating on the moves towards a 'scientific' understanding of the nature and practices of economic developments and the triumph of political economy, or the heroic impact of innovators and inventors such as Hargreaves, Arkwright, Crompton, Wedgewood, Boulton, Watt, Stephenson and many others.[3] The first British academic to actually use the term in its present context was Arnold Toynbee in a series of lectures to undergraduates at Oxford given between 1881 and 1882 which were published under the title *Lectures on the Industrial Revolution in England* in 1884. Indeed it was Toynbee's integrative approach that examined the effect of changes to British agriculture, population growth, industrial development and, importantly, the impact this had on the conditions of the

---

1 Rondo Cameron, 'A New View of European Industrialization', *The Economic History Review*, Second Series, Vol. 38, No. 1, (1985) pp. 1-23. See also by the same author, 'The Industrial Revolution: A Misnomer', in Jurgen Schneider, (*ed*). *Wirtschaftskräfte und Wirtschaftwege: Festschrift für Hermann Kellenbenz* (5 vols., Stuttgart: Klett-Cotta, 1981), v, pp. 367-76.

2 Anna Bezanson, 'The Early Use of the Term Industrial Revolution', *Quarterly Journal of Economics*, XXXVI (1922), pp. 343-9; Claude Fohlen, *Qu'est-ce que la révolution industrielle?* (Paris: Laffont, 1971), pp. 16-20. J. J. Fazy, *Principes d'organisation industrielle pour le développement des richesses en France* (Paris, 1830), p. 271. Travers Twiss, *View of the Progress of Political Economy in Europe since the Sixteenth Century* (London, 1847), p. 226.

3 See, for example, Andrew Ure, 'This island is pre-eminent among civilized nations for the prodigious development of its factory wealth'. *The Philosophy of Manufactures. An Exposition of the Factory System of Great Britain* (London, 1835), p. 6.

working class and his conclusion was that it was the advent of capitalist competition that was the significant feature of this change.[4] This 'class' centred approach to the impact of the Industrial Revolution was taken further by the widely read work of John and Barbara Hammond in the first decades of the twentieth century.[5] On the purely economic front the first criticism of the uniqueness of the event came from Joseph Schumpeter whose analysis of long-wave cycles provided the argument that similar 'revolutions' had, in fact occurred previously.[6] Similarly historians during the inter-war period emphasised the gradual nature of change across the industrial sphere even after 1750 pointing out in the case of Sir John Clapham that several areas of manufacturing remained unchanged by 1850, whilst Carus-Wilson and John Nef argued for the significance of major changes dating back to the thirteenth century in the case of the former and the Tudor and Stuart periods for the latter.[7]

This gradualist approach remained the state of the debate until the 1960s when a series of re-interpretations emerged. In the immediate post World War II era T. S. Ashton's *The Industrial Revolution 1760-1830* was somewhat ambiguous as to the accuracy of the term suggesting that economic change is rarely if ever 'revolutionary' but rather an accumulation of practices affecting intellectual and social as well as economic change, yet conversely this small but highly influential book did successfully re-establish the view that the eighteenth century was the crucial turning point.[8] Building somewhat on Nef's work W. W. Rostow offered the attractive allusion of tentative beginnings leading to an acceleration of growth which he appropriately termed 'take-off' akin to an aircraft leaving the runway into full flight. Whist Deane and Cole began to seriously interrogate the statistical data across a range of features of economic and social change suggesting that notions of a 'take-off' were a gross over-simplification, but that the pace of change did quicken from the end of the seventeenth century.[9] Eric Hobsbawm by the middle of the 1960s was in no doubt that something revolutionary took place in Britain from the middle of the eighteenth century suggesting indeed that what this constituted was one of the most important events in the history of the known world up to that point.[10] Crucially it was in the modern work of Hobsbawm that the crossover began, from the emphasis purely on the economic transformation into social consequences of dramatic change, and this mantle was brilliantly explored in

---

4   Arnold Toynbee, *Lectures on the Industrial Revolution of the Eighteenth Century in England* (London, 1884; reprinted 1920), especially pp. 64-73.
5   J. L. Hammond and Barbara Hammond, *The Town Labourer, 1760-1832* (London, 1917); Idem., *The Skilled Labourer, 1760-1832* (London, 1919).
6   Joseph A. Schumpeter, *Capitalism, Socialism and Democracy*. (New York: Harper & Row, 1942).
7   J. H. Clapham, *An Economic History of Modern Britain*, i, (Cambridge: Cambridge University Press, 1926), p. 143-5. E. M. Carus-Wilson, 'An industrial revolution of the thirteenth century', *Economic History Review*, 11 (1941), pp. 39-60. X J. U. Nef, *The Rise of the British Coal Industry*, i. (London, 1932), p. 165, Nef, 'The Progress of Technology and the Growth of Large-Scale Industry in Great Britain, 1540-1640', *Economic History Review*, 5/1 (1934), p. 24.
8   T. S. Ashton, *The Industrial Revolution, 1760-1830* (Oxford: Oxford University Press, 1948).
9   Walt Whitman Rostow, *The Stages of Economic Growth: A Non-Communist Manifesto* (Cambridge: Cambridge University Press, 1960). Phyllis Deane, *The First Industrial Revolution* (Cambridge: Cambridge University Press, 1967) pp. 117; Phyllis Deane and W. A. Cole, *British economic growth, 1688-1959: Trends and Structure* (Cambridge: Cambridge University Press, 1962).
10 Eric Hobsbawm, *Industry and Empire, from 1750 to the Present Day*, (Harmondsworth: Penguin, 1968), p. xi.

INTRODUCTION

Edward Thompson's *The Making of the English Working Class*, which brought to vivid life the world of ordinary working people amongst the impact of devastating transformation.[11] More will be said about the historiographic influence of Thompson in the course of the foregoing discussion but it is worth noting here that this book left an enormously powerful impression on the way historians perceived this vitally important period whether one agreed with his findings or took issue with them. In more recent years the consensus of the arguments has been that academics have been more circumspect when discussing 'revolutionary' change. Musson for example in the 1970s suggested that the short shock of transformative change that a revolution would comprise was not tenable when examining the period, whilst firstly Knick-Harley and then Nick Crafts argued that very often the economic growth rates attributed to the period from the end of the eighteenth century up to 1830s do not support the conclusion of any 'take off' at all and as a consequence bring to the fore once again the questioning of the possibility that an 'Industrial Revolution' ever happened.[12]

Yet this was not in fact the true state of the ensuing historiography, the term continued to be used, but in more refined and specific ways. The position adopted in the study below is that change was more often determined depending on the region examined and indeed the industrial sector under investigation. Thus although the rates or aggregate totals of economic growth were themselves downgraded in terms of importance, nonetheless, as Hobsbawm noted years before, it was the process of transformation which had been started at some point in the second half of the eighteenth century which was the crucial feature which was in fact a watershed of historic proportions and affected everyone it touched.[13] Unquestionably, Britain was at the end of the seventeenth century and in the first decades of the eighteenth in a very favourable position compared to its major European competitors vying for commercial and trading ascendency. The agricultural base was solid enough to provide conditions for stable demographic growth and an existing workforce which was as capable and proficient as any on the continent. It had a huge advantage in terms of the availability of the vital raw material of coal as a means of providing not only fuel but ultimately as a source of power. As an island nation it was relatively secure and free from the continental machinations which appeared on an almost yearly basis in Europe. It possessed a vast colonial and imperial territorial mass with which to extract primary products and export finished goods on very favourable terms, and had a political and economic system which appeared to be geared to exploit these favourable advantages to the maximum. These are often the key features which those contributing to the historiography appear to agree on, but still find it difficult to come to any definite conclusions about what all this really represented in terms of its overall significance and, importantly, in relation to what was about to happen over the course of the next century. Yet within this

---

11 E. P. Thompson, *The Making of the English Working Class* (London: Littlehampton Book Services Ltd., 1963).
12 A. E. Musson, *The Growth of British Industry* (London: B. T. Batsford Ltd., 1978), pp. 8, 62-5, 107- 14, 139-142. C. Knick Harley, 'British industrialisation before 1841: evidence of slower growth during the industrial revolution', *Journal of Economic History*, 42/2 (1982), pp.267-289. N. F. R. Crafts, *British Economic Growth during the Industrial Revolution* (Oxford: Oxford University Press, 1985), ch.1; Idem, 'British economic growth, 1700-1831: a review', *Economic History Review. 1983/2*. See also N. F. R. Crafts and Knick Harley, 'Output growth and the British industrial revolution: a re-statement of the Crafts-Harley view', *Economic History Review*, 45/4 (1992), pp. 703-730.
13 E. Hobsbawm, ibid.

vast and mesmerizingly detailed but often conflicting historiography there is little known about when this course of change actually began. This is where the present study strives to enter into the discussion, insofar as that it was the impact of a dramatic change in attitudes of those in positions to determine the manner in which the organisation and actual practices of the productive process were to be carried out. Thus the principal concerns here are three inter-connected features of this process of change. Firstly, the nature of economic thinking needs to be considered in the decades leading up to the moment when the new practices began to be introduced. It needs to be ascertained just how different the new proposals were to the more traditional economic system that was in place and what they actually consisted of. Secondly, this study will examine the new practices involved in a specific industry, in this case the cotton textile sector in the North-West of England. It will look at who was making these changes, their reasons, what they actually consisted of and, crucially, how they were received by the emerging working class who were affected by the changes. It was these communities of working people who felt the full influence of the changes being enacted, some of them impacted remarkably quickly, others took more time to develop, but overall these communities were transformed and it is how the emerging working class encountered and dealt with this process which is one of the primary concerns of this study. Thirdly, this period under discussion was one in which the political culture of the nation was undergoing a significant transformation and it was often one in which questions relating to how the economy operated, how it could be improved, and the overall economic direction of the country were placed at the centre of the debate. This involved the nature of power and how it was to be used and, indeed, by whom. This is important because if the new men instigating the changes were to have lasting success they would need political support to make their practical innovations permanent and legally binding.

It is acknowledged within the historiography of the development of industrial capitalism that the North-West and specifically Lancashire played a crucial role in the engine of economic change in eighteenth-century Britain. However, there exists surprisingly little rigorous study into the effects of this change on the region's inhabitants during this period of social and economic transformation. In 1724 Defoe described Manchester as "the greatest mere village in England";[14] by 1780 the town and the North-West generally was becoming the template for the new industrial system. This was a system that was deploying factors of production in a radically new and methodological manner along lines of classical political economy. Yet in 1740, again in reference to the existing historiography, there are precious few indications of imminent transformation. The key question therefore is what features can be detected that reflect the changes that impacted on the local population of the North-West in the period between 1740 and 1780? One, now traditional, method of attempting to detect societal change is to examine displays of popular protest and disaffection, and this is an area that the proposed study will use as a means of relating just how the working people of the region reacted to circumstances which to them were of enormous importance. They realised quite early in the process just what the changes being attempted by the masters would mean and they resorted in some cases to displays of protest, which encapsulated direct action, and in others they used quite sophisticated methods of collective organisation.

---

14 Daniel Defoe, *A tour thro' the whole island of Great Britain, divided into circuits or journies* (London: JM Dent and Co, 1927 Everyman edn.), Vol. ii, p. 261.

Introduction

This book builds on previous research. Between 1990 and 1993 I was the Senior Research Associate working on a project looking at social protest and community change in the West of England, 1740-1840. This was funded by the ESRC and jointed sponsored by the Universities of Birmingham and Liverpool and headed by Professor Adrian Randall and Andrew Charlesworth respectively. It was the source of subsequent publications. This book is designed to carry the knowledge and expertise gathered during the previous project into what is under-researched geographical area. Between 1760 and 1800 Lancashire and North West underwent a dramatic economic and social transformation. The foundations that were laid in this region at this time were to change the essential fabric of this country in a variety of ways. The classical prerequisites to the development of a truly capitalist industrial economy are the existence of the mechanisms of marketing organised to sustain a stable or growing population, an explosion in the growth of manufacturing, increased urbanization and the existence and expansion of a dynamic entrepreneurial and powerful merchant middle class. All these were to be found in the development of the North-West in the first half of the eighteenth century and beyond. However, apart from the well-trodden path of progress in the production of cotton goods, little has been researched or written about the changes affecting the population and, importantly, the communities of working people in the North West. In some small way this study hopes to redress this imbalance.

It is not in dispute that from the second half of the eighteenth century the applied and theoretical economic structure of Britain underwent significant change. The classic example of this has been traditionally depicted as coming in the cotton sector of the textile trade and, more specifically, located in the North West. But why did this take place in the North West? It is the contention of this research that it occurred due to a series of interconnected developments starting with the arrival and eventual dominance of a relatively new type of textile master; the 'fustian masters' who saw their opportunity emanating from the so-called 'Manchester Act' of 1736. This allowed these new masters to expand into the calico sector. Fortuitously, this came at the start of what economic historians such as McKendrick, Mockyr, Crafts and De Vries have described as the *domestic* industrial revolution. These new masters began to apply capital to the fustian and smallware sectors of the cotton trade. It is an indisputable fact that under the capitalist system of the three factors of production only the price of labour is capable of being meaningfully controlled by the capitalist. Hence keeping down the cost of labour became a priority as did the terms of employment, conditions and productivity of the work being performed. This research attempts to show that these masters did this in the North West especially in terms of the spinning and weaving undertaken by workers. The traditional practices of these workers were under severe threat by the 1750s and they reacted by resorting to combinations. This came at the same time as living conditions and costs, especially of food, were rising, with protests singling out attempts to maximize profits by middle men, corn factors, millers, brewers and, of course, farmers. Here we see how the capitalization in both essential provisions and the terms of work practices combined in the 1750s to provide a highly unstable and volatile social environment. However, these developments were not peculiar to the North West, similar developments were taking place in other textile areas associated with the production of woollen cloths, most notably the West of England and the West Riding of Yorkshire. Yet there the traditional worker practices and customs were maintained for much longer than in the

North West. Arguably the Manchester masters resolved to alter the existing nature relations between employer and worker as soon as the realisation began to become apparent following the 1736 parliamentary ruling. Certainly by 1747 workers had become sufficiently concerned as to amend the role of their nascent trade union, known at the time as the 'box club'. From this point through to the 1750s their resistance to the masters become much more concerted. By 1758 the masters sought to move more aggressively against their workers. If the 1736 Manchester Act had served to clarify the existing statutes concerning cotton goods, then what they attempted in 1758 was to make new law, on this occasion bypassing parliament and appealing to the highest judiciary. As we shall subsequently discover, when they did so they were extremely fortunate or well informed in making this appeal to the Lord Chief Justice, who was openly critical of the monopolistic nature of mercantilism. To a significant extent what Lord Mansfield did on this occasion decided the dispute between the employers and their workers to the unambiguous advantage of the Manchester industrialists. Yet crucially the magistrates of the North-West, (many of whom would have been sat on the Grand Jury at the Assizes presided over by the Lord Chief Justice), as the traditional arbitrators in disputes between masters and men, received the message sent by Mansfield's ruling loud and clear. Over the next four years worker resistance was crushed and the field was clear for the new masters. Then at the conclusion of the Seven Years War in 1763 not only were the domestic trade and European exports available for exploitation but now also the vastly increased British Empire. It was from the end of 1760s that the main innovations were deployed in the cotton trade, especially in spinning and weaving, with the precedent now fixed and clear that the masters were free in law to force their practices on resistant workers. This will be the core of the foregoing investigation and it is the establishment of its evidential value of such a hypothesis that concerns this research.

A key conceptual problem to be investigated is whether the purity of Edward Thompson's 'moral economy' model holds good in light of the pressures being faced by labouring communities in the North-West at this pivotal period of industrial and social transformation. In Thompson's classic model the moral economy was the tried and tested method open to the crowd to display and act on behalf of perceived grievances and blatant injustice. According to Thompson and backed up by historians of the early modern period such as Buchanan Sharp, Keith Wrightson and more recently Andy Wood[15] these customary practices were sanctioned not only in long-standing common law and the Book of Orders but also in statute law. By those displaying social protest in this manner, this relationship of a justification to act was perceived as deriving from the ancient rights of the 'free born Englishman' as contrasted with the tyranny of other nations. They existed and laboured in trades in harmony with a consciousness of a moral economy which they understood sanctioned them to protect their customary rights and justified their actions accordingly. Thompson was of the belief that it was the perceived right of the crowd to nudge the powerful into acting in support of the crowd's legitimate demonstrations and actions, especially in terms of access to the essential necessaries of life, without which they faced

---

15 B. Sharp, *In Contempt of all Authority*, (London: Breviary Stuff, 2009 edn.) Keith Wrightson, *English Society, 1580-1680*, (London: Routledge, 1982) *Poverty and Piety in an English Village, Terling, 1525-1700* (Oxford: Clarendon Press, 1995) *Earthly Necessities. Economic Lives in Early Modern Britain, 1470-1750*, (New Haven: Yale University Press, 2000). A. Wood, 'The Place of Custom in Plebeian Political Culture', *Social History*, 22, 1, Jan. 1997.

starvation. This was unquestionably about power: the powerless invoking their only recourse to apply pressure on the powerful. However, for Thompson the model was quite pristine and well defined in its operation. It was for example legitimate for the crowd to go after corn factors, millers, farmers etc. who may have been contravening accepted customary rules against forestallers, regraters and engrossers. Outside of these fairly tight parameters Thompson's paradigm was unwilling to broach. Increasingly, however, in the course of preliminary research this 'pure' model appeared to be in need of expansion in the case of the North-West. Here industrial change seems to have been indelibly intertwined with the customary practices of the moral economy prevalent throughout Britain at this time. Therefore the key exercise here is to show that the former practices of the labouring and artisan communities in the North-West underwent change linked to modified work practices and how this is related to traditional displays of protest associated with the moral economy. Before outlining how this process appeared to be developing, a brief discussion of the pertinent historiography is appropriate. The essential aim of this overview is to discover from little used source material what was happening in one of the economically socially dynamic parts of Britain during a period (1740-1770) when some of the most intense change and social tension throughout the whole of the eighteenth century was taking place. It also reflects the added and somewhat topical interest of how a society copes with the dramatic and at times violent periods of change from a well-entrenched (or traditional) social and economic system to a relatively and occasionally unsettling new set of processes. This, many (historians) would argue, is where the study and practice of history comes into its own. In this sense the task is the pulling together the various strands of empirical research and historiographic evaluation.

1
The Economic System in 1750s Britain

It is a common perception that for most of the eighteenth century British trade and commercial policy was based on the principles of mercantilism. However, it needs to be stated at the outset that the policies associated with mercantilism varied from country to country across Europe and that the British variant went through significant change, from the version commonly attributed to that initiated in the sixteenth century to that which existed in the middle of the eighteenth century. Undoubtedly, there was considerable thought being given to the nature of trade and commercial practices of Britain in the first half of the eighteenth century.[1] It is convenient but ahistorical to criticise the mercantilist system based on comparisons with how trade, commerce and the introduction of the discipline of economics subsequently developed. Ostensibly, mercantilism was a system of trade and commerce that evolved over time but was primarily concerned with the security and protection of the state, its inhabitants and the preservation of British political culture. As a means of organisation in the British context, mercantilism was remarkable and historically noteworthy in that from its earliest manifestation it was centralised and quite uniform in its application by the state. It was a practice common in Europe from the 16th to the 18th centuries. The central aim was to stimulate governmental regulation of the national economy by augmenting state power at the expense of rival national powers.

Mercantilism has suffered the obloquy of successive thinkers on economic policy from Adam Smith onwards, but it should be remembered that its constituency and influence did not end with the publication of *Wealth of Nations* in 1776. Very powerful economies such as the United States and Germany followed strict protectionist policies promulgated by the central state towards the end of the nineteenth century and into the twentieth. For all that can be said regarding anti-monopolies and *laissez faire*, the fact remains that in terms of fashioning national economic policies, the central state constituted one of the largest monopolies of them all.

According to conventional mercantilist beliefs, the only true measure of a country's wealth and success was the amount of precious metals (gold or silver) it possessed. If a nation had more gold than a rival did, it was necessarily more affluent. This idea had important implications for economic policy. The best way of ensuring a country's prosperity was to strictly limit imports and encourage exports, thereby generating a net inflow of foreign exchange and exploiting the country's gold stocks. Such ideas were attractive to pre-industrial governments. Accumulating precious metals was believed to be necessary for a strong, powerful state. Britain specifically implemented policies that were designed to protect manufactories and traders and make the most of available income. The Navigation Acts restricted the ability of other nations to trade between Britain and its colonies, and were a classic example of state regulation under a mercantilist system. There were, however, other important ingredients to the

---

1 D. Defoe, *The Complete English Tradesman I*, (London, 1726) *The Plan of English Commerce*, (London, 1730); J.Vanderlint, *Money Answers All Things*, (London, 1736); G. Berkeley, *The Querist* (London and Dublin, 1735-1737); M. Postlethwayt, *Britain's Commercial Interest Explained and Improved*, two Volumes, (London, 1757).

operation of mercantilism in practice and the core fundamentals of its beliefs. In Britain Thomas Mun (1571-1641) wrote extensively on trade and national commercial policies. He was among the first to propagate the role played by the exportation of services, or invisible items, as valuable areas of trade in themselves, and made early overtures in support in the deployment of capital. He proposed ways of balancing trade as a "means to enrich a kingdom" by means of exporting more than importing. For Mun if a nation spends more than it makes then overall national wealth will decrease. Exports should be increased by decreasing imports. This could be best achieved by utilizing all available resources, promoting domestic productive capacity, export goods by using British resource means, and finally if a commodity is seen as too expensive in a local market consumers will attempt to buy from elsewhere if possible.[2] Following on from Mun's pioneering work, by the late seventeenth and early eighteenth centuries the belief grew that the idea that hoarding precious metals by the state or individuals was erroneous. Such national valuables needed to be put to work by investment in order to accrue even greater value.

This position was taken further by William Petty when he argued in *The Treatise on Taxes and Contributions* (1662) that intrinsic value is down to the labour taken to produce a given commodity. By the 1690s, Petty's work had aroused significant interest in the nature of the role of the central state. Of particular interest were Petty's theories and analysis on taxation policies, the balance of trade and national wealth, the velocity, supply and circulation of money, the role of interest rates and international trade and the range and extent of government investment. Pretty much the whole package of what should concern a modern economist.[3] By the 1760s, businessmen and early industrialists were becoming increasingly interested in related areas such as the availability and cost of labour; the introduction of significant and extensive investment in industry; the application of innovation and science to industrial needs, enhancements to national and local infrastructure to improve the transportation of commodities and people, and the necessity to reconsider the social and legal relations to industrial development.[4]

Mercantilism could be simplistically defined as constituted of the three 'Bs'; bullion, boats and bodies. Bullion or valuable but easily transferable precious metals were required to construct and maintain the Royal Navy which was pivotal to the survival of the nation. However, the success of the Royal Navy and its pre-eminence as the 'Senior Service' meant that these commodities were also needed to pay for any involvement Britain may have which required the use of armed forces. From the post-sixteenth century Civil War period Britain possessed a very small standing army, hence in the case of an armed conflict on

---

2 Thomas Mun, *A Discourse of Trade from England unto the East Indies*, (London, 1621) and *England's Treasure by Foreign Trade* (London, 1664).
3 Tony Aspromourgos, 'The life of William Petty in relation to his economics', *History of Political Economy 20*: 337-356 (1988) Eli Heckscher, *Mercantilism*. London: (London: Allen & Unwin, 1935). Charles H. Hull, (ed.) *The Economic Writings of Sir William Petty*, (London: Routledge/Thoemmes, 1899). Terrence Hutchison, 'Petty on Policy, Theory and Method' in *Before Adam Smith: the Emergence of Political Economy 1662-1776*. (Oxford: Blackwell, 1988). W. Letwin, *The Origins of Economic Science*. (London: Methuen, 1963).Ted McCormick, *William Petty and the Ambitions of Political Arithmetic* (Oxford: Oxford University Press, 2009). Guy Routh, *The Origin of Economic Ideas*. London: (London: Macmillan, 1989) .Joseph A. Schumpeter, *A History of Economic Analysis*. London: (London: Allen & Unwin, 1954).
4 Sidney Pollard, 'Investment, consumption and the Industrial Revolution', *Economic History Review*, Second Series, Vol. 11, No. 2, (1958), p. 215.

land she relied on being able to purchase the services of an army from overseas. This may have been an inconvenience for an aspirant major player on the stage of continental European power, but Britain was not that; and the lack of a permanent substantial army meant an enormous saving in terms of national assets. As an island nation geographically separated from the on-going struggles of continental Europe the belief was that as long as Britain maintained her navy she was relatively secure. The understanding that Britain was not permanently militarised filtered down to the ordinary people who made up the 'lower orders'. They lauded the fact they were 'free-born Englishmen' and not held in thrall by a large-scale armed force controlled and directed by the central state to cower or suppress the civilian population, as was the case, for example, of ordinary men and women in France.

Boats, however, not only refers to the Royal Navy, but also another method of raising revenues and collecting money by the importing and exporting of goods by means of an extensive maritime navy. It is unquestionably correct that from so-called Glorious Revolution of 1688 until 1815 Britain was engaged in series of conflicts; usually, but not exclusively, with France. However, although the Royal Navy was a vital and much needed means of securing the survival of the nation, in fact the British merchant fleet was the way in which such defence was achieved. All imports and exports were carried by the merchant fleet on a truly global scale. However, the British, following the lead of the Dutch, did not import commodities purely for domestic use, but an increasingly valuable aspect of British mercantilism was the re-export of imported goods. This was especially so in the case of Britain in the re-export of goods from the Empire or colonies. For example, the following is a list of commodities entering Britain from the Thirteen Colonies of North America, many of which would be re-exported.

New Hampshire	Cattle, lumber, fish, and fur
Rhode Island	Cattle, corn, lumber, and ships
Massachusetts	Fish, whale products, fur, timber products, metals and metal products, raw wool, and ships
Connecticut	Flour, dried meat, fish, rum, and iron bars
New York	Fur, timber, foodstuff, cattle, horses, beer, fine flour, flax, and iron bars
New Jersey	Cattle, flax, Indian corn (maize), wheat, and flour
Pennsylvania	Foodstuff, wheat, corn, apples, dairy cattle, glass, wine, beer, rope, and bricks
Delaware	Furs, tobacco, meat, grain, flour, bread, barrel staves, lumber, horses, cloth, and iron
Maryland	Flax, grams, corn, tobacco, fruit, vegetables, fish, iron, lumber, clay, bricks, beaver, and ships
Virginia	Wheat, flax, tobacco, corn, and iron
North Carolina	Tobacco, wheat, corn, forest products (tar, pitch, lumber), barrel staves, furs, metals, wine glass, and exotic birds
South Carolina	Rice, indigo, beef, silkworms, cotton, furniture, lumber, some tobacco, grapes, wine, olives, raisins, capers, and currents
Georgia	Rice, clay, pottery, cotton, indigo, tobacco, fruit, barrel staves, and pork

It was crucial in the mercantile system that the state maximise its revenues, thus goods coming into the country were subject to an import duty, and this was effectively passed onto the domestic consumer at first hand, but could be subject to an export duty if the goods were to be traded to another nation. Hence, the state collected revenues from the operations of the maritime fleet for both goods entering and exiting the country although it had in effect contributed nothing to the intrinsic value or, indeed, production of such commodities. It was this aspect that so exasperated Adam Smith. He made the distinction between capital accumulation and revenue accumulation. The former employs productive labour whilst the latter utilises unproductive labour. According to Smith, "Investment (the utilisation of capital) sets to work productive labour... The proportion between capital and revenue... seems everywhere to regulate the proportion between industry and idleness. Wherever capital predominates, industry prevails: wherever revenue, idleness."[5] Thus, the call from Smith was clear, government should keep interference in the role of trading, manufacturing and commercial activity to a minimum and cut back as far as possible in setting tariffs and duties on the flow of trade. What we see in Smith's strictures is the birth of the modern term 'capitalism' and its usage as a process and, above all, a set of guiding principles. However, his view was one that obviously ran totally opposite to the role of the state envisaged by mercantilists. Yet it was in fact a stance that had been gaining ground and being put into actual practice in the North-West from the 1740s.

Finally, 'bodies' refer of course to the citizens of the country. For the functioning of mercantilism, the role of the population was to staff the military and maritime fleets and to produce goods for the maintaining of national needs such as food but also to produce manufactures that could raise revenues. Eighteenth century British society was strictly hierarchical with the greatest wealth; be it coming from speculation in products from the colonies or from lucrative places created out of the 'revenue state' system reserved for the most powerful elites. However, gradually the role of manufactures gained increasing importance as we move towards mid-century. Land ownership and rentals were still the benchmark of visible elite status and social position, but more and more influence was being given over to the application of capital to produce goods for sale and profit. It was still a highly protectionist system with strict controls enforced by the state on what could be sold domestically so as not to damage the necessary acquisition of state revenues, and also to maintain a trading advantage over international competitors. Thus, a skilled worker could not ply his trade in France or Spain as this would be construed as giving a possible advantage to a rival power. Whatever advantages Britain possessed or could acquire as a military, commercial, trading or manufacturing power had to be protected at all costs.

By mid-century the 'middling sort' were gaining more influence as Edward Thompson tells us in his essay 'Patricians and Plebs':

> ... by mid-century they [the rising middle classes] were numerous enough- certainly in London and also in some large towns- to be no longer dependent upon a few patrons, and to have acquired the independence of the more anonymous market. There is a sense in which a middle class was creating its own shadowy civil society or public sphere.[6]

Thompson rightfully asserts that the middle class were probably a hundred years away from gaining significant political influence and power – in this area, they

---

5   A. Smith, *Wealth of Nations I*, pp. 319-320, see also pp. 314-316, (London: Penguin, 1999)
6   E. P. Thompson, 'Patricians and Plebs' in *Customs in Common*, (London: Merlin, 1991) p. 32.

were still largely dependent on the patronage of the elites no matter how much they may resent the fact – but they were by the 1750s gaining economic power and influence.[7] It was from this growing *bourgeoisie* that the pressure for economic change was most forcibly mounted. However, much of what follows below is concerned with the changing relations between employers and labourers in a specific manufacturing sector, at a precise moment when the transformation began in an explicit geographic location. Here, the north-west of England and, more precisely, the region immediately surrounding Manchester, the middle class manufacturers attempted to change the worker/master relationship decidedly to the advantage of the new masters who were consolidating their influence in the light cotton trade. We shall see that there were particular reasons why this change was required on the part of the masters. However, its needs to be stated that what made the events of the later 1740s into the 1750s even more galling for the labouring population was that these changes came after a period of improvement in the general living standards and relative independence of ordinary people. Thompson, for example, argues that the decades immediately preceding the 1750s and '60s were a time of great benefits to the labourers. As he tells us:

> The eighteenth century witnessed a qualitative change in labour relations whose nature is obscured if we see it only in terms of an increase in the scale and volume of manufacture and trade. This occurred of course, but it occurred in such a way that a substantial proportion of the labour force actually became *more* free from discipline in their daily work, more free to choose between employers and between work and leisure, less situated in a position of dependence in their whole way of life, than they had been before or than they were to be in the first decades of the discipline of the factory and of the clock.[8]

If we accept Thompson's position here, this locates the changes during the later 1750s and into the 1760s in even greater relief and makes them of major historical significance. This was so because they came just at the moment when working people were passing through a period when labour relations had reached their apogee and in a sector of manufacturing they were never to see again.

The relations in the mercantilist system between the elites, the middling sort, made up of gentry, professionals, men of commerce and up-and-coming manufacturers, and those groups below them was complex in eighteenth century society. The elites set policy, waged and went to war, and discussed great affairs of state. The middling sorts effectively ran the country in the day-to-day mundanities and in the provinces. It was to these groups that the lower orders had first-hand dealings, but it was to the elites that they expected legal and moral guidance. In the case of disputes between masters and men, these would be set at the foot of the justice of the peace. Here there developed a breach between the 'gentry' and the manufacturers of the middling sort. In 1738 in a letter signed by an 'Englishman' written to the Secretary of State, Lord Harrington, the writer complained of those woollen manufacturers who had attained the status of 'gentry', part of the accepted duties of which was to serve on the bench of the magistracy. "Whenever a tradesman is made a justice a tyrant is created." When these men were asked to arbitrate on cases relating to issues directly affecting working people they frequently were seen to be "beating down the wages of the

---

7 Thompson, ibid pp. 30 and 32.
8 Ibid p. 38.

poor" and paying them in truck, even though this was technically illegal. The writer suggested that the workers needed their issues to be addressed by the independent elites; the "men of great fortunes" in the form of a commission of enquiry "to attend to the evidence of the poor weavers."[9] Thompson was probably correct to suggest that the paternalistic and protectionist aspect of mercantilism was being distanced by the manufacturing middling sort when they considered the labouring class beneath them. Further, it would certainly appear that working people no longer expected such feelings or consideration from their employers, yet they still seem to have regarded the elites as retaining paternalistic qualities. At the beginning of the Seven Years War in 1756, the Palatinate of Chester wrote an address to the King. The language used reveals the nature of the expected relationship between the monarch and his people.

> Conscious, therefore, of your majesty's wonted justice and paternal affection for your people, we dutifully hope, that your majesty will kindly, and duly, consider the present unhappy situation of these once flourishing kingdoms… [Which] induce us to unbosom our thoughts to your royal consideration; not doubting redress from our grievances from a king who loves to be esteemed the father of his people.[10]

Exactly how real or meaningful the elites took this position of paternalism to heart and put into practice is immaterial, in the sense that if enough of the lower orders believed it to exist then, to a large extent, it served its purpose. Token gestures, such as discussing labour/employer relations in Parliament or pronouncements upholding existing laws against forestalling would be enough to sustain the belief that the groups at the very top of society had the well-being and protection of the masses in their thoughts. However, it was in the provinces and regions that the *loci* of conflict and its resolution were centred and where the initial indications of change can be seen. To a significant extent it fell to the magistracy to attempt to mediate between contending parties and to maintain order. It will be seen in the course of this study that the attempts by working people, either in seeking to maintain their customary work practices or in efforts to dissuade hucksters in the provision markets, resulted in (sometimes quite violent) protest as a means of showing to the local authorities, in no uncertain terms, their evident and very real grievances. Yet their displays should alert the historian to the fact that they were responding to a perceived threat which they believed they had the right to do. If the crowd could be assertive in its own defence so too could those of the middling sort whose thoughts increasingly turned to profits and making both human and monetary capital operate more effectively in their interest. They would produce the argument that they did this not merely for their own pecuniary benefit, but for the betterment of the nation as a whole. It is worth repeating, as it will become a point of focus and analysis later, that ultimately how subsequent developments unfolded came down to how the magistracy dealt with these competing social and economic factions in times of stress and change.

Social historians of the eighteenth century have noted that when the crowd displayed discontent in the form of protest or indeed riot, they did so in the understanding that this was a demonstration to the authorities to uphold their (dwindling and increasingly eroding) paternalistic responsibilities. These responsibilities were popularly viewed as entrenched in the traditionalist values

---

9 National Archives, Kew, State Papers Domestic, 36.47.
10 *Gentleman's Magazine,* vol, 25, 1756, p. 477.

of the protectionist nature of the mercantilist state.[11] It was, in essence, because of what they regarded as their natural, inalienable right, of being a 'free born Englishman', to herald this much used phrase, that the authorities offered some licence to the 'lower orders' to openly demonstrate their grievances and to act in order to mitigate the circumstances of the grievance. To ordinary working people this is what the existing state system had done for centuries. The problem was for those manufacturers who, as we noted, in the later 1750s were aiming to maximise the profitability of their capital and enhance productivity, the labourer was seen as *too* free. Thompson again expresses this more appropriately than many historians of the genre.

> ...this is the century [the eighteenth] of the advance of "free" labour. And the distinctive feature of the manufacturing system was that, in many kinds of work, labourers (taking petty masters, journeymen and their families together) still controlled in some degree their own immediate relations and modes of work, while having very little control over the market or over the prices for raw materials or food. This explains something of the structure of industrial relations and of protest, as well as something of the culture's artefacts and of its cohesiveness and independence of control.[12]

For this new breed of masters there was a need to re-shift the balance of labour relations in their favour, in effect changing the existing state system into one in which they possessed more control. This ran directly in the face of the customary nature of work practices among the cotton weavers in Lancashire. Thompson makes the vital point that an important part of the motivations of the 'lower orders' of their promoting the application of the 'free-born Englishman' to their actions was to capture some the constitutionalism which the elites shrouded themselves. Working people were conscious that the elites claim for social and political leadership rested on their (and the nations) prescriptive customary rights and privileges. If this were indeed the case they could had few logical or moral objections for the lower orders attempting to assert and retain their customary

---

11 E. P. Thompson, *Customs in Common*, (London: Merlin, 1991); G. Rudé, *The Crowd in History: A Study of Popular Disturbances in France And England, 1730-1848*, (London: Serif, 2005 edn.); A. Randall, *Riotous Assemblies, popular protest in Hanoverian England* (Oxford: Oxford University Press, 2006); A. Randall, 'The Industrial Moral Economy of the Gloucestershire Weavers in the eighteenth century' in J. Rule (ed.), *British Trade Unionism, 1750-1850*, (London: Longman, 1988); J. Rule, *British Trade Unionism: the formative years*, (London: Longman, 1988); J. Rule, *The Experience of Labour in Eighteenth-Century Industry*, (London: Croom Helm, 1981); J. Bohstedt, *Riots and Community Politics in England and Wales, 1790-1810*, (Cambridge, Mass.: Harvard University Press, 1983); J. Bohstedt, *The Politics of Provisions: Food Riots, Moral Economy, and Market Transition in England, c. 1550-1850*, (Aldershot: Ashgate, 2010); P. King, 'Edward Thompson's Contribution to Eighteenth-Century Studies. The Patriarch-Plebeian Model Re-examined'. *Social History*, xxi(2) (1996); N. Rogers, *Crowds, Culture and Politics in Georgian Britain*, (Oxford: Clarendon Press, 1998); D. Rollison, 'Property, Ideology and Popular Culture in a Gloucestershire Village, 1660-1740', *Past and Present* xciii (1981); D. Rollison, *The Local Origins of Modern Society: Gloucestershire 1500-1800* (London: Routledge, 1992); N. Landau, *The Justices of the Peace*, (Berkeley: University of California Press, 1984); R. W. Bushaway, *By Rite: Custom and Community in England 1700-1880*, (London: Breviary Stuff, 2011 edn.); B. Sharp, *In Contempt of all Authority*, (London: Breviary Stuff, 2009 edn.); K. Wrightson, *English Society, 1580-1680*, (London: Routledge, 1982); K. Wrightson, *Poverty and Piety in an English Village, Terling, 1525-1700*, (Oxford: Clarendon Press, 1995); K. Wrightson, *Earthly Necessities. Economic Lives in Early Modern Britain, 1470-1750*. (New Haven: Yale University Press, 2000); A. Wood, 'The Place of Custom in Plebeian Political Culture', *Social History*, 22, 1, (Jan.1997).

12 Thompson, 'Patricians and Plebs', in *Customs in Common*, op cit, p. 74.

rights. However, this was not how the Lord Chief Justice (himself a noted and vocal supporter of the elite's customary rights) saw the situation. He sided firmly with the new masters of Manchester in the cotton sector, which in an important sense takes us briefly back to the historiography of the emergence of the middling sort. This focuses on the nature of patronage and client status of the emerging middle class in Hanoverian Britain in relation to the gentry and aristocratic elites. The argument runs that indeed they were becoming a vital and increasingly powerful group as the eighteenth century moved on. However, this was a very slow process. Many years ago John Cannon suggested that the middle classes not only prospered in the eighteenth century but they did ultimately begin assume and construct political alternatives to elite political culture and hegemonic control. Yet this challenge came at the very end of the century.

> ...the questions to be explained seem to me to be almost the opposite of Marxist historiography – not how did they not come to control government, but why did they not challenge aristocratic domination until towards the end of the century?[13]

The nature of the clientage to the aristocratic and gentry elites by the middling sort is a point reinforced by John Brewer, who tells us that all those who provided services for the rich, "relied for their living on a culture centred upon the Court, Parliament and the London season."[14] The point to recognise in the case of the emergence of the Manchester textile middle classes is that they were not subject to the same degree of clientage as those from London or, indeed, of other sectors of the middle classes who owed their position and financial security on the fees paid to them by their elite patrons. From the outset, as we shall discover in the next chapter, these men were independent of clientage and elite patronage and sought to alter the existing rules, especially in the terms of trade, but also in attempting to alter existing legal and political relations in their favour. Thus we need to examine in more detail just what forces were emerging to challenge the existing beliefs regarding Britain's commercial and trading position and how this related to the perceived needs of the rising manufacturing groups of the North-West.

---

13 J. Cannon, *Aristocratic Century: the Peerage of Eighteenth-Century England*, (Cambridge: Cambridge University Press, 1984) p. ix.
14 J. Brewer, 'English Radicalism in the Age of George III', in J. G. A. Pocock (ed.) *Three British Revolutions*, (New Jersey: Princeton University Press, 1980), p. 339. See also by the same author, 'Commercialisation and Politics', in N. McKendrick, J. Brewer, and J. Plumb, *The Birth of Consumer Society*, (Bloomington: Indiana University Press, 1982).

2
The Spread of Alternative Views of Trade and Commerce

It would appear from the stance of conventional economic history, and the development of practices associated with the industrial revolution in the second half of the eighteenth century in particular, that Britain was in an economically advanced and dominant position in terms of a comparison with, say, France. Yet that was not necessarily how contemporaries saw these developments. From the concluding years of the 1750s into the 1760s there was growing pressure to affect change on the political, social and economic fronts in Britain. Before looking in more detail at the nature of this pressure, especially on the economic front, it is worth considering by way of a comparison just why this was important at this particular time. The main reason is that although the Tories as a functional political entity were rendered effectively redundant and emasculated of power until 1760 and the accession of George III, Britain was still an inherently conservative country. The belief in the value of customary practices – that is to say, practices and means of conducting affairs that had proved their effectiveness over several generations – was well enshrined in British political, social and, indeed, legal culture. To be sure, there were differences over policy and emphasis, especially amongst the Whigs, but the essentials of the conducting of politics and commerce remained effectively locked in a world view that had hardly changed since 1688 and the so-called 'Glorious Revolution'. This date is a particularly important one for those alive at any part of the eighteenth century as it symbolised the end of one of the most turbulent periods in British domestic history whereby three generations had known little but a tyrannical monarchy, rebellion, civil war, regicide, a dictatorial republic, a restoration and yet another monarchical crisis.[1] Yet more recently, the historiography has lessened the impact of the developments leading up to 1688 and focused on the maintenance of traditional institutions in terms of their social, political and religious constancy rather than their disruption, which was such a feature of the 1960s and 1970s interpretation.[2]

However, in both readings of developments it followed that extolling customary practice as a safe means of conducting affairs of state, affairs of law and affairs of commerce was a natural means of national self-preservation. The mercantilist system fitted perfectly with this perception of customary practice as

---

1 J. H. Plumb, *The Growth of Political Stability in England, 1675-1725* (London: Palgrave Macmillan, 1967) p. 1
2 C. Russell, *Parliaments and English Politics, 1621-1629* (Oxford University Press, 1979); G. R. Elton, *Studies in Tudor and Stuart Politics and Government*, 3 vols. (Cambridge: Cambridge University Press, 1974-83); J. S. Morrill, *Cheshire, 1630-1660* (Oxford: Oxford University Press, 1974), and *Reactions to the Civil War, 1642-1649* (London: Palgrave Macmillan, 1982). These titles are selected from a vast literature. See, however, L. G. Schwoerer, 'The Bill of Rights: Epitome of the Revolution of 1688-89', in J. G. A. Pocock, *Three British Revolutions: 1641, 1688, 1776*, (New Jersey: Princeton University Press, 1980), pp. 224-43; and M. Goldie, 'The Roots of True Whiggism, 1688-'94', *History of Political Thought*, (Cambridge: Cambridge University Press, 1980): 195-236; L. Colley, 'The Politics of Eighteenth-Century British History" *Journal of British Studies*, Vol. 25, No. 4, (Oct., 1986), p. 368, and the same author, *In Defiance of Oligarchy: The Tory Party, 1714-60* (Cambridge: Cambridge University Press, 1982), pp. 3-23.

it appeared to function over a long period, to the apparent benefit of everyone, especially the state, who gleaned their effective funding not only by levying taxes domestically but also by charging duties on goods entering the country and again when they were sold domestically or re-exported via the *entrepôt* system. In the short term this suited early eighteenth century governments well as it provided a regular and trustworthy source of funding for the frequent wars that Britain became involved in, a further example of the practice of what John Brewer termed the 'fiscal-military state'.[3] Thus it appeared – especially to those in power, or those with a direct stake in the existing system – that the state could only effectively function financially by maintaining the mercantilist system. Yet it was recognised by those who studied or were directly involved in trading matters that the system did not function as efficiently as it should.

As we move out of the formative system of trade and commerce of the later seventeenth century into the eighteenth century, two interconnected aspects were the primary interest of commentators. One was concerned with the theoretical and applied aspects of how the process of economics operated in its totality with regard to the British system of trade. There were calls for a much greater and in-depth understanding of all aspects of the system, and we will examine this feature later in the chapter. However, another major concern was the nature of commercial and trading co-ordination at the level of the state and how the particular variants of trade, manufacturing and commercial activity in the different regions of the country could be accessed and heard at the level of the central state, in order to influence its key policy decisions. One of the key problems was seen to be the lack of input as to the needs of specific branches of trade and the apparent closed nature of viable access to how policy was introduced and overseen at the level of national government. This in fact was recognised early as under the existing system it was effectively impossible to gain access to, let alone influence, the closed environment of government policies on trade and commerce. This was partly due to the nature of the factionary politics of the ruling Whigs, who were keen to keep as much hold on the making of key decisions as possible. A significant part of the problem was the role of the Board of Trade. In the early to mid-1690s Davenant and Whiston both put forward schemes for an independent Committee of Trade, to be established in order to mitigate the glaring deficiencies of government policies of commerce and trade, it would operate as a form of commercial parliament, comprised, either by election or appointment, of the leading representatives of all the major commercial, manufacturing and trading interests of the nation.[4] The Board of Trade that was established in 1696 was decidedly not independent and, in fact, was effectively an adjunct committee that reported in closed session only to the Privy Council and not even to parliament, and whatever influence it had was removed by the reforms of George III in the 1760s in his bid to eradicate the Old Whig factionalism and to make the British civil service more coherent. The desperate need of some viable form of allowing the trade, commerce and manufacturing interests to be heard in a non-party independent central authority led, between 1750 and the 1770s, to calls again for a Committee of Trade,

---

3 J. Brewer, *The Sinews of Power: War, Money and the English State, 1688-1783*, (London: Hutchinson, 1988), *passim*.

4 J. Whiston, *A Discourse on the Decay of Trade* (1693). Such a Committee of Trade "a yet fairer light, and insight ... (and) redress all those mal-administrations and non-improvements of trade which ... cannot so easily fall under a sufficient parliamentary inquiry". p. 4; see also Davenant, British Library, Harley. MSS, 1223, I, fols.187-89 (c. 1695); also see R. M. Lees, 'Parliament and the Proposal for a Council of Trade, 1695–6', English Historical Review, LIV (1939) 44-47.

equipped with a professional and well-trained personnel with direct access routes to all trading interests from across the nation.[5] Yet at this time such calls came to nought.

In fact, in Britain what we would describe as macroeconomic policy was firmly locked within the paradigm of mercantilism and all the facets which we associate with such policies, such as setting the value of the currency in relation to other currencies, domestic and foreign trade flows, import and export tariffs, and, hence, price controls and controls on levels of consumption of certain products, the granting of joint stock enterprises, taxation and the setting of interest rates, were controlled by the succeeding governments throughout the whole of the mercantilist period. However, some relatively new and small capitalist entrepreneurs in the North-West were beginning to shift the mercantilist paradigm with the microeconomic methods they were applying. A major reason for this was a distinctive change in attitudes towards, and the application of a radical set of approaches to, the factors of production, especially labour. Mercantilism on the one hand was, in essence, a means of gaining through trade the basic military security of the state and, on the other hand, protecting the commonwealth of the kingdom at large. It had been adapted over many generations to the peculiar needs of Britain, 'boats, bullion and bodies', but was essentially a collectivist vision of what was best for everyone – regardless of rank or station – throughout the entire nation. However, a fresh approach based partly on the early works of thinkers such as Grotius, Bernard Mandeville and Pufendorf, who looked at the Dutch patterns of trade and commerce, was stressing a more individualistic attitude as to how entrepreneurs and businessmen should conduct their affairs, which would, crucially, attempt to minimise the involvement of state in their profit making ventures.[6] Indeed, as early as 1711 in Britain *The Spectator* was arguing that the crux of a flourishing enterprise, and what was beneficial to the trading prospects of the nation as a whole, lay with the price of labour.

> It is the very Life of Merchandise to buy cheap and to sell dear. The Merchant ought to make his out-set, that he may find the greater Profit upon his Returns; and nothing will enable him to do this like the Reduction in the Price of Labour upon all our Manufactures. This too would be the ready Way to increase the number of our Foreign Markets: the abatement of the price of the Manufacture would pay for the Carriage of it to more distant Countries; and this consequence would be equally

---

5   M. Postlethwayt, *Great Britain's True System* (1757), pp. 9-13, 34-45, 57-66, 247-49; for example, "we have a Board of Trade, but it takes no immediate cognisance of the commerce of the kingdom...almost merely ... for political use". pp. 192-193. T. Mortimer, *The Elements of Commerce, Politics and Finances*, in *Three Treatises* (1772), The outline of his 'Eight Point Plan' on pp. 192-200.
6   C. L. Carr, (ed.), *The Political Writings of Samuel Pufendorf* (Oxford: Oxford University Press, 1994); Henry Clark, (ed.), *Commerce, Culture and Liberty: Readings on Capitalism Before Adam Smith*, (Indianapolis: Liberty Fund, 2003); E. G. Hundert, *The Enlightenment's Fable. Bernard Mandeville and the Discovery of Society*, (Cambridge: Cambridge University Press, 1994); J. Bell, *Hugo Grotius: Historian*.(Ann Arbor: Michigan University Microfilms, 1980); Hans W. Blom, (ed.): *Property, Piracy and Punishment: Hugo Grotius on War and Booty in De Iure Praedae- Concepts and Contexts*. (Leiden: Brill, 2009), H. W. Blom, L. C. Winkel, *Grotius and the Stoa*. (Assen: Van Gorcum Ltd, 2004); P. Borschberg, *Hugo Grotius, the Portuguese and Free Trade in the East Indies*, (Singapore and Leiden: Singapore University Press and KITLV Press, 2011); Stephen Buckle, *Natural Law and the Theory of Property: Grotius to Hume*. (New York: Oxford University Press, 1993)

beneficial both to the Landed and Trading interests.⁷

Yet this approach at this point had no real coherent body of theory, the nature of political economy and *laissez-faire* would have to wait until 1776 and the publication of Adam Smith's *Wealth of Nations* and those economists who followed him. Yet by the 1740s, 1750s and into the 1760s the flaws in the mercantile approach were being increasingly outlined and the belief in customary practices that lay at its base was simply being ignored as new methods were being applied. What began to be stressed was a phrase that would become so common as to require little explanation and, indeed, became a buttress of the capitalist system itself, but was in the mid-eighteenth century hardly used: '*private enterprise*' or the pursuit of private gain as untouched as possible by the interfering hand of government. Such a position would, of course, be taken by Smith and form the bedrock of his view that the eventual achievement of private gain would lead to the widespread benefits to the wider community and, indeed, the entire nation, through the operation of the 'invisible hand' guiding a free market economy instead of the regulations and overtly interfering visible hand of the state. This was in fact a dramatic change in prevailing contemporary attitudes. What Smith did in 1776 was to give codified expression to a growing set of opinions and arguments, (and actual practices in the North-West) which were getting more vociferous by the year.⁸ In fact, although these developments leading up to and beyond the enormously influential work of Smith are not the focus of this particular study, we do have to take note of what Smith was advocating, if only to compare and contrast this with what was being put forward by the earlier advocates of change. Thus it was the views of those producing the thinly veiled attacks on the mercantilist system up to the 1750s that is of primary concern here, and, importantly, how they were put into practice at a microeconomic level in the North-West. As we shall see in due course, the weavers of Lancashire believed it necessary to convert latent instruments of self-protection from 1747 into organisations of effective resistance to the actions of the capitalist manufactures. There is no record of them believing they had the

---

7 *The Spectator*, Letter Number 232, (26 November, 1711), pp. 384-385.
8 See for example, H. Forster, *An Enquiry into the Causes of the Present High Price of Provisions*, (London, 1767), M. Postlethwayt, *Britain's Commercial Interest Explained and Improved*, (London, 1757), J. Vanderlint, *Money Answers All Things*, (London, 1734), G. Berkeley, *The Querist*, (Dublin, 1737), E. A. J. Johnson, *Predecessors of Adam Smith*, (New York: P. S. King, 1937), Anon, *Remarks upon the Serious Dissuasive from an Intended Subscription for Continuing the Races*, (London, 1733), D. Hume, (ed. J. Rotwein), *Writings on Economics*, (London, 1955 ed.), J. R. McCulloch, *Essay on ... the Condition of the Labouring Classes*, (Edinburgh, 1826), F. Moore, *Considerations on the Exorbitant Price of Provisions*, (London, 1773), Anon, *Considerations on the Policy, Commerce, and Circumstances of the Kingdom*, (London, 1771), W. Temple, *A Vindication of Commerce and the Arts*, (Bristol, 1758) and the same author, *An Essay in Trade and Commerce*, (London, 1770), A. Young, *The Expediency of a Free Exportation of Corn*, (London, 1770), Anon, *Propositions for the Improving the Manufactures, Agriculture and Commerce of Great Britain*, (London, 1763), Anon, *The Causes of the Dearness of Provisions Assigned*, (London, 1767), Anon, *The Occasion of the Dearness of Provisions and the Distress of the Poor*, (London , 1767), J. Tucker, *Elements of Commerce*, (Bristol, 1755), and by the same author, *Four Tracts on Political and Commercial Subjects*, (London, 2nd edn., 1774), Anon, *Propositions for Improving the Manufactures*, (London, 1763), Anon, *Considerations on a Bill for A General Naturalization*, (London, 1748), P. Murray, *Thoughts on the Money, Circulation and Paper Currency*, (London, 1758), J. Steuart, *Inquiry into the Principles of Political Economy*, (Edinburgh, 1767), J. M. Low, 'An Eighteenth Century Controversy in the Theory of Economic Progress', *The Manchester School*, XX, (1952), and A. W. Coats, 'Changing Attitudes to Labour in the Mid-Eighteenth Century', *Economic History Review*, New Series, Vol. 11, No. 1 (1958), pp. 35-51.

need to do so before this date, and they did so because the masters were changing the customary work practices. But where did these new masters get their ideas from to put into practicality the need to tighten their control over the workforce?

For centuries, indeed traced back to the Greek stoics and the writings of St Paul, and maintained throughout the medieval period, the Tudors and the turmoil of the seventeenth century Europe, was the belief that the pursuit of purely individual gain would lead to avarice and passionate, selfish greed, to the detriment of the wider community, hence a price was deemed just when it was seen be fair to both the seller and the buyer, (in essence a *moral* economy). In the capitalist paradigm the pursuit of self-interest results, at worst, in the relatively harmless chase for individual profit and, at best, in producing a peaceful harmony which is essentially a civilising force. Such a position began in embryonic form in the writings of John Locke at the end of the seventeenth century. Although defending the mercantilist state Locke also stressed the predominant rights of individual entitlement especially in relation to property and its value, indeed he produced a rigorous defence of the pursuit of what he believed an individual was entitled to by virtue of the value of property.[9] This of course flew directly in the face of previous notions that the reckless hunt for self-interest or individual profit at all costs could/would be detrimental to the community at large, that, in effect, the interests of the wider community should be protected above those of individual self-interest. Indeed, even Smith himself seemed to doubt the overall social benefits which would accrue from the widespread pursuit of self-interest when he noted that, although eventually wider society would improve through the pursuit of self-interest, many of these individualist motivations were despicable in themselves.[10] Smith's contemporary, David Hume, suggested the positive political effects of the beginnings of economic self-interest when he wrote that the baronial powers decreased when they stopped spending huge amounts of money on military retainers and dependants, who had their own aspirations of power and communal mischief making, and more on acquiring luxuries from people who had no agenda but to make money.[11] From which Hume deduced that people acting in their own self-interest would become industrious, diligent and prudent, having even greater political effect as they would also become reliable, predictable and responsible citizens, (in short less volatile and riotous). Hence society as a whole would benefit as its members would attain genuine liberty and yet be orderly and peaceful. Hume argued the pursuit of self-interest produces even greater advantage in terms of the general elevation of taste and sensibilities across society and an improvement of its behaviour and manners.[12] For Smith the attainment of natural liberty could only be achieved through an economically competitive setting with the least interference possible, it was for him as natural

---

9   John Locke, *Two Treatises of Government*. Cambridge Texts in the History of Political Thought. (ed. Peter Laslett), (Cambridge: Cambridge University Press, 1997). John Locke, *Political Writings*. Cambridge Texts in the History of Political Thought. (ed. Mark Goldie), (Cambridge: Cambridge University Press, 2002). John Locke, "Two Tracts on Government." in *Political Writings*. Cambridge Texts in the History of Political Thought. (ed. Mark Goldie), (Cambridge: Cambridge University Press, 2002). John Locke, "Essay on the Law of Nature" in *Political Writings*. Cambridge Texts in the History of Political Thought. (ed. Mark Goldie), (Cambridge: Cambridge University Press, 2002).
10 A. Smith, *The Theory of Moral Sentiments*, (London: A. Millar, 1759).
11 D. Hume, *The History of England*.6 vols. (London: A. Millar, 1754-62).
12 D. Hume, *Political Discourses*. (Edinburgh, 1752).

as the need for survival which is with us from birth until death. Yet he warned that the dark side to this could be the activities of the unscrupulous trader or artisan, or indeed corrupt government official, who sought to pass off shoddy or overpriced services. To this again his answer was the attainment of genuine and truly open competition and the removal of, as much as possible, official interference.

However, there were also contemporaries who challenged the existing knowledge of the actual practices, not only of the state's involvement in commerce and trade, but also how to build intellectual bridges between the various branches of these activities. In short, the understanding of economics. One such was Joseph Massie who in 1760 wrote to the Duke of Newcastle, the Prime Minister. Massie's chief concern was that this lack of knowledge and understanding would be detrimental not only to the ability of that class of merchants and traders who enriched the country, but eventually to Britain itself. At the outset of his piece he noted,

> Some writers have considered commerce a *science*, and endeavoured to deduce the knowledge of it from axioms, maxims etc., while many others have treated it as a branch of *history*, and given narratives of transactions, occurrences etc., but the former have made only light essays on the elementary part of commercial knowledge, and the latter have only scraps of commercial history, or at most, have only compiled small parts of it.[13]

This, according to Massie, led to considerable confusion, as the various component parts are not understood in relation to their total effects. This was, he pointed out, due to a lack of the basic means of gaining an understanding either through empirical research (scientific) or the use of historical precedents. Thus far, said Massie, it appeared impossible for anyone to be able to get to grips with what was actually taking place from the national perspective because they are not "enabled to study" from a scientific, historical or both points of view at once. As for commercial writers, although "they have considered commerce either as a science, or as a branch of history, but produced a confused picture because they have mixed personal with national affairs, and blended principles, history and practice together."

> Under these circumstances, it is impossible to generally promote the knowledge of commerce as a national concern; for such knowledge cannot be acquired until the necessary means are not only ascertained, but properly collected together; and they should have been ascertained at the first, because a general partition of commercial knowledge would have followed in course, and the many difficulties now attending the subject, might have been thereby avoided.[14]

Massie called for the application of empirical research in order to rectify what he termed a "distorted and ill-marked picture" regarding contemporary

---

[13] J. Massie, *Representation Concerning the Knowledge of Commerce as a National Concern; Pointing out the Proper Means of Promoting such Knowledge into this Kingdom*, (London: T. Payne, 1760) p. ii. For earlier forms of attempting to quantify as well assess the political and economic importance of trade to the country see, J. Hoppit, 'Political Arithmetic in Eighteenth-Century England" in *Economic History Review*, New Series, Vol. 49, No. 3 (Aug., 1996), pp. 516-540, and by the same author but with specific reference to Joseph Massie, see 'The Contexts and Contours of British Economic Literature, 1660-1760", *The Historical Journal*, 49, 1 (2006), pp. 79-110.

[14] Ibid

understanding of the relationship between the interests of the state and those of the commercial and trading sectors. These resulted in the perpetuation of "false ideas" in desperate need of rectification.[15] Of equal significance for Massie was that not only did so-called experts on commercial matters not apply the correct methodological tools to examine the totality of areas relating to the national economic interest, the work they put out was little read or understood by the public at large. This lack of real and meaningful knowledge gained through reason and research was a situation, he warned, that if not addressed would be inevitably detrimental to both the trading and commercial sectors but also the nation as a whole because,

> The causes whereof are, there not having either the *elements of commercial knowledge* to inform them of the rules of right and wrong therein, or a proper commercial history to inform them of the past and present states, etc. of the several branches of *British* manufactory and commerce; by which means, they have been kept under some sort of uncertainty, as mariners would be, in long voyages, without either a compass or a quadrant; for they neither could know what course to steer, nor how to avoid being retarded and tossed about by the winds of contrary opinion.[16]

Indeed, according to Massie this lack of understanding of what was in effect economics was of crucial importance to all the citizens of the country regardless of their class or status or occupation, as he explained:

> ... the knowledge of commerce *as a national concern*, is also very interesting to all ranks and degrees of people in Great Britain, that it is quite unnecessary to specify in this place, the several reasons why all proper endeavours should be used to facilitate the acquisition of such knowledge; for the rich know and the poor feel that their welfare depends upon the prosperity of commerce, which is the strongest general reason imaginable for promoting the knowledge of it as a national concern.[17]

It was the responsibility of the government to make the acquisition of knowledge of economics a priority, because, he argued, only government officials adequately educated in the full understanding of trading and commercial matters could be the proper arbitrators, certainly the trading sector on its own was clearly incapable of doing so as "...most of the commercial regulations which have from time to time been made by the Legislature, were prayed for by some merchants or traders, and petitioned against by others."[18]

However, Massie also hints at a crude understanding of forms of the 'terms of trade' and 'comparative advantage'. "...the ability of one nation to carry on trade with other nations doth chiefly and generally depend upon nearly as great quantities of the commodities and manufactures of such one nation being consumed by peoples of other nations, as that nation consumes of their commodities."[19] This is not as forceful or explicit as the tenets of political economy but it was implicitly prescient of the work of David Ricardo some sixty years later. But lying just below the surface of Massie's point was the view that the openness of trade was not only dependant on the ability of the products to be

---

15 Ibid, p. iii.
16 Ibid p. vi.
17 Ibid p. vii.
18 Ibid p. 3.
19 Ibid pp. 10-11.

exported by merchants and freely consumed by their customers, (as this would undoubtedly result in the growth of domestic and international trade and profit), but also that those individual governments should endeavour to make this practice part of the their national trading policy, rather than focusing solely on their desire to acquire tariffs or, as in classical mercantilism, precious metals on which to base their currencies. This in Massie's view was shown to be a dangerous prospect, as his reading of history had shown. Here he was probably thinking of the rises of inflation in the mid- to late-Tudor period when the national monetary policy was solely reliant on the capacity of the navy to take Spanish gold and silver and had the effect of debasing the value of the currency and inflating prices whereby real wages fell by as much as 60%. In Massie's words:

> All the mines in Peru, Mexico and Brazil do not annually yield gold and silver sufficient to pay for the foreign commodities which yearly are consumed by the Spaniards and Portuguese; and as to other European nations, which have scarcely any other gold and silver than what was extracted from those mines, and gained by them in a long course of trade, it is manifest that they cannot for a continuance maintain their foreign trade upon any other terms than those exchanging commodities and manufactures with each other, so long as they gain proportionally by others.[20]

This being the case, argued Massie, governments should attempt wherever and whenever possible to facilitate the free and smooth movement of trade and not impose harsh debilitating duties and tariffs, unless absolutely necessary as a means of retaliation on, say, a country that is imposing harmful protective duties on British commodities exported openly and freely.

> This being the case, it is evident that Princes and States are under the necessity of permitting to consume the commodities and manufactures of other countries wherein the consumption of their commodities and manufactures is the like manner permitted; and that Princes are also under a necessity of retaliating upon an unfriendly nation, whatever injuries their subjects suffer in consequence of prohibitions or high duties being laid upon the commodities and manufactures which those subjects send to such unfriendly nation...[21]

With the disparities in the corn trade specifically of concern because of the apparent social disruption they caused, which appeared to be proliferating throughout the 1750s, Charles Smith published his *Two Tracts on the Corn Trade* in 1758.[22] Smith suggested that it was not the avarice of farmers, millers, bakers or middlemen that were the main problem but the vagaries of the crops and inclement seasons that result in shortages and, at times, with diseased crops. He noted the North-West as being an area which in the previous few years had been beset with shortages of grain. According to Smith the key problem here was that the region as a whole (apart from relatively small areas of Cheshire) did not possess grain growing arable land sufficient to naturally supply the larger urban areas, and thus the market and distribution of grain supply rested on the corn merchants, "Purveyors, Layers, Badgers, Kidders and Carriers." Who,

---

20 Ibid, p. 11
21 Ibid, p. 11
22 C. Smith, *A Short Essay on the Corn Trade, and the Corn Laws*, (London, 1758), see also by the same author, *Three Tracts on the Corn Trade and Corn Laws*, (London: J. Brotherton, 1766).

admitted Smith, despite the old statutes may have succumbed to "some evil practice having crept in amongst them."[23] However, given that the sale life of corn is limited and the product is prone to spoiling, the possibility or such people rigging the market are strictly limited, regardless of the penalties in place provided by the old statutes prohibiting forestalling, engrossing and regrating. It simply was not worth the risk for these middlemen or farmers to risk the wrath of the crowd and the authorities for a little more profit. Also when they do, for example, forestall grain they run the risk that when the price has reached its optimum some other middleman may step into the void and flood the market rendering their schemes a major financial loss of their capital. On this specific topic Smith has some views, he tells us:

> Having mentioned the word capital, it may not be improper to observe, that to carry on every branch of the Corn and Flour-trades, a much larger sum of money is required than may be commonly imagined, but will easily be believed, when it is remembered, that the whole is paid for in present money, and though some part may be returned within a month, yet the whole, by those who have any considerable trade, is not returned more than three or four times in a year; and he cannot in plentiful markets lay in a stock, but is obliged to buy in proportion to his sales in short markets, will find his trade turn out to little account.[24]

Smith's key point of argument, however, was that in those parts of the country where the supply of grain is imperative due to the relative lack of local produce, the existing laws, both in common and statute law, the assize of bread and the fixing of prices by magistrates, did more harm than good. In the conclusion of one of his reflections on the existing laws, Smith had this to say: "The purport of all that hath been said is this, as the variety of seasons will always prevent the Price of Corn being fixed by law, and could it be done, it would be attended with inconveniences..."[25] Yet by far the loudest argument amongst those who considered commercial and trading matters was not for the investigative research of economics and a more open trading policy as advocated by Joseph Massie, or the relaxing of the existing statutes and practices in common law suggested by Smith, but the opposite. In fact the strongest call was to maintain of the protective devices implicit in the mercantile system for the benefit of society as a whole and particularly the weakest or poorest. Indeed, some accused Britain's enemies of making vast profits at her expense by dint of the commercial policies being *too* liberal and open. These advocates placed not only national security firmly at stake with regard to Britain's trade but also the parlous nature of the increasing levels of poverty amongst the labouring population.

To give one example of the resistance to the opening up of international markets in 1740, a pamphlet which appeared in the *Gentleman's Magazine* virulently attacked the state of trade, specifically the largest branch of British trade: the woollen industry. The anonymous author, said to be a prominent London draper, also outlined the shortage of money and the growing problem of poverty, all of which stemmed directly from what he perceived to be the decline in the wool trade and the existing practice of exporting raw wool abroad: "...because, by the loss of our woollen trade in other nations, the balance is against us. In France English guineas are as common as Portugal pieces here. It

---

23 Ibid. p. 17.
24 Ibid. pp. 17-18.
25 C. Smith, *Three Tracts on the Corn Trade and Corn Laws* p. 92.

is evident by the scarcity of our coin. Many London traders agree that they never knew anything like present want of money" due to the decline in the woollen trade, says the author, "which used to give circulation to all other branches of trade" and was a crucial source of foreign exchange, and "...having the balance of trade on *our* side, whereas now our specie is exported for foreign goods."[26] With regard to the rising levels of poverty and unemployment, the writer tells us that one contemporary study, undertaken by an unnamed Peer, suggested that there were a million people claiming relief who were capable of working in 1736, "...and every parish knows they have increased ever since. Let anyone examine those towns where woollen manufacture has been carried on, and he will see the most flourishing reduced to beggary."[27] However, the author was adamant that even though the numbers of the poor claiming relief will impact the wealth of the landed gentry, reducing the wages of those labourers who are still working was not the answer. In a remarkably enlightened, indeed modern interpretation the author warned, "If you lower the price of labour you lower the value of land and obstruct the circulation of commerce, the more the lower the wages, the less money the labourers have to purchase their products of the earth."[28] The numbers of the poor will, our author tells us continue to rise: "Some time ago our poor amounted to 1,400,000; the decay of our trade since and the severity of last year may have increased them to two million..."[29] This was a critical situation that needed immediate redress in order to prevent a major crisis. The short-term answer, he argued, was to suspend the export of wool as a raw material and prevent other powers, most notably France, from making a profit. Because if such a policy was not forthcoming, our author calculated, "it appears the nation loses no less than 42 million sterling yearly, before what the landed interest suffers by the poor, and rates, which, by the decay of our manufactures, will become so numerous, that the revenues of all the lands will not be sufficient to maintain them."[30] Inevitably, there will be conflict yet again with the French.

> [France] are making preparations for open enmity, and then the mask will be taken off. The only thing to be considered is their capacity to put their designs into execution. And what should prevent the execution of their designs, if instead of taking proper measure for our safety; we furnish them with the means of accomplishing it? We have seen what riches arise

---

26 'The Consequences of Trade", *Gentleman's M'agazine* vol. X, October, 1740 and November 1740, pp500-502 and 549-552, p. 502. For other examples in the period covered in this chapter see *Gentleman's' Magazine*, Vol. XVII, December, 1749, p. 557. *Gentleman's' Magazine*, XXVII, June, 1757, pp 291-292, again same volume, December, 1757, pp. 601-602, and again December, 1757-January, 1758, p. 632. *Gentleman's Magazine,* Vol. XVIII, January, 1758, pp. 5 and 9-1'3, and again same volume, February, 1758, pp. 60-67, and pp. 124-126, and May, 1758, pp. 229-231, and June, 1758 'A Vindication of Commerce", by Mr Bell, pp. 299-302. *Gentleman's Magazine*, Vol. XVIIII, February 1759. review of the book, Anon, *Populousness Oeconony, The Wealth and Strength of a Kingdom*, or 'Popular Economics", "The piece is rather declamatory than argumentative, but it seems to animated with an honest zeal for the public good, and a warm benevolence to mankind." p. 88.
27 'The Consequences of Trade', *Gentleman's Magazine* Vol. X, October, 1740 and November 1740, pp500-502 and 549-552, p. 502. See also John Basset, *Chronicum Rusticum-Comerciale*, ed. John Smith, 2 vols. (London, 1747), vol. i, p. 351; N. C., a Weaver of London, 'The Great Necessity and Advantage of Preserving Our Own Manufactures' (London, 1697); cited in W. H. Moreland, *India at the Death of Akbar* (London, 1920), p. 270.
28 Ibid p. 551.
29 Ibid p. 549.
30 Ibid.

> from trade, and how inseparable riches and strength are from each other, and yet we suffer the French to enrich themselves by a trade, which they cannot carry on without our leave, while we grow weak by the loss of it.[31]

The writer of the article in the *Gentleman's Magazine* went as far as to suggest that the French king was the greatest stock jobber of them all and thus held in his power the effective functioning of the whole of the British trading structure.

> And what should prevent the execution of their designs, if instead of taking proper measure for our safety; we furnish them with the means of accomplishing it?
> We have seen what riches arise from trade, and how inseparable riches and strength are from each other, and yet we suffer the French to enrich themselves by a trade, which they cannot carry on without our leave, while we grow weak by the loss of it. We are sensible of public debts, yet we load ourselves with taxes when we might make others pay them; while their finances are not only disencumbered, but their King, as they are fond to boast, is continually putting money into our funds, and by the help of our wool, will soon engross so large a share of them, that by drawing out, will leave us defenceless... a general discontent is a natural consequence of a general decay of trade... It will better become us to check their [the French] greatness, and recover our own trade, which cannot be done without putting a stop to the exportation of our unmanufactured wool. The only sensible question is not whether it be necessary to do it immediately, but *how* it can be done.[32]

Thus in the first half of the eighteenth century leading up to Smith's *Wealth of Nations* there were increasing calls for a reappraisal of trading and commercial policies which were growing louder as the century progressed, from reformers on one side and those who demanded stricter application of the protective mechanisms inherent in the mercantilist system on the other. Yet these calls were tempered by some of the tactics of the merchants in the sector of essential provisions. Throughout the 1750s there were spasmodic but fairly frequent outbursts of the popular protest against food shortages and high prices, which as we have seen prompted a great deal of attention of commentators on both sides of the argument. The type of problems the authorities had to deal with can be encapsulated in an incident that occurred in London in the summer of 1757, just prior to the new harvest of grain coming onto the market. In August the corn merchants of London sent a memorial to the Privy Council allowing them to export grain. They had, they said, imported grain in a time of shortage as the market price had fallen below what they had initially paid, and they now sought leave to re-export the grain "thereof in foreign parts, where it bears a considerable price, and will perish if not disposed of."[33] The Lord President of the Council then began inquiries as to the legitimacy of the corn merchant's request. The Lord Mayor reported that he believed in fact that the corn merchants had formed a combination to fix the price of wheat in London markets, and moreover pledged not to sell any flour to bakers unless their terms were met. The Privy Council then issued a summons to all the corn merchants ('mealmen') to attend a full meeting of the Council in order to be questioned. In the meantime the Council deliberated what should be done. Present were the Lord President of the Council, Earl Granville, the Lord Chancellor, the Earl of

---

31 Ibid p. 549.
32 Ibid.
33 National Archives. Privy Council Registers, PC2 Vol. 105, ff 571, (9/8/1757).

Hardwick, the Attorney General, Earl Camden, Lord Chief Justice Mansfield, Home Secretary Holderness, and Secretary of State William Pitt. The upshot was to invoke the old statutes, specifically 25 Henry VIII, which would have laid the merchants open to indictment and imprisonment, although Mansfield added useful evidence of where his sentiments lay by saying he doubted the old acts legality, and it should not be used "unless all other expedient should fail and the necessity become very great."[34] Hence the threat to invoke the old statute was to be exactly that; a threat, and of course the corn merchants backed down.

A significant economic criticism was that the mercantilist system seemed to breed monopolies for key operators in certain sectors, (such as the above attempt by the London corn merchants), roughly corresponding to the particular part of the world the imports originated, hence the furore over the operations of the East India Company later in the eighteenth century and the charge frequently levelled at government ministers that they and their friends lined their pockets through corrupt practices via the sector of government under their control. However, this growth of imperial commerce highlighted a further problem concerning the availability of capital: specifically industrial capital. Much more money could be made relatively quickly by deploying capital in an overseas venture than could be made by investing in canal building or speculating on the success of domestic industrial ventures. The point is that the mercantilist system effectively encouraged this and hence deprived the domestic market of capital reserves. One of the key pillars of the growth of modern industrial capitalism was the availability of capital or savings to be taken up through loans. Yet speculation in foreign ventures was maintained throughout the first half of the eighteenth century, even after the mopping up of the South Sea Bubble which drowned so many investors in 1720. In effect what was developing in Britain as a result of their over-reliance on the apparent effectiveness of mercantilism was that financial markets became established but not financial institutions – despite the existence of the Bank of England – to oversee both their financial viability and incorruptibility and backed up by legally binding rules and regulations.[35] This further stymied the efforts of those seeking to start up or expand their domestic enterprises through increased capitalisation via their formal access to funding through an established institutional sector. As Sir Arthur Lewis, an early thinker on national economic development, wrote:

> It is the habit of productive investment that distinguishes rich from poor nations, rather than differences in equality of income or differences in the respect accorded to wealthy men... The really significant turning point in the life of a society is not when it begins to respect wealth, as such, but when it places in the forefront productive investment and the wealth associated therewith.[36]

Joint stock companies could and did exist in the eighteenth century, either by special charter, as in the case of the East India Company, or through the granting

---

34 Ibid. ff 578, (23/8/1757).
35 L. Neal, 'How it all began: the monetary and financial architecture of Europe during the first global capital markets, 1648–1815', *Financial History Review*, Volume 7 / Issue 02 / October 2000, p. 118. In fact a Stock Exchange did not exist until the mid-1770s, and the effective incorporation of investors through the Joint Stock Companies Act of did not take place until 1844, although even then investors still carried unlimited liability and this was not fully addressed until a Limited Liability Act was placed on the statute book in Britain in 1855.
36 Cited in P. Mathias, *The First Industrial Nation: An Economic History of Britain, 1700-1914*, (London: Methuen, 1969) p. 14.

of parliamentary permission, as in the case of those capitalists constructing a canal or turnpike, dock enlargement (such as at Liverpool) or a waterworks. But such investors were liable to all the debts incurred and attracted only the more substantial investors and usually formed into a trust of significant numbers to shield the risk. According to Sidney Pollard writing in the mid-1960s:

> Most of this earlier capital was invested in commerce, in finance, in farming, and in stocks of manufactured goods and raw materials, and what was noteworthy in the next two generations was, not so much the absolute (and probably also relative) growth in the quantity of capital, but a change in its composition: the emergence, for the first time, of large concentrations of fixed capital.[37]

Yet by the 1750s, and indeed into the 1760s, the individual middling sort of entrepreneur found it difficult to initially raise capital and to keep the enterprise afloat till profits began to accrue. It was not the fact that merchant and clearing banks did not exist, but that these tended to lend to their close network of clients in and around London. A middling sort of Manchester entrepreneur, especially those recently established, would in all likelihood be excluded, and such institutions in the north were only just beginning to develop their businesses and the widespread access to bank business loans from such bodies lay some way off in the future.[38] In any case the level of sureties demanded by such banking houses made it again difficult for the moderate cotton textile master to secure loans purely on the basis of vague claims to future profits.[39] To a certain extent the new Manchester men devised a means of overcoming these obstacles, however they were initially assisted by the nature of industrial development in the branch of textiles they were involved in before the 1770s, when the advent of the widespread growth of factories took off. In the 1740s and 1750s their need for substantial amounts of fixed capital may have been limited but not unattainable. Their enterprises in the 1750s were still reliant on the functioning of the outworker system, the point was that the changes they made to this system directly led to the next and more advanced stage of industrial development in the North-West which would demand more fixed capital outlay. Curiously, the raising and deployment of capital on the eve of the industrial revolution is not a topic that energised economic historians who examined the features of growth or what W. W. Rostow famously called 'take off', even after the publication of François Crouzet's, *Capital Formation in the Industrial Revolution*, in 1972.[40] There are significant studies of capital formation once take off had taken place, but little on how this process was initiated and the problems faced by early

---

37 S. Pollard, 'Fixed Capital and the Industrial Revolution in Britain' *Journal of Economic History*, Vol. 24, Number 3, 1964, p. 299.
38 In fact it was not until 1771 that the first bank was opened in Manchester, that of Byrom, Sedgwick, Allen and Place.
39 There has been some work done on how finance was raised in the eighteenth century, indeed in eighteenth century Lancashire, but this tended to focus on the raising of finance through variations of mortgages either on real estate or long leasehold property. See B. L. Anderson, 'Provincial aspects of the financial revolution of the eighteenth century' in *Business History*, Vol. 11, Issue 1, 1969, pp 11 to 22, and by the same author, 'The Attorney and the Early Capital Market in Lancashire', in J. R. Harris, (ed.) *Liverpool and Merseyside. Essays in Economic and Social Historyof the Port and Its Hinterland*, (London: Frank Cass and Co., 1969), 'Aspects of Capital and Credit in Lancashire during the Eighteenth Century', (University of Liverpool, M.A. Thesis, 1966).
40 F. Crouzet, *Capital Formation in the Industrial Revolution*, (London: Methuen, 1972).

entrepreneurs.[41]

The lack of a viable institutional arm to link the growth of national financial markets with the growing international financial markets underscored a further hindrance to the creation of a buoyant domestic investment capital market, which indicated the reluctance of governments to encourage usury. Ever since Edward I had expelled the Jews in the first half of the thirteenth century Britain had not possessed a dependable mode of mass borrowing on credit. Even well into the eighteenth century the term usury was tainted as some form of rash speculation that would only advantage the person giving the advance and usually at exorbitant rates of interest. Indeed the statutes forbidding usury were not repealed until 1854.[42] Yet acts of usury, whereby funds could be raised, did take place, usually by individuals in the form of annuities, paid in annual instalments to the person obtaining the loan, to be paid back with considerable interest (often double the actual monies loaned) at the death of a wealthy relative and guaranteed by the lender who would then take out a policy of life insurance on the person receiving the loan.[43]

This was not the means of raising capital used by the Manchester cotton merchants. Traditionally loans and advances to purchase raw materials were organised in the North-West by the larger (originally linen) drapers of Manchester and some of the larger towns such as Bolton. Clearly the use of credit facilities was important, given the time lapse from purchasing the raw cotton to be warehoused, then distributed to the domestic spinners, then on to the weavers, the finished pieces then to be collected by the master's agents or chapmen, and finally sent either to London to be sold or (increasingly from the 1720s and '30s) exported via Liverpool. This whole process would take several months from the inception of the transaction to the point of receiving payment for the finished materials. The traditional larger merchants, such as the Chethams', Joshua Browne, or Nathaniel Walker of Manchester, or Thomas Marsden of Bolton, would put out the cotton wool to the spinners, onto the weavers and debit the costs of both materials and wages against the expected or contracted value of the finished goods in London, on which he would draw bills of exchange or, indeed, cash. Men such as these also acted as informal bankers discounting other people bills of exchange for cash for a given remittance of four pence per pound sterling which he would settle with his London goldsmith. They could also be acting as creditors to smaller masters, again either in the form of bills of exchange to be drawn under a certain stipulation of time in London or

---

41 S. D. Chapman, 'Fixed Capital Formation in the British Cotton Industry 1770-1815', *Economic History Review*, (1970); S. D. Chapman, 'Fixed Capital Formation in the British Cotton Manufacturing Industry' in J. P. P. Higgins and S. Pollard, *Aspects of Capital Investment in Great Britain, 1750-1850*, (London: Methuen, 1971). N. Crafts, *British Economic Growth during the Industrial Revolution*, (Oxford: Clarendon Press, 1985). C. H. Feinstein, 'Capital Formation in Great Britain' in P. Mathias and M. M. Postan, (eds.), *The Cambridge Economic History of Europe, Vol. IIV, The Industrial Economies, Part I*, (Cambridge University Press, 1978); C. H. Feinstein, 'National Statistics, 1760-1920', in C. H. Feinstein and S. Pollard, (eds.), *Studies in Capital Formation in the United Kingdom, 1750-1920*, (Oxford: Clarendon Press, 1988). J. Mokyr, 'The Industrial Revolution and the New Economic History", in J. Mokyr, (ed.) *The Economics of the Industrial Revolution*, (London: Allen and Unwin, 1985). S. Shapiro, *Capital and the Cotton Industry*, (New York, Ithaca: Cornell University Press, 1967)

42 *Hansard*,17 & 18 Vic. c. go: "An Act to repeal the Laws relating to Usury and to the enrolment of Annuities."

43 See S. Campbell, 'The Economic and Social Effect of the Usury Laws in the Eighteenth Century" *Transactions of the Royal Historical Society*, Fourth Series, Vol. 16 (1933), pp. 197-210.

alternatively cash, in both cases at a 'tolerated interest'.[44]

However, by the 1720s and 1730s, the situation had changed for the merchants, factors and clothiers in the North-West cotton industry due to the growth of Liverpool as a port for receiving raw materials and sending out cargoes and, importantly, the manner of financing import/export operations. It would appear that, given the limiting alternatives, the Manchester merchants involved in a variety of enterprises throughout the North-West began to adopt the innovative financing structures that gradually developed in Liverpool as the port began to grow. It was here that we see the evolution of the role of the 'supercargo' as a person who would be placed in charge of the safe passage of the freight, its sale and the purchase of the return cargo, often the raw materials required by the merchants of the North-West. Insurance was limited at this time, as was the means of raising large amounts of capital, as we have seen. The way round these difficulties was by means of pooling resources and risks by buying shares in sea-going ventures, especially when part of the goods exported belonged to the Manchester cotton masters. As early as 1714 some Manchester cotton masters were becoming involved in overseeing the export of their own goods to the Americas and Caribbean, so long, that is, as they shared the risk with the Liverpool merchants. So we see three merchants, Thomas Touchet and John Dyson from Manchester, and Matthew Wilson of Wortley Forge, near Sheffield, taking out cargo space in 'dry goods' on a vessel bound for the Caribbean. The terms were no payments for the passage outbound, but a charge of five shilling per hundred pounds value of cargo for the return back to Liverpool. Fustians were among the outbound cargo and raw cotton, sugar and tobacco on the return voyage.[45] These merchants were pooling their resources to ensure the sale of their products and to import necessary raw materials, and in so doing were spreading any risk that pursuing such a venture as an individual would carry. In a sense they were pooling their capital and, as such, were setting a precedent for future cotton merchants of Manchester. Yet they were doing more inasmuch as the leading Manchester merchants began to finance loans to ship cargo and receive necessary imports, not only with other merchants in the cotton sector but with the Liverpool merchants. By the 1720s and 1730s these Manchester men had set up warehouses and handling offices in Liverpool itself.[46] One ship's manifest of 1729 shows that cotton checks, cotton dimities, cotton strips, dyed pillows, linen checks, Kendal cottons, sheeting linen, fustians, dyed jeans, printed cottons, coal, pipes, nails and bottled beer were all purchased on credit on the outward sail, and oil and barrel staves were collected from Boston for the passage home, (worth in total £1,200). These transactions were conducted in four different currencies: pounds sterling, and Bermuda, Boston and Irish notes.[47] These men also increasingly began to become involved in another lucrative but more sinister cargo, that from the 'middle passage' with cotton goods deported to the West African coast and slaves carried on to the Caribbean and the American colonies.

Thus, the merchants of Manchester had arrived at the solution to the raising of capital through co-operation and spreading the risk by the investment of small sums among several 'partners' as an informal trust fund. By this means they were

---

44 *Palatinate Papers, Lancashire,* P. L. 6, 36/109, (1684-1688); 36/120 and again, P. L. 7, 130, (1720).
45 *Palatinate Papers, Lancashire,* P. L. 6.58/6; P. L. 7. 126, (1714).
46 *Palatinate Papers, Lancashire,* P. L. 6.70/25; P. L. 7, 141. (1727-28).
47 *Palatinate Papers, Lancashire,* P. L. 6.69/21; 71/36; P. L. 7. 142, (1729).

able to gain access to their precious raw materials. The relative success of this device would not have been lost on these men. They also realised that although they might be in competition with other merchant clothiers in terms of their means of accruing profit, they all had their well-defined methods in the manner of how they applied their trade, the use of chapmen and local agents. Yet in terms of the acquiring of the raw cotton and the dispatching of the finished goods, they seem to have operated a tight network of closed collaboration. In this sense, they began to control the putting out system, (at times even the supply of the means of production in terms of the provision of hiring out looms to weavers), the production itself, the finishing of the various types of cotton clothes, and the distribution and sale of fustians and the smallware sectors of the cotton trade.

This began on a small scale, but grew in the 1720s, 1730s and 1740s so that by the time we arrive at the 1750s these Manchester (and Liverpool) men had become very powerful economic figures controlling many if not most of the cotton districts of the North-West and the livelihoods of several thousand workers. Yet even at the end of the 1730s one contemporary was noticing the difference between the old, traditional type of cotton master and the new men. The older type of merchant did not especially concern himself with "Dress, Servants, Equipages, Wine, Entertainment, etc.", but lately:

> ...though it must be confessed that of late they have departed rather too much, some of them of the younger sort, from that simplicity, neatness and frugality, which their ancestors valued themselves for and with very good reason.[48]

They also began thinking of the expansion of the trade – of which the effects on the workers of the North-West will be examined in detail in due course – and these merchants were greatly assisted in terms of widening possibilities by national political policy. This was especially the case regarding the expansion of the opportunities for the export of cotton goods via the enlargement of the British Empire. This growth in the opportunities presented by increased export potential will be the central focus of the next chapter, but a confluence of circumstances began to enhance the prospects of the cotton masters of the North-West and indeed probably acted as a stimulus to their motivations to revise the structure of their production methods.

We will examine the speed and impact of changes made through innovations in the cotton sector in later chapters, which deal specifically with the nature of social protest in the 1750s and 1760s, however there were changes afoot before these dates which are worthy of note. As stated earlier the modern capitalist system is suggestive of an array of distinct ingredients which allow the capitalist to facilitate the maximisation of capital outlay by improving methods of production and out-competing potential rivals. One of these distinctive ingredients was the coming of the factory system, which involved the concentration as well as the division of labour in a specific location and the application of machinery to make the productive process more efficient. Throughout the 1720s, 1730s and 1740s pioneer entrepreneurs were gauging the profit potential of expanding trade and, crucially, investment capital appears to have been available. The question remains which came first: the re-organisation of the proto-industrial system itself through the removal of workers customary practices? Or was it the huge incentive to reorganise production methods offered

---

48 *Burton Manuscript*, Vol. vii, p. 45, Manchester Central Reference Library.

by the possibility of expanding overseas markets? Or could it have been the examples of the impact of early efforts of concentrating production in factories? These early moves towards the coming of the factories before the 1760s were a truly nationwide phenomenon, from Belfast, Drogheda and Dublin in Ireland to Glasgow and Edinburgh in Scotland, and in England from Newcastle upon Tyne, Carlisle and Kendall in the North through to York, Leeds, Manchester, Liverpool and Sheffield down to Chester, Nottingham, Leicester and Birmingham, to Norwich, Colchester, Northampton, Tewkesbury, Gloucester and Bristol and Watford, London, Mitcham and Weymouth on the South coast.[49]

The earliest examples of the concentration of labour in factories in Britain came early in the eighteenth century through their use in the workhouses as a means of reducing the poor rates, where the labour was most amenable to discipline and where it was to be found naturally assembled and concentrated. In 1721 Elias Barns wrote to the Board of Trade and Plantations to suggest the use of children in poor-houses to spin cotton and flax.[50] Although these early attempts had the double advantage of making money for both the originator of the scheme and for the government, they did not materialise into a viable concern for the enormous profits, and indeed power, of the monopoly in the importation of fine Indian calicos by the East India Company. John and Thomas Lombe had built a silk factory in Derby in 1721, but this appears to have been the only private purely capitalist venture before the 1740s and there is no record of any similar attempts in the cotton sector. Yet what these early efforts indicated first of all was the obvious fact that there needed to be a means of increasing the efficiency of providing a reliable and fast supply of yarn to the weavers. The weavers were always reliant on the spinners for their supply of yarn in any of the branches of the textile trade. This was the initial blockage in the whole productive process, there had to be found a more efficient way of producing an adequate supply of spun thread. In some ways the fact that early improvements on the weaving side, such as John Kay's flying shuttle, did not have the rate of uptake that their labour saving value demonstrated until much later in the eighteenth century testifies to the priority of innovation in spinning that needed to be accomplished. The logic of the situation was such that it mattered little if the weavers could produce cloth more efficiently and faster if they were still reliant on the older inefficient means of producing warp and weft. However, from the mid-1730s Lewis Paul and John Wyatt began their scheme of designing a multi-spindled frame to use on any textile yarn, but they found that the most adaptable and efficient was cotton. They received their patent in 1738 and by 1742 the first water powered cotton spinning mill was operational in Northampton mainly for use in the manufacturing of hosiery.[51] Yet the profits at this early stage did not merit the significant capital outlay or take into sufficient account the volatile costs of the raw material, nor did the midlands offer the same type of traditional labour inherently trained for the cotton sector found in the North-West or indeed the sophisticated infrastructure of knowledgeable merchants concentrated in Manchester or the large scale import/export port facilities of Liverpool. Another mill at Leominster in Herefordshire was founded 1748 by Daniel Bourn and this time there was a connection with an "eminent

---

49 See Wadsworth and Mann, op cit p. 434.
50 The National Archive, Kew, *Journals and Papers of the Board of Trade and Plantations* (C.O. 388/22 Q.151 and Q. 159 see also C.O. 388/23 R. 29.)
51 Johnson Letters, Birmingham Reference Library, undated, 1742 Cave to Paul, (185,462).

tradesman" of Manchester named Thomas Bourn.[52] Yet this enterprise seemed to have suffered the same fate of the Northampton venture, as it ceased operations in 1754 when it burnt down.[53] The link with Lancashire and the North-West came in the early contacts between Paul and Samuel Touchet in 1742.[54] Touchet had commercial and family links to the cotton trade in Manchester and had offices in London for distribution but initially began the operation of a spinning mill in Birmingham in 1744 but with little success, and Touchet and his partner, Holden Bowker, took over the running of the mill at Northampton. By 1748 Touchet seems to have control of all Paul's patent spinning machines but he could not, once again, make sufficient profit to make the ventures viable and by 1755 was making such a loss that he washed his hands of the whole enterprise.[55]

This was the state of advance of factories and, especially, innovations until we get to the 1760s when, at this time, viable examples were developed in the North-West. However, in the intervening period the incentive to begin this process of radical transformation in the cotton textile sector in Lancashire came by way of a vital alteration in Statute Law which was to have a direct impact on the fortunes of the cotton industry in the North-West, which we will consider in chapter six below. Yet another vital factor was the effects of one of the most decisive and impactful wars in British history in terms of the opening up the nation's potential for global trade, and it is the consideration of this that we now turn our attention.

---

52 *Whitworth's Manchester Advertiser*, (January 9, 1759).
53 *Manchester Mercury*, (November 5, 1754).
54 Cited in Appendix C, Robert Cole, *The Paul Papers*, in *The Life and Times of Samuel Crompton: Inventor of the Spinning Machine Called the Mule: Being the Substance of Two Papers Read to the Members of the Bolton Mechanics' Institution*, Gilbert James French, Robert Cole. P. 264, (Manchester, 1859).
55 Wadsworth and Mann op cit pp. 444-445.

3

The Seven Years War and the Onset of Modern Imperialism

The onset of the Seven Years War in 1756 did not come at a particularly propitious moment for Britain, especially on the economic front as international and domestic trade had been somewhat flat in the mid-1750s, but then it is hard to find a war that ever came at a propitious time for the countries involved. If we take the export of cotton goods as an example of the period under scrutiny here, 1749 was the peak year with 357,289 lb of cotton exported; however, in 1750 the figure had shrunk to 64,405 lb. In 1754 it had risen again to 175,678 lb, but in 1755 it had reduced again to 144,901 lb.[1] Indeed, early in the war Lord Chesterfield, a confidant of Secretary of State, William Pitt, (the fiercest imperial warmonger of them all), writing to his close friend Solomon Dayrolles, perceptively suggested: "In my opinion, our greatest danger arises from our *expense*, considering the immense National Debt."[2] It was perceptive because Chesterfield knew only too well what the subsequent costs could involve. It was not so much the fact that Britain would be spending most if not all of her income conducting the war in North America and elsewhere in the world, but with the precarious European situation (given the nature of having a German as a monarch) and the lack of Britain possessing a practical standing army, that inevitably loans by way of the issuing of treasury bonds would be needed to pay for troops to defend Britain's and her allies interests in the European theatre and very possibly elsewhere in the world. This would saddle Britain with an enormous debt once the war was over, whether indeed she won or lost. The potential commercial impact of the war was not lost on government ministers, as Secretary of State Holderness, a close colleague of Pitt's explained:

> I am convinced you will agree with me in one principle, that we must be merchants while we are soldiers that our trade depends upon a proper exertion of our maritime strength; that our trade and maritime force depend upon each other, and that the riches that are the true resources of this country depend upon its commerce.[3]

Britain used most of the available income between 1756 and 1763 in pursuance of the war. In fact this appeared to be widely known at the time. In an address to the King from the County Palatine of Chester in September, 1756, they noted the increase in taxes, "which are grievous, the national debt immense; that our trade daily lessons, though they multiply; by which we fear, we may be too soon disabled from raising the necessary supplies for the support of your Majesty's and our country's rights."[4] However, at its conclusion British politicians knew they had to spend more than the national income in order to service the debts incurred by the war. This resulted in an increase in the amount of income

---

1 *Custom House Accounts, Records of the Board of Customs and Excise*, (Customs 3), Public Records Office, Kew.
2 Letter from the Earl of Chesterfield to Solomon Dayrolles, (June, 1756), printed by John Bradshaw, (ed.), *The Letters of Philip Dormer Stanhope, Fourth Earl of Chesterfield*, (London: Swan, Sonnerschein and Company, 1905) p. 1146.
3 Cited in J. Corbett, *England in the Seven Years War*, (London: Longmans, Green, and Co., 1907) Vol. i, p. 189.
4 *Gentleman's Magazine*, (September, 1756), p. 477.

devoted to public spending in the years immediately following the war. Although initially costly, in this way Britain purchased the 'second' empire by effectively spending more on the debts but at lower interest rates than her defeated enemy. Yet the debts had to be in part repaid and interest charges certainly had to be addressed to those of the landed elites who had purchased bonds during the war. The result was that in years following 1763 the government attempted to share out the burdens of debt both domestically and among its colonies. In the former, not unexpectedly, this resulted, in the short term, in serious social protest which eventually forced the government to back down,[5] and in the latter, within twenty years, in the rebellion of the Thirteen Colonies of North America.

As for the conflict itself, it was in essence a continuation of previous, yet clearly unresolved, conflicts from earlier in the eighteenth century and, arguably, the end of the seventeenth century. These were, firstly, the war of the Spanish Succession from 1701 to 1713, and then the war of the Austrian Succession, from 1740-1748. In both cases the French felt hard done by. By the early 1750s in North America the French, in alliance with the native Indians, had begun to move up Ohio Valley with the aim of encircling the Thirteen Colonies and meeting up with their countrymen in Canada. As could be expected, this created alarm not only in the Thirteen Colonies but obviously in Britain. The suspicion grew that the French grand plan was to stretch British forces to breaking point by setting off a series of infractions throughout the British Empire, in North America, the Caribbean, Africa, India and the Far East, as well as applying pressure in Europe for other strategic reasons. This conflict was effectively the first truly world war. One of the chief strategists in this period of British overseas imperial expansion, both for commercial ends and to assume global power, was William Pitt. He was one of the first national politicians to clothe himself in populist 'patriotism', attacking Walpolian corruption in the 1730s, the impact of increased Hanoverian subsidies used in Germany in 1740s, and in the 1760s the limitations of the Peace of Paris that ended the Seven Years War. He was less prone to be seen to be politically pragmatic, compromising or 'expedient', preferring to pursue and assume the populist position that Britain's national interest must come first in all government policies and this should be done from a position of military strength. Because he was not part of the powerful Whig family cliques and more of an outsider he was able to complete the circle of being a relevant political operator in royal court influences, high politics at cabinet level and populist opinion 'out of doors'. The outcry when he was dismissed by George II in April 1757 was deafening and his popularity increased even more when the King was forced to recall him in June the same year.

During and after 1759 and the year of a string of victories in North America, Pitt did little to discourage the populist suggestion that these were down to his policies and commitment. The reality was more likely that it was down to the successful and steady build-up of the Royal Navy, which effectively prevented the French from re-equipping their beleaguered North American forces. However, in any case, for the French the main theatre of the war was in Europe, but for the British it was from the outset the larger picture of the possibility of imperial expansion. By 1760 the war in North America was effectively over, resulting in a British victory and the complete control of French Canada.

---

5   See D. Walsh, 'The Cider Tax, Popular Symbolism and Opposition in Mid-Hanoverian England', in A. Randall and A. Charlesworth, (eds.) *Markets, Market Culture and Popular Protest in Eighteenth-Century Britain and Ireland*, (Liverpool: Liverpool University Press, 1996) pp. 69-91.

Similarly, in India the British assumed control of the war early into the conflict. In fact India was the greatest prize of all of the gains that Britain accrued as a result of the Seven Years War, with the French after the Peace of Paris in 1763 agreeing to use their stations at Mahé, Pondicherry and Chandernagore only as trading posts and never again to maintain troops there. Pitt's main contribution to the success of Britain during the Seven Years War was less his relatively passive involvement in decision making at the highest level, but rather his passionate pursuit of the need to neutralise the French by building on Britain's already substantial empire. He was important in another sense simply by the fact that for most of the war he was in office and was a populist figurehead that the majority of the 'middling sort' as well as articulate lower orders could rally behind, which had not been the case during the War of the Austrian Succession some ten years previously.[6]

Because of the debts incurred at the conclusion of hostilities in 1763 trade and commerce for Britain took on even greater importance than before the Seven Years War, but things were changing and the old certainties were disappearing. The Whig political hegemony which had been pre-eminent since the House of Hanover assumed the British throne was much less emphatic with the accession of George III, who now brought the formerly ostracised Tories back into the political fold. The Whig party – as far as the term 'party' is a relevant term for any period in the first half of the eighteenth century – was always divided among the leading factional alliances which, although forever shifting, remained essentially true to the basic Whig principles: a check on the powers of the monarchy and the pre-eminence of Parliament, acceptance of nonconformist individualism, its urban electoral base and the primary importance of trade over, say, the traditional Tory landed interest. However, the added strain of the debt incurred by the late war and the apparent switch in political ideology and increased visibility of the new king brought forth increased criticism. A new phase of popular political radicalism emerged which was not confined to disgruntled opposition polemicists but was increasingly vocal over a range of issues. Issues not now confined to high politics but embracing trade and government corruption, nepotism, sinecurists, placemen, government contractors and high profile state pensioners created largely for services rendered to previous political cliques.[7]

The popular cry was 'Wilkes and Liberty'; but liberty from what, and why choose John Wilkes as a figurehead for such a radical outcry? In 1762 George III dismissed the government of the Duke of Newcastle. William Pitt, who was widely perceived as the key leader and reason for the imminent victory over France, had resigned the year before on the appointment of the Earl of Bute as Secretary of State and the reluctance of the new government to declare war on Spain. More than this, however, was the fact that the monarch was seen to be

---

6   R. Middleton, *The Bells of Victory: The Pitt-Newcastle Ministry and the Conduct of the Seven Years' War, 1757-1762* (Cambridge: Cambridge University Press, 1985).

7   F. O'Gorman, *The long eighteenth century: British political and social history, 1688-1832* (London: Arnold, 1997), G. Rudé, *Wilkes and Liberty: a social study of 1763 to 1774.* (Oxford: Oxford University Press, 1962), J. Brewer, *The Sinews of Power: War, Money and the English State, 1688-1783*, (New York: Alfred A Knopf, 1989) P. Langford, *A Polite and Commercial People, England 1727-1783*, (Oxford: Oxford University Press, 1992), R. Porter, *English Society in the Eighteenth Century*, (London: Allen Lane 1982), R. Price, *British Society, 1680-1880: Dynamism, Containment and Change*, (Cambridge: Cambridge University Press, 1999), N. Rogers, *Crowds, Culture and Politics in Georgian Britain*, (Oxford: Clarendon Press, 1998), P. Thomas, *John Wilkes: A Friend to Liberty*, (Oxford: Oxford University Press, 1996).

becoming directly involved in political decision making at the highest level. This appeared to run directly contrary to the Settlement of 1688 and was likened to the despotic actions of the French King, which by extension was portrayed as dangerous because one of the principal reasons why the war was being fought in the first place was to maintain the liberties of the 'free born Englishman'. This was compounded by George III when he appointed his old tutor, the Tory Earl of Bute, as the leader of his new government. If this was not bad enough for the interfering monarch, it was made even worse by the utter incompetence of Bute as Prime Minister, as typified by the introduction of new fiscal policies that ran directly against perceived English freedoms and rights, as for example with the Cider Tax of 1763.[8] John Wilkes was MP for Aylesbury and directed all his venom inside and outside the House of Commons against Bute and, by extension, the King. Bute was doomed for reasons other than his political limitations – which were considerable – in that he was seen as being a mere puppet of the King: by being Scottish with the name of Stuart, and due to his alleged affair with the King's mother. He was in this sense an easy target and Wilkes made a meal of him, especially in *Issue 45* of the his periodical the *North Britain* which directly attacked the Peace of Paris which ended the Seven Years War and directly accused Bute of being incompetent and not acting in Britain or her allies best interests, which by implication meant being soft on French interests or at least offering comfort to a defeated foe. Wilkes himself had no specific political programme, he did not support universal suffrage although, through 'virtual representation', believed that the views of ordinary Briton's should be heard, but he was in favour of giving the Parliamentary franchise to the rising industrial areas of Birmingham, Leeds and Manchester. It was through the ruthless persecution of Wilkes by his opponents – especially the King and his party – that galvanised support across the country and made this such a serious radical turn in terms of sea-change in British political culture.

Between 1763 and 1770 the support for Wilkes ranged much further than his London base. There was support for the Wilkesite cause in the North-East, many of the port areas across the country, and many of the emerging industrial areas.[9] When Wilkes returned from exile in France in 1768 his name was put forward as a candidate in the Middlesex Parliamentary election and he won, with support including innkeepers, small craftsmen, shopkeepers, and even labourers. As Paul Langford has commented although Wilkes's political programme was limited to vague statements concerning 'liberty' it possessed a resonance that many ordinary people could identify with, as the Middlesex election proved:

> It was perhaps the most famous single election result in the history of English parliaments, and the Middlesex freeholders who brought it about did so in a spirit of plebeian libertarianism which confounded respectable opinion. It was conventional in the eighteenth century to pay lip-service to the broad base of properties politics. In practice, men of very small property rarely found their way onto the political stage. In 1768 for a short, tempestuous time they crowded it out, with chastening effects on those accustomed to play the principal roles.[10]

This year of the general elections in 1768 was to have great significance in the North-West, but the immediate nature of the political turmoil was to a

---

8 See Walsh op. cit.
9 See O'Gorman op cit p. 225.
10 Langford, op cit pp. 377-378.

significant extent mirrored by the dire economic situation that faced the government after the victory in 1763. British debt had almost doubled from £74 million in 1756 to £133 million in 1763. The servicing of these debts was consuming evermore of the British gross domestic product and dramatically affecting her balance of payments, to the extent that by the end of the Seven Years War it was approaching 40% of total government expenditure.[11] Thus, although in some respects the Seven Years War was the last fought with mercantilism as a backdrop, crucially for all the contending parties, especially the two main protagonists, Britain and France, the result would have a profound bearing on the state of their respective nations' future trading and commercial prospects. For France this proved ultimately disastrous but for Britain it meant the she was now capable to look elsewhere in her now vast empire to find amenable markets for her trade. In future wars would be fought with either emerging or fully formed industrial capitalism as a key economic goal of victory. Yet in the short term the economic imperative of expanded empire was something of which the merchants of the North-West could take advantage, but arguably the greatest prize, the Indian sub-continent, proved to be singularly difficult to grasp, and ultimately would only be achieved once the cherished colonial markets of America became less amenable to British control.

British economic interest in India had begun in the sixteenth century. The British East India Company received its royal charter from Queen Elizabeth in 1600 and began to set up trading posts at Bombay, Madras and Calcutta. India's ruling Mogul Dynasty initially attempted to keep European traders under control, however by the eighteenth century the Mogul Empire was collapsing and was to be replaced by dozens of small states, each headed by a ruler or maharajah that had broken away from Mogul control. In the context of the Seven Years War the French allied to disgruntled local rulers and attempted to stretch the British hold over key territories, but in 1757 Robert Clive led East India Company troops in a decisive victory at the Battle of Plassey. After a revolt of the native princes in Oudhand, Bengal was again put down by Clive and their territories incorporated in 1764. From that date, until 1858, the East India Company was the effective controlling power in India. However, the British government did have some significant input. These were hammered out by negotiations culminating in 1767 whereby it had to export a fixed amount of British goods to India including, importantly, finished cotton goods. The company was to have its dividends regulated to the amount of 10% and was ordered to pay £400,000 to the Treasury for two years. All the possessions accrued before, during and after the Seven Years War the Company was allowed to retain and if the dividends fell to under 6% it was not obliged to pay the government subsidy. India became one the most important export areas of British goods for the next two centuries.[12]

---

11 P. G. M. Dickson, *The Financial Revolution in England: A Study of the Development of Public Credit*, (London: Macmillan, 1967), p. 10. and Brewer op cit. pp. 114-115. See also, J. F. Wright, 'British Government Borrowing in Wartime, 1750-1815', *The Economic History Review*, New Series, Vol. 52, No. 2 (May, 1999), pp. 355-361.

12 H. Alavi, 'India: The Transition to Colonial Capitalism', in H. Alavi *et al.* (eds.), *Capitalism and Colonial Production*, (London: Croom Helm, 1982). P. Bairoch, *Victoires et déboires: Histoire économique et sociale du monde du XVIe siècle à nos jours*, (Paris: Gallimard, 1997). N. Chanda, *Bound Together: How traders, preachers, Adventurers, and Warriors shaped Globalization*, (New Haven: Yale University Press, 2007) F. Clairmonte, *Economic Liberalism and Underdevelopment: Studies in the Disintegration of an Idea*, (New York: Asia Publishing House, 1960). T. Das, Review of *The Economic History of India: 1600-1800, American Historical Review* 51.2

For the cotton trade of the North-West this came just at the right moment. Not necessarily due to the immediate export potential of Lancashire manufactured cotton goods to India, but because of the restrictions imposed in the directional flows of Indian produced goods to the territories now firmly under the control of the British as result of imperial expansion after the conclusion of the Seven Years War and the Peace of Paris in 1763. At this point the French and the Spanish were out of the picture and cotton goods produced in Britain could serve not only the expanding domestic market but also markets in Europe, Africa, the Caribbean and, effectively, the whole of the Americas as well as to a large extent the Far East. This was of course greatly enhanced by the continued operation of the Navigation Acts which meant that all goods coming out of and going to the British colonies had to be transported in British ships. All this further boosted the advocates of the mercantile system at the moment that Britain was attempting to service the huge debts incurred in the fighting of the late war. High quality Indian calicos were still being exported but effectively under license from the East India Company, from which the British government of course took its duties. The rate of these duties was an effective reduction of high quality Indian cotton goods sold in Britain, but the increasing demand for these types of products was a potential boost to the inferior quality domestically produced cotton goods. Whenever Indian cotton goods came into Britain the main aim was to collect the duties on their re-export. However, the fact was that in terms of competitive advantage quality Indian cotton goods could be produced much cheaper than British goods and this was something the masters of Lancashire attempted to redress. The quality problem was something the British manufacturers could begin to address with improved mechanisation, but in the 1750s and 1760s it was the unit labour costs of British produced cotton goods which made direct competition with Indian cotton products difficult.[13] However, there were savings to be made in the relative costs of producing cheap cotton products in Britain in contrast to the better quality of Indian produced calicos, even though the relative wages and social overhead costs, such as importing the raw materials into Britain and the improved transport, were higher in Britain than India. This was primarily due to the enhanced productive capacity in terms of unit labour costs of British labour compared to Indian labour, and was to prove the guiding principal of the Lancashire cotton-manufacturing masters.

(January, 1946), pp. 312–314. A. G. Frank, *Re-Orient: Global Economy in the Asian Age*, (Berkeley: University of California Press, 1998). P. Kennedy, *The Rise and Fall of the Great Powers: Economic Change and Military Conflict from 1500 to 2000*, (New York: HarperCollins, 1989). D. S. Landes, *The Unbound Prometheus: Technological Change and Industrial Development in Western Europe from 1750 to the Present*, (Cambridge: Cambridge University Press, 1969). R. Marks, *The Origins of the Modern World: A Global and Ecological Narrative*, (Lanham, MD: Rowman& Littlefield, 2002). E. Moe, *Governance, Growth and Global Leadership: The Role of the State in Technological Progress, 1750-2000*, (Aldershot: Ashgate, 2007). R. Mukerjee, *The Economic History of India: 1600-1800*, (Allahabad: Kitab Mahal, 1967). P. Parthasarathi, 'Rethinking Wages and Competitiveness in the Eighteenth Century: Britain and South India', *Past & Present* 158 (1) (Feb., 1998), pp.79-109. F. Perlin, 'Proto-industrialisation and Pre-colonial South Asia', *Past and Present* 98 (1) (Feb., 1983) pp. 30-95. K. Pomeranz, *The Great Divergence: Europe, China, and the Making of the Modern World Economy*, (New Jersey: Princeton University Press, 2000).

13 S. Broadberry, and B. Gupta, 'Cotton Textiles and thee Great Divergence: Lancashire, India and Shifting Competitive Advantage', 1600-1850, (Conference Paper at the conference, 'The Rise, Organisation and Institutional Framework of Factor Markets', 23-25 June, 2005, Department of Economics, University of Warwick, 2005) and P. Parthasarathi, 'Rethinking Wages and Competitiveness in the Eighteenth Century: Britain and South India', *Past & Present*, 158 (1) (Feb., 1998), pp. 79-109.

This involved an assault on all the processes of production from spinning the raw cotton, to weaving and finishing towards the end of the 1750s. But the concentration of the masters for the introduction of new work practices was initially targeted on the spinning of the cotton thread. Principally because this was the most labour intensive of the processes and in need of technical innovation (which duly arrived) and the discovery that the types of workers needed in this sector (women and children) were the easiest to control and discipline.

The Lancashire manufacturers were also assisted by the heightening popularity of cotton goods in terms of female fashion and the production of male shirting.[14] This growth of domestic consumerism has been a recent feature of the historiography of British economic development from the middle of the eighteenth century.[15] Yet in respect of the main argument being presented here,

---

14 L. Baumgarten, *What Clothes Reveal: The Language of Clothing Colonial and Federal America*, (New York: Yale University Press, 2002). A. Bissonnette, *Fashion on the Ohio Frontier 1790-1840*, (Kent State Univerity Museum, 2003). A. Buck, *Dress in Eighteenth Century England*, (London: Holmes & Meier, 1980). C Willet Cunnington and P. E. Cunnington, *Handbook of English Costume in the 18th Century*, (London: Faber, 1957). M. Delpierre, *Dress in France in the Eighteenth Century*, (New Haven: Yale University Press, 1998). Tandy and Charles Hersch, *Cloth and Costume 1750-1800 Cumberland County Pennsylvania*, (Carlisle: Cumberland County Historical Society, 1995). A. Ribeiro, *A Visual History of Costume: The Eighteenth Century*, (London: B. T. Batsford Ltd., 1983). A. Ribeiro, *Dress in Eighteenth Century Europe: 1715-1789*, (London: Holmes & Meier, 2002). A. Ribeiro, *The Art of Dress: Fashion in England and France 1750-1820*, (New Haven: Yale University Press, 1995). D. Roche, *The Culture of Clothing: Dress and Fashion in the Ancien Regime*, (Cambridge: Cambridge University Press, 1996). N. Rothstein, *Barbara Johnson's Album of Styles and Fabrics*, (London: Thames & Hudson, 1987). J. Tozer, and S. Levitt, *The Fabric of Society: A Century of People and Their Clothes 1770-1870*, (Manchester: Laura Ashley, 1983). A. Adburgham, *Shopping in Style: London From the Restoration to Edwardian Elegance*, (London: Thames & Hudson, 1979). A. Backhouse, *The Worm-Eaten Waistcoat*, (York, 2003). C. H. Crowston, *Fabricating Women: The Seamstresses of Old Regime France, 1675-1791*, (North Carolina: Duke University Press, 2001). E. Kowaleski-Wallace, *Consuming Subjects: Women, Shopping and Business in the Eighteenth Century*, (New York: Columbia University Press, 1997). B. Lemire, *Fashion's Favourite: The Cotton Trade and the Consumer in Britain 1660-1800*, (Oxford: Oxford University Press, 1991), and the same author, *Dress, Culture and Commerce: The English Clothing Trade Before the Factory, 1660-1800* (London: Palgrave Macmillan, 1997). C. Gillespie, (ed.), *A Diderot Pictorial Encyclopaedia of Trade and Industry*, (London/New York: Dover Publications, 1959). N. McKendrick, J. Brewer and J. H. Plumb, *The Birth of a Consumer Society: the Commercialization of Eighteenth Century England*, (Bloomington, Indiana University Press, 1982). E. Sanderson, *Women and Work in Eighteenth-Century Edinburgh* (London: Palgrave Macmillan, 1996).

15 W. A. Cole, 'The measurement of industrial growth', *Economic History Review*, 2nd ser., XI (1958), pp. 309-15. N. F. R. Crafts, *British Economic Growth During the Industrial Revolution* (Oxford: Oxford University Press, 1985), and the same author,"Economic Growth", in J. Mokyr (ed.), *Oxford Encyclopaedia of Economic History* (Oxford: Oxford University Press, 2003), vol. 2, pp. 137-145, N. F. R. Crafts, S. J. Leybourne, and T. C. Mills, 'Trends and cycles in British industrial production, 1700-1913', *Journal of the Royal Statistical Society*, ser. A, 152 (1989), pp. 43-60. R. S. W. Davies and S. Pollard, 'The iron industry, 1750-1850', in C. H. Feinstein and S. Pollard, (eds.), *Studies in capital formation in the United Kingdom, 1750-1920* (Oxford: Clarendon Press, 1988), pp. 73-104. P. Deane, 'The growth of British industry' *Economic Journal*, 46 (1956), pp. 493-500. P. Deane, 'The output of the British woollen industry in the eighteenth century', *Journal of Economic History*, 17 (1957), pp. 207-23. P. Deane and W. A. Cole, *British economic growth, 1688-1959: trends and structure* (Cambridge: Cambridge University Press, 1969 2nd edn.). C. H. Feinstein, 'Capital formation in Great Britain', in P. Mathias and M. M. Postan, (eds.), *The Cambridge Economic History of Europe*, VII (Cambridge: Cambridge University Press, 1978), pp. 28-96. C. K. Harley, 'British industrialization before 1841: evidence of slower growth during the industrial revolution', *Journal of Economic History*, 42 (1982), pp. 267-89. W. G. Hoffmann, *British industry, 1700-1950* (Oxford: Blackwell, 1955).

this debate about whether the industrial revolution was fired by domestic consumer increase or by enhanced export potential, is largely irrelevant given that in either case demand for Lancashire cotton products would have been boosted after 1763. It is highly likely that it was a combination of both these aspects along with the advent of more disposable income by the middling classes and upper echelons of the skilled workers, who were being directed to the purchase of both domestically produced commodities and those imported from the now burgeoning empire.

The Seven Years War had a significant effect on the moment of the explosion into a fully-fledged *capitalist* economy in Britain. It may not have been directly triggered when the second Peace of Paris agreement was signed but it made the circumstances much more advantageous. From 1759 the war in North America and the Caribbean was effectively over, this meant that the cotton plantations of the Southern Colonies and the Caribbean islands, now controlled by the British, could safely plan for increased production without concern for French interference or harassment. British control of the major trading stations of West Africa meant there were now both a ready and constant supply of slave labour and a captured market for British cotton goods. The stable colonial situation and enhanced export potential meant that the demand for raw cotton would increase in Britain and likely at more favourable prices. India was under British control from 1764 and all imports and, crucially for Lancashire, the distribution of Indian cotton exports were being organised by the East India Company, falling in line with trading policies dictated in Westminster. This was not only a boost to the merchant navy which would make handsome profits moving Indian goods out of and all imports into India, but also to the Lancashire cotton merchants who now knew that the superior Indian cotton products would be prohibitively priced in Britain, Europe and anywhere else in the world where Britain determined the sales of goods from the sub-continent. But the outlook for British produced goods was much improved because, as we have seen, relative demand both domestically and internationally had been increased substantially as a result of the recent conflict.

In fact, the production methods employed by the East India Company were not dissimilar to those in Britain. The consolidation of East India Company power after the 1760s did not initially lead to decline in textile exports from India. British cotton industries were undoubtedly growing but not to the extent that it would in the next fifty years and high quality Indian fine textiles were in great demand in Europe. So the company was keen on expanding textile exports from India via the *entrepôt* system. Before establishing political power in Bengal and Carnatic in the 1760s and 1770s, the East India Company had found it difficult to ensure a regular supply of goods for export. The French, Dutch, Portuguese, as well as the local traders, competed in the market to secure woven cloth. So weavers and supply merchants could bargain and try selling the produce to the best buyer. In their letters back to London, Company officials continuously complained of difficulties of supply and high price. However, once the East India Company established political power after the Seven Year War, it could assert monopoly trade rights. It proceeded to develop a system of management and control that would eliminate competition, control costs, and ensure regular supplies of cotton and silk goods. This it did through a series of careful stages. Firstly, the company tried to eliminate the existing traders and brokers

---

J. Hoppit, 'Counting the industrial revolution', *Economic History Review*, 2nd ser., XLIII (1990), pp. 173-93.

connected with the cloth trade and establish a more direct control over the weavers. It appointed a series of paid servants called the *gomastha* to supervise weavers, collect supplies, and examine the quality of cloth, not that dissimilar to the chapmen used in the Lancashire cotton industry. It prevented Company weavers from dealing with other buyers. One way of doing this was through system of advances. Once an order was placed, the weavers were given loans to purchase the raw material for their production. Those who took loans had to hand over the cloth they produced to the *gomastha*. They could not take it to any other merchant or deal with any other company other than the East India Company.

As loans flowed in and the demand for fine textiles expanded, weavers eagerly took the advances, hoping to earn more. Many weavers had small plots of land which they had earlier cultivated along with weaving, and the produce from this took care of their family needs. Now they had to lease out the land and devote all their time to weaving. Weaving, as in England, required the labour of the entire family, with children and women all engaged in different stages of the process. Soon, however, in many weaving villages there were reports of clashes between weavers and *gomasthas*. Earlier supply merchants had very often lived within the weaving villages or been in close proximity, and had a close relationship with the weavers, assisting their needs and helping them in time of crisis. The new *gomasthas* were outsiders, with no permanent social links with the village. They acted arrogantly, marched into villages with sepoys and peons, and reprimanded and punished weavers for delays in supply – often beating and flogging them. The weavers lost the power to bargain for price and sell to different buyers; the price they received from Company was often wretchedly low and the loans they had accepted tied them to the Company. Thus in many places in Carnatic and Bengal, weavers left their villages and migrated, setting up looms in other villages where they had some family members. Elsewhere, weavers along with the village traders revolted, opposing the company and its officials. Over time many weavers began refusing loans, closing down their workshops and resorting to subsistence and agricultural labour. Now, by the final third of eighteenth century, India too was prime export target for the receiving of Lancashire cotton goods.[16]

For an ideal growth pattern under a capitalist system economists refer to 'total factor productivity'. This is where all the three (four if you include information) factors of production (land, labour and capital) are increasing at the same time. Classically the capitalist only has effective control of one of the factors of production, the cost, discipline and productivity potential of labour. However, during and after the Seven Years War the emerging capitalists of the North-West were making rapid strides towards having much more control over their raw materials in terms of both their availability and the potentially reduced costs through bulk buying and inducing economies of scale in terms of increased supply and the deployment of the raw materials on their terms. Thus

---

16 D. A. Farnie, *The English Cotton Industry and the World Market* (Oxford: Oxford University Press, 1979). P. Parthasarathi, *The Transition to a Colonial Economy: Weavers, Merchants and Kings in South India, 1720-1800,* (Cambridge: Cambridge University Press, 2001). O. Prakash, 'Bullion for Goods: International Trade and the Economy of Early Eighteenth Century Bengal', *Indian Economic and Social History Review,* 13 (1976), pp. 159-87. S. Chaudhury, 'European Companies and the Bengal Textile Industry in the Eighteenth Century: The Pitfalls of Applying Quantitative Techniques', *Modern Asian Studies,* 27 (1993), pp. 321-40; O. Prakash, 'On Estimating the Employment Implications of European Trade for the Eighteenth Century Bengal Textile Industry — A Reply', *Modern Asian Studies,* 27 (1993), pp. 351-2.

performance of one of the factors of production was now enhanced for these cotton merchants. We have also seen that their control of the flow and deployment of capital was steadily improving as they joined in *ad hoc* partnerships to deliver short and long-term capital requirements for the collection, distribution of the raw cotton, the spun thread, the weaving, dying and, ultimately, dispatching both to domestic and overseas markets. However, their control of the productivity, discipline and, most crucially, cost of labour as a factor of production was also beginning to be re-appraised and to come further under the control of the cotton masters in the North-West, and the ensuing struggle is, in essence, the basis of the argument that follows.

The Seven Years War was a major event in the developments of eighteenth-century Britain, after it the development of capitalism could and would proceed incrementally quicker. It still needed a coherent body of theory, but the certainties of mercantilism were no longer universally accepted and both David Hume and Adam Smith were busy sharpening their pencils. Politically, the old Whig guard was gone and popular radicalism had been born, and in terms of British overseas interests, imperialism was becoming the foreign policy of capitalism.

4

Employer and Worker: Agency and Class

The protectionist nature of the mercantile system in the proto-industrial phase was, it must be reiterated, a long-standing feature of the relationship between masters and labourers, be they skilled, semi- or unskilled. In urban centres the skilled craft workers were protected by the guild system, which was seen as vital to protect the status, wages, apprenticeship rules and the so-called 'mysteries' of a given craft. In non-urban or semi-urban areas workers organised their own protective devices by means of the friendly society, a method by which for a certain, usually small, regular financial contribution a worker and his family could depend on some relief in times of work shortages, illness, incapacity or death and burial. Often these friendly societies were termed 'box clubs', so called because the contributions would be collected and secured in a locked box by a designated member and these, it was believed, were early forms of trade unions.[1] Thus on the surface they would appear to be an unassuming early form of self-help for the labouring population, but the danger was that these lower orders were organising themselves – forming 'combinations' – bringing with it aspersions of conspiratorial intent. This threat alone could turn employers into believing that the workers were attempting to wrench away the masters control of the discipline/wages etc. of a particular trade to their advantage. The key fact was, as we shall discover in due course, that the attitudes of many of the labouring population was to regard their employer masters with suspicion and distrust, and often they had good cause for doing so.

The key point to realise at this juncture in the discussion however is that the labouring class attempted to assert and retain their independence, (or at least limit their dependence on their employers), which they believed had been customary since at least the establishment of the Tudor acts of 1512, (4 Hen. VIII c. 5.), 1514 (6 Hen. VIII c. 3) and the more famous Elizabethan Statute of Artificers of 1562, (5 Eliz. I c. 4). The Acts sought to enshrine the rights of labourers in terms of apprenticeship, wages, restrictions of movement overseas, (to potential enemies of the Kingdom), of trades vital to the national interest. These pieces of legislation set the benchmark of customary practices which labourers and artisans throughout the country assumed were protective devices in their common interest. Hence, in the course of over two hundred years many, if not all, of the labouring population of Britain were of the view that the preservation and maintenance of their customary practices were a *right*, enshrined, certainly in common law, if not in statute law. Thus in this sense when they attempted to ensure the maintenance of their customary rights by resisting they were to all intents and purposes acting out of a response to what they perceived as an attack on them as a *class*. In this way it mattered little if their recourse to resistance was over a trade dispute or the forced enclosure of commons or the attempts of corn merchants to fix the price of grain and flour, the effect was the same; they perceived themselves both subjectively in terms of their understanding and knowledge of their customary rights to an objective and very real affront by another more powerful class. Of course many employers and men of property did not see this relationship in quite the same way, which again can be extrapolated as an understanding that was determined by *their* interest or

---

[1] J. Rule, (ed.) *British Trade Unionism, 1750-1850: The Formative Years*, (London: Longman, 1988).

class position. However, before we examine the divergence, and indeed hardening of the employer/labourer relationship around mid-century, we have at this point to briefly consider the relevant historiography surrounding eighteenth-century social and especially hegemonic correlations. A more detailed discussion of the historiography of the concept of moral economy will follow in the next chapter, but the nature of the topic under examination in this chapter demands some dialogue about the character of the debate.

Even after over half a century since its publication this topic of the emergence of class and, more specifically, the working class is still strongly influenced by Edward Thompson's *The Making of the English Working Class*,[2] and, indeed, his other pieces of scholarship on this topic. The defining period for the 'making' of the English working class was from the 1790s when the objective reality of their position was recognised by many working people which was coupled with a body of radical theory based on actual long-term and short-term historical developments, not least those arising from the French Revolution of July, 1789. A working class consciousness began to be formed which understood the need for a concerted response; to mount a political struggle to ameliorate their economic subservience to the practicalities of capital and the theory of political economy which supported it. Hence, for Thompson modern capitalism – which was becoming ever more pervasive from the 1780s – had to be in place before a working class was itself formed; in essence the existence of and the threats posed by the factory system (even for those such as handloom weavers who were not yet in the factories) and working people's relationship to the capitalists (as owners of the means of production) who controlled it. These features had to evolve before a true working class, (waged labourers who owned nothing but their ability to labour), could be said to have been formed. Working people began to think of themselves and the world in which they lived increasingly in class terms. Thompson wrote in the preface of *The Making of the English Working Class*. "Class is defined by men as they live their own history, and, in the end, this is its only definition."[3] Thus it is an understanding of the ramifications of changing circumstances into which the working class were placed that made them become aware of their class position in relation to other classes, which they were obviously in a subordinate position in terms of social, political and economic power.

But what of the situation before the 1780s and 1790s; the conditions before the circumstances were in place to forge the working class in a meaningful (Thompsonian) sense? How do we refer to the working people in these phases of development? There has been some work that does suggest that class, (class identities, solidarities and action), can be seen as far back as the late medieval and into the early modern periods.[4] Indeed Andy Wood has suggested that "social historians have been mesmerized by that single definition of class-identity. The assumption that 'true' class consciousness can be manifest on the level of the nation-state has led historians to find in the early modern period one

---

2   E. P. Thompson, *The Making of the English Working Class*, (London: Littlehampton Book Services Ltd., 1963).
3   Ibid p. 7.
4   Note the work of Andy Wood, 'Subordination, Solidarity and the Limits of Popular Agency in a Yorkshire Valley *c*.1596-1615', *Past & Present*, 93 (1) (Nov., 2006), pp. 41-72, and 'The Place of Custom in Plebeian Political Culture: England, 1550-1800' *Social History*, Vol. 22, No. 1 (Jan., 1997), pp. 46-60, and, 'Fear, Hatred and the Hidden Injuries of Class in Early Modern England', *Journal of Social History*, Vol. 39, No. 3, (Spring, 2006), pp. 803-826.

of the main barriers to the operations of class."[5] For Wood, particularly in the early modern period class identities are clearly visible in the local environment, within the communities of working people. They are features which came to especial prominence in the period after 1650 and again clearly in the 'Thompsonian' phase of the 1780s and 1790s, when the Industrial Revolution was in full swing. Yet traces of them, claims Wood, were to be found from the late medieval period when some particular threat appeared to put established customs and traditional practices at risk. At these moments the community of working people to all intents and purposes were acting in a class-based way, in defence of what they believed – their basic rights as workers – were under attack by forces that required countering by collective displays of resistance. Hence the basis of 'class' resistance was conservative in its most literal sense, to conserve and preserve what had made these communities of ordinary working people viable, independent and, indeed, functional both economically and socially. By engaging in resistance against the powerful they were invoking their potential or latent power of the defence of what they saw as their inherent, intrinsic and commonly held rights; the rights, as noted previously, of what came to be known as the 'freeborn Englishmen'.[6] They were displaying a common identity of interest which was uniquely their own. Yet this need not necessarily be opposed to more powerful interests within the state in terms of an all-out threatening challenge to power, but to nudge the more powerful into an understanding that what was happening was wrong in a specific situation or in immediate circumstances. This leads to the interpretation more associated with social and cultural historians and indeed anthropologists, which is encapsulated most elegantly in the work of James Scott.[7] For Scott peasant lives are constantly re-negotiated under a series of accepted veneers which he terms 'transcripts' or accepted cultural and social norms of behaviour and acceptance; deference and inherent (but often hidden) hostility. For Scott, deference is but a façade and part of the public transcript of accepted behavioural patterns and, to a significant extent, it is negotiated between the giver and receiver of deferential behaviour. But this accepted and negotiated façade can slip and reveal the hidden transcript lying just below the surface of widespread popular resistance, which all the members of the labouring communities understand and are aware of. Thus the hidden transcript can serve as a brake on the authoritarian influence of the elites and reveals a cultural milieu deeply embedded within the lower orders which is widely understood within such communities and is an element that can explode into open resistance. Thus in Scott's interpretation of the operation of these peasant societies is one of semi-permanent, but constant testing of the existing elite authority and potential resistance to it when it appears to overreach its boundaries. Thus peasant societies, according to Scott, possessed an agency of coping with seemingly unending subservient powerlessness. Displays of deference to social superiors were crucially part of the façade to ensure the elites

---

5   A. Wood, *Riot, Rebellion and Popular Politics in Early Modern England*, (*Social History in Perspective*), (Basingstoke and New York: Palgrave Macmillan, 2002) p. 26.
6   See for example, M. Bush, 'The Risings of the Commons in England, 1381–1549', in *Orders and Hierarchies in Late Medieval and Renaissance Europe*, ed. Jeffrey Denton, (Basingstoke: Palgrave Macmillan, 1999), pp. 109, 111, 112, 113-4.
7   See for example, J. C. Scott, *Domination and the Arts of Resistance: Hidden Transcripts* (New Haven: Yale University Press, 1992 Ed.), and by the same author, *The Moral Economy of the Peasant: rebellion and Subsistence in South-East Asia*, (New Haven: Yale University Press, 1976), and *Weapons of the Weak: Everyday forms of Peasant Resistance*, (New Haven: Yale University Press 1985).

never got too close to becoming aware of what the real feelings of the lower orders actually were: mistrust, suspicion and resentment. There is a lot to be said for Scott's interpretation, given the inter-connected nature of these relatively small communities of working people who were without formal political, social or economic power in conventional terms, but who did possess the power to influence their community peers and their families and were ready to mobilise themselves for the defence of attacks on their customary rights in the North-West in the later 1740s into the 1750s. As we shall discover in the final chapters below, displays of deference also possessed an important relevance in the contests for political power, where paternalist rituals were enacted in order to demonstrate what political interests could offer in exchange for the support of working people.

At this point, however, we need to get back closer to the period under investigation and return again to what Edward Thompson had to say about early (pre-1780s) displays of 'class' feelings. When discussing a series of measures attempting to place a strict limit on the actions of the 'loose and disorderly' persons, particularly at election times, Thompson tells us how for Walpole at the height of powers in the 1720s even this was too much for the great man. That even the Whigs, with their effective political monopoly of all power at the national or local level, realised the limitations of their authority to enforce attempts to limit popular expressions of discontent, he writes:

> Any licence afforded to the crowd by the Whigs during these years arose less from libertarian sentiment than from a realistic sense of what those limits were. And these limits, in their turn, were imposed by a particular equilibrium of forces which cannot, in the end, be analysed without recourse to the concept of class.[8]

Thus, although at this point he appears to be sympathetic to the use of class as a viable explanatory concept, Thompson warns against the old enemy of many historians, that of anachronism, who read back to the past modern interpretations of a potentially illustrative concept. Thus we must at all times be aware of the historical specificity of the use of class in terms of its appropriateness to the period to which it is being applied. This is primarily because in the language of the time the term 'class' was not used as a category of social location. Yet there were undoubted social categories and often the 'lower orders' or 'common people' were referred to, as we shall discover, in derogatory terms by their 'social betters', hence there was an understanding of an early form of class difference and distinctiveness. 'Class' begins to appear regularly in terms of common linguistic usage in the decade after the 1790s, which again was Thompson's starting point for the birth of class. Yet as we see from the work of Scott and Wood, there can be an appropriate utility to class as an explanatory concept in attempting to disentangle the essence of peasant communities and those of early modern Britain. Thompson himself refers to the 'heuristic category of class' in terms of its usage in pre-industrial revolution circumstances because, 'no alternative category is available to analyse a manifest and universal historical process.'[9]

> This emphasizes, however, that class, in its heuristic usage, is inseparable from the notion of 'class-struggle'. In my view, far too much theoretical

---

8 E. P. Thompson, 'Class Struggle without Class', *Social History*, Vol. 3, No. 2 (May, 1978), pp. 133-165, p.146.
9 Ibid, p. 149.

attention (much of it plainly a-historical) has been paid to 'class', and far too little to 'class-struggle'.[10]

From what has been discussed above it is clear that historians of popular protest have willingly and validly employed the application of class as an explanatory concept in periods prior to the eighteenth century and thus a key to understanding the circumstances prevailing in the North-West in the struggle between masters and workers during the crucial years between 1747 and 1770 is one that is appropriate to be discussed in class terms. As Thompson tells us, "we can read eighteenth-century social history as a succession of confrontations between an innovative market economy and the customary moral economy of the plebs."[11] Indeed, these struggles seem to have reached the notice of those at the very apex of the elites. In a draft of his speech to the official state opening of Parliament in December 1757, the King made mention of this prevailing 'spirit of disorder': He was particularly concerned about disharmony among the lower orders and the effect this could have on maintaining enthusiasm for the War effort.

> I have had such ample experience of the loyalty and good affections of my faithful subjects towards me, my family and government in all circumstances that I am confident they are not to be shaken. But I cannot avoid taking notice of that spirit of disorder which has shown itself amongst the common people in some parts of the Kingdom. Let me recommend to you to do your part in discouraging and suppressing such abuses; and for maintaining the laws and lawful authority. If anything shall be found wanting to explain, or enforce what may have been misunderstood, or misrepresented, I am persuaded it will not escape your attention. Nothing can be so conducive to the defence of all that is dear to us as well as reducing our enemies to reason, as union and harmony amongst ourselves.[12]

There is, however, a further feature of the theory of class that has to be discussed in relation to the viability of its usage before the phase of capitalist industrialisation, and this is the related concept of 'agency'. This refers to the will and demonstrable effects of the working class to act in their own interests. Instead of relying or expecting an agency outside the parameters of the working or labouring classes, (such as a magistrate, a member of the local or county elites, or indeed the state itself), to act to redress an anomaly or grievance on their behalf, the working class had, in significant numbers, come to the inescapable conclusion that they *themselves* must act as the agency of change in order to redress their disputes. This was the point at which, for Marx, the working class move from a 'class-in-themselves' to a 'class-for-themselves'.[13] It

---

10 Ibid.
11 Ibid. p. 155
12 National Archives, Kew, State Papers Domestic, 36, Vol. 138, ff 162-163, (December, 1757). In fact from November into December, 1757 there were serious riots in East Anglia. the Midlands, Yorkshire and Staffordshire. See *Gentleman's Magazine*, 'Thoughts on the Late Insurrections', which were primarily caused, according to author by the engrossing (enclosures) of farms. (December 1757) pp. 601-602.
13 The extent however, that this distinction is directly attributable to Marx is hotly debated among social and political theorists. See E. Andrew, 'Class in Itself and Class against Capital: Karl Marx and His Classifiers', *Canadian Journal of Political Science / Revue canadienne de science politique*, Vol.16, No. 3 (Sep., 1983), pp. 577-584. See also T. Dos Santos, 'The Concept of Social Classes', *Science and Society 34* (1970), 181; H. Draper, *Karl Marx's Theory of Revolution: The Politics of Social Classes* (New York: Monthly Review Press, 1978), 40-41, 349;

serves to indicate the point at which evolving capitalism had reached, in that the lines of demarcation have become drawn into much sharper relief between the capitalists as a class and the working class, in effect the working class are becoming or have become class conscious. Yet even by Marx's definition this does not preclude the existence of class before this stage is reached, rather it emphasises, quite specifically, the need for certain pre-conditions to be manifest to make the working class politically viable as an opposition to the capitalists and become potentially a revolutionary force. Then they would be competent to overthrow or at least challenge the power of capitalism as the economic basis of society, and also recognise the state as a pivotal feature of the supporting political superstructure. When this 'political' element is realised the working class have matured into gaining full class consciousness. Thus the latent power of the working class is innate, but it is a power which the forces of authority and the working class themselves begin to increasingly realise is potentially effective and indeed as necessary as capitalism as a system becomes more exploitative. Not long after Thompson's formation, or 'birth', of the working class we see evidence of this from a working man, albeit one member of the working class who was a committed radical. In 1810 the Manchester Committee of Working Men was formed in light of a serious slump in the cotton trade, and a year later the Oldham handloom weaver, John Knight, wrote a paper in response to a petition signed by 40,000 Manchester workers which had been dismissed by Parliament. Knight outlined the key problems facing the working class, "...considering the number of petitioners and the extent of their sufferings was it not possible that some reasonable portion of hope should not have been founded on these circumstances." He noted that Parliament could and did interfere in fixing the assize of bread, regulating the price of corn and fixing the wages of the weavers of Spitalfields, as well as the journeymen tailors of London, augmenting the salaries of clergymen and judges, and for regulating commerce.[14] He then put his case directly:

> This Committee are utterly at a loss to conceive on what fair ground legislative interference can be improper under circumstances so necessitous...if laws can be made to regulate the necessaries of life, laws should be enacted for regulating the wages by which such provisions must be purchased, especially when (as in our case) such wages have lost all reasonable balance and proportion....The moral to be drawn from these events is that the House of Commons, as is at present constituted or appointed is unfit to manage your affairs...had you possessed 70,000 votes to elect members to sit in that House, would your application have been treated with such indifference, not to say inattention? We believe not. You are urged to exert yourselves to recover the right of electing representatives and extending the franchise.[15]

Here we see Knight calling for the working class to operate for themselves and gain political representation; to gain some form of political power and force their grievances on the existing order. This was the type of agency – and possibly even

---

G. A. Cohen, *Karl Marx's Theory of History: A Defence* (Oxford: Clarendon Press, 1980), 73-76. N. Poulantzas, *Political Power and Social Classes* (London: New Left Books, 1973), 74-76, and A. Przeworski, 'Proletariat into a Class: The Process of Class Formation from Karl Kautsky's *The Class Struggle* to Recent Controversies,' *Politics and Society* 7 (1977), 343, 367. K. Marx and F. Engels, *Collected Works* (New York: International Publishers, 1976), Vol. i1, 187.

14 All of which would have been known to the working class of the North-West in the 1760s.
15 National Archives, HO. 42.117, (Fletcher to Ryder, 21/11/1811).

more direct confrontation – for the working class to take action for themselves. In its language and, importantly, its meaning it was not dissimilar to that being used by the leaders of weavers' resistance in the North-West in the later 1750s. Knight's statement also fits classically into what Wood has defined as the distinction between agency and structure, which he characterises thus, "the relationship between agency (that is, the capacity to assert meaningful control over the circumstances of one's life) and structure (the means by which social structures exert prior material and political inhibitions upon agency)."[16] In Knight's address we see exactly this in operation, thus out of struggle the working class become more and more subjectively aware of their subservient (objective) structural position and discover the need to act as agents for themselves and, in so doing, define and sharpen their class consciousness. Again Edward Thompson phrased this perfectly when he said:

> Indeed, class-struggle is the prior, as well as the more universal, concept. To put it bluntly: classes do not exist as separate entities, look around, find an enemy class, and then start to struggle. On the contrary, people find themselves in a society structured in determined ways (crucially, but not exclusively, in productive relations), they experience exploitation (or the need to maintain power over those whom they exploit), they identify points of antagonistic interest, they commence to struggle around these issues and in the process of struggling they discover themselves as classes, they come to know this discovery as class-consciousness. Class and class-consciousness are always the last, not the first, stage in the real historical process.[17]

Thus a significant point to note regarding the development of class and class consciousness is whether the degree of working class activity, organization and will-to-act (agency) indicated what they understood to be an assault on the existing political culture, norms and structures. Hence a key question, and indeed one of the central themes of the discussion that follows, is just how developed was the agency of the working class to organise and actively engage with the forces of authority, and/or their social superiors and employers, in order to affect change purely in this class sense. In this context it matters little whether or not they succeeded, more that they were willing to attempt to act for themselves as a class. However, moving to the central core of this chapter we need to consider what employer/worker relations were like in the period under discussion and, more saliently discover what can be gleaned of worker attitudes towards their employers.

As we saw in chapter two, there was pressure to change aspects of the mercantile system in the first half of the eighteenth century. This was especially so with the overtly protectionist aspects concerning the myriad of levies, tariffs, customs and duties imposed on imports and re-exports and on the customary practices protecting workers against employers who aimed to change the basis of existing (and often long-standing) contracts between them. Mainly these challenges came from commercially minded (urban) Whigs who sought license to expand their influence – and, of course potential profits. The fact was that under the mercantile system there were occasions when the 'crowd, mob, lower orders or common labourers' did force a change in policy or the maintenance of

---

16 A. Wood, 'Subordination, Solidarity and the Limits of Popular Agency in a Yorkshire Valley c.1596-1615', *Past & Present*, 93 (1) (Nov., 2006), pp. 41-72, p.43.

17 E. P. Thompson, 'Class Struggle without Class', *Social History*, Vol. 3, No. 2 (May, 1978), pp. 133-165, p.149.

existing policies that served to protect working people. The nature of change in the cotton sector of the North-West in the later 1740s into the 1750s will be the main focus of study in due course. However, the key area occasioning disputes in the first half of the eighteenth century was to be found in the woollen industry, which was by far the largest single sector of employment, income and exports of all the British proto-industrial sectors. The main woollen industrial areas in Britain throughout the eighteenth century were in East Anglia, moving down into north Essex, the West Riding of Yorkshire and the West of England, chiefly around west Wiltshire, east Somerset and central and south Gloucestershire, with some specialist centres in Devon. The workers of the West of England were particularly forthright in the need to protect their customary practices in terms of charges-per-length of piece, apprenticeship rules, types of cloth woven, its length, picks of warp and weft, the dressing and finishing procedures of the material. Likewise, some master clothiers attempted at various times to challenge these customary methods of work and impose new practices, especially when the trade was booming or alternatively in a serious slump. Thus we see outbreaks of protest by the workers in defence of the attacks they perceived coming from the masters (clothiers) to what they saw as their long-held traditional rights.

There were serious outbreaks of protest and, indeed, violence occurring fairly regularly not long after the Hanoverians ascended the throne in 1714. Workers in the woollen sector were active in forming box clubs and engaging in industrial disputes in East Anglia and Devon in 1715. These grew decidedly dangerous with the workers at one point brandishing pistols, clubs and swords to force the authorities to act against recalcitrant clothiers who had cut the rates of pay for piecework, so dangerous and serious, in fact, that the Privy Council had to step in to broker a peace between the contending parties. In Devon the worsted and serge workers formed trade unions to fend off pay cuts in 1717 and these again resulted in very serious rioting escalating at one point in attempts to demolish houses of the disputing clothiers.[18] They ignored the magistrates attempting to read the Riot Act and instead communicated directly with the officer in charge of the troops trying to keep the peace. There was more trouble in Devon, at Tiverton in 1720, when the main issue was the use of Irish woollen thread which would have denied the work of the weavers' wives and daughters. This Irish wool was burned ceremoniously and again there was evidence that the workers were prepared to use arms.[19] In Somerset in 1725 there were serious disputes over wages and by this time the clothiers were demanding that something be done about the escalating violence and advance of trade unions. In 1726 Parliament acted by allowing magistrates to fix workers' wages according to the old Tudor statutes, and at the same time denying clothier's who happened to be Justices of the Peace to be party to such arbitration. By the same token they imposed serious sentences to workers who were found guilty of entering or destroying industrial goods or buildings, by threatening capital punishment or transportation. Importantly, Parliament also made worker combinations illegal.[20] This appears to have had little effect as more disputes flared up in West Wiltshire around Frome, Melksham, Bradford upon Avon and Trowbridge. Along with Gloucestershire, this was the region which seems to have been most active in

---

18 See A. Randall, *Riotous Assemblies: Popular Protest in Hanoverian England,* (Oxford: Oxford University Press, 2006) pp. 137-138.
19 Ibid, p. 138.
20 Ibid. pp. 138-139.

protecting worker rights as we move into the later 1720s and through to the 1730s. The target again were those masters trying to change customary practices, and we see here a magistrate attempting to broker a form of arbitration between masters and workers, with some success, at least in the short term.[21] Indeed, one commentator accused the clothiers of the Melksham/Trowbridge districts of attempts of 'incorporating themselves' so that "they might with greater strength bear down on the already oppressed manufacturers" by, in effect, forming a monopoly to fix all dealings with the woollen workers.[22] Once more the government got involved and sent down commissioners to investigate the circumstances, and they found that several magistrates urged the workers to petition parliament to remedy their case. There was also support coming from the landowners and local gentry who were similarly aware that continued disputes would result in social disruption, loss of work and earnings for the labourers, and would eventually impact the rising poor rates and, by extension, their pockets.

Clearly, worker attitudes towards employers in the Hanoverian period was one of suspicion, as witnessed by the outbreaks of anger and violence, but also one in which the 'common people' were readily prepared to confront what they saw as injustices being perpetrated against them. Thus in the later 1720s and into the 1730s magistrates throughout the West of England were equipped to set the workers' wages, only in some cases to see these ignored by the clothiers. This tense situation that existed exploded again in Wiltshire. The circumstances were similar to those previously outlined whereby during a brief recession in trade – when food prices were generally rising – a clothier from Melksham imposed a lower piece-rate pay and was rumoured to be paying his workers in truck, (a means of payment where the workers received tokens or actual food and drink instead of cash), which, if allowed to continue, would surely mean that other clothiers would do exactly the same throughout the clothing districts. Violence was again reported, the house of a clothier who had initiated the first attempt to reduce pay was totally destroyed. Troops again arrived, arrests were made and magistrates again attempted to placate the warring factions. Of those arrested three were sentenced to death as a demonstration that the authorities would only tolerate so much, whilst again it was urged that magistrates do all they could to arbitrate fairly in matters of contract and disputes between masters and men. Yet there was evidence that the clothiers themselves were visiting weaver's houses in the night to threaten and intimidate them and further were using the troops as a means of direct attack on the weavers and fomenting the trouble between the contending groups.[23] The upshot was, as noted above, an Act of Parliament to empower all magistrates to act as impartial arbitrators in disputes between masters and labourers.[24]

It is at this point that we witness the sharpening divide amongst men of business regarding what should be the proper way to deal with workers and how the authority of masters must be reconsidered. This will be important as we examine the circumstances of the disputes in the North-West later in the century

---

21 Ibid. p. 139.
22 Anon, *The Devil drove out the warping-bar; or, The snap-reel snap'd...*, (London, 1727) p. 8.
23 Ibid. See the Informations given on oath of John Say of Bradford upon Avon, weaver; James Hellps of Bradford upon Avon, weaver; Richard Hall, broadcloth weaver of Limply-Stoak in the parish of Bradford upon Avon; John Marks, broadcloth weaver, of Bradford upon Avon, December, 1726 to January, 1727. Appendixes, pp. 21-29.
24 Geo I, (c 23), Woollen Manufacture Act, 1726.

in chapter seven below, but it is worth noting here that it was no accident that the opening salvoes of the debate of the old and the new attitudes took place in the West of England in the wake of almost twenty years of ongoing disputes and worker resistance to change of any kind. Resident here was one of the foremost influential national voices on all things commercial, trading and manufacturing in the shape of Josiah Tucker. Writing in 1757 and in the middle of a long and ongoing series of disputes between master and men in the West of England and indeed in the North-West, the soon to be Dean of Gloucester held forth on his views of working people. He compared the dependent outworkers of the West of England with the much more independent workers of the West Riding of Yorkshire. There, said Tucker the middle men were in effect self-employed agents of clothiers, and thus being independent are "all rivals, all animated with the same desire of bringing their goods to market upon the cheapest terms and of excelling one another."[25] In the West Riding the journeymen weavers they serviced were:

> Likewise ... being so little removed from the degree and condition of their masters, are likely to set up themselves; by the industry and frugality of a few years, have no conception that they are embarked in an interest opposite to that of their masters, or that they are called upon to enter into clubs and combinations against them. Thus it is that the working people are generally moral, sober and industrious, and that a riot or mob is a thing hardly known amongst them.[26]

Whereas in the West of England (and, by extension, the North-West) the master clothiers buys and controls all the raw materials and all the processes involved in the production of the finished fabric: "That is, he is master of the whole manufacture, from first to last, and perhaps employs a thousand persons under him."[27] This, for Tucker, was a seething conduit for mutual contempt, and such attitudes were held and acted upon similarly by the employers: "because they [the working class] ought to be kept low and not to rise up in competition with their superiors."[28] For their part the workers "think it no crime to get as much wages and to do as little for it as they possibly can, to lie and cheat, and to do any other bad thing, provided it is only against their master, whom they look upon as their common enemy, with whom no faith is to be kept."[29] This was a description of employer/worker relations under the capitalist system that could have been written at any time during the series of crises that can be found in the period during the consolidation of capitalism in Britain, from the 1790s until the later 1840s or at the very end of the nineteenth century amongst the semi- and unskilled workers, or indeed in the period from the turn of the twentieth century until 1945 in some of the old staple industries.

Tucker was writing his opinions at the end of the 1750s, but we get a clearer view of how he may have reached these views if we briefly examine the historical context of the situation in the West of England over the previous twenty years. In one corner we have the archetypical paternalist magistrate, Thomas Andrews, and in the other the disgruntled clothier, William Temple,

---

25 Josiah Tucker, *Instructions for Travellers; A Brief Essay on the Advantages and Disadvantages which respectively attend France and Great Britain with Respect to Trade,* (Dublin, 1758,) pp. 36-38.
26 Ibid.
27 Ibid.
28 Ibid.
29 Ibid.

from Melksham, calling for the old customary practices to be confined to history. The exchange is interesting in that we see in sharp relief the contrasting values of the two positions. This remarkable argument took place over eight weeks in the *Gloucester Journal* and neither party were prepared to give an inch, so bitter was the dispute and so important were the points at issue.[30] Such was the interest caused by this exchange that both the diatribes were subsequently published.[31] It was Temple who opened up the exchange by challenging Andrews's judgement in accusing the clothiers of being oppressors of the labouring classes. "...when we see *Ignorance* and *Vanity*, or *Malice* and *Knavery*, stand up as Champions of a licentious Rabble, (patronized by a Magistrate [Andrews] who ought to suppress them) ... impose on the *Weak* and *Unthinking*, and deceive the *Judicious* by bold Assertions."[32] Temple said that there were upwards of 150 clothiers in and around Melksham, Bradford upon Avon and Trowbridge and that Andrews had tarred them all with same brush as oppressors of the weavers. They were accused of detaining or paying them low wages, or paying them in truck in lieu of wages, combining together to fix low wages until the weavers are 'starving in their thousands'. Of these 150 masters Temple, whilst suggesting that "never was a body of men of any sort in the World, who deserved the epithets of *Just* and *Honourable*," admitted that there may be some "who not behave to the *Poor* with that Humanity and Tenderness they ought."[33] However, it did not take Temple long to say what he really thought of the woollen workers of the West of England.

> The Cause of the *Poor* is popular, and apt to bias many thinking judicious Persons, who would not have much to do with them. The World would have quite a different Opinion of the manufacturing Populous from what perhaps they have, if they were acquainted with their *Indolence, Idleness, Debauchery, Frauds* and *Dishonesty*, so well as the *Clothiers* who employ them... they (the woollen workers) and their adherents ought to be looked upon by every honest Man as a Body of *Villains*, who have forged Lyes, [sic] and trumped up Falsehoods in order to render the *Clothiers* odious, palliate their own *Guilt*, and have a Plea for their own Wickedness.[34]

Yet he admits that one master, who was now a magistrate, used to 'kick, cuff, beat and abuse' his workers as well as "stop their Wages and defraud them in the most base flagrant Manner."[35] Nevertheless, according to Temple, the weavers "are the most feeble, weak and impotent of all the Manufacturers."[36] He mocked the fact that the weavers struggle on subsistence wages, or that government and local taxes, levies, tariffs and duties eat into their earnings, in fact according to Temple "the poor have such high Wages, as to furnish them with the Means and Instruments of Luxury and Idleness." Thus the logic according to Temple was clear, "if the Poor can acquire enough in a Part of their Time to be luxurious, and debauch the rest, certainly their wages cannot be low, nor can they feel any

---

30 *Gloucester Journal*, December 19, 1738; January 9, 1739; February 7, 27, 1739.
31 W. Temple, *The Case as stands between the Clothiers, Weavers and other Manufacturers, with regard to the late Riot etc*, (London: T. Cooper, 1739). T. Andrews, *The miseries of the miserable: or An Essay laying open the decay of the fine woollen trade, and the unhappy condition of the poor Wiltshire Manufacturers, by a gentleman of Wilts*. (London, 1739).
32 W. Temple, *The Case as stands between the Clothiers etc*, p. 3.
33 Ibid. p. 5.
34 Ibid
35 Ibid. p. 6
36 Ibid. p. 12.

burden from Taxes..."³⁷ Then Temple suggested a remedy. "The only way to make the Poor sober, industrious and obedient, is to take away the means of Idleness and Intemperance, such as high Wages..."³⁸ Temple concluded by asking what the solution should be and he offered the answer.

> ...what remains to be done? But for the *Gentlemen* and *Magistrates* to treat the *Clothiers* more respectfully, and speak more kindly of them for the future than they have done formerly. Also to aid and encourage them in the Reduction in the Price of Labour...and necessary for the Preservation of our *Foreign Trade*. We must by some Means or other, reduce the Price of Labour, that our Manufactures may find a Vent in Foreign Markets; for it is our Foreign Trade, or Exports, the Riches of our Nation depend.³⁹

Clearly, Temple did harbour particularly critical sentiments towards the labour force, yet, as we shall discover when we examine the situation in the North-West, this was exactly the tactic employed by the cotton masters from the later 1740s and into the 1750s. Importantly, it was his view that labour was a key element in the ability of those directing an enterprise to control as an essential means of production. In adopting this position he was forward thinking, even if some areas of his critique appear to suggest a rather heartless and intolerant autocrat. However, returning to the theme of employer attitudes of the later 1740s, Temple's strong, indeed antagonistic views were tempered by an opposing set of values, extolled by a more traditionalist country gentleman, and magistrate, Thomas Andrews who, in a direct counter to the views of Temple, looked to the beneficial effects of customary practices and in the process counters every one of the clothier's claims. Crucially, Andrews, as a point of logical argument, makes use of the moral economy as a concept to hang the oppressive masters. He began by suggesting there were two ways of conducting business that are damaging to the interests of those involved in industry. The first was by pursuing a venture that could be in some way hurtful to the community at large. The second was by "taking *unreasonable* profits at a useful occupation." The intimation was that this was exactly what the West of England clothiers were doing. The remedy Andrews proposed was that:

> ...too great Plenty of that Sort of People who live by Selling the Necessaries of Life and Trade to the Community, as it must be attended with a Deficiency of *honest Gains* to many of them, often put petty Traders upon such acts of Oppression and Dishonesty to gain a Livelihood, as are greatly hurtful to our *Manufacturing Poor*. This general Rule then ought to be observed in Great Britain, to let our Poor have a comfortable Subsistence at the *cheapest Rates* we can, to improve our *Lands* and encourage the raising of Wool on them; to keep our Poor industriously at Work on *Manufacturing* it all in its native Soil; and to send the Cloth to Foreign Markets, and sell it for what it will yield...whereas the Suffering our *Wool* to be run, or letting it, or our Cloth lie long unwrought or unsold at home, for the Sake of keeping up the Price, set our Poor to Idleness and will ruin all our Trade.⁴⁰

Andrews then went on to reassert the basic principles and reasoning behind

---

37 Ibid. pp. 17-18.
38 Ibid. p. 20.
39 Ibid. p. 53.
40 T. Andrews, *The miseries of the miserable: or An Essay laying open the decay of the fine woollen trade, and the unhappy condition of the poor Wiltshire Manufacturers, by a gentleman of Wilts*. (London, 1739). pp. 11-12.

mercantilist protectionism and to urge that these should be applied towards the labouring classes. The basic necessaries of life should be sold to the lower orders at the cheapest possible rates, "for these poor Wretches do not want to grow rich, but the Bread for Themselves and their Families", and echoing the suspicions of the working class towards the claims of the Anti-Corn-Law-League one hundred years later, "...consequently, *Lowering* the Necessaries of Life to them if effectively done, will be equal to an Advancement of wages."[41] The sentiments offered by Andrews were not isolated to one or two more humane traditionalist paternalists. When the next phase of the struggle in the West of England took place there were many more gentlemen and landholders who were sympathetic to the plight of the woollen workers. However, as with the nature of advancing trade and the practices of commerce, the controllers of industry were gaining the momentum and it was the values and attitudes of Temple regarding the labouring classes that were winning the day. An extraordinarily similar position was adopted in the early 1750s, when Tucker was asking, "Whether the Manufacturing Poor in any Country as so debauched and immoral as in England?"[42] Echoing the view of Victorian manufacturers a hundred years later, he perceived the lower orders as possessing the mentality of children; and children who needed to be taught hard lessons for their own good, but more for the good of the nation's prosperity. He went on to suggest – and using the term 'class' on this occasion – that the principal disadvantage to truly enhancing the trading performance of Britain was "The want of subordination in the lower Class of People." He forcefully argued that if this situation was allowed to continue it would have "dreadful consequences, both in a Commercial and Moral View."

> If they are Subject to little or no Control, they will run into Vice: Vice is attended with Expense, which must be supported either by a high Price for their Labour, or by Methods still more destructive. The End of all is Poverty and Disease; and so they become a loathsome Burden to the Publick.[43]

Yet in terms of the general theoretical model of mercantilism, it was the position of Andrews that most suitably fitted the model. As we have seen, as it evolved from the decline of feudalism – in Britain dating from the end of the fourteenth century and the centuries after – the basic requirement of the mercantilist system as the means of conducting trade and commerce coupled with essential needs of the state was protectionist. The nation needed wealth (bullion) to be able to secure itself, it needed a navy to protect Britain's shores and to conduct trade safely and it required its population to be protected to conduct trade and industry in order to be able to acquire the bullion needed for national security. Loop language of course, but a discourse very familiar to a mercantilist. In the social structure of the Tudor and Stuart periods there was the dichotomy between town and country. The corporate town also saw their salvation in miniature versions of mercantilism, whereby they protected themselves from outside competition, but crucially the system also meant that if they succeeded in protecting themselves, then their population would gain by being fully employed, to the benefit of

---

41 Ibid. p. 25.
42 J. Tucker, *Reflections on the Expediency of a Law for the Naturalization of Foreign Protestants in Two Part: Part Two, Important Queries*. (London: T. Trye, 1752) p. 40.
43 J. Tucker, *A Brief Essay on the Advantages and Disadvantages which Respectively Attend France and Great Britain with Regard to Trade with some Proposals for Removing the Principal Disadvantages of Great Britain. In a New Method*, (London: George Faulkner, 1757) p. 23.

themselves and the town. Importantly, they would not be claiming poor relief, which is why they imposed or sought to impose the strict Laws of Settlement. In the country, the same set of circumstances prevailed, yet here there were not the Charters of Incorporation. Yet they still felt it most satisfactory to get as many of the able bodied to work as was possible. If the hard-liners like Temple had their way and wages were reduced and the hours of work increased then undoubtedly there would be a sharp rise in those claiming relief, as many workers would be unable to gain an adequate living. In Rochdale, Lancashire, for example, in the trading slump year of 1700, trade had dropped off by two thirds and the poor rates had risen from £700 per year to £1,069.[44] At the same time a petition from the Lancashire cotton traders was referred to a Committee of the House of Commons, considering a bill for the "more effectual punishment of vagrants and sending them whither they ought to be sent."[45] In the West of England in 1702 due to scenes of protest and unrest, Parliament passed an Act outlawing the payment of workers' wages in truck; needless to say, it was largely ignored by the clothiers.[46]

Indeed, it may be coincidental, possibly even cynical to suggest that the kindest and most encouraging considerations expressed by the elites towards the labouring classes appear to have been most forthcoming in times of war or national crisis. When things returned to normality so, apparently, did the need to extract as much work out of them as possible. A better example would be difficult to find than the developments of 1745. From 1740 until 1748, the British were yet again involved in yet another war on land and sea. The War of the Austrian Succession was the last battle in which a King of England and, indeed, his son were actually on the battlefield. In May 1745, the Duke of Cumberland suffered a humiliating defeat at the hands of the French, which dramatically lifted their morale and sent the message that the British mystique of militaristic infallibility was put under serious strain. The French then attempted to build on the British setback by creating a domestic diversion by arranging for the Stuart 'Young Pretender', Charles Edward Stuart to invade Britain and raise an army of disaffected Scots. This duly happened in July, 1745. The outcome was that although the Jacobite forces got as far as Derbyshire in their bid to return Britain to a Catholic monarchy, once the British forces re-grouped the Jacobite threat was over. The final *coup-de-grace* came in April, 1746 when, at the Battle of Culloden, their forces were routed by the Duke of Cumberland. However, in the immediate aftermath of the crisis in December 1745 an article appeared in the *Gloucester Journal*, and was reprinted in the *Gentleman's Magazine*, which eulogised the 'common people'. "By the common people I don't mean *idle poor, sturdy vagrants*, who are rightly called the *vermin* of a commonwealth; but the industrious and laborious poor, such as maintain themselves and their families by their labour, follow some lawful calling, and are willing to take pains to get an *honest livelihood*." Clearly these were not the type of labourer that Temple described in 1739, as the *'idle* and *debauched...the drunken Punk,* the *tattling Gossip...*the idle vociferous *Fuddle-Cup.'*[47] Or as a Gloucestershire farmer affirmed '...there is no country in the world in which the poor are more idle, dissolute, drunken & insolent'.[48] Yet the opposite view was can

---

44 *Journal of the House of Commons,* vol. xiii, (1700), pp 269-270.
45 Ibid.
46 Acts of Parliament, 1 Anne, st. 2, c. 18; 9 Anne, c. 30.
47 Temple, op cit., p. 15.
48 *Gloucester Journal,* (8 December, 1766).

also be found, particularly in the aftermath when the crisis of the Pretender had been resolved. According to the writer 'Popularis' in 1745 the labouring classes: '...are the people that constitute the *power* and *strength* and form the character of any nation...'[49] With regard to their rights and importance to society:

> Whatever therefore contributes to destroy the lives or lessen the numbers of such profitable members of society, whether it be by war or plague, famine or luxury, must be looked upon with a heavy judgement, and whoever treats them with contempt, makes them uneasy by oppression, or would deprive them of their rights, should be deemed an *enemy* to the *commonwealth*. It is wholly for the sake if *these people* that *government* itself was ordained, and for *these* its utmost *care* must be exerted.[50]

The article continued:

> And this much I will venture roundly to affirm, without coming to particulars, that the *commonality of this nation* are in themselves *brave, generous, honest, sensible, good natured* and *industrious*. They always *mean right* and would always *do right* if they were not misled and imposed on by false knaves and impudent liars. The[ir] worst enemies have acknowledged them brave and generous; and there is not a day but produces instances of their *good nature* and *humanity*. These are most amiable qualities, and a *great pity* it is they are not *encouraged*; but much *greater* they should be corrupted or abused. There is another quality which makes them still more valuable, and that is their *industry*.[51]

The sometimes bitter struggles of the weavers of the West of England to retain their customary practices continued throughout most of the rest of the eighteenth century. There were more skirmishes between the weavers of West Wiltshire throughout the early 1750s and serious disputes in Gloucestershire between master and woollen workers. The upshot again was that the magistrates were sanctioned by parliament to maintain the practice of setting the rates of wages and adjudicating in disputes between masters and men that had been passed in Statute Law in 1728. The clothiers then responded with a huge petition from Somerset, Wiltshire and Gloucestershire to amend the existing legislation protecting the weavers set out most recently in 1756, the upshot of which was a bill to "better regulation of the woollen manufacture", to repeal the role played by the magistrates, and to allow market forces determine the price of labour.[52] This was countered by a deposition presented to the House of Commons in person by some delegates of the broadcloth weavers from Gloucestershire. They, in turn, were supported by a petition from some of "the gentlemen and landholders from several parishes ... in Gloucestershire for, and on behalf of themselves, and many other gentlemen and landholders of the said parishes representing the several bad consequences... they apprehended would arise, in case a bill should pass to divest the justices of the power to regulate the weavers wages..."[53] The result was that the Act of 1728 was repealed, but laws laid out a level of fines to be paid by the clothiers if they were found to be in breach of the terms of the contract entered into by themselves and the weavers. Yet with no teeth to ensure the behaviour of the clothiers, the only recourse the weavers

---

49 *Gentleman's Magazine*, (December, 1745), pp 654-656.
50 Ibid. p. 655.
51 Ibid. p. 655.
52 'History of the Last Session of Parliament' *Gentleman's Magazine*, (1758), pp. 9-13.
53 Ibid. p. 11.

would have would be to hope they found a friendly magistrate to arbitrate the dispute impartially. Thus, by 1757 the levels of protection the woollen workers of the West of England had struggled for since the first Hanoverians acceded to the throne were gone.

These developments were widely publicised, especially in the press of the West of England and London, and it is known that the Manchester cotton masters had agents and indeed some of their own representatives in London at this time.[54] Thus, although the values and pragmatic economic needs of the masters appeared to be gaining momentum in terms of the imperative of national commercial priority, this by no means meant that the labouring classes were cowered into submission. They still held that the preservation of customary practices were not only a guarantee of their established rights, but also were integral contributions to how they saw the functioning of the industrial system in Britain in terms of balance and fairness. In what might be termed in short an industrial moral economy. The labouring classes still held that although the masters were the providers of their work and income in the proto-industrial system, they were also likely to attempt to out-manoeuvre them and circumvent the established practices at every opportunity. It was also clear, from Parliament's ruling of 1757 – if any more evidence was needed – that the masters firmly held the reins of power in this relationship. Unmistakably then, by the later 1750s the nature of the changing attitudes towards commerce and the use of labour were quite literally becoming more challenging for many working people. On the one hand the opportunities for profit were increasing, but on the other the drive by the state to extract every penny in duties, levies, customs and taxes was squeezing these proto-capitalists. Hence the increased calls for a complete re-think of the role of the state in free commercial enterprise. It further made the need of the masters to make their labour force not only cheaper in terms of the wages paid but also to make them more productive. This situation would undoubtedly create tensions but so strong was the need to remove as many impediments as possible – such as inconvenient Parliamentary Statutes, and paternalistically inclined local magistrates – so that the masters may pursue their aims and objectives (and profits) in order to eradicate the traditional relationship between masters and their labourers. Yet the masters were aware that paternalist sentiments still held sway in the counties amongst both Whig and Tory gentlemen and these were still powerful political figures nationally, but the growing economic power was increasingly in the rapidly developing urban centres and, as we shall see at the very end of this study, in Lancashire the Manchester men were making a claim for asserting their political input as 1770 approached.

This sense of the importance of industry was underscored as the Seven Years War was drawing to a conclusion. Now for many in positions of national political power, after Britain had effectively been at war for virtually twenty three years, there was a desperate desire to enhance the state's income from trade and commerce: to re-stock the national coffers and recover from the enormous national debt that Britain now faced. To a significant extent this fitted well with a new breed of master manufacturer who wished, out of basic necessity, to rid the industrial process of these outdated and awkward values held by the labourers

---

54 *Journal of the House of Commons*, Vol. xxix. pp. 957 and 1019, (1758), also *Whitworth's Manchester Advertiser*, (June 20, July 11, 1758) also, A. P. Wadsworth and J. De Lacy Mann, *The Cotton Trade and Industrial Lancashire, 1600-1780*, (Manchester: Manchester University Press, 1965 edn.) pp. 243-248.

and to replace them with a more modern set of attitudes and practices that were pragmatic and – from working people's perspective – became a much more ruthless set of procedures. However, nothing was more entrenched in the mind-set of the labouring classes than the operation of the 'moral economy' and however much the masters may wish to supplant this, they would find it difficult. Before we move on to discussing how the struggle shifted to the textile workers of the North-West, we must understand in rather more detail just what the precepts of the moral economy actually were.

5
The Moral Economy in Theory and Practice

The first and probably most important point to state at the outset is that for most of eighteenth century Britain the moral economy was not an alternative economy, but something that was to a significant extent inherent to the operation of the mercantile system. If anything, certainly in the final third of the century, it was political economy that was the rising alternative view of how an economy ought to be organised, both at the macro and microeconomic levels. We have gained a hint thus far that at the level of single enterprises, (the microeconomic level), the new practices were gaining adherents among the commercial, manufacturing and trading classes from the later 1720s, and we shall discover shortly that this was to have a major impact in the North-West. One point that needs to be clarified from the outset, however, is that the connotations which lead to thinking (and believing) that the moral economy was a view that perceived the interaction of trade, industry and commerce as one that was primarily designed to be morally beneficial. And thus the obverse that political economy was by dint of its supposed 'discovery' of scientific 'laws' of how economies operate under a full blown capitalist system was devoid of morality. This is clearly not the case. Under the mercantile system, and especially so as we move through the eighteenth century, the desire to make profit was just as strong as it was under the capitalist system, with the theoretical and applied strictures of political economy in place a hundred years later. The key difference was the ability of those who believed themselves to be the victims of the ruthless pursuit of profit were able to mount viable resistance to its widespread application. Furthermore, when that resistance occurred there were those in positions of power and authority who understood why they were resisting in the first place, if not categorically sanctioning the actions of the resistors. Likewise, Adam Smith and the political economists who followed in his wake believed profoundly that their system possessed a moral imperative for the betterment of society as a whole, as long as the application of a structured, inescapable, scientifically proven set of economic laws which they and the rest of Enlightened Europe had discovered were put in place and allowed to function unfettered by governmental intervention. Indeed, a case can (and very often has) been made to show this is essentially correct. Yet it became correct because the capitalist system evolved into the dominant means of organising and giving credence and offering explicit exemplars to not only the national, regional, local and individual economic structures and enterprises, but to the manner in which society itself began to be organised, and the way in which political and legal power sanctioned these momentous changes. The system became a self-encased paradigm: a thought and belief system where, once one was inside, its laws and patterns of behaviour became obvious and resistance totally illogical. However, to those ordinary people – workers, labourers, the lowers orders eking out a life just above subsistence in the 1730s, 1740s, 1750s and 1760s when food prices were rising – there were no 'laws' of political economy fully established at that time to point out to them the errors of their ways. Had they been in place, it would have been explained to them that because the laws of supply and demand under a capitalist system are immutable, it was irrational to argue against scientifically proven truisms, thus their resistance was irrational. Again, to use the analogy from T. S. Kuhn's *Structure of Scientific Revolutions*, although the paradigm-shift was under way by the mid-eighteenth century, it had not yet reached its terminus.

However, it must be stressed that the labouring classes fully understood the nature of the market, and they had been in a position to observe it since the accidental and tragic effects of the hideous plague of the mid fourteenth century which effectively created the manumission of the old feudal bonds. Increasingly, former peasants became waged labourers, but free, independent, waged labourers, whose wages would fluctuate according to the market and, of course, how good they were at their labour. Likewise with the marketing of provisions, this too could be subject to the fluctuations of weather, bad harvests, ruined crops because of pestilence, and, of course, unscrupulous merchants in all branches of the retail and wholesale sectors, which could inflate the price and adulterate the product. Yet it was to prevent the perversions of the unscrupulous employer, merchant, retailer or wholesaler that the Tudor and Stuart Acts were put in place, to give at least the appearance of fairness, backed up in statute law and indeed common law. Thus these customary practices became engrained in the functioning of the market and society, and, importantly, in the consciousness of the lower orders: that they were protective devices for the defence of the weakest, least powerful members of early modern British society, and it was this system that was the foundation of the moral economy. What historians – after the Chartist polemicist Bronterre O'Brien initially coined the phrase in 1837 – termed the 'moral economy' was in fact the normative economic practice in terms of conducting trade and marketing for two hundred and fifty years as we arrive at the mid-eighteenth century. Thus, although it was a practical device to prevent abuses, it also became engrained in the understanding of the labouring classes and those of the gentry authorities who sought to uphold it for the benefit of all in the community. This was done partly on humanitarian and paternalistic grounds, (for some it may have been spiritual), but not exclusively. It was also enacted as a form of insurance to maintain the strict hierarchical nature of the natural 'organic' early modern view of society, and above all to preserve and protect not only the property of substantial holders of property, but crucially their power. Thus it was at one level paternalistic but also patriarchal, in that it strongly reinforced the strict and rigid hierarchy of (especially rural or semi-rural) eighteenth century society as a form of social control. A labouring class was required to till the fields, artisans to make the furniture, build houses, make cloth for clothing and so on, but also crucially to man both the Royal Navy and its merchant counterpart, thus the very real need of the security, wealth and well-being of the country. This valuable commodity – the labouring classes – required protecting from itself running crazy in a property-destroying riot and threatening the established order, as much as from the unprincipled manipulators of the market. Yet they were given license to make the authorities aware of breeches to the established conditions should a trader or employer contravene or attempt to circumvent the codes of practice of the system. This, of course, did not prevent people from attempting to pervert these traditional practices to increase their market share and profits – and probably some succeeded for a time – but they knew, as did the rest of society, that if detected and caught they faced the wrath of the crowd and indeed the law. Thus, the nature and widespread consequences of the free market capitalist system as a widely and accepted means of trading, marketing and, importantly, as a means of production was completely unknown to any member of early modern society, its workings had not been developed nor had the 'laws' been formulated with which to control the processes. It was not just an alien concept or an attack on the basis of free labour by greedy or unscrupulous masters; it simply did not exist in its free market, nineteenth century form. To reiterate, this was primarily because the necessary driving forces as prerequisite factors to its creation had not yet developed. The fact that there existed at any given time some who would attempt to enhance their profits along lines that would have been completely acceptable to those who later advocated free market capitalist economics, was the reason why the statutes against such practices had been put in place from the economic crisis of the early sixteenth century. By the mid-eighteenth century however, as we have seen above, the basis of labour, its control, cost, productive capacity and, importantly, the establishment of the immutable discipline of the industrialist who was paying good money for the production of his commodities began to come under much closer study. Now in the post-1763 age, when the floodgates of the potential of benefits of overseas trade became a major national priority, the practicalities of competition to capture an ever larger market share plus the tantalising possibility of enhanced profitability which could be ploughed back as capital to create even greater productive capacity and personal prosperity, were forcing merchants (in the provision sectors as well as the industrial), traders and industrialists to re-think their relationship with the market and with labour. The first salvos of this transformation were to be felt in the way that human capital was to be utilised and it began to become apparent that this aspect was as important in terms of its application and benefits to those in control of it as financial capital. If anything, it was this realisation, and then the initial attempts at the introduction of new work practices that vaulted the system from its proto-industrial form into the beginnings of the modern capitalist process.

Thompson himself dealt with some of these issues in two long essays, 'The Moral economy of the Crowd in the Eighteenth Century' and 'The Moral Economy Reviewed' in his book *Customs in Common*.[1] Not to put too fine a point on this topic, a prevailing view from the mid-eighteenth century was that those who sought to profit in times of dearth or high food prices by engrossing, forestalling or regrating a commodity, or, indeed, as we would assert in this study, attempted to change the customary practices of industrial labourers, did so purely out of self-interest and certainly not out the interests of the workers or their communities. Such people were tainted as greedy, selfish, avaricious and indeed anti-social in terms of the general good for the whole community, or to give its contemporary term the 'commonwealth'. This historical definition of the 'commonweal' as the pursuance of the health, safety, and basic necessaries of life of a community meant the preservation of the common good of literally everyone in that community, and by their actions of demonstration and protest in attempting to maintain these facets it is clear the so called 'lower orders' perfectly understood this. Those who enclosed formerly common land, who aimed to make a profit when times were most precarious, or who shattered the customary work practices that served hundreds and hundreds of small semi-industrial hamlets where the inter-relationship of the community rested naturally formed bonds of a type of self-contained primitive socialism, were highly likely to be considered hostile to the interests of the ordinary labouring poor. Even if the budding capitalist entrepreneur had the belief that in the long run there would be wider societal benefits, this was unlikely to be believed or understood by those who were on the receiving end of 'reforming' strategies. This need to

---

1 E. P. Thompson, 'The Moral Economy of the Crowd in the Eighteenth Century' and 'The Moral Economy Reviewed' in *Customs in Common*, (London: Merlin, 1991) pp. 185-258, and pp. 259-351.

reform the old economic practices was a view that undoubtedly became increasingly acceptable among those engaged in commerce, trade and industrial enterprises by the time we get to the end of the Seven Years War. However, the watershed of the formal marriage of new, pragmatic, applied practices and the fledgling body of the theory of political economy was not yet consummated, as Thompson reminds us:

> It is perfectly possible that *laissez-faire* doctrines as to the food trade could have been *both* normative in intent (i.e. Adam Smith believed they would encourage cheap and abundant food) *and* ideological in outcome (i.e. in the result of their supposedly de-moralised scientism was used to mask and to apologise for other self-interested operations)... The Tudor policies of "provision" cannot be seen, in a modern sense, as an "economic" strategy only: they depended also of theories of the State, of the reciprocal obligations and duties of the governors and governed in times of dearth and of paternalist social control; they still, in the early seventeenth century had strong religious or magical components. In the period 1700-1760, with the dominance of mercantilist theory, we are in a kind of middle passage of theory. The magical components of the Tudor theory became much weaker. And the social location of the theory became more ambiguous; whilst some traditionalist gentry and magistrates invoked it in time of dearth the authority of the theory was fast eroding as any acceptable account of normal marketing practice.[2]

Thus by the time we get to the end of the Seven Years War, a conflict of interests is developing at State level. On the one hand, George III brought the Tories back from their isolation and many of those who followed them into the governmental parliamentary lobbies were still believers in the organic basis of customary obligations and paternalistic responsibilities, such as the natural equilibrium of society but, on the other hand, the pressing need of the State was to encourage overseas trade and commerce as much as possible, even to the point of exporting grain to get the nation out of the cycle of debt that twenty three years of war had brought. Such policies were grasped encouragingly by the men of commerce and industry throughout the country, but this also, as the former realised only too well, would put them on a collision course with many of common people, who were fiercely protective of their customary rights, and this is what duly happened. Yet increasingly the focus of attention began to intensify, both theoretically and in practice, as we saw in the early writings of Joseph Massie, and indeed the increasingly influential French physiocrats on the nature of the economy as entity in itself rather than whether it should be a conduit for the maintenance of traditional moral imperatives, or indeed whether an economic system should be socially fair or equitable at all.

This brings us to an extremely important point, which is did those involved in the business of trading or industry, and, importantly, those charged with maintaining civil authority both in a national and local sense – magistrates, politicians and judges – become aware of these growing forces of change to the traditional economic practices? Consequently this begs the crucial question that if they were understanding of the necessity for change, what reasoning was being applied to justify the changes? More will be said of the aspects of law and in particular the role played by the Lord Chief Justice Mansfield in chapter nine below, but here we need to make some important points of context, and this affects specifically contemporary arguments relating to the marketing of

---

2 Ibid. p, 269.

provisions. In the early 1980s a research project was undertaken at the University of Cambridge to re-asses the importance of the early phases of the development of political economy. Isvan Hont and Michael Ignatieff edited the results in the book *Wealth and Virtue*. In the essay 'Needs and Justice in *Wealth of Nations*', they take issue with Thompson's application of the moral economy in terms of its contemporary philosophical relevance. They accused Thompson of setting Adam Smith as the leading philosopher and economist who broke the back of the old moral economy and, by implication, being the villain of the piece. This Thompson did by putting "the Smithian position into sharp relief, crediting him with the first theory to revoke the traditional social theory attached to property."[3] They go on to suggest:

> To the extent that favouring an adequate subsistence for the poor can be called a moral imperative, it was one shared by paternalists and political economists alike... On the other hand, to call it the moral economy is to portray it simply as a set vestigial moral preferences innocent of substantive argument about the working of markets. In fact so-called traditionalists were quite capable of arguing their position on the same terrain as their political economist opponents. Indeed, and this is the crucial point, debate over market or 'police' strategies for providing subsistence for the poor divided philosophers and political economists among themselves no less deeply than it divided the crowd for Smith.[4]

Two points need to made here. Firstly, as has been attempted to be shown above, from at least the later 1720s voices were raised about the need to re-assess the role of state in the functioning of trading, industrial and private commercial practices, and by the end of the Seven Years War these voices had become much louder, not only in Britain but across Europe. In fact what Smith did in 1776 with the publication of *Wealth of Nations* was to simply amalgamate a growing body of critical reasoning coming from Britain, from the European Enlightenment and from the physiocrats of the previous thirty years, and to codify this into a highly influential body of not only theory but also economic practice. It became so rapidly influential, indeed not only on those sectors involved directly with commercial, trading or industrial business, but crucially those politicians – such as Burke and the Younger Pitt – who were, from the middle of the 1780s and at the loss of the American colonies, beginning the process of re-thinking national macroeconomic practices.[5] Indeed, Burke afforded the laws of political economy to be divine when he wrote in his pamphlet, *Thoughts and Details on Scarcity...*, in the famine year of 1795 that: "We, the people, ought to be made sensible, that it is not in breaking the laws of commerce, which are the laws of nature, and consequently the laws of God, that we are to place our hopes of softening the Divine displeasure to remove any calamity under which we suffer, or which hangs over us."[6] In fact Burke was already involved in the repeal of the old statutes before the publication of

---

3 I. Hont and M. Ignatieff, 'Needs and Justice in *Wealth of Nations*', in I. Hont and M. Ignatieff (eds.), *Wealth and Virtue*, (Cambridge: Cambridge University Press, 1983), p. 43.
4 Ibid, p. 43.
5 Ibid. p. 18. Pitt attempted to streamline tariffs and reduce the burdens on those merchants importing and distributing commodities from abroad and laying out the foundations of what a free trade policy could resemble. Burke was already involved in the repeal of the old statutes before the publication of Smith's Wealth of Nations in 1772, and a bill drawn up partly by Burke to repeal the old statutes was in fact passed, with Burke being central to its success in 1772.
6 E. Burke, *Thoughts and Details on Scarcity. Originally Presented to the Right Hon. William Pitt, in the Month of November, 1795*, (London, 1800) p. 32.

Smith's *Wealth of Nations*. In 1772 a bill, drawn up partly by Burke, to repeal the old statutes was passed, with Burke being central to its success at that time. Yet although this is evidence that the pressure to change the central role of the state in the protectionist mechanisms associated with classical mercantilism was growing, it did not prevent prosecutions under common law of those middle men, 'jobbers' and 'badgers' who sought to inflate the price of provisions in times of shortage by regrating, engrossing or forestalling of given commodities that were the vital necessaries if life.

The second point of note to the position of Hont and Ignatieff comes from Thompson himself when he said:

> It is in fact Hont and Ignatieff, and not Thompson, who wrote that "by 1776, Smith remained the only standard bearer for 'natural liberty' in grain",[7] a spectacular mis-statement which they reach by confusing the British context with the French context in the aftermath of the *guerre des farines*. As for portraying the "moral economy" as "a set of vestigial moral preferences innocent of substantive argument about the working of markets", the trouble is, once again, the vulgarity of the crowd. They were not philosophers. They did, as my essay shows, have substantive and knowledgeable arguments about the working of markets, but about actual markets rather than theorised market relations. I am not persuaded that Hont and Ignatieff have read very far in the pamphlets and newspapers – let alone in the crowd relations – where these arguments will be found and I do not know what business they have to put me, or the crowd, down.[8]

A further, indeed central, point in the argument that will be developed in the following chapters is that of the legal position of the moral economy and the maintenance of customary practices from the mid-eighteenth century onwards. These centred on two crucial areas of contemporary understanding and the resulting decisions and actions in terms of the conflict between those politicians at the highest levels of the State, both those in Government and in Parliament, who sought, like Burke, to rid the law, government and society of all the old statutes and attitudes. Such views were tempered by those who wished that the old statutes be re-enacted or re-stated in order to uphold the moral economy and customary practices. Additionally the position of leading law officers, (particularly Mansfield), who made judgements on the basis of the circumstances of particular cases and of the body of relevant statute and common law as they interpreted it. In fact in the localities the penalties against those 'jobbers', 'badgers' and middlemen who sought to inflate prices in times of shortage on a range of commodities that were regarded as essential to the maintenance of the necessaries of life continued to be enforced after the 1772 repeal of the old statutes under common law, especially in those years of particular shortages and hardship. Yet one thing was clear and that was that as a result of the repeal of 1772 there existed among some at the highest level of state the power to begin the process of liberalisation towards a more capitalistic version of market forces. Moreover, it was evident that in those areas of the country which had easy access to wheat-growing arable areas there would be an outflow of the surplus to other parts, and indeed, at times, for export abroad at a bounty paid to the exporters. It was here that middlemen flourished and the propensity for nefarious actions to

---

7   I. Hont and M. Ignatieff, 'Needs and Justice in *Wealth of Nations*', in I. Hont and M. Ignatieff (eds.), *Wealth and Virtue*, (Cambridge: Cambridge University Press, 1983) p. 18.
8   E. P. Thompson, *Customs in Common*, (London: Merlin, 1991) p. 275.

disrupt the free passage of grain to the market would most likely occur. Yet, as we have seen, Charles Smith reminded his readers (and historians) that the area's which were most at risk of shortages and manipulation of the market were those parts of the country where there was little or no grain-producing arable land, of which the North-West was one. Charles Smith attempted to argue that given the figures of productivity derived from its consumption, there should not be any severe shortages of grain if the trade was organised properly in terms of the supply of the product and the obvious demand for such a staple as grain. As he said: "Now, it seems very clear, could the prices at which Corn may be said to be *cheap, reasonable* or *dear*, be ascertained, it would be of great use in determining what alterations might be made, with propriety, to all or any of the present Corn-Laws."[9] However, this proved to be something beyond the capabilities of anyone involved in the corn trade itself and had to be left to the interventions of the local and national authorities. There was undoubtedly a desire to attempt to find a remedy to the ongoing problems associated with the social disruption and tensions created by food dearth and wildly fluctuating prices. But, if anything, these were proving to be getting worse in the second half of the eighteenth century, just, in fact, at the moment that the pressures were growing for the removal of all the false impediments to the free movement of the grain trade, as determined by the intervention of magistrates or the enforcement of penalties allowed under common law. These periods of dearth and disturbances associated with high prices included, apart from the 1750s; 1766-7, 1771-3, (when the old statutes were repealed) 1776, 1780, 1782-3, 1789, and virtually the whole of the 1790s into the early 1800s.[10] It was at these times, when shortages, (indeed famine in some cases), and high prices in essential food products were directly affecting the labouring classes the most severely, that Adam Smith and his followers, both academic and in high governmental office, as Thompson reminds us, were at their most strident in the need for a total liberalisation of the corn trade. These included the abandonment of any sanctions against those that would attempt to enhance profits when the lower orders were at their most vulnerable as in the famine years of the 1790s.[11] Their central argument was that if one allows the price to rise naturally without any impediments or interference it will stimulate capital accumulation which will be then utilised, in what was clearly a profitable enterprise, in bringing more land into cultivation, the introduction of more efficient methods of production and giving much better yields. Thus eventually all the needs of consumers would be met. The major problem with this version was that time between the periods of high prices and possible conditions of near starvation and those of abundance.

Hence, the debate surrounding trade and commercial liberalisation was fully exposed by the situation now facing Britain in the immediate aftermath of the Seven Years War and the years that followed, but the actions of the lower orders and the circumstances of severe dearth would keep this a living issue until the early nineteenth century. The economic reality – whether the original framers of the old statutes were aware or not – was that commodities, vital or otherwise, will leave areas where there is little opportunity for their purchase (because of high prices) to places where there is sufficient money in sufficient numbers to make a profit. That is the essence of business, be it advanced capitalism or its

---

9 Smith, op. cit. p. 77.
10 A. Charlesworth, *An Atlas of Rural Protest in Britain, 1548-1900*, (Beckenham: Croom Helm, 1983) Chapter 3, pp. 63-116.
11 Thompson, *Customs in Common*, pp. 278-284.

proto-industrial version. Most of the time, at any point in the eighteenth century, those members of the labouring classes below the rank of skilled, time-served artisan (and at certain times even these groups) were existing extremely precariously in economic terms, barely above subsistence. For those who could only gain seasonal employment or were effectively labourers operating solely when work was available, as many in the proto-industrial sector often were, high prices or the alteration of the terms of their contracts to the advantage of their employers could be disastrous. Thus, when this situation was threatened or actually took place, the only recourse they had was to demonstrate by way of social protest. Again, Edward Thompson phrased what has been discussed here in the last two chapters most succinctly when he said:

> The "relationship of people to food" involves systems of power, property and law. Conflict over entitlement to food might be seen as a forum of class struggle, if most historians were not too prissy nowadays to use the term. It may also be seen as a forum for the conflict of interests, "Town" versus "Country", as manufacturing workers, woollen workers, or colliers, confronted farmers and dealers.[12]

The observation that needs to be underscored is that the customary practices and the limitations to exploit the masses in the vital area of essential provisions enshrined in the old statutes and common law, which have been termed the moral economy, acted as a safety net for the lower orders. And they were only too well aware that this was the case. They saw it as a crucial mechanism of defence against the unscrupulous and they invoked what power – and they possessed precious little real power either in the market place or anywhere else – they had to its maintenance. This will be a topic that will re-surface in discussions in future chapters, however, we must, at this point, return to the nature of the debate surrounding the value of the concept of the moral economy to the patterns of industrial change.

The key conceptual problem to be investigated in this chapter is whether the purity of Edward Thompson's 'moral economy' model holds good in light of the pressures being faced by labouring communities in the North-West at this pivotal period of industrial and social transformation. In Thompson's classic model the moral economy was the tried and tested method open to the crowd to display and act on behalf of perceived grievances and blatant injustice. According to Thompson, and backed up by historians of the early modern period such as Buchanan Sharp, Keith Wrightson and more recently, as we have seen above, Andy Wood,[13] these customary practices were sanctioned not only in long-standing common law and the *Book of Orders* of 1631 but also in statute law. By those it affected, and this is a point worth reiterating, this relationship was perceived as emanating from the inherent rights of the 'free born Englishman' as contrasted with the tyranny of other nations, most notably France. They existed and laboured in trades in harmony with a consciousness of a moral economy which they understood sanctioned them to protect their customary rights and justified their actions accordingly. Also for Thompson the most important aspect was the belief that it was the perceived right of the crowd to nudge the

---

12 Ibid. p. 287.
13 B. Sharp, *In Contempt of all Authority*, (London: Breviary Stuff, 2009 edn.); K.Wrightson, *English Society, 1580-1680*, (London: Routledge, 1982), *Poverty and Piety in an English Village, Terling*, 1525-1700 (Oxford: Clarendon Press, 1995) *Earthly Necessities. Economic Lives in Early Modern Britain, 1470-1750* (New Haven: Yale University Press, 2000); A. Wood, 'The Place of Custom in Plebeian Political Culture', *Social History*, 22, 1, (January, 1997).

powerful into supporting their legitimate demonstrations and actions, especially in terms of access to the essential necessaries of life. The crowd believed that they were entitled to perform such actions legitimately as an essential part of the commonwealth. As we have also suggested this was unquestionably about power: the powerless invoking their only recourse to act on the powerful. However, for Thompson the model was to be applied to specific situations and to be well defined in its operation. It was, for example, legitimate in his reading of the moral economy for the crowd to go after corn factors, millers, farmers, etc. who may have been contravening accepted customary rules against forestallers, regraters and engrossers and who, by their actions, threatened the well-being of the many, and often the most vulnerable. Outside of these fairly tight parameters Thompson's model was less willing to broach. Increasingly however, in the course of research for this study, this 'pure' model appears to be in need of expansion in the case of the North-West. Here industrial change seems to have been indelibly intertwined with both the need to access the necessaries of life in the provision sector of the moral economy prevalent throughout Britain at this time *and* the protection of their customary industrial practices. The key exercise here therefore is to show that the former practices of the labouring and artisan communities in the North-West underwent changes linked to modified work practices and how this is related to traditional displays of protest associated with the moral economy. Before outlining how this process appeared to be developing a brief discussion of the pertinent historiography is appropriate. The essential aim of this overview is to set the context of the discussion to follow in later chapters when we will discover from little used source materials what (if anything) was happening in one of the economically and socially dynamic parts of Britain during the onset of one of the most intense periods of change and tension at any time during the eighteenth century.

Historiography

In one of the most recent additions to the historiography of popular protest Adrian Randall, in *Riotous Assemblies, popular protest in Hanoverian England*, points out that it was not mere economic dislocation creating social tensions that the early historians of riots used as a starting point, but rather power relations. Put simply it concerns the tensions between those who held power of various kinds and those who, on the surface at least, possessed virtually no outward or visible signs of power. In this, as we have seen above, Randall is following in the formidable footsteps of Edward Thompson. There are two important concepts initially introduced by Thompson which were taken up by Randall as the guiding methodology of his book and are also of much relevance to what is being discussed here. The first is the idea of the existence of a 'field of force' whereby elites are forced to face up to their responsibilities by the actions of the crowd. The second is the persistence of a moral economy, which again allows for the crowd to act in defending its customary rights against those who may attempt to deprive, coerce, manipulate or merely ride roughshod over the just and fair claims of working people. It was the decline of the latter, replaced as it was by political economy, and the effective removal of old statutes and attitudes ensconced in common law that was to prove the most contentious and damaging to the emerging working class.

Without entering into a full-scale critical assault on Thompson, what Randall does quite early in the book is to provide a useful historiographical survey of how historians of protest have interrogated the Thompson thesis and reinterpreted it into their own work. To a significant extent this is what Randall does, but not before offering a full critical review of the pros and cons of the various positions. John Bohstedt was one of the first to refine the Thompson model by including a third element, the shopkeepers and employers (the so-called 'middling sorts') often in opposition to the customary rights of plebeians, with agents of authority attempting to control the conflicting factions. This tripartite model, to a large extent, is supported by Peter King, a specialist in eighteenth century crime and punishment. However, the chief danger with these tri-polar models is that they themselves need to be refined, lest they be easily confused with an anachronistic view of class in a full-blown capitalistic society. As noted in the previous chapter, this view of class would only be complete with widespread development of middle and working class consciousnesses, as in the post-1790s period when Thompson originally suggested the working class was 'made'. However, it was often against these middling sorts that the crowd were prone to vent their wrath in the earlier period. Randall reminds us that it is not the role of historians of protest to develop models of social order *per se*, but rather to place into historical context the kind of protest being engaged in and locate comparisons and contrasts. Let us attempt to clarify some important points regarding the use of the concept of moral economy. Thompson's classical use of the moral economy concept was, as Randall usefully reminds us, primarily concerned with power: of the relatively powerless to exert some influence on those members of the authorities who possessed the power to apply sanctions against those attempting to subvert the common good. However, power can be detected at various levels and this does not necessarily need to include the overt coercive power of the threat of criminal penalties – although these do have to come into the equation at certain points. There can be social power which was a vital part of eighteenth century social structure and mobility, whereby it was not necessarily what one knew or how much property one possessed – although neither of these would do any harm – but *who* one knew and how this intimacy could advance one socially through the various levels of status to gain access to the really powerful. Eighteenth century society, as much as any society in British history, was all about patronage and making the right connections, and this could open the doors to real political power and, by extension, personal wealth. Few of the middling sorts would ever get real access to this type of power either in the urban context – although this was growing as the century developed – or at the level of the country gentry. It could also at a lesser social level be about economic power. The labouring classes possessed unquestionable levels of independence that their nineteenth century counterparts could never imagine, yet they were reliant on their employers to provide them with work, to pay them agreed amounts in wages, and on the merchants and shopkeepers to provide them with reasonably priced goods and provisions. Often it was these same men who controlled the poor relief, thus another bone of contention as to where their real interests lay. Working people also needed access to the rapidly disappearing common land, often for the provision of water and fuel in the winter. If one sees power as a graph in terms of levels of relative dependency, then the lower orders were at the bottom and were almost entirely at the mercy of the groups above them who possessed various levels of economic power, as well as, of course, the magistrates, who possessed some legal power and, crucially, the power to arbitrate between contending parties. No matter how socially inclusive and self-contained these labouring communities were, they would still be touched at some point with those with much greater power and they had to learn to negotiate this fact in order to survive. In a sense this takes us back to the discussion in the previous chapter where James Scott's 'transcripts' of peasant communities which utilise displays of deference in order to conceal a sense of communal solidarity in labouring societies which placate those above them – the powerful – by reinforcing their belief they are in control. When in fact lying not far below the surface, in these labouring communities there are feelings of suspicion and hostility towards their social superiors which can erupt into demonstrations of class agency and social protest if the societal and economic balance is upset.

Hence a tripartite model can be effectual in understanding the nexus of protest with the moral economy, certainly around the mid-eighteenth century. As Randall tells us:

> What, critics ask, of the middle classes, who, as employers and forgers of a new 'civil society' were intimately concerned with the effects of popular protest? Thompson recognised that, *de facto*, his model had a third 'leg' namely the middling sort. To Thompson the employers and shopkeepers were certainly involved in the problem: indeed they too often *were* the problem. Artificially raising prices or lowering wages, and thereby disturbing the equilibrium of social relations. Indeed, there is a real sense in which his model resembles the triangular 'scales of justice' with the crowd on the one side and the employing and marketing classes on the other, both looking to the magistracy and government at the top of the scale for approval, action or arbitration.[14]

As noted, Peter King also looked at the problem of whether the moral economy needed to be re-drawn as a tripartite model rather than the a bipolar model as demonstrated by Thompson. King suggested, even after the re-working of his model in the essay 'Moral Economy Reviewed' in 1991, that for Thompson there are problems relating to how and when he had effectively marginalised the middle classes in the original article which made it hard to explain the emergence of a new, self-conscious urban middle class presence from the 1790s onwards. Thompson admitted that his bipolar model has more relevance to rural or proto-industrial areas than to London and the larger corporate towns. Also, and this is important for the study here, King maintains that this suggests Thompson's model as well as being more appropriate to the rural rather than urban "also signalled the possibility that his model works better for the period before 1760 than for the period after it."[15] David Levine was even more direct in his criticism of Thompson's lack of consideration of the urban middling sorts, their size, relative growing importance throughout the eighteenth century, and where they fit into the moral economy model. As he says:

> It is germane to note that the rise of the 'town gentry' – who were often dissenters and who were engaged in trade, services and manufacturing – is still left unexamined in Thompson's survey in the long eighteenth century. The bourgeoisie seems to be missing from the historic moment of its birth...Clearly the quantitative boundary of the political economy is no less ambiguous than the qualitative boundary of the moral economy of propriety; one wants to have a perspective which embraces both morality

---

14 A. Randall, *Riotous Assemblies*, op cit. p. 6. See also by the same author, 'The industrial moral economy of the Gloucestershire weavers in the eighteenth century', in J. Rule, *British Trade Unionism, 1750-1850: The Formative Years*, (London: Longman, 1988).

15 P. King, 'Edward Thompson's Contribution to Eighteenth-Century Studies. The Patriarch-Plebeian Model Re-examined'. *Social History*, xxi (2) (1996), p. 225.

and economics in the same field of vision. Thompson provides us with this kind of perspective from the bottom-up; but he never fits it together with a complementary one from the top-down. This oversight, I think, impoverishes the force of his analysis.[16]

If this is so then the present study may hopefully offer Professor Levine with a more accommodating perspective. However, to return to the essence of the moral economy model as it can be applied to understanding the situation facing the mid-eighteenth century labouring classes and whether, indeed, it can accommodate an 'industrial' perspective at all. Randall saliently reminds us that it is not the aim of historians of social to protest to "construct, through the matrix of disorder, a comprehensive model to explain all the alignments, nuances, and distinctions of the social order."[17] Moreover the main aim for historians of social protest is to attempt to historically contextualise the nature and basis of what the leading actors were attempting by, first of all, striving to alter the balance of customary practices with their own alternatives, and those who were resisting these attempts. This said, Randall also suggests that if the lower orders were not yet developing a fully-fledged 'class consciousness' then neither were the middling sorts, who being forced with a choice to either remain in their fixed urban and semi-urban parochial worlds or join the rapidly encompassing trends of national conformity through, at one level, the on-going 'consumer revolution'. In essence, the key question is whether a pattern of protest and conflict emerges and what forms does this take; the bipolar or the tripartite including the various elements of the middling sorts? Randall's answer is to confirm a refined bipolar model. This is an exemplar whereby the actors are, as we move past mid-century, being influenced by a number of features that stretch their positions into either an embrace of 'modernism' – and, in effect, the capitalism of the political economy hue – or as the protectors of customary values. In a sense it is immaterial which branch of eighteenth century social grouping they belong to, the key element is their attitude, based on either of the two propositions noted above and, further, the basis upon which they reach their decisions on how they will act. They are caught in milieu of conflicting predispositions, but the essential bipolar model is the one that confirms their presence in the on-going field of conflict between those who see the changes as necessary and 'progressive' or deeply damaging and detrimental, not only to the labouring classes specifically but to the very nature of the society which they inhabit and the on-going pressures they experience in their day-to-day lives. Hence if a member of eighteenth century society is engaged in some aspect of the marketing of provisions (either as traders or consumers) or in the industrial sphere (as labourers or employers) this to a significant extent will be determined by the situation they are facing and ultimately regulate the course of action they take. Thus for Randall the concept of the moral economy is one that can be applied to proto-industrial protest, as he says:

> I would argue that there are persuasive reasons for utilising these sorts of bipolar models, in conjunction with Thompson's original formulation of the moral economy, in examining the character of popular protest in Hanoverian England, given that they can be extended more widely to other forms of protest beyond food riots.[18]

---

16 D. Levine, 'Proto-Nothing: *Customs in Common* by E. P. Thompson', *Social History,* Vol. 18, No. 3, (1993) pp. 381-390, p. 387.
17 Randall, op. cit. p. 8.
18 Randall, op cit p. 9.

Historians like David Rollison and Dror Wahrman have also come, via their very different research routes, to confirm the bi-polar model by noting how the rise of national consumer culture impacted and informed attitudes and, indeed, split opinions between those who favoured the traditional, older forms of localistic social and economic interaction and that of increasingly regional or indeed nationalistic tendency towards 'modernity'. Such conflicts of the shock of the new set against the stability of the tried and trusted, the local as opposed to national bi-polar trends can also be found in the work of Nick Rogers, Norma Landau and Bob Bushaway.[19] Randall concedes the value of all these various approaches in what was a rapidly changing society but correctly asserts that none of them essentially diminish the fundamental basis of the original Thompson model. However, Thompson himself remained sceptical. He castigated Keith Snell for attempting to apply the moral economy concept to those seeking to assert rights to settlement in order to receive relief under the old Poor Law, and extends this to the general application of the poor laws.[20] "But where are we to draw the line", he comments on Snell's model to attempt to extend the range of the moral economy, "... to the general application of the poor laws to yearly hirings' and 'fair wages', and even to 'popular consumption', fashion [and] leisure activities."[21] However, he is less assertive with Randall's application of the moral economy concept into areas of industrial dispute, as he says of its usage in earlier work of Randall's: "I am more than half persuaded by this [Randall's] argument."[22] The key point to make here is that in the North-West in the latter years of the 1750s, there was a combination of both provision protest occurring alongside ongoing industrial disputes and the two appeared to have merged together, a phenomenon that the Thompson model takes no account of.

The nature of the debate surrounding the application of the moral economy may well be wrapped in a web of complex theoretical perspectives, but in direct historical terms it needs to be remembered that for the proto-industrial labouring classes their positions were by far the most vulnerable. Thompson's first great foray into the social history of the eighteenth century working class was, as we have noted, the *Making of the English Working Class*, which locates their birth with the gaining of an agency to act on their own behalf by dint of acquiring class consciousness from the later 1780s into the 1790s and beyond. Yet even this process had to show signs of developing before these dates and what follows in the chapters below may offer some shred of an understanding about when and why this was taking place. From the later 1740s and into the 1750s the labouring classes of the North-West were being subjected to their first exposure to the attempted changes being wrought by the new merchant advocates of advanced capitalist ideas and especially their application. The effects of these changes were

---

19 J. Bohstedt, *Riots and Community Politics in England and Wales, 1790-1810*, (Cambridge, Mass.: Harvard University Press, 1983); See also *The Politics of Provisions: Food Riots, Moral Economy, and Market Transition in England*, c. 1550-1850, (Aldershot: Ashgate, 2010) remains fixed with the view that a tripartite model of the moral economy is most appropriate, but for alternatives see N. Rogers, *Crowds, Culture and Politics in Georgian Britain*, (Oxford: Clarendon Press, 1998); D. Rollison, 'Property, Ideology and Popular Culture in a Gloucestershire Village, 1660-1740', *Past & Present* 93 (1) (Nov., 1981) pp. 70-97; and by the same author, *The Local Origins of Modern Society: Gloucestershire 1500-1800* (London: Routledge, 1992); N. Landau, *The Justices of the Peace*, (Berkeley: University of California Press, 1984 edn.); R. W. Bushaway, *By Rite: Custom and Community in England 1700-1880*, (London: Breviary Stuff, 2011 edn.).
20 Snell, K. D. M. *Annals of the Labouring Poor*, (Cambridge: Cambridge University Press, 1985) pp. 99-199, 103.
21 Thompson, *Customs in Common*, p. 339.
22 Ibid.

to re-order the world of the cotton workers and their communities. They attempted to defend themselves by forming combinations (early form of trade unions and collective action) which was an indication of their shared community of interests, and their community of values; which was a visible display that their way of life and what they, as a self-identifying social group, believed were important, and at that time the key ingredients of which were being threatened. Their actions were informed by the need to act collectively in demonstrations of resistance, and were at times a defiant justification of the position they had taken up against the masters. They still appealed to those social groups above them, (initially, at least), such as magistrates for legitimation of their actions and did not overtly engage in a political discourse to assert their grievances, but it was a demonstration of their latent power as communities of fellow-minded men and women and of their trade, hence there were elements of 'agency' present. The process of struggle in the North-West from the later 1750s, into the 1760s and beyond began the process of nudging them ever closer to developing a working class consciousness through this experience of class struggle as we approach the 1780s and 1790s. Again, to reiterate, at this stage of development they engaged in these actions to defend their intrinsic values as labouring communities. They were, in one sense, the conventional community values of people of similar rank and status living in a socially defined locality, but they were also the community values of those engaged in the various process of cotton manufacturing. This process of class definition had to start somewhere, and it is the details of this process that will be the core theme of the final chapters of this study. However, at this point we have to examine how the cotton sector began to take on such a pre-eminent role in the industrial development of the North-West.

6
The Development of Cotton Manufacturing in Lancashire

It was believed at the end of the eighteenth century that the production of cotton textiles was first introduced to the North-West by protestant migrants fleeing persecution from Northern Europe in the mid-sixteenth century.[1] Whatever the truth of this, it is clear that by the end of the Tudor period and the beginning of the reigns of the Stuarts the production of cotton goods was flourishing in Lancashire.

The organisation and modes of operation of the textile industry in Lancashire from its origins at the end of the sixteenth century were modelled on the classic forms found in Italy and Flanders from the end of the thirteenth century.[2] Again in terms of its initial organisation it was a hierarchical system based largely on access to credit and working capital. This was effectively a warehouse system whereby the raw materials (and sometimes the materials required for production) were bought by the merchant, stored, and then distributed to workers to spin the thread and make the product in their places of business or, more likely, their homes. The woven cloth would then be collected, sent on to the finishing processor, and then sent back to the original warehouse before being distributed to the end buyer. Like other areas of commerce and trade from the later medieval period, in the cloth industry there grew up a cartel or monopoly system whereby only those with licenses could operate in the trade and this severely limited the levels of the imports of raw materials and the export of the finished products. All this was bound up with the needs of European monarchs and princes to acquire loans and give privileges to organisations like the Hanseatic League, Merchant Adventurers and, later, the various joint stock companies (such as the Levant Company or the East India Company, operating under licence from the central state) and, as such, was by necessity bound up with the vagaries of the constantly shifting alliances and European politics generally. The English textile trade received an enormous boost with the opening up of the Atlantic trade in the second half of Elizabeth's reign. Yet forms of monopolies remained in all sectors of the trade even at the end of the sixteenth century, including amongst the weavers of the corporation guilds. Exempt from these however, were the textile areas of the West Riding of Yorkshire and Lancashire. At this time cottons were regarded as a branch of the woollen industry though it is likely that 'Manchester cottons' contained an element of the vegetable fibre as they were termed 'cotton wool'. From the 1640s, Manchester and the Lancashire region generally began to be known for the manufacturing of linen goods and fustians (a heavy fabric of cotton weft and linen warp) and these being distributed to the London cloth merchants for export.[3] This allowed specialism to develop along the broad topographical location taking a line from Manchester in the south east of the region though Bury, Bolton, Blackburn, Whalley, Clitheroe up to Lancaster, to east of this and into the West Riding of Yorkshire. Here the principal manufacture would be predominantly woollen fabric and to the west

---
1 T. Walker, *Review of some of the Political Events ... in Manchester*, (Manchester, 1794) pp. 23-24.
2 G. W. Daniels, *The Early English Cotton Industry*, (Manchester: Manchester University Press, 1920) pp. xxiv-xxviii.
3 Ibid. pp. 7-9.

linen and cotton. From being a scattering of producers and merchants at the end of the fifteenth century by the middle of the seventeenth century it was known that textile production was one of, if not the principle trade of Manchester and the north-west. The numbers involved were already substantial by the early eighteenth century. In 1713 the number of people involved in the linen industry alone across the whole of the region was put at 60,000 in a petition presented to Parliament, with probably at least three times as many involved in the production of cotton fabrics.[4] As for those of the lower orders who were engaged in the trade it appears that from an early date they were not averse at making their feelings known against perceived abuses from employers. This is evident in a counter petition in support of a statute passed by Edward VI which allowed wool to be sold to staple merchants or those who were actually engaged in its manufacture. In 1577 the merchants and middlemen petitioned that this latter category not be enforced so that only they could buy and sell wool. The ordinary workers, ("poore cotegers") made it known in their petition that if the middlemen had their way "the trade would be driven into a few riche men's hands, so that the poore shall not be paid for their worke, but as it pleaseth the riche."[5] Their success, however, was only limited and by the early seventeenth century the buying and selling of both the primary and end products lay in the hands of a few very wealthy and powerful people in Manchester.[6] These men were the early proto-capitalists of the cotton trade in the North-West: the Mosleys, Wrigleys, Tippings, James Rillston, Edward Hanson, and, of course, the Chethams. They were referred to by a variety of names, as clothiers, mercers, linen merchants, drapers or simply cloth merchants, but were the forerunners of Manchester commercial middle class urban elite.[7] They began to amass significant capital by selling finished cloth to the shipping agents and merchants of Chester and Liverpool in their own region, and Hull and London outside. In the ports they would buy or collect their raw materials of cotton, flax and linen yarn which they would sell on credit to the county manufacturers and small-scale clothiers. It is known that by the early seventeenth century these large Manchester merchants had agents and representatives in London, with all the opportunities for expansion which would have been available in the nation's largest city.[8] It is important to note that the potential for expansion in the seventeenth century was limited. There was some export and, of course, the necessary import of raw materials but the nature of the commercial basis of the mercantile system at this point meant that both the imports of raw cotton and the export of the finished cloth would be strictly limited to the monopolised large Companies established under royal license. In the case of the importation of raw cotton this was controlled by the Levant Company. Thus there were strict limits to the opportunities for commercial expansion for any of relatively wealthy Manchester merchants such as the Chethams, for example, with regard to export growth due to the monopolies established by the larger Companies in London and in Europe. It would appear that most of the business they conducted was

---

4 *Journal of the House of Commons*, (1713) Vol. 17, p. 377 and again JHC Vol.16, pp. 311-324
5 State Papers Domestic, Eliz, Vol.117(1577) p. 38.
6 Chethams Library, Manchester Court Leet Records, Vo.1 pp. 203-4, 245, Lancashire and Cheshire Wills, New Series, Vol.28 p.15
7 Ibid. pp. 31-33, and A. P. Wadsworth and J. De Lacy Mann, *The Cotton Trade and Industrial Lancashire 1600-1780*, (Manchester: Manchester University Press, 1965 edn.) pp. 29-53.
8 W. E. A. Axon, *Manchester a Hundred Years Ago* (Manchester, 1887) a reprint of *Ogden's Description of Manchester*, (Manchester, 1787) p. 43.

with the domestic markets, including Ireland.⁹ The amount of circulating capital within the region was limited to the provision of the various types of thread to be woven by the smaller county clothiers. These in turn would distribute this to their travelling chapmen and then on to the various domestic weavers in and around Manchester, Bolton, Blackburn and so on, and passed on again to the more remote parts of the region.

Hence, the pattern at this stage of development is more akin to a form of clientage whereby there would be established a chain of face-to-face relationships from the top down to the lowest small-scale, yet still largely independent domestic spinner. It was this process that prevailed at this early stage, rather than the employer/worker matrix, with all its attendant disciplines and loss of independence that industrial capitalism brought with it. Throughout most of the seventeenth century and for at least the first four decades of the eighteenth century, the organisation of the industry was reflective of the type of clientage relationship whereby the large Manchester or Bolton master clothier would place an order to his range of smaller masters in the out-townships and semi-rural hamlets. There he passed the work on to his core of regular spinners and weavers and the kind of cloth to be woven, its weight and picks-per-square-yard and of course, the price per piece to be paid on the satisfactory completion of the work. The cotton workers would be in no doubt of who the masters were and the gulf of status and power that lay between them in terms of social hierarchy, and, of course, the fact that they were dependant on them for their livelihood. But it was essentially a fee-based system through the chain from the top down. Thus, the weavers can be viewed as a type of self-employed artisan performing the work to order, yet remaining effectively independent and free to work for whosoever they chose as long as their work was deemed of good quality.

We will discuss more on the nature of the early cotton workers shortly but first it will be useful to gauge just how profitable cotton manufacture was for these larger Manchester master clothiers. We know from the estate records of one of these substantial Manchester merchants in the mid-sixteenth century that the profits could be considerable. If we take the example of a middling rank Salford merchant, Henry Wrigley, who was a dealer mainly in fustians, but probably not in the same scale of turnover as the larger merchants such as the Tipping's or Chetham's. Wrigley began in the trade as a chapman, one of the intermediaries who linked the raw cotton once it arrived in the Manchester warehouses with the numerous labourers throughout the North-West region. He did well and began to operate for himself and by the 1620s appears to have been well established. From the mid-1620s Wrigley maintained a London office until his death in 1658, and in 1646 we have an estimate of his assets. He had fustians in his London warehouse worth £5,143, and payments outstanding of £5,134 and he held cash to the value of £10,402 with bad debts standing at £1,801, making a total of £22,479, which in today's money was worth £3,191,000,000.¹⁰ Crucial to these larger early merchant capitalists were their intermediaries who were the link between the raw cotton being brought by the larger merchants from London and Bristol and the general body of spinners and weavers. It was these men who gave out the raw materials and possibly furnished the workers with looms which they either hired or, like the raw materials they bought on credit with the

---
9 Wadsworth and Mann, op cit. p. 33.
10 National Archives, Kew. County Palatinate Notebooks, Lancashire, (1645-1646) Book iv, pp. 102-104.

network of intermediaries (chapmen) acting as the conduit between the larger town-based merchants and the cotton workers who produced the goods. Thus on their circuit of producers in the plethora of semi-rural weaving hamlets scattered throughout the North-West, they would supply the raw materials and pick up any of the finished woven cloth pieces and forward them on to the warehouses of the larger town-based merchants. The payments per piece would be made to the weavers minus the deductions for the previously supplied raw materials, and so the pattern would be maintained. Yet these larger merchants had the advantage of access to the raw materials, which they could buy in bulk and stockpile, this made a profit in its distribution to the intermediary, who in turn would make their mark up as it was distributed to the workers on credit. Likewise, the large merchants controlled the distribution of the finished goods to the network of purchasers in London and elsewhere, where once again they would sell for a profit. Thus in one way that was similar to the encroaching factory system in the second half of the eighteenth century whereby the producers were isolated from access to the raw materials of their trade and the consumers of the finished products. Effectively by the end of the sixteenth and into the seventeenth centuries these intermediate chapmen had become localised employers in their specific districts and towns. Now with their own chapmen and specialising in the various types of cotton cloth of that district, the various types of linen/cotton weave: Blackburn greys, bedsticks, checks, hollands, gowns, ginghams, the smallwares for neckcloths, shirting and handkerchiefs and then the fustians: Augsburgs, bombazines, diapers, dimities, drawboys, jeans, Manchester cottons, counterpanes, petticoats, printed fustians, pillows, quilts and stripes.

As for the cotton workers themselves it was, as noted above, with the absence of craft guilds in the North-West relatively easy to enter the trade. The seven years apprenticeship was required to become a weaver, the actual outlay in terms of the means of production was quite cheap even by the standards of the day. A loom could be bought on credit and would cost from between 6 to 12 shillings, it would be located in the upstairs room of the cottage preferably with large windows to let in maximum light. The implication of the name 'domestic industry' suggests it would involve the rest of his family, for whom a spinning wheel would cost about a shilling and hand cards only coppers.[11] To give some idea of the amount of workers involved in the trade in the mid-seventeenth century we can ascertain from Poll Tax returns in 1660 that in the townships and hamlets in and around Oswaldtwistle, Accrington, Huncoat, Rossendale and Haslingden there were 654 households, of which 5% held land over the value of £20 per year; 10% held land valued between £10 and £20; 22% land valued between £5 and £10 and 63% under £5. In Accrington itself, of the 96 household heads 7 were described as clothiers (male weavers) and 13 as websters, (female weavers). Of these household heads there was one clothier who had three apprentices living in his house, another had two and another had one apprentice. However, there were other journeymen weavers living in these houses aged over 16 years; two had five of these and there were others with smaller numbers. The estimate appears to be that the number of those whose occupation was mainly agricultural and those engaged in cotton textiles were equally spread across this part of Lancashire[12] This pattern appears to have been typical of that across the whole region for the remainder of the seventeenth century and, indeed, into the early eighteenth century. Thus by end of the

---

11 Wadsworth and Mann, op cit. p. 49.
12 J. Tupling, *Economic History of Rossendale*, (Rossendale, 1927) pp. 163, 168, 178-179.

seventeenth century cotton textiles was established across the North-West, but it still was no match for the size and wealth creation of the woollen sector. A large part of the reason for this was that the woollen merchants were fiercely protective of their share of the national trading position, and were not at all ready to relinquish this to their cotton rivals. Nor does it appear that until the start of the eighteenth century that the larger cotton merchants were particularly keen to challenge the interests and superiority of the woollen sector.

What needs to be established at this point is that although the cotton industry was growing, indeed flourishing, in the North-West, it was not producing pure cotton fabrics, but rather a variety of cotton mixes. The reason for this lay with the monopolistic privileges of the East India Company who enjoyed to protection of the state in ensuring that only the finest pure cotton calicos were imported from the Indian subcontinent, either for domestic sales to the up-market end of the wealthiest customers or for re-export as dictated by the national policy of mercantilism. However, this began to be legally challenged by those involved in both the silk and woollen interests at the end of the seventeenth century. From 1691, the monopolist advantages held by the East India Company in the importation and, indeed, control of textiles was attacked by a powerful group of London merchants who petitioned the King demanding that the Royal Charter given to the Company be dissolved and replaced with a more equitable version especially of those involved in silk and woollen production. In 1700 Parliament passed an act banning the importation of fine printed calicos and a penalty imposed on anyone buying or using them for either soft furnishings or clothing.[13] The response of the East India Company unsurprisingly was to import plain calicos and then print them in this Britain. This was countered by another Act of 1703, which forbade the importation of plain calicos. However, all this flurry of litigation and legislation largely amounted to nought, as it was all effectively a dead letter, as people still demanded the finest calicos and they continued to be imported and sold. The next phase was from 1719 when parliament was bombarded with petitions initially demanding that something be done to halt the textile trade as a whole being dominated by imported foreign calicos. The profits of which were either going into government funds or to an elite set of jobbers who possessed a stake in the East India Company to the detriment of domestically produced textile products that so many throughout the kingdom relied upon and so much employment depended and was the primary industrial exported commodity. The result was an act of 1721 that prohibited both the wearing of domestically produced printed calicoes or cotton mixtures or their more expensive and finer quality Indian produced counterparts. The 1721 Act was aimed to protect Britain's traditional woollen industry from competition from new manufacturing areas which were starting to produce printed cotton cloth. This Act was the outcome of a string of petitions to Parliament during 1719-20, mainly from the regions where woollen manufacture had always been strong, for example, the South West, the West of England, East Anglia, and the West Riding of Yorkshire. The threat, however, was now perceived to be not necessarily from the East Indian Companies importation of expensive calicos, but rather closer to home. The chief complaint of the petitioners was that the entire woollen industry was threatened by competition from the home producers of cotton-based fabrics as well as from overseas imports, and that unemployment and hardship were growing among those whose livelihoods depended on wool production. The key reasoning behind this was that although domestically

---

13 11 and 12 William III, c. 10, (1700).

produced cotton mixes lacked the quality of the Indian calicos they were much cheaper and were clearly being bought in significant enough volume to pose a real threat to the woollen sector. The 1721 Act therefore attempted to protect woollen manufacturing by banning the wearing of various types of cotton cloth. In due course, and as a result of further petitioning, Parliament had to accept that it was unfair as well as impossible to extend complete legal protection over to the woollen industry, hence, as with the earlier attempts by the woollen sector, the 1721 Act became effectively a dead letter.

With the lessening of legislation governing the textile trade there was, by the 1740s, an increase in those attempting to become involved in the profits of cottons, fustians as well as worsteds. In order to maximize their potential these new men opted for the new relationship of employing workers from the start to the finish of the productive process. These new men, who were driven to abandon traditional practices, were, according to Richard Guest writing in 1823, known as 'fustian masters' and it was they who were to be the dynamic force in the transformation of the industry and those engaged in it.[14] The reason for this upsurge in activity came in 1736 when the masters of Lancashire, Cheshire and Derbyshire petitioned Parliament for clarification of the various Acts of Parliament which were the outcome of those numerous petitions to Parliament during 1719-20 and 1721, mainly from the regions where woollen manufacture had always been strong, as noted above. It would appear on the face of it that this kind of regulation clearly presented serious problems in the up-and-coming cotton-producing districts around Lancashire, Cheshire and in Scotland, but it is also suggestive of the advances they were making as a rising trading sector. In the short term it also had an adverse effect on merchants in Bristol, Liverpool, Lancaster and London, for example, whose businesses very much depended on the import of raw cotton from the American colonies. It would appear strange to suggest that in fact the Act of 1721 actually was of benefit to the staple cotton industry of Lancashire as 'pure' cotton goods were not, or very rarely, actually being produced. In Lancashire the products comprised of various cotton mixes, mainly with linen, but also with wool. Clarification was called for as to exactly what fabrics were included and excluded in the new act and this was quickly forthcoming.[15]

Excluded under the terms of the 1721 act were muslins, neckcloths and fustians. Thus, the act of 1721 served to stimulate trade in the variety of cotton-based goods being produced in the North-West and as noted this grew steadily throughout the rest of the 1720s into the early 1730s. However, contention remained regarding precisely what was legal and what was prohibited. The point of clarification was to know whether it was illegal to wear domestically produced printed fustians. Thus, another petition appeared in 1735 to ascertain exactly what was permissible, but this petition did not originate in the North-West, but from Norwich. Here, it would seem, the local woollen interest had placed newspaper stories suggesting that the wearing of printed fustians was illegal under the terms of the 1721 act. That this was not the case meant little as merely the rumour was enough to impact sales of printed fustians. Now the Manchester merchants began to be active. A petition was drawn up from the fustian manufacturers of Lancashire, Cheshire and Derbyshire requiring parliament to be clear on the matter and explaining in detail and for all to hear and understand

---

14 R. Guest, *A Compendious History of the Cotton Manufacture*, (Manchester, 1823) p.11.
15 G. W. Daniels, *The Early English Cotton Industry*, (Manchester: Manchester University Press 1920) pp. 21-23.

exactly how the act of 1721 affected them.[16] The upshot was that the 1736 Manchester Act gave the manufactures unquestioned legality for their processes. From this point on exports of cotton-based goods began to increase steadily to Ireland, Europe and especially to the Caribbean, the Americas and Africa. From a figure to the value of £9,605 in 1729, by 1739 this had risen to £14,324. By 1750, the value was placed at £19,667, but by 1759, the figure was now £109,358.[17] On the import side, the figures show in 1730 that 1,545,72lbs of raw cotton entered the country. By the end of the Seven Years War, this figure had more than doubled to 3,870,392lbs.[18] The Manchester Act of 1736 can be viewed as the recognition by parliament of the importance of cotton manufacture to national trade and prosperity, and, importantly, effectively cleared up all doubts about any restrictions. The Act was therefore vital in paving the way towards the mechanisation of the cotton industry and its mass production in factories later in the century. Clearly the mood of central government was changing in regard to the need to stimulate domestic trade and the act of 1736 was direct action by the state to encourage the cotton sector, but it did something else. It effectively encouraged new 'fustian masters' to get into this now very lucrative and expanding branch. These men initially entered the trade in the country districts with relatively small amounts of capital and using credit from the larger, longer established merchants of Manchester and Bolton. They dealt in small quantities as first, but began to expand as the trade flourished and in turn gravitated to Manchester itself, opening warehouses and employing their own chapmen as the intermediaries to liaise with the country weavers. In a remarkably short space of time, these new men began to challenge the control of the traditional cotton merchants, but they also began to attempt to re-organise the way cotton manufacture operated in the North-West.

At this stage it is worth offering a paragraph about what these more remote cotton areas of the North-West were actually like. They came in various sizes in terms of population, from the quite large, as in the case of Manchester and its immediate out townships, to the small, such as the tiny hamlet of Rough Hey, about two and a half miles from Oswaldtwistle and five miles from Accrington. There was a water powered cotton spinning factory operational at Rough Hey in 1782 and its ruins can still be seen today. There are about 25 surviving cottages, but again more ruins can be seen of about the same number. Thus the working population of spinners and weavers would not be more than about a 150. They would alternate their work during the year between some employments for the local pasture farmers, but their principal occupations were in the production of cotton commodities, from the spinning of the warp and weft to the finishing of the cloth. There were no shops, no church or chapel and the nearest public house was about two miles away. The nearest grain merchant and miller was at Blackburn, seven miles distant, too far to make regular journeys for refined flour, so some of their number would go and purchase the grain or meal in bulk once every month or so. Hence this community had to be self-sufficient in a range of normal everyday activities and the point was they had to inter-relate and co-operate with each other. They would mill their grain or meal with the ancient method of a quern, probably for all to use. If anything this was as near to a primitive socialist community as one could get; each family dependent on the others for their food, their clean water, their beer, their work and basic

---

16 *Journal of the House of Commons,* Vol. XXII, (1735) 9 Geo II, c. 4 p. 551.
17 Wadsworth and Mann, op cit. p. 146.
18 Daniels, op cit. p. 24.

livelihood. This was still the case when the first factory was built, as long as it was reliant on water power, but when they were transferred over to steam these remote settlements were no longer needed and mill owners wanted a greater concentration of labour and to be closer to the network of roads and canals connecting them to the major centres of trade and commerce. The majority of the proto-industrial workers at Rough Hey would be forced to either stay and scratch out a living in a place in decline or move to where there was more regular work. Thus the old community, its traditional value system and its communal inter-relationships was effectively destroyed. It was for reasons such as these and the independence these workers felt they possessed, coupled with customary work practices that had been operational for centuries, that these people resisted the changes wrought by the encroaching capitalist system.

Crucial to the growth of the cotton industry in the North West in the first half of the eighteenth century was the growth of Liverpool both as a port of entry of raw materials and exit of the finished products, and also its significance in the slave trade. In fact the prerequisites were already in place when the cotton industry began to grow significantly in the North-West. It was the Portuguese who began to use slave labour in their imperial possessions, not only in the Caribbean but in their expansion into Brazil; other nations however, were not far behind. In the case of the British the slave trade from West Africa had been furnishing labour for the Caribbean sugar trade from the second half of the seventeenth century and this set the precedence for the expansion and use of slaves for the sugar plantations and cotton fields of, firstly, the Caribbean plantations and then the Southern Colonies in North America. Sugar was the initial commodity and a source of huge profits for Britain, but the Atlantic Eastern Seaboard's chief economic role was to act as the service sector for the West Indies, providing black slaves for the plantation labour. However, by the 1720s the huge profits derived in Britain from the production, shipping and re-export of sugar had deteriorated, and the British comparative advantage evaporated. This was chiefly due to the French use of the island of Saint-Domingue – modern Haiti – and the Spanish control of Cuba that ended British trading superiority, and new areas of exploitation were required. Tobacco and cotton, grown again in the West Indies, but also capable of large-scale production in the Southern Colonies of America were obvious replacements, again with the use of black slaves as the primary source of labour. However, the American colonies were also demographically expanding, both with voluntary and involuntary migrants and, of course, slaves. In addition to West Africa, the American colonies began to be important market areas for British produced goods, especially cotton.

It was on the back of this growth in trading alternatives to sugar that witnessed, from the 1720s, the establishment of Liverpool as a rival port to London and Bristol. Its proximity to Manchester and the hinterland of the North-West was an obvious advantage to Lancashire merchants. Yet by the early decades of the eighteenth century it had developed the use of the relatively sophisticated 'supercargo' system whereby the types of commodities exported and those imported could be mixed among several operators and the overall risks shared and costs reduced. In 1700 the population of Liverpool was placed somewhere between 5,000 and 6,000 people. It was estimated to be 12,000 in 1730, 18,000 in 1740 and 22,000 in 1750, which made it slightly larger than Manchester and Salford at around the same time.[19] The evidence suggests,

---

19 Wadsworth and Mann, op cit. pp. 510-511.

however, that at this stage of development most of the raw cotton was still coming from the West Indies. It was not until the deployment of Eli Whitney's cotton gin in the 1790s that cotton production in North America was developed on a truly industrial scale. This process had begun, however, from the later 1740s and was growing steadily through the 1750s.[20] Thus, we have seen that a regular supply of the raw materials for cotton textile production had been established by the 1750s, and also that new men were being attracted to the trade after the 1736 Manchester Act. The next stage of this study examines how the traditional work practices operated and how, from the middle of the 1750s, these customary practices came under serious threat.

We have seen that by the 1750s there began the onset of a foreshadowing of the established patterns and a set of alternative ideas emerged setting the foundations of classical economics and commerce.[21] As we have also seen above this period was the high point of the elder Pitt's imperial expansion and a series of petty conflicts culminating in the enormous growth of the British Empire at the conclusion of the Seven Years War in 1763. At this stage of development Britain became effectively an 'export led' economy furnishing both the new and established territories with goods either produced in Britain or the re-exportation of commodities from British-controlled parts of the world. It was at this time that ideas began to be formulated and conceived on how best to accomplish maximum commercial benefit, not only for the state but those who controlled the productive, commercial and distributive processes.

---

20 C. Knick Harley, 'Slavery, the British Atlantic economy and the Industrial Revolution', *University of Oxford, Discussion Papers in Economic and Social History*, No. 113, (April, 2013) pp. 23-24.
21 For this see the work of N. Mckendrick, J. Brewer and J. H. Plumb, *The Birth of Consumer Society* (Bloomington: Indiana University Press, 1982), J. Mokyr, (ed.), *The British Industrial Revolution: An Economic Perspective*, (Oxford: Westview Press, 1999 edn.), N. F. R. Crafts, *British Economic Growth During the Industrial Revolution*, (Oxford: Oxford University Press 1985).

7

The Changing Nature of Work Practices

The developments described thus far are indicative of an attitudinal shift taking place in the first half of the eighteenth century. Under the mercantile system, there already existed an established and well-used set of procedures to ensure a fair and just relationship between masters and workmen. If a worker had a grievance, he or she could present their case before a magistrate who would give his ruling impartially according to the facts. Arbitrary actions, conspiracies of any kind or private collusions were not encouraged. In this way, worker's combinations were suspicious in terms of their potential to undermine the accepted conventions of the state and its authority. Workers had neither the right nor the status to independently force their terms on employers, which could be construed as interfering and disruptive of the trading potential of the state. Employers likewise understood the nature of the relationship with their workers and were duty bound to accept that the state was traditionally protective of customary work practices. Yet this did not preclude them from attempting to evade the established practices or from giving vent to expressions of exasperation. For example, during the long disputes between the woollen workers and their masters in the West of England in the later 1720s into the 1730s, one master published an essay in response to an article entitled *An Essay on Riots*, printed in the *Gloucester Journal* in December, 1738. In the response the writer complained:

> But whilst the *Clothiers* are in the hands of the *Grand Inquisitor*, who proudly sits on his Tribunal examining, and censuring their Conduct, and calling the Aid of the Secular Arm to punish them; whilst he exercising all his Malice, and spitting his Venom on them, they may draw some Consolation even from his very Poison...In the 13th year of George I, an Act of Parliament was past, impowering the Justices to determine all Disputes between the *Clothier* and *Manufacturer* according to their Direction. The Act we speak of might be shewn to be very deficient, and want many amendments.[1]

Clearly then by end of the 1730s some masters were already questioning the appropriateness and adequacy of magistrates having the power to determine how they conduct their businesses. By the 1750s we see the wider onset of a foreshadowing of these established patterns and concrete alternative ideas emerged, setting the foundations of classical economics and commerce.[2] The nature of Britain utilising the assets at the end of the Seven Years War, in terms of her economy furnishing both the new and established territories with goods either produced in Britain or the re-exportation of commodities from British-controlled parts of the world to the rest of the globe, meant that, even more than in the past, the potential of overseas trade was seen as a national priority. This was given even greater importance as the reckoning took place in relation to the

---

1. Philanthes, *Case between the clothiers, weavers and other manufacturers with regard to the late riots in Wilts, 1738*, (London 1739) pp. 4. 6. An *Essay on Riots* appeared in the *Gloucester Journal*, 19 December, 1738.
2. For this see the work of N. Mckendrick, J. Brewer and J. H. Plumb, *The Birth of Consumer Society* (Bloomington: Indiana University Press, 1982), J. Mokyr, (ed.), *The British Industrial Revolution: An Economic Perspective*, (Oxford: Westview Press, 1999 edn.), N. F. R. Crafts, *British Economic Growth During the Industrial Revolution*, (Oxford: Oxford University Press, 1985).

growth of the national debt. Debates and ideas began to be formulated and conceived on how best to accomplish maximum commercial benefit, not only for the state but also for all those who possessed some control of the productive, commercial and distributive processes.

It was within this maelstrom of change that the cotton industry of the North-West found itself at the beginning of the Seven Years War. Now that the conditions for change and growth had been improved dramatically with the passing of the Manchester Act in 1736 and ease of access to port facilities afforded by the growth of Liverpool, the new masters entering the trade at this point had significant advantages. Their capital outlays were modest, yet their potential profits could be substantial and they already had the wherewithal to combine together to arrange for larger loans and financial services should the need arise. Yet the potential for even larger profits was a tantalising prospect, if they could effectively organise the trade to their satisfaction. Everything seemed to be in place. There were no corporate guilds to hold them back and impose their ancient privileges. They were relatively free of the larger Company and larger merchant houses that dominated London, as they had their own textile merchant centre in Manchester and seemed to have an abundance of the labour necessary to accomplish all aspects of cotton production, from the spinning of the thread, to weaving and bleaching, and the printing of the finished pieces. There were of course some drawbacks. They did not possess the transport links or marketing facilities that the metropolis possessed and this was especially problematic for the adequate collection and distribution of certain foodstuffs, especially grain, as well as the enhanced distribution and collection of their stock in trade, textiles. These men were proud of their individualism, their willingness to back themselves and their enterprises with capital and their nonconformist, no-nonsense work ethic. Many of them were self-made; they had been apprentices to Manchester drapers and merchants, served their time as intermediate chapmen and learned the business the hard way. No one had given them their position by virtue of hereditary privilege or through a network of elite connections, and whilst, when the occasion arose, they may have had to display deference to the local landed gentry and their socially high-born betters, it did not mean they had to respect them or expect any help from them. These men were in a hurry to get on, and 'woe betide' anyone who stood in their way. In the example of the provisioning of Manchester these men were the first to successfully challenge the monopolistic privileges of the trustees of Manchester Grammar School who controlled all grain milling in the area, an object which even the Lord of the Manor, Sir Oswald Mosley, could not achieve in 1732.[3] Their goal was not only to enhance their profit making potential but also to make Manchester the principal commercial centre of the North. They were beginning to turn their minds to political activism by supporting candidates to sit in the House of Commons who could achieve in law the necessary conditions which would assist their economic aspirations.

According to Richard Guest, writing in 1820s, the Manchester merchants were, by the 1740s, expanding their industry by giving out more raw materials and receiving back the woven fabrics, but he also tells us that by the 1750s there was a new set of masters: "second-rate merchants called fustian masters", mainly operating in the country districts but still based in Manchester.[4] In the cotton

---

3 *A History of the County of Lancaster:* Volume 4 , 'Townships: Manchester (part 2 of 2)' (1911), pp. 230-251.
4 R. Guest, op cit., p. 9

industry, although some were involved in fustians, a significant number were trading primarily in smallwares and cotton checks which were principally related to the out-townships around Manchester and country districts of Lancashire. These local centres would have been Stockport, Wigan, Bolton, Blackburn, Preston and Lancaster in the far north of the region, although in the case of the latter two they would be forced to make changes. In terms of the export of these products, even during the most intense period of naval conflict throughout the Seven Years War, their prospects were improving. In 1755 cotton checks were exported to the value of £54,345, by 1756 this figure had risen to £84,992, and in 1757 they had risen again to £101,318. Working of the purchasing power index this figure now equates to £1,181,000,000,[5] and a significant amount to be shared by a relative few enterprising entrepreneurs. Profits then could be good even in this relatively minor branch of the cotton-manufacturing sector, but potentially be even much better. The success of these smallware checks was mainly down to their export to Africa and the Caribbean, where brightly coloured fabrics were popular, and, by the end of the 1750s with the French navy now virtually non-existent, British exporters had the whole field to themselves, as well as the growing domestic market for shirting, handkerchiefs, and neckcloths.

Let us now consider the nature of labour in this growing sector. The kind of work done by the cotton workers in the two centuries prior to the 1750s has been noted above, and we have also seen the struggles encountered by the woollen workers in the West of England in attempting to keep a grasp on their work practices and what they believed were their customary rights. The great benefit of the artisan outworker system was its flexibility. There were literally hundreds, if not thousands, of workers throughout the North-West, all capable of performing the requisite tasks to a reasonable quality, with rates of pay established. The terms of their employment status is interesting and was akin to a form of clientage connection rather than the strict master/servant relationship associated with the factory system. In the seventeenth century the classical description of the Manchester merchant draper was that of buying (and selling) the raw materials, sending these out via his intermediaries (chapmen) to then be spun into thread, winding, warping and weaving. All these were specialised tasks and some of them were regarded as skills demanding a seven years apprenticeship. The chapmen would then return with the woven fabric to the Manchester warehouse, where it had to undergo finishing, calendaring (making the material smooth and even), perching (inspecting for flaws), bleaching, dyeing, and then cutting. These tasks at the end of the productive process could again be outsourced to self-employed finishers or, if the merchant was one of the larger merchants, they may have used their own waged labourers. As for the outworkers, they came in various grades according to the skills they possessed. The spinners were classified as the least skilled workers, then warpers, and the weavers were regarded as the most skilled. This position of clientage, rather than master/servant is most clearly seen as a matter of legal arrangement based on established laws of contract.

As we have seen, the intermediate chapmen distributed the raw materials to their respective workers on behalf of a merchant, and in due course collected the woven fabrics and paid the weavers for their work. As this system became established, two distinct types of worker emerged. There were those who

---

5 http://www.measuringworth.com/ukcompare/

became dependent on the relationship with the merchant and his chapmen, and those who were less dependent. The first group tended to be small family units located in the scattered hamlets throughout the country districts adjacent to the towns, whose turnover tended to be moderate, but the second group tended to be located in and around the larger cotton centres and could combine with other workers to produce larger amounts of the finished fabrics. The former type of workers received the raw materials from the chapmen and simply produced the woven fabric, possibly on a rented loom, but the latter bought the raw materials on credit from the masters via his chapmen and worked on their own looms, and were thus effectively self-employed. If the master was unhappy with the work, he could bring an action in law or more likely find other, more reliable outworkers. Likewise, if a weaver, for whatever reason, was not content with the treatment he received from the masters or his chapmen he could work for someone else. However, there were only a finite amount of merchants but there were thousands of weavers, spinners and warpers. Thus, the advantage always lay with the masters. But if a master short-changed or underpaid a worker, he was effectively in breach of his contract and, as with the dissatisfaction of the finished product, the law served now to protect the labourer, in that he too could seek a magistrate to redeem the money that he believed he had owing to him. On occasions masters complained that the workers were embezzling the raw materials, possibly to make extra fabric lengths for a future sale. It was in such situations that we see the clientage relationship as it operated. No matter how much in reality the worker was dependent on the master for their work, in a strict legal sense, they worked for themselves and were thus responsible for the work they produced and, by extension, liable for any damages or bad work produced if the master wished to force the issue. Likewise, if a master believed he was being short-changed with the raw materials he could bring the case before a magistrate for adjudication. The master could take two legal routes at this point. The first option was a criminal action under the terms of the anti-embezzlement laws, the second was a case heard as a breach of contract, which constituted a breach of equity law, and it would be heard on those terms. This also served to protect the worker as although this was a dispute regarding payments, (or possibly wages), in strictly legal terms this was suggestive of a contract dispute between equals and not one between master and servant.

We have noted the relative freedom of the North-West region from the restrictions imposed on a range of manufacturing sectors by the absence of guilds, but there were exceptions. The places where the guilds still operated were Wigan, Lancaster, Liverpool and Preston. In these places, up until the seventeenth century at least, the privileges of the guilds and their freemen to buy and sell produce only to those affiliated to the guild was maintained. This meant that attempts by the Manchester clothiers to forge an inroad into these towns and the surrounding areas were limited. Nonetheless, there were still plenty of 'open' districts where the outworker textile trades could be carried on. Yet even here the old statutes surrounding apprenticeship regulation were adhered to. The situation changed in the mid-1630s. After a plague had ravaged Preston in 1630, to the extent that almost 60% of its population were dead, men from outside the town and outside the influence of the guild began to undertake business in the textiles trades. The guild merchants then lodged a complaint to the Privy Council outlining their grievance that the terms of the guild were being breached. The Privy Council sent the matter to three justices, who came out in favour of the non-guild traders. The Preston Guild Company appealed and three other justices once again found against them, saying in a clear re-affirmation of the need to protect the labourers:

> The several trades are rather to be continued (being in remote places from Preston) that suppressed, for that many thereby purchase relief for themselves and their families where otherwise they would live very poorly or be cast onto the country or go abegging ... the private end and benefit of some few of the inhabitants of the Town of Preston who, some of them, are conceived to be within the penalty of the statute, they not having served seven years apprenticeship, and they being rich and able men where they live, strive to reap that benefit for the themselves to the impoverishment of the multitude.[6]

The law came down clearly on the side of those in the country seeking to carry on producing and making a living, but it also came down strongly supporting those who, although operating outside of the guild, were serving an apprenticeship. Thus, the law favoured those who had been apprenticed rather than men who, although rich, were unwilling to give the same privileges to those outside of the chartered guilds geographical boundaries as to those who were fortunate enough to be apprentices inside. However, this was no seventeenth century socialist utopia being acted out but rather a pragmatic appraisal of the effect of a large number of people suddenly being thrown out of work would have on the level of poor rates. In the short term this had little effect in Preston, the guild continued to enforce its privileges within the trading limits of the geographic area of the town. Whilst this might serve to protect the tradesmen and merchants of Preston, its long-term use was limited in effectiveness, as the larger Manchester merchants simply bypassed Preston and sent work (and money) to those areas not controlled by any guilds. Preston and Lancaster through attempting to preserve their guild status became time-locked cocoons while the economic advances elsewhere in the region passed them by. What needs to be stressed at this point is that in both the corporate towns and in the non-corporate areas that lay outside their control, the system of apprenticeships was maintained in order to ensure that the quality of the product remained consistently satisfactory.

Developments in the other corporate town, Liverpool, were overshadowed by events which drowned and dwarfed those attempting to hold on to the ancient restrictions. It would appear that several London merchants had moved to Liverpool after the plague and fire, shortly after the Restoration, and then again to escape from the chaos of the French Wars. As we have seen, towards the end of the seventeenth and into the first half of the eighteenth century the port and city exploded in a frenzy of economic activity, which left the guild with merely a form of limited localised political control. As 1750s approached all the old corporate towns – Liverpool apart – fell behind their non-incorporated rivals, both in terms of population and commercial activity.

There then developed, from at least the early seventeenth century, a remarkably free and open pattern of trade and commerce in the North-West. There further developed a variety of differing types of clothing masters, some large scale, based in Manchester, Rochdale, Bolton and Blackburn, and many smaller masters, with much more limited capital, sometimes acting on their own or sometimes acting as intermediaries or chapmen for the larger merchants in the various kinds of cotton fabrics. The larger Manchester merchants would supply

---

6 *Preston Pilot,* 'Local Sketches' (April, May, 1875, and 12 October, 1889).

the smaller independent merchants with raw materials, purchased on credit against the value of the finished fabrics which would be sold back to them. Alternatively, they would employ their own intermediaries to supply their network of spinners and weavers in and around Manchester or, indeed, further into the countryside, once again the woven fabrics would be sent back to their warehouses. In both cases the masters were free to trade and deal with whomever they chose. It is noteworthy that there was at least one woman, Mrs Dickinson, who was prominent in the trade in Manchester, who carried on the same procedures as the men, and had the same links with the London merchant houses, and there were women occupying the same role in the countryside as more modest merchants.[7] The weavers may take the raw material, spin it, wind it into thread, and then weave it, or they may just take the spun thread off the chapman and weave the fabric. It would largely depend if they possessed an extended family large enough and with the requisite skills to be able to spin and wind the raw cotton. Both the larger merchants and their smaller counterparts may directly employ factors or agents themselves who would in turn get the cotton spun, wound and woven in their workshops, probably employing workers for those tasks. This type of operator could be termed a 'merchant-manufacturer' because he had the capability – and necessary capital and wherewithal – to carry out both tasks. The whole system was, although complex in terms of its organization, remarkably flexible as several different kinds of productive devices were available to be used in the case of glut of orders or the more staid times of business. At the actual labouring end of the trade, all were to a greater or lesser extent dependent on the merchants who served them the raw material and took the woven fabric at an agreed tariff of payments-per-piece (or, as it was termed at the time, per 'end'). Ultimately, all were dependent on the large Manchester merchant with his warehouses, offices and contacts, agents, shippers and dealers in Liverpool and London. It was calculated in 1696 that in the immediate vicinity of Manchester alone there were 40,000 employed in the various branches of manufacturing cotton goods.[8]

What is noticeable in the pre-factory stage of industrialisation is the lack of synchronisation of labour as a factor of production and the apparent inability of employers to enforce the necessary disciplines for effective co-ordination in all manufacturing sectors save, possibly, the silk and pottery industries. In the later 1750s Josiah Wedgewood had leased the Ivy Works in Burslem, Thomas Whieldon had leased Lombes's silk factory in Derby, and there was also another early example in Preston of a silk weaving factory. These three served as precedents for the future of production in Lancashire cotton dating from even earlier in the eighteenth century.[9] There was also a textile factory operational between 1681 and 1713 at New Mills, near Dunfermline, Scotland that employed 700 workers and a piper to keep them amused, and its own prison to keep them in check.[10] In this sense, the way forward for those merchants who wished to change the ancient outworker system had been revealed, but the problem was going to be how to get so many workers re-organised into a set of more accommodating mentalities, disciplines to force them to fit into the new

---

7 PRO, *Palatinate Papers*, Lancashire, P. L. 6, 44/52, see also Wadsworth and Mann op cit., pp. 81-82.
8 This evidence comes from the panic created by the shortage of specie money due to the revaluing of the coinage in 1696. *Historic Manuscripts Commission, Kenyon Mss*, (1894) p. 410.
9 PRO, *Palatinate Papers*, P. L. 6, 51/93, (1704)
10 Wadsworth and Mann, op cit., p. 108.

system. The entire culture of the workers would have to be radically changed and their conditioning to the terms of industrial capitalistic techniques would undoubtedly be a painful transition. Most strikingly, these changes would result in their loss of independence and, indeed, their community's entire way of life. Clearly, this process would be a protracted one and this would in all probability result in disruption and worker protest and resistance, but it was something that, if accomplished, would ensure a distinct upturn in the potential profitability for the entrepreneur. This nature of worker independence was something that was noticeable in the conduct, behaviour and attitudes of English working people. As we saw in chapter four when examining the attitudes of clothiers like William Temple and the reaction of the West of England woollen workers to the attempted changes to customary work practices in that region, working people were not easy to manipulate to the will of a progressive master. As the future Dean of Gloucester, Josiah Tucker put it in 1745, when describing the workers of the West of England:

> And in fact, with regard to the morals of the *poor* at present, far from exaggerating the matter, it must be acknowledged, times were never worse. For the *lower* class of people *are at this day* so far degenerated from what they were in *former* times, as to become a matter of astonishment, and a proverb of reproach. Such brutality and insolence, such debauchery and extravagance, such idleness, irreligion, cursing and swearing, and contempt for all rule and authority...our people are *drunk with the cup of liberty*. They enjoy to a degree unknown to our forefathers, who lived in a state of vassalage and dependence, little better than that of bondage and slavery; and who by this means were habituated to think, that it *was above their sphere*, and fitting only for their *superiors*, to gratify themselves in scenes expensive pleasures and criminal diversions. But their *posterity* have been growing up into freedom for several generations back, and are now become entirely independent, and matters of themselves and their own actions. Their minds and inclinations are now let loose to *think*, and to *judge*, and *do* as they please.[11]

Clearly such people needed to be taught some intrinsic lessons on how to behave and to know their place. By the early 1750s, the production of cotton fabrics, their finishing, and printing was by far the largest industrial sector in the North-West. In 1751, before a Committee of the House of Commons enquiring into the legitimacy of Lancashire fustians in not contravening the Act of 1721 outlawing the manufacturing and indeed wearing of pure cotton products, it was claimed by one manufacturer that at Blackburn he employed 3,000 people working 600 looms. The overwhelming majority of the fabric produced was printed, and termed fustians, in order to circumvent the 1721 Act, and the evidence of such witnesses to the clear growth of the industry in the North-West was enough to see that Parliament saw no need to pursue the matter.[12] Clearly, this was now a significant branch of manufacturing and employer of labour. Certainly, by the 1770s, they outnumbered the smallware merchants, but it was in the mid-1750s that these new men in both the fustians and smallware sectors, referred to by Guest, began in earnest their attempts to re-organise the industry, particularly in terms of the role of labour.[13] It is likely that this process of changing the role of labour from the clientage and the relatively independent

---

11 J. Tucker, *Six Sermons*, (Bristol: Felix Farley, 1745) pp. 70-71.
12 *Journal of the House of Commons*, Evidence of Robert Livesay, vol. xxii, (1751) p. 567.
13 Daniels, op cit., p. 39.

relationship noted above to, effectively, wage labourers had started from the later 1740s, but by 1756-57 the new masters began to adopt a much more aggressive position towards the cotton workers, especially in terms of their customary work practices. What these new men realised was that labour was a commodity, just like their capital and raw materials, and, indeed, just like the finished product. It required monitoring, organising and, above all, supervision so that if the work was unsatisfactory or overpriced it could be regulated to their advantage. Such an important commodity such as labour required discipline. Such correction could not be given if trust was placed in the workers hands, no matter how long their traditional practices had been in place. Without concern to the older masters, modern times required new systems if profit was to be maximised; the workers would always try to turn the situation to their advantage if left to their own devices, work when they pleased, practice 'St Monday' and attempt to assert themselves.

What is noticeable about the Lancashire cotton workers was their relative lack of disputes with the masters in previous periods. Apart from the odd petition warning of some transgression by some masters there is hardly any mention of any major industrial disagreements in the sixteenth or seventeenth centuries and the traditional masters appear to have been satisfied with the organisation and practices of the labourers. In one sense this is unsurprising, given the part of the reasoning behind the old Tudor and Stuart statutes was to keep wages in check but at the same time adequate for all grades of workers engaged in the trade. The key point is that both sides could call for redress and arbitration by magistrates; the one for bad work or the embezzlement of materials, the other for non-payment or under-payment of monies owing for work produced. It was also quiet in the first three to four decades of the eighteenth century but, as we shall see in the next chapter, the cotton workers began to be concerned over the posturing of what Guest described as the "second-rate merchants". In an attempt to counter the potential problems there is evidence that the weavers had initiated a trade union with the view to forming a combination out of their existing mutual 'box club' from 1747, in an effort to combat the masters. Contrast the situation in the North-West with that of the West of England. As we have seen, here there had been severe disputes going back to the time when the Hanoverians ascended the throne. Therefore, in Lancashire, unlike the West of England there was no recent experience of organising a dispute to defend what they saw as an assault on their common value system and basic rights of the weaving communities. Yet clearly, by 1747 and the establishment of the rules of their organisation they had clearly more than a suspicion that the new masters were attempting to alter the traditional terms of employment.[14] Nor would the conflict and organisational activities of

---

14 Manchester Central Reference Library, *The Worsted Small-Ware Weavers' Apology, Together with all their Articles, which either concern their Society or Trade. To which is added a Farewell Discourse, made by their First Chair-Man. All faithfully collected together, by Timothy Shuttle.* (Manchester, 1756), also see; Wigan Reference Library, *The Linen and Cotton Broad-Ware Weavers' Apology: Humbly addressed to the Gentleman Manufacturers of Manchester, And all others whom it may concern. By a Well-Wisher to Trade.* (Liverpool, 1758) A definition at this point may be necessary. The term 'Apology' in the discourse of this document, does not mean the conventional remorse, rather it is intended to convey the 'reasons' why such a society was needed to come into existence. Although published in 1756, it is clearly dated that the first 'article' agreed to by the initial members dated from 1747. A further interesting point was suggested by Alfred Wadsworth, suggested in *The Cotton Trade and Industrial Lancashire, 1600-1780*, (Manchester: Manchester University Press, 1965 edn.) that it was unlikely that the two 'Apology's would have been written by the weavers themselves, but more likely by a middle class sympathiser, which, if

other cloth workers have been unknown to the operatives of the North-West. This was due not only to the fact that their disputes were noted in the regional and national press, but first-hand knowledge could have been gleaned from those skilled workers on the 'tramp'. This was a system whereby when there was a shortage of work in a labourers' own locality the time-served, fully indentured worker would obtain a 'clearance' or 'document', also known as a 'blank', from his local box club to allow him to travel all over Britain to obtain work. They would know a list of places to stay ('houses of call'), usually a public house or, alternatively, the 'club house' where they would be given refreshment, a place to rest and maybe find work. It is known for example that the woollen workers of Devon had a tramping system from 1700 and the Taunton weavers from 1707.[15]

However, we need to be clear at this point just what these cotton workers were seeking to defend. Effectively, within the structure of the weaving of cotton, there were three grades. The first were termed the undertakers, these were the leading weavers who were the most experienced, who ran their own shop, supervising the spinning, warping, the cleaning of the finished cloth and the training of as many as seven apprentices, as well as weaving the fabric themselves. In taking the responsibility of training the apprentices, the undertaker would receive a fee from the parents of the young person, as young as eleven or twelve years of age. This fee was not only to pay for the child learning the trade, which could serve as employment for the rest of their lives, but also because the child would often live with the undertaker, or at least be fed by them. Then there were the journeymen, who had served the statutory seven years apprenticeship, but were less experienced and who may work a second or third loom on their own in partnership with the undertaker. It was alleged by the masters when the disputes materialised that the undertakers were taking on people as journeymen for a fee who were not fully time-served in contravention of the statutes, doing so when work was plentiful to cash in on the glut of orders.[16] Whether there was any truth to these allegations is in one sense moot. Firstly, it would be ultimately detrimental to the undertakers if the work produced by the interloper was bad – thus needing constant supervision and rectifying. In addition, if others in the cloth producing community became aware of the abuse, then they risked being ostracised from the fellowship of the weavers' self-imposed mechanisms of protection, such as their primitive friendly societies, of which more will be said in due course. Yet this was clearly an issue, as it was mentioned in the regulations drawn for their protective combination of 1747. The only conditional proviso being for taking on a journeyman or journeywoman who had not served the full seven years was that if they had enjoyed their apprenticeship at fifteen years of age when they could be indentured after six years. Finally there were the apprentices, who would learn all the so-called 'mysteries' of the trade and at the end of seven years were clear to practice the trade on their own behalf. Often the apprentices would live with the undertakers, or at least close by. After serving their apprenticeship term they were given the 'document', 'clearance' or 'blank' noted above, countersigned by other undertakers to support their claim to have served the requisite length and be capable of carrying on the trade to satisfaction. The 'blank' would have to be

---

so will be of relevance to the next chapter.
15 See E. J. Hobsbawm, 'The Tramping Artisan', *Economic History Review,* New Series, Vol. 3, No. 3 (1951), pp. 299-320, New Series, Vol. 3, No. 3 (1951), pp. 299-320. See also , S. Webb and B Webb, *A History of Trade Unionism,* (London: Longmans, 1894) pp. 438-9.
16 Daniels, op cit., pp. 40-41

paid for by the now indentured weaver and costs varied from the various locations, but it was reported to be four pence.[17] Once this was paid his or her name was entered into a register and they were free to work either as an undertaker or as a journeyman or journeywoman and, as we have seen, were free to go on the 'tramp' should the need arise.

One must remember that in the Lancashire countryside, possibly several miles from the nearest township or large town, these places were effectively self-contained communities. The undertakers may have leases to farm a smallholding, or at least be expected to join in the agricultural work of the surrounding community when the seasons demanded. Thus there was an order and balance to their lives in which everyone knew their role and the nature of the communities demands as a self-contained unit. For the undertaker the crucial phase was to get adequate quantities of spun yarn to weave. If there was a blockage in the production of sufficient spun yarn this could be financially costly, thus young women and children were vital to producing the necessary amounts of spun yarn. However, the role of women in this community were probably the most interesting of all its members. As well as the necessary domestic duties of child rearing, cleaning and cooking, the woman would be expected to brew beer, maintain adequate food supplies, such as quern the grain and flour, then make the bread, possibly churn milk for butter and cheese, and further, she would be integral to the industrial employment of the family unit. Importantly, and apparently unique to the textile industry in the North-West, she too, as we have seen, could be a time-served skilled weaver, and, indeed, be entrusted to train her own apprentices and thus be categorised as an undertaker.[18]

From the time of the appearance of the first 'articles' of regulations set out in the *Weavers' Apology* in 1747, until 1756 when they were published, the situation between the masters and workers had deteriorated. One accusation made by the weavers was that the new masters had begun to employ workers who had not served a full apprenticeship and, further, that they were employing young people as apprentices who, in fact, were not learning the trade, but actually producing goods offered for sale at reduced wages. The growing concern of the weavers in the combination is made clear by the increased stringency of their later 'articles'. In one of these later articles it was announced that no member should work for a master in the smallware sector who had not been operational before 1753, as those entering after this date were perceived to be those who were the most ruthless and least tolerant of the weavers' traditional practices. The inference is that it is from this date that the workers began to feel increasingly threatened. If a worker did work for one the new masters there would be repercussions. They would be deemed "unfair and not stood by." In addition, all the so-called 'apprentices' now working for the new masters were to be classified as 'unfair' and not given the privileges or "Right to this our said Branch."[19] Yet the tide of commercial opinion seemed to go against the workers and in favour of those masters who were endeavouring to sweep the old system away. In 1757, just at the moment that the new merchants and masters of the North-West were tightening their grip on the supply of the essential products of provisioning and their costs and, in the industrial areas, on the 'rationalization' of work processes, once again that prodigious contemporary commentator Josiah Tucker, now the most reverend Dean of Gloucester, came forth with his views

---

17 *Small-Ware Weavers' Apology*, op cit.
18 Ibid.
19 Ibid.

on the British worker in an essay published in 1758.

> The Complaints against the Morals of the manufacturing poor become louder every Day, and certainly demand, if any Thing doth, the serious Attention of the Legislature. Combinations of Journeymen to extort exorbitant Wages. This money is spent on Drunkenness and Debauchery...their Unfaithfulness to their Trust – the Badness of their Work, whenever their Masters have great Demand, and dare not turn them off – the increasing number of the Poor...A certain very ingenious Gentleman, and himself a great manufacturer in the Clothing Way, had attended to them with great Assiduity; and is engaged in a Scheme which he intends to exhibit to the Publick, of a very singular Nature, for the Reformation of these Abuses. He has carefully observed, that in exceeding dear years, when Corn and Provisions are at an extravagant Price, then Work is best and cheapest done – but that in cheap Years, the Manufacturers are idle, Wages high, and the Work ill-done. He has carried out these Observations through many years back; and confirmed them by the Testimony of several great Writers upon Trade. *Therefore* he infers, that the high Duties, Taxes and Excises upon the Necessaries of Life, are so far from being a Disadvantage to Trade...that they are eventually the chief Support of it – and ought to be higher still, in order to oblige the Poor either to Work or Starve.[20]

If ever the new merchants of the North-West both in the industrial sector and in food provisioning needed a manifesto on what they should do, then Tucker provided it for them. He went on to directly attack those in control of "Our Monopolies, publick Companies, and Corporate Charters, [that] are the Bane and Destruction of *Free Trade*"[21] In an extraordinary, and economically prescient and modern passage, Tucker not only advocated the free movement of people, but the actual encouragement of immigration into Britain, because by not allowing foreigners to settle is "another Material disadvantage to *English* trade." He explained in graphic detail what later economists have termed the crucially important actions of the 'elasticity of labour'.

> Foreigners can never get rich in a Strange Country, but by working cheaper or better than the Natives. And if they do so, though individuals may suffer, the Publick is certainly a Gainer; as there is so much Merchandize to be exported on cheaper Terms, or so much saved to the Merchant, whereby he may afford to export the cheaper. Not to mention, that by this Means the Price of Labour is continually beat down, Combinations of Journeymen against their Masters are prevented, industry is encouraged, and an Emulation excited. All of which are greatly for the public Good.

To this Tucker added that the capitalist employers should openly seek to expand their enterprises by 'outsourcing' (to use the modern vernacular) to where the labour was cheapest in order to undercut the profits of the French, and, if necessary, moving out of one region and into another, or indeed to the "South-West of Ireland" where "the Price of Labour is as cheap in these Parts, as anywhere in *France*."[22] To add even more to the nirvana of the new merchants,

---

20 J. Tucker, *A Brief Essay on the Advantages and Disadvantages which Respectively Attend France and Great Britain with Regard to Trade with some Proposals for Removing the Principal Disadvantages of Great Britain. In a New Method*, (London: George Faulkner, 1757) pp. 34-35.
21 Ibid. p. 26.
22 Ibid. p. 40.

now imbued with the overtly capitalist ethic of the rapacious gathering of profits through the application of stringent disciplines on their workpeople, Tucker suggested that they be entrusted with direct *political* control of the workers. He said that in all the industrial areas new localised politico-legal Courts should be initiated, to be called "Guardians of the Morals of the Manufacturing Poor". Qualifications for this device of overt social control were designed by Tucker to suit the new masters perfectly.

> The Qualifications of each Member of this Court to be as follows; 1st, that he employs not less than twenty Manufacturers on his own Account, the greater part of the Year. By this Regulation, the most eminent, as well as the most concerned, will be the only Persons admitted. 2dly, That each member subscribes a certain Sum, suppose two Guineas at least, every Year, towards the good Purposes hereafter to be mentioned; but that they be admitted to receive the Legacies and Donations of others. 3dly, That each Member be a married Man, in order to set the good example here recommended. The Aim of this Court to be to discourage Vice, Idleness and Debauchery, and to encourage Industry, Probity and Fidelity, in the lower Class of People.[23]

What Tucker was in fact advocating was making the capitalist entrepreneurs magistrates and giving them total control to police their workers in accordance with rules and values that they saw fit, which would have the effect of completely nullifying the impartial arbitration of the old style justices to any of the complaints of the workers enshrined in the old Tudor and Stuart statutes. Yet it was more than this. Such a body, suggested Tucker, should control all the alehouse licences, be able to inflict corporal punishment on their recalcitrant workers and be in direct charge of all their leisure pursuits.[24] Tucker was providing for the new masters (and indeed the more traditional masters) a licence to act more stridently and forcefully towards their workers, to instil their forms of discipline, but also further – along with other anti-mercantilist proponents – offering them the economic justifications for such actions. In short, to be able to control every aspect of the workers existence, rendering them utterly dependent, and indeed utterly submissive to the will of their masters.

Such were the times and the changing attitudes that the workers of the North-West were now facing. We shall detail the events of what took place in the region between 1756-1760 shortly, but first we must briefly examine just what the masters were attempting to change and what nature the workers defence mechanisms entailed. In Manchester and the other large weaving centres, the weavers formed localised branches consisting of those workers who were employed the leading merchants. This they termed their 'trade society', who were in contact with the larger, indeed, region-wide, 'weavers' committee' that served the interests of all the weavers throughout Lancashire. Although these bodies had existed from at least 1747, and standing orders and notes were taken from that time, there were no set of official rules or articles of governance until 1756. Wadsworth and Mann argue that these were articulated by a middle class sympathiser. This person they suggest was the dissenting vicar of Failsworth, Robert Robinson. In any event, the weavers appear to have been prepared for some measure of defence and were organised by 1756. A roll was taken at meetings with weavers and the 'shops' they represented, they appointed a treasurer and a chairman who served for the duration of three months, any

---
23 Ibid. p. 35.
24 Ibid. pp. 35-37.

grievances were to be put forward formally in writing and all meetings were held in private behind closed doors, probably in a public house, with the last man in attendance acting as a doorman. Anyone arriving drunk or swearing or placing wagers would receive the chairman's censure and be barred from future meetings for two months, members were not even to be allowed to sit down at meetings with their hats on:

> For if we consider this Society, not as a Company of Men met to regale themselves with Ale and Tobacco, and talk indifferently on all Subjects; but rather as a Society sitting to protect the Rights and Privileges of a Trade by which some hundreds of People (I might say Families) subsist; and see that no Violence or Encroachments be offered either to *it* or its Dependents.[25]

All of which indicates a formality of procedure and a seriousness of purpose. The society was formed at the level of the district, township and parish, each branch established a 'box' to collect funds and to "communicate and inform, the Society of any Things necessary to be done." Each branch nominated a president, clerk and steward, and they were paid expenses for their time doing the business of the society.[26] This suggests an extraordinary degree of organization and quite sophisticated co-ordination for the time. Here were workers' combinations for the whole of the region, sub-divided into branches at all localities, co-ordinating with their respective larger town societies, who in turn liaised and were in contact with the main leadership branches in Manchester. All the various branches of the cotton weaving trade were now being represented by their respective societies, the check weavers, the worsted small-ware weavers and the broad-ware weavers.[27] This began to raise concerns in government, especially pertinent at this particular point as the Seven Years War was not going at all well.[28] Given the nature of the widespread worker anger throughout the textile areas, not only in the North-West, but also in the West of England where the weavers took their battle to Parliament over a dispute that had been simmering since 1755. Here, they initially won their right for magistrates to set their rates of pay in 1756.[29] However, the clothiers mounted a stiff campaign of resistance and got the Act repealed in March, 1757.[30] In the West of England, however, the workers stuck to their traditional methods of petitioning Parliament for redress of grievances, with the support of sympathetic magistrates, and there were few indications of co-ordinated region-wide combination; different, then, to the situation in Lancashire, where the masters chose this moment to strengthen their grip on the trade, only to see a response in kind from the workers. In their 'Articles' of 1758, the broad-ware weavers proved that the masters were lengthening the woven pieces without adjusting the prices paid. Previously the piece length was warped at 80 yards to the piece

---

25 Manchester Central Reference Library, BR 677 S18, *The Worsted Small-Ware Weavers' Apology, Together with all their Articles, which either concern their Society or Trade. To which is added a Farewell Discourse, made by their First Chair-Man. All faithfully collected together, by Timothy Shuttle.* (Manchester, 1756). p. 25
26 Ibid. p. 12.
27 Ibid. pp. 12-13.
28 National Archives, Kew, State Papers Domestic, SP 36 Vol. 136, ff 84-85 (1757); SP 36, Vol. 136, ff 117, (June, 1757); SP 36, Vol. 136, ff 186, Letters from Wigan, (11/8/1757); SP 36, Vol. 138, ff 48, letters from Wigan (1757), ff 45-47, Riots at York, (2/9/1757); SP 36, Vol. 138, ff 127-129, Riots at Liverpool, (22/11/1757).
29 29 Geo II, c.33.
30 See Randall op cit, pp. 149-150.

whereas in 1757-58 this had now risen to up to 96 yards to the piece. Not only had they changed the piece-length, but masters now expected the increase do be done in the same time but with inferior raw materials, meaning that they could weave the old piece-lengths much faster in the past for more money which, in real terms, given the shortage and rising costs of provisions, meant now they were losing up to a third of their income compared to the recent past. Given the outgoing costs for actually working pin-winding, loom rental, buying candles; the worker was left with 4 shillings and three pence per week on which to live; pay house rental costs and buy food for his wife and children.

> Now I will leave it for anyone to judge how such a Family as this must live Seven Days, upon Four Shillings and Three Pence, even supposing it all to go for Provisions, and set Rent, Fire and Clothes, and even all other necessaries aside, which will make better than Two Shillings of the Money, and must be had somehow or other; I do affirm that there is not one Weaver in Six, the whole Trade through, that will make Half a Piece of this sort of Work in one Week. I have seen such a family as this I am speaking on (and can bring living Witnesses to testify it) that have lived Four Days out of Seven, upon nothing but Water Gruel without ever a bit of bread to it.[31]

Crucially, in the initial articles, the weavers' society of the North-West considered whether they were in breach of common law. This was likely because of the example of a weaver being charged in 1754 with being a member of a combination and brought before a magistrate.[32] However, the articles contained a thinly veiled threat; they asserted that if they were in breach they were justified in their actions. In itself this is interesting on several levels. Firstly, it reveals that in the mindset of the weavers at this time, even if the law prohibited their actions, their situation was such that it demanded they take that risk no matter what the outcome may be. Secondly, it also reveals that, in common with historical and popular perceptions of liberty, if an act is clearly and demonstrably against the public interest then it can justifiably and legitimately be opposed. Thirdly, this displays the resolve of large number of workers drawn from the whole of the North-West region to defend themselves because of the concerted attempts by the masters to change the terms of their working relationship, which to these weavers was a very serious and dangerous situation. In the drawing up and, indeed, through the publication of their articles, they made plain the basis of their principles and, of direct relevance to this study, there is clear evidence that industrial workers could be imbued with a sense of the moral economy as discussed in chapter five above. They said of those in positions of authority who may be asked to arbitrate on their actions:

> ...a grand Objection that may be made to the whole, and that is, That it will be acting too much against Common Law, to which I answer, That we have hitherto been acting more so, than we shall, when once Unity, Order and Decency is established amongst us. For when Gentlemen and Magistrates of the Law sees a Trades-Society acting upon Principles of Justice, and ordering their Affairs by the strictest Rules of Decency, they

---

31 *The Linen and Cotton Broad-Ware Weavers' Apology*, (1758), Cited in Wadsworth and Mann, op cit. p. 350.
32 J. P. Earwaker, (ed.), *The Constables' accounts of the Manor of Manchester: from the year 1612 to the year 1647, and from the year 1743 to the year 1776*, (Manchester: Cornish 1891) Vol. iii, p. 65.

will rather revere than punish such a Society.[33]

Their basis, then, was justice based on prescriptive, traditional customary practices which, indeed, they believed could be sustained in both common and statute law and this, they further believed, could be proven. A further significant passage links the classical moral economy based on resistance to the manipulation of the marketing of provisions with their industrial struggle. They pointed out that it was the increased cost of provisions which was a motivating factor in their need for self-protection, coupled with the large profits now being enjoyed by the cotton merchants, who had amassed such "large and opulent Fortunes as hath enabled them to vie with some of the best Gentlemen in the County. But with regard the poor Workmen, it hath been quite the reverse." This was a connection with not only the perceived assault on their customary industrial practices by the new masters, but also with their ongoing protest at the increasing cost of food. This again is a direct connection and indeed evidence of a contemporary understanding of arguments associated with the traditional methods of state protection (the moral economy) as being a motivating factor in their need to combine together to enhance their bargaining position and unity of purpose. Their suspicion, shared with others of the region, was that the merchants of Manchester played a substantial role in being responsible for both these conditions (the cost of provisions and changes to work practices) the workers were now facing. What appears to have been a further incentive to combine into a protective society was the success over the centuries of the corporate guilds. The workers of the North-West contrasted their position with the relatively favourable position of the Spitalfields silk weavers of London who enjoyed collective protection and had a reputation of fierce independence, and they would have been further aware of other regions where no such organisations existed, and they probably would have known or have been given word of the struggles that had recently taken place in the West of England. "The Manufacturers hath acquired immense Riches, and purchased large Estates, and can live with almost equal Grandeur to a Peer of the Land." Needless to say the masters were concerned, but the weavers sought to assuage this.

> Our Meeting once a Month hath given Offence to some of our Masters... We make use of this Opportunity to acquaint them that instead of injuring them either by attempting to raise or Prices, or any other Ways; that we have seen with Patience other Trades, such as Carpenters, Bricklayers etc., raise theirs upon account of Provisions being more than one third dearer than usual; I say, we have seen others do it, and at the same Time are sensible that ours is as hard gotten Bread as theirs.[34]

The aim of the weavers was to protect entry into the trade and maintain adequate skills acquired by apprenticeships and enshrined in the Tudor and Stuart statutes, as well as pointing out that real wages were worth only two-thirds their value of twenty five years before. Furthermore, the new masters were accused of taking those children of the poor and engaging them as 'apprentices' when in reality they were a source of unindentured cheap labour, and also their use of un-apprenticed small farmers who were being increasingly recruited in the times of year when little farm labour was needed. Given that in the mid to late 1750s provision prices were rising and reasonably paid work was becoming more difficult to find, it is not surprising that the temporary farm workers were a target

---

33 *The Worsted Small-Ware Weavers' Apology*, op cit. p. 27.
34 Ibid pp. 29-30.

in the cotton sector. But one suspects that the farmer-weavers as a group had been part of the cotton manufacturing processes for some time. Some indeed may have served some limited apprenticeship as a young person, but specifically what they were accused of by the end of the 1750s was taking any work on any terms from the masters, thus undermining the standing of the full-time cotton workers:

> For it is such as these, who, for some Seasons of the Year, have taken Work upon any Terms or Wages rather than stand still when they could find no Employment in either Barns or Fields, and what they thus make a Practice of, others who had no other Dependence but Weaving, were soon obliged to comply with.[35]

Possibly it was the new masters who were seeking out such temporary workers and were doing so as a means of reducing the piece rates throughout the industry which, if indeed was the case, confirmed the suspicions of the full-time weavers. Thus, if times were as hard as the weavers maintained, the farmer-weavers would get any work at any price they could in order to make a living, and masters were gleefully exploiting the situation to the detriment of all grades of weavers.

However, the accusation regarding the poor apprentices was even more serious. The 1758 *Broad-Ware Weavers' Apology* makes the case that "Strangers and Foreigners, who have come into the Town and taken Parish Apprentices out of all the Towns round about, purely for the Sake of a little Money." It was asserted that the masters had taken as many as a dozen at a time and worked so hard that ultimately they were fit for nothing but poor relief:

> And as such Numbers could not be kept without Employment, and they being but Children and consequently could not perform work as they ought, their Masters were obliged to take Work for them on such Terms as the Employers were pleased to propose to them; to make amends for which, the poor Children have been as it were sold into worse Slavery, and harder Bondage, than the Negroes in our *English* Plantations in *America*; some of them have been, through such hard Slavery and worse Usage, rendered such shocking Objects of Commiseration and Charity, as to soften the Heart even of Tyranny and Oppression itself, and have thereby for ever after commenced either Cripples, Beggars, or Paupers, to the no small Detriment of the Landed Gentlemen.[36]

If this was the case it was little wonder that the Lancashire weavers were angry and determined to defend their position. All this resentment at the manner which the masters had attempted to change customary practices provoked the necessity to form combinations, with or without the sanctity of the law, in the belief that the magistrates would see what the masters had resorted to and thus be persuaded by the weavers' side of the argument. This was coupled with the pragmatism that if the present situation was allowed to continue it would unquestionably hit the county elites in their pockets because, inevitably, the poor rates would rise, as the broad-ware weavers' apologist argued as the workers "are with Sorrow constrained to fly to the Parish for Relief, which hath at present raised the Poor Rates to such a Height, as in some Degree, to effect even the

---

35 *The Linen and Cotton Broad-Ware Weavers' Apology*, (1758), cited in Wadsworth and Mann, op cit. p. 316.
36 Ibid, p. 349.

Landholders themselves."[37]

Clearly the masters' belief was that the time was right to bring in these wholesale new work practices. They appeared to getting encouragement from influential writers such as Tucker and their feeling was that the law was on their side. A crucial element of their argument was that it was a national necessity to change the economic basis of the worker/employer relationship. If this indeed proved to be the case, then the position of the workers in attempting to defend what they understood to be their prescriptive right in maintaining their customary practices would be under serious threat. The maintenance of the Tudor and Stuart statutes was the cornerstone of their argument and their fight. If they lost this then the way would be clear for the masters to openly employ anyone, time-served or not and on terms that they completely determined. This preservation of the apprenticeship rules was the only means the workers had of controlling the numbers in their trade and, from their point of view, making sure that all of their kind received some work at reasonable rates of pay. Losing this right would probably mark the end of all their privileges and their status as independent workers, and the masters would be free to bring forward changes and innovations to improve the production process and organise the trade on terms which best suited them, including the rates of pay. Yet, as we have seen, the weavers were flying against a torrent of new thinking regarding trade and manufacturing. The working relationship was no longer to be seen as a partnership between master and worker, but rather one where the employer demanded complete and total control of all aspects of the manufacturing process, those that performed the work and crucially what they believed the work was worth.

Yet this was now to be done solely on terms dictated by the masters and not the clientage relationship of the previous two hundred years. The onset and increasing application of more modern capitalistic approaches to industrial manufacturing also meant that competition would increase, to gain the most orders and most reasonable returns of capital invested, to, in short, maximise profits in order to potentially create even more investment capital, which would of course create even more profitability. The masters could clearly see a growing demand for their products, both through domestic sales and, possibly even more importantly, the potential for high profits which could be derived from the growing export market. What they believed was of immediate, paramount importance was to iron out any impediments to the supply side of the production process. The irrepressible Dean Tucker was, of course, clearly aware of these developments. He spoke directly in favour of those masters who were attempting not only to rescind the old practices, but to innovate and introduce ever more cost-cutting processes at the micro-economic level, and to extol its undoubted benefits. He laid it out in his own phrase, 'step by step', to allow even the most economically inarticulate reader to be able to grasp the significance: "And the first Step is, that Cheapness, *caeteris paribus*, is an Inducement to buy, and many Buyers cause great Demand, – and that great Demand brings on a great Consumption; – which great Consumption must necessarily employ a vast Variety of Hands."[38] Tucker was of course also aware of worker resistance and that as the relationship between the capitalist and worker developed as an

---

37 Ibid, p. 350.
38 J. Tucker, *Instructions for Travellers*, (Dublin, 1758 edn.) pp. 32-33. Clearly an early statement of the need to increase aggregate demand and one that John Maynard Keynes would have been proud of.

increasingly concentrated and capital intensive process, it will inevitably be a source of conflict. Referring specifically to the woollen industry the capitalist clothier is:

> One Person, with a great Stock and large Credit, buys the Wool, pays for the Spinning, Weaving, Milling, Dying, Shearing, Dressing Etc. Etc. That is, he is the Master of the whole Manufacture from first to last, and perhaps employs and thousand persons under him. This is the clothier, whom all the Rest are to look upon as their Paymaster. But will not also sometimes look upon him as their Tyrant?[39]

Tucker also presaged the view that, undoubtedly, class tensions would be heightened and somewhat pragmatically goes on to say that the master, no matter how much humanity he may possess in himself, will inevitably by the imposition of such a system be "naturally tempted by his situation to be proud and overbearing, to consider his People as Scum of the Earth, whom he has a Right to Squeeze whenever he can..."[40] Hence the workers began to look upon their masters as a class of people who were their common enemy. Tucker even augured the attitudes of workers concentrated in a factory environment. Unlike the condition found with the independent and largely self-employed workers of Yorkshire, who Tucker believed "being so little removed from the degree and condition of their masters",[41] operated with little overt animosity to the master clothiers, but in the West of England and the North-West, especially after the coming of the factories, this, according to Tucker, would result in class animosity of the most violent kind.

> And as great numbers of them [the working class] work together in the same shop, they will have it the more in their power to vitiate and corrupt each other, to cabal and associate against their masters, and break into mobs and riots upon every occasion.[42]

Such was the nature of considered opinion of those who examined the changing economic condition of Britain towards the end of the 1750s. Let us be clear on the impact of commentators such as Tucker in advocating the need to radically change the practices of productivity at a microeconomic level. What was being argued here was that if Britain was to advance in terms of trade, commerce and manufacturing, and build on the enormous advantages that imperial expansion brought with it, coupled with the widening consumer market domestically, then such dramatic adjustments had to be made. If not Britain would in all likelihood be overtaken in areas of trade by a foreign rival who would be prepared to make these necessary changes. Also these views would have been widely circulated via national journals such as the *Gentleman's Magazine* and the *Annual Register*, especially as the latter was edited by that staunch advocate the free trade, Edmund Burke, who was also the chief contributor from its first publication in 1758.[43] Then there were the growing numbers of local and national newspapers who may also have carried these views.[44] Hence by the later years of the 1750s

---

39 Ibid. pp. 37-38.
40 Ibid.
41 Ibid.
42 Ibid.
43 See for example T. W. Copeland, 'Edmund Burke and the Book Reviews in Dodsley's Annual Register', *Publications of the Modern Language Association*, Vol. 57, No. 2. (Jun. 1942), pp. 446-468.
44 According to Jeremy Black "Between 1690 and 1780 the number of newspapers printed annually

there was a widening circulation of information relating not only to the need and desirability of change but also to the ways that this could/should actually be brought about. The tide seemed to be increasingly favouring the nascent industrial capitalist and the workers appeared to be dangerously incapable of understanding the significance of these changes and the value to national commercial growth this would bring.

However, although the master may have been influenced by the imperative of change, the ordinary cotton workers of the North-West do appear to have become aware of the transformation of opinion regarding the defence of their customary practices, and they realised that they must not alienate the (Whig) commercial basis of the country by attempting any overt form of coercion. They knew that the conspiracy laws were tight, and Britain was, of course, in the middle of an enormously expensive and precarious war and a vital means of maintaining and ultimately attaining a successful outcome of the conflict was through the finance generated by increased trade and commerce. They were conscious from experience that the Whig triumph since 1714 had been buttressed by trade and they also must have been cognizant that the district of the North-West was not an area looked on particularly favourably by the Whig elites in London, given the support for the Pretender both in 1715 and 1745 throughout the region. Trade was the key means of the Whigs holding on to power nationally and the masters of the North-West were as aware of this as anyone, as Frank O'Gorman tells us:

> The fact that the middling orders, especially in the towns, remained for so long willing to accept the continuing supremacy of a social and political system dominated by the aristocracy and gentry should occasion no surprise. After all, there was nothing in the Whiggism of the eighteenth century to inhibit the pursuit of wealth or diminish the value of commerce. Indeed the Hanoverian regime was supremely well disposed towards finance, commerce and industry, recognising their vital importance to the nation, to its security and to its ability to finance the wars...The first half of the eighteenth century witnessed a dramatic expansion in commercial activity. Between 1714 and 1760 shipping increased in tonnage by around 30 per cent, the value of exports by 80 per cent, re-exports by 50 per cent.[45]

Thus, the workers embarking on a confrontation with the masters through their combination were well aware they had to tread carefully. They certainly did not what to create the impression that they were in any way antagonistic towards the interests of commerce or trade. As the writer of the 'Broad-Ware Weavers' Apology' made clear:

> Now I would not be thought, from what I have said, to be an Enemy of Trade and Commerce, being very sensible that it is one of the greatest Blessings this Nation ever enjoyed; and I likewise do acknowledge, that such Gentlemen as have, and now do, launch out their Money in Trade, do not only deserve the Thanks of the Public, but ought to reap the Benefit of their Labour, by acquiring moderate Fortunes for their Descendants: But then it must be allowed on all Hands, that the Poor Mechanic, by whose hard Labour and Industry, the Trade in general is supported, and carried on, and ought to be entitled by the Laws of Reason

---

in England rose from less than a million to fourteen million, a growth far in excess of that of the population." *History Today*, Volume 36 Issue 10 October 1986, p. 1.
45 O'Gorman, *The Long Eighteenth Century*, op cit., p. 109.

and Equity, not only to comfortable Maintenance, but to have it in his Power to lay up some trifle for the Support of his family, either in case of old Age, Sickness, Death or any other Mortality...but I have not only shewn above, that it is at present entirely out of their Powers to do, but that every one that is acquainted with them can witness, that the greatest Part of them cannot get the Common Necessaries of Life...[46]

There are some revealing elements to this statement. Firstly, the writer makes it clear that those deploying their capital are entitled to their rewards, but secondly, and this more than a hundred years before Marx, they understood that the true value of all commodity production is the labour used to produce it. But, of course, so too did the masters, which is precisely why they had to gain much tighter control of the means of production. Yet, crucially, at the conclusion of this statement a clear link is made between the nature of the ability of the weavers to make an adequate living and the fact that they can barely afford the 'common necessaries of life.' Thus this is clear evidence of the industrial struggle being directly related to the marketing of provisions: of, in short, a moral economy dictating their action in their efforts to combat both these threats to the communities and their lives.

Thus the struggles between the textile workers of the North-West, which had been simmering since the later 1740s into the 1750s, were now about to become even more fraught. The cotton workers of the North-West recognised not only the symbolic value of the apprenticeship clauses enshrined in the Elizabethan and Stuart statutes, but also the practical implications of their removal. If they were nullified it would have meant that they had no control whatsoever *as to* who entered the trade and the terms on which they were employed. This was, then, a serious threat to not only their independence as workers but to the future conditions of employment with the masters. Previously this relationship was to a significant extent based on mutual respect and trust, albeit tense and one where each side was always suspicious of underhand tricks by the other. Yet there was a sense of freedom where if the worker was unhappy with terms offered by the master he could opt to find another employer via the number of chapmen and undertakers that would always be moving through his district. Likewise, the master had the pick of skilled workers who were scattered in and around Manchester and, indeed, the whole region. If these old statutes were removed then the power would be solely with the masters, and eventually the whole trade would be controlled by them and the perceived 'rights' of the workers would be gone, and it was highly probable they would be gone for good. This struggle in the final analysis was concerned with power and it was one which the workers simply could not afford to lose, which is why they went to such lengths and were so determined to organise their trade in the defence of their perceived rights. However, the touch paper to set off the displays of protest was initially the escalating price of provisions which is where we must now turn our attention.

---

46 *The Linen and Cotton Broad-Ware Weavers' Apology*, (1758), cited in Wadsworth and Mann, op cit. pp. 350-351.

8
Social Protest in Lancashire in the 1750s: Provisions

One of the (possibly unintended) effects of the Reformation of the sixteenth century was that it gave ordinary people – the so-called commons – the license to openly protest over a perceived grievance. During the medieval period ordinary people possessed few, if any, rights. They could resort to the law, but this was chiefly with regard to civil disputes usually between people of the same social status. All this was made more complicated with the relationship between the secular authorities and those of the Catholic Church, and in the final analysis the Church trumped the state. Pivotal to the understanding of how medieval Catholicism operated was that it was left to the clergy to signify what constituted a sin and who were the sinners. Only the clergy had the power to decide whether or not a person was fit to be placed in a position of grace, they were effectively the conduit between mortals and the almighty, which endowed them with enormous power. Only they knew and understood the mysteries and interpretation of the word of God and only they were the direct line of communication. Ordinary people had to suffer their lot, it was, after all, where God has placed them, and their rights in terms of both the secular and religious authorities were minimal. Above all they should know their place; demonstrations of anger or of protest were most definitely not to be encouraged. The Reformation removed many of the mysteries and superstitions surrounding not only spiritual beliefs but also secular. Increasingly, the trend was to embrace reason rather than magic. It also meant that for the first time people could now read the word of God for themselves, and it also meant that people believed they had rights, inalienable rights, both in law and between themselves and their Maker. Importantly, these rights were now guaranteed in both statute and common law and also, crucially, before God. Of course, there had been revolts and widespread demonstrations of social protest before the Reformation, such as the events of 1382, or surrounding the adulteration or high price of provisions, but now many ordinary people believed that they possessed the right to make their feelings known. To many nonconformists and Protestants of any denomination a return to Catholicism equated a return to a system where ordinary people held few rights, and where their fate was sealed by forces beyond secular control. Such a system, it was thought, lead people into believing in superstition, magic and a general debasement of human capabilities, which cowed them into subjection. Yet, conversely, in the highly contested state of religious belief of which eighteenth century Europe was far from immune, for Catholics this was the one true faith and they were virtually unshakeable in their commitment to their religion. For protestants – and Britain was most decidedly, in terms of its political culture, a protestant nation – a return to Catholicism was a step backwards from the manifest liberties they enjoyed, including the right to protest.

The Politics of Provisioning

The Tudor and Stuart statutes regarding the regulation of trades and, above all, apprenticeship rules and wage rates were perceived as vital ingredients of protection for working people. But they also fitted with what the mercantilist state required: that workers skills should only be available for the benefit of Britain and that wages should not be allowed to be determined solely by either the masters or the workers, but by impartial magistrates in the case of a dispute. Similarly, from 1580 and, explicitly, in 1630, the Book of Orders laid down the role of magistrates in securing adequate supplies of the 'necessaries of life' and that these should be presented for sale in an untainted, unadulterated form. Also, that designated places for the sale of foodstuffs should be provided and that the poor or those buying only small amounts should be allowed first access. This was done to offset the possibility of regrating by a large merchant buying a large amount or all of the produce in a market where the price was low and selling the product in another market where they could gain a much higher price. There were also laws concerning those who attempted to circumvent the protection enshrined in the *Book of Orders*. Forestalling grain or corn, (holding it back from the market), or any commodity of provision was illegal both in common and statute law, as was engrossing, (buying large amounts of a commodity such as grain while it was still growing) and regrating. All these contributed to the belief among the common people that they were being protected and, that they possessed rights, including, crucially, the right to make visible social protest. However, riots, although they were a semi-permanent feature of eighteenth century society, were not something that the authorities wished to be seen condoning. Indeed, the Hanoverians had only just arrived and it was felt necessary by the state to place on the statute book a Riot Act "for the prevention of tumults and riotous assembles",[1] it did little good as riots carried on as if the Act had never been passed. However, by the mid-to-late 1750s it appeared that both the national and local authorities were becoming less tolerant of displays of civil disturbance. Whether, on the one hand, this was due to the progressively loud clamour for a reduction of state protection afforded by the mercantile system which may have given those in search of higher profits a justification and in turn served to trigger off concerted demonstrations of crowd anger or, on the other hand, simply because the crowd were becoming increasingly belligerent, it is difficult to say, it is likely that it was a combination of the two.

Widespread and at times serious public disturbances did, however, appear to conform to a certain pattern. At the bottom of the 'socially acceptable' table were those riots that had been deliberately orchestrated to attain a given end. These were usually election or political riots, where one side – either Whig or Tory – fired up a crowd (usually by the copious application of drink) to demonstrate their opposition to a rival. Although confined to election times and in so called 'open' contests, these were among the most distasteful of all public demonstrations and were often portrayed as revealing the crowd to be little better that a flock of sheep following the lead of a local demagogue or, worse, a 'rent a mob'. Nevertheless, they were an enduring feature of eighteenth century political culture and were taken to be one of the unfortunate but tolerable offshoots of a system that although was effectively corrupt did produce a relatively stable political regime.[2] There were also more spontaneous riots. These tended to be in a more urban setting and were usually a response to an event or some form of sleight. Thus there could be theatre riots, turnpike riots, militia riots, riots against

---

1   I George I, st.2 c.5.
2   However, as we shall see in the final chapters below, there was a remarkable example of these types of riot at the very end of the period under discussion that occurred in the North-West which was to be of major significance.

public whippings, riots of footmen, riots at hanging days when the crowd would attempt to rescue the corpse of the recently executed to save the body from the anatomists' knives. There were of course religious riots, against Catholics or Jews, various types of Dissenters, Quakers, Methodists, and so on. There were riots of specific trades, such as the Newcastle keelmen in 1750, or various disputes among agricultural workers, not least enclosure riots. Then there were riots surrounding provisions. Of all the disturbances of the eighteenth century those occasioned by some grievance surrounding aspects of food were most numerous. There were serious food riots or 'risings of the poor' in 1709, 1740, 1753, 1756-57, 1766-67, 1773, 1782, scattered throughout the 1790s and 1800-01.

What elevated food riots above the rest was firstly, the disparate nature of those involved, ranging from Cornish tinners, to Gloucestershire shearmen, to Staffordshire potters, to Lancashire weavers, to London sailors and dockworkers. All the lower orders affected felt a commonality of purpose. Secondly, on the one hand, there was a sense of entitlement to demonstrate their grievance by the crowd and, on the other, often this was (on occasions grudgingly) accepted by the authorities, both nationally and locally. What motivated the crowd was that an individual or small group attempting to exploit the mass of ordinary people when they were at their most vulnerable purely for the sake of selfish greed. This is why for Edward Thompson the food riot was the epitome of the operation of the moral economy. The logic of this situation was not lost on those at the very height of government, as Lord Chancellor Hardwick explained to the Duke of Newcastle and the Chancellor of the Exchequer, Charles Townsend, during the great riots of September 1766, that the most important consideration was the need for prompt action.

> So that unless His Majesty should upon this emergency exert his Royal Authority to prevent further exportation of wheat: His Majesty's own subjects would be in danger of starving whilst foreigners are supplied with bread ... and that given that Parliament was prorogued and if the matter was to wait until they were met, the mischief and evil would have taken place and the grievance be past all possibility of remedy.[3]

According to this analysis the crowd seemingly was justified to demonstrate and nudge the authorities into action. In a scene of confrontation some years earlier, in Bristol in 1753, the situation became so dangerous that it probably went some way to confirming to those at the very top of the pyramid of power that the actions of the crowd needed to be tempered. Part of the problem was the mercantilist policy itself. At one level it sought to protect the masses from violent swings in prices, yet at the same time the policy encouraged the export of commodities, including grain, by offering bounties on exports. If the price of grain exceeded a certain figure then an embargo would be placed on all exports, but this had to be activated by a standing order in Parliament. If, as in 1766, Parliament was in recess, then exports could continue no matter how high the prices were domestically, thereby ensuring a bonanza in profits for the grain merchants. Thus, the people became very nervous of grain exports when, domestically, the prices were rising and grain was in short supply. Often the local authorities stepped in to offset potential trouble but on other occasions this could result in very dangerous breakdowns of civil order. In order to present such a situation the civic authorities and, indeed, the forces of local justice would give

---

3 British Library, *Newcastle Papers*, ad ms 32977, (25/9/1766) Townsend to Newcastle, ff 151.

the crowd as much leeway as possible in an attempt to placate them and redress their immediate grievances. One such situation took place in Bristol in 1753; here there was very serious confrontation between the middle class merchants and the weavers and colliers from the surrounding countryside. At this time Bristol was not only the second largest port in country after London, but also the second largest city in the kingdom. It also possessed a reputation of being a riot-prone area. The city was encircled by weavers in nearby Gloucestershire and Somerset and the notorious Kingswood colliers on either side of the main London road entering Bristol.[4] In 1709 two hundred colliers entered Bristol and would only disperse when they had the assurance that the price of corn would be reduced, which it duly was. Five years later there were serious riots at the accession of George I in 1714. Between 1727 and 1729 the weavers on the outskirts of Bristol were extremely active in attacking masters who they accused of underpaying their normal rates. This culminated in a gun battle in which seven weavers were killed in September, 1729.[5] Thus the relationship between the labouring population of Bristol and its immediate vicinity, the civil authorities and, indeed, many of the commercial middling sorts was tense, as indeed it was throughout the West of England as we approach the 1730s, 1740s and 1750s. Moreover, throughout this period there was effectively a continuous battle between the lower orders and the local (and at times national) authorities regarding the main turnpikes servicing the city. These disputes were not ended until 1755 when the Act of Parliament that allowed the turnpike to function lapsed and all were allowed unfettered entry into Bristol.

The early 1750s witnessed a series of bad harvests and some serious outbreaks of livestock diseases. Provision prices continued upwards and there were reports of workers on the verge of starvation.[6] On 21 May 1753, the colliers of Kingswood entered Bristol demanding that the council enforced their right to set the price of grain at affordable levels. The city council met with four of the colliers' leaders and agreed to set fair prices as soon as was possible. When this was agreed many of the protesters were satisfied and set to return to their homes. At this point a rumour began to circulate that a ship, The Lamb, was due to set sail for Ireland fully laden with grain. The colliers and others of the labouring population returned to Bristol on May 25 resolved to 'rescue' the ship and sell the grain at popular prices. It was then that the local shopkeepers and merchants of Bristol, heartily sick of the reputation and intimidation of the Kingswood colliers, decided to confront them. Probably part of the reason they chose this moment to do so was the arrival of a troop of Scots Greys from Gloucester. In the ensuing struggle four of the rioters were killed and thirty taken prisoner. The crowd then attempted their release and also took five of the local merchant's prisoner in reprisal. Three of these were quickly freed by the troops but two were taken by the colliers back to Kingswood.[7] Within days,

---

4 R. Malcolmson, *A Set of Ungovernable People: The Kingswood Colliers in the Eighteenth Century*, No. 2 in the Kingswood History Series, (Kingswood, 1986 edn.)
5 British Library, Add. MS. 47032, 47033, f. 22. Egmont Papers, Historical Manuscripts Commission, Egmont Diary, vol. i. See also J. Latimer, *The Annals of Bristol in the Eighteenth Century*, (Bristol, 1893), p. 275.
6 See for example, *Gentleman's Magazine* for July and August, 1753, p. 343 Women of Taunton destroying mills, p. 389, threatening letter sent to John Prankard, of Milburn Port, Somerset, "John Noake, I assure you and other farmers, if you do not fall the corn, we will arise and burn you in your beds."
7 Letters of Mayor Clements to Newcastle, 21 May and 15 May 1753, and affidavit of John Hones, 21 May 1753, PRO, SP 36/122; *Felix Farley's Bristol Journal*, 26 May 1753, lists the names of

however, the colliers released their prisoners and the general feeling of support for the condition of colliers among the general population of Bristol is witnessed by the raising of a subscription for the relief of the starving labourers as well as the provision of medical services for fifty of the colliers injured in the fracas.[8] Yet in spite of the displays of conciliation, some of the labouring population remained embittered. There were reports that the colliers had sealed off the main London road to all traffic in and out of the city. A woollen draper, John Brickdale, was an especial target of the crowd, as he was one that had joined the merchants in their attack against the colliers earlier in May and he was also foremost in the turnpike riots of late July 1749.[9] Brickdale was secretly taken out of the city and placed in protective custody in Lincoln's Inn, London and, unwilling to risk a trial, he moved out of Bristol and into Somerset. Meanwhile a coroner's inquest found him guilty of the murder of one of the colliers of 25 May.[10] In a letter from the Mayor of Bristol to the Duke of Newcastle the request was that the conviction of Brickdale be quashed and this was duly affected in November 1753.[11] This demonstrated to the crowd that, although in the moment of their heightened state of agitation they may get some redress, if it was clearly shown they had gone too far, which the developments at Bristol seemed to reveal, then in the aftermath of especially violent riots the local and national authorities were only willing to bend so far to accommodate demonstrations of anger. This made it clear to the crowd that there would be serious repercussions. Yet the crowd were in the firm belief that they had the inalienable right to show that they were being dealt with unfairly and appeared willing to to uphold their rights of popular demonstration despite the risk of capital charges possibly being levelled against them.

Indeed, they were so convinced that they possessed the right to protest and to take matters into their own hands that they were prepared to take up arms against the civil and military authorities and against those they believed were attempting to make the price of food prohibitively high for the sake of temporary high profits in a period of shortage. To give a flavour of the desperation felt by the crowd on such occasions and to offer an illustrative demonstration of the need of the national and local authorities to be vigilant in such cases due to the danger of civil unrest they presented, the following is an eye-witness account of an incident in the West of England which typifies the nature of how the lower orders could exert their latent power in the face of what they saw as a breach of the moral economy regardless of personal safety. This event took place on the Wiltshire/Somerset border in 1766, during one of the most serious and widespread episodes of food rioting at any time in the eighteenth century. In it we get a sense of not only the mood, motivations and recklessness of the crowd, driven seemingly to distraction by hunger, but it is also evidence of their willingness to risk even death in their efforts to gain redress. On this occasion a group of up to two thousand, looking for reluctant millers, were on the east-west turnpike near Frome at around noon when they

---

the captured rioters. For more on the opposition to the export of grain and similar riots, see Thompson, 'Moral Economy', op cit, *passim*, and R. B. Rose, '18th Century Price Riots and Public Policy in England', *International Review of Social History*, VI, 287 (1961).
8   *Felix Farley's Bristol Journal*, 2 June and 8 September 1753.
9   Letters of 5 August and 15 September 1749, PRO, *State Papers Domestic* SP 36/111.
10 Letter of Attorney General to Newcastle, 2 June 1753, PRO, SP 36/122; and Hugh Valence Jones to Newcastle, 2 June 1753, BL, Add. Mss' 32732.
11 PRO, *State Papers Domestic*, SP 36/124, ff. 39 Petition of John Brickdale to the Duke of Newcastle, (15/11/1753).

were stopped by Thomas Prowse, the county Member of Parliament for Somerset, and several other gentlemen. Prowse was in a particularly favourable position, being described as a known paternalistic parliamentarian and described by Horace Walpole as the "most knowing and the most moderate of the Tories."[12] He had been returned as the county member for Somerset on five occasions and was well known for his restrained and sympathetic attitudes towards the lower orders and their problems. He made a speech to the assembled crowd, telling them that he would strive to see their wants redressed if they would disperse. At this those in the front of the crowd directly facing Prowse told him they "had not eat a Morsel of Bread for three Days, but had subsisted on Grain etc., and their Wives and Families were in the same miserable Condition."[13] The spokesman of the crowd continued,

> We looked upon it that Providence fought on our side, and that if we ventured never so great a hazard, we could not be much hurt, so when we found we could not gain possession by storming, we made a fire at some distance, where we could not be discovered, and when properly lighted, we carried it, under cover of a party, to set fire to the thatched hovel joining the mill, having at the same time dispatched a messenger to our battery with our intention, so desired they would support the fire as brisk as possible, while we put our design into execution, which was soon done, without being discovered till on fire. This so greatly alarmed our enemies that they fled...and soon gave us possession, so having taken the flour, and done what mischief we could, we dispersed home, some boasting of their exploits, others dreading the consequences of such proceedings: says one, 'I don't care much about the consequence, I would as soon be hanged as starved, and another, damn me if I don't wish the French would come, I would be on their side, another by God, we could but be poor then, and Damn me, if I would not go down with some of the rich.[14]

In such situations, not even considerate paternalism could stem the rage felt by the crowd. This offers a vivid picture of what lengths the ordinary people of the eighteenth century would go to in order to defend what they believed were their inalienable rights, and as noted above, demonstrate their often suppressed but on occasions very real power. As Edward Thompson said in his first Moral Economy article:

> While this moral economy cannot be described as "political" in any advanced sense, nevertheless it cannot be described as unpolitical either, since it supposed definite, and passionately held, notions of the common weal – notions which, indeed, found some support in the paternalist tradition of the authorities; notions which the people re-echoed so loudly in their turn that the authorities were, in some measure, the prisoners of the people. Hence this moral economy impinged very generally upon eighteenth-century government and thought, and did not only intrude at moments of disturbance. The word "riot" is too small to encompass this.[15]

In effect what Thompson and the social historians who have been influenced by his work are saying is that, as we move through the 1720s up to the 1750s, ordinary people were sensing and indeed witnessing a change in the economic

---

12 H. Walpole, *Memoirs of the Reign of King George the Third*, Four Volumes, vol. I, (London, 1894 edn.), pp. 67-68.
13 *Western Flying Post*, (29 September, 1766).
14 *Salisbury Journal*, (29 September, 1766 and 6 October, 1766).
15 E. P. Thompson, *Customs in Common*, op cit. pp. 188-189.

façade of British commercial practices. They were feeling first-hand the morally corrosive control of the increasingly important financial imperatives that were taking root in this society now increasingly governed by 'market forces'. In their world, the sense of justness and open-handed dealing was clearly under attack, and therefore also under attack was their access to the market for basic provisions and the customary practices of their ways of work. Faced with social destruction, what else could be left to lose? To them bread literally was the staff of life and work was the only means of getting it; they knew little, if anything, of the vague promise offered by Adam Smith's 'invisible hand' which would elevate them to a point of economic utopia. They gradually realised that this was a concerted attack specifically on them, the labouring population, and increasingly on their position as a 'class'. From the 1750s and 1760s, the state and the authorities of civil control also seemed to be embracing the pursuit of individual profit above the needs, values and concerns of the labouring classes. Moreover, this was taking place in a seemingly growing number of localities, the West of England, the agricultural belt of the Home Counties, the metal working Midlands, the Potteries and, where the industrialisation process was becoming operational, in the North of England. The period they were entering from the 1750s was one that involved a very real battle between the shared communal values of so many labouring people throughout Britain on the one hand and, on the other, not only their ways of life, but their entire patterns of livelihood and abilities to purchase and consume the necessaries of life. They saw these changes as very real and personal attacks on them, the ordinary 'commons', and it was little wonder that they fought with such resolve to hold onto their long-standing customary practices and communal ways of life. For many working people faced with the dramatic changes taking place, the pure pursuit of profit was an unworthy and hollow goal, especially if it came at the cost of destroying patterns of community lives that had existed for centuries. This was not about the fact that the people in business deserved to make a profit, but rather they should not exploit the most vulnerable in doing so.

In Lancashire the situation regarding the marketing of provisions was made more complicated by the relative lack of available locally grown produce, especially corn. In most other areas of England the occasion of dearth was in some senses exacerbated by the fact that the people could see the crops growing around them, but in the North-West this was not the case. Effectively, all provisions had to be brought into Manchester from outside. This situation created problems throughout most of the 1750s especially in the shortages of key provisions such as grain, but also meat, dairy products and potatoes. We have seen that the high price of provisions had triggered displays of anger at Bristol in 1753; there were also murmurings of discontent at Liverpool and Manchester.[16] The problem of an inefficient and, at times, ineffective transport system, coupled with the steadily rising population meant that even at the best of times supplying the provision needs of the North-West was problematic. There was also the fact that real wages were falling due to the progressive increase in duties collected by the state and the rise in prices for a range of necessary provisions including sharp rises in the price of meat.[17] The most prosperous decade for the labouring population of Lancashire was the 1730s when work was plentiful and prices

---

16 T. Smollett, *History of England, from the Revolution to the Death of George the Second*, (London, 1804 edn.) vol. iii, p. 360.

17 For example one of the most reviled of the new duties was the Beer Act of 1761 which appeared to be specifically targeted at working people. *Beer Act, 1761, (2 Geo. 3) c. 14.*

relatively low.[18] It was likely that this is the decade which the workers of the North-West were referring to when in 1756 they recalled just how much real wages had fallen in recent memory.[19] Liverpool was regularly importing grain from the later seventeenth century and in 1690 took in cargoes from Bridgwater, Padstow, and Barnstaple as well as from the more accessible central Wales all laden with wheat, oats and barley.[20] Later in the eighteenth century grain was arriving through Liverpool from as far as the Isle of Wight and Dorset,[21] and in 1756, the Corporation of Liverpool borrowed £2,000 to purchase corn, which was sold to the poor at cost price.[22] One writer in the *Gentleman's Magazine*, presaging the words said to Prowse in 1766 at Frome, said that the poor were faced with the stark and "dreadful alternative of being starved or hanged".[23] The region had been at the forefront of the Pretender's march south in 1745, and there were some, high and low born who were supportive of this threat to the Hanoverians.[24] In the aftermath the resulting recriminations meant that tensions were high. That this remained so is evidenced by the subscription which was raised by the leading inhabitants of Manchester in order to keep the peace in 1749, amounting to £1,023.[25] This may have been a prescient step because in September 1750 a riot by people protesting at the public whipping of criminals occurred.[26] By 1753 the rising prices, initially triggered by merchants holding back grain from the market in order to gain from the government bounty paid on corn exports, resulted in the disturbances at Bristol as we have seen, but there were also reports of smaller displays of crowd anger at Manchester and Leeds. In the latter, Smollett tells us:

> ...a detachment of the King's troops were obliged in their own defence to fire upon the rioters, eight or nine of whom were killed on the spot; and, indeed, so little care had been taken to restrain the licentious insolence of the vulgar by proper laws and regulations duly executed under the eye of the civil magistracy, that a military power was found absolutely necessary to maintain the peace of the kingdom.[27]

In July 1753, at Manchester, the journeymen joiners and carpenters struck for a pay increase, they were soon followed by the bricklayers and labourers. The *Gentleman's Magazine* reported that, "A great number of them were this afternoon before justice Birch, who earnestly told them to return to work till the next quarter-sessions, for the common wages, and then the bench of justices would take that affair under consideration; but they were not in the least satisfied with what the justice said; so that building is at present entirely suspended in this place."[28] Also in September the weavers of Manchester were in dispute with Manchester College regarding the latter right to impose a tithe of 4d per loom

---

18 Cited in Wadsworth and Mann, op cit., p. 357, *Autobiography of William Stout*.
19 See page 99 above.
20 Liverpool Reference Library, *Port Books,* E. 190, 1351/1, (1690).
21 *Williamson's Liverpool Advertiser*, (2/7/1756) and *Manchester Mercury*, (4/8/1767).
22 *Williamson's Liverpool Advertiser*, (5/11/1756).
23 *Gentleman's Magazine*, (December, 1758), p. 5.
24 'A True Account of Mr. John Daniel's Progress with Prince Charles Edward in the Years 1745 and 1746 Written by Himself.' Walter Biggar Blaikie, 'Origins of the 'forty-Five, and Other Papers Relating to That Rising' *Scottish History Society, Second Series*, Vol II, pp 175-193.
25 Manchester Constables Accounts, vol. iii, p. 356. See Appendix One below for the names of the subscribers.
26 *Gentleman's Magazine,* (28 September, 1750), p. 427.
27 T. Smollett, op cit., p. 361.
28 *Gentleman's Magazine*, (6 July, 1753) pp. 342-343.

every Easter, and before a special sitting of the Lancaster Assize they won their case.

There was a slight stabilisation of prices in 1755, but the poor weather throughout the spring of 1756 resulted once again in acute shortages. The merchants of Manchester wrote to the Privy Council at the end of November saying that the situation was so dire that not only the poor were suffering but also the artisans and manufacturers, and explaining how the area was overwhelmingly dependent on supplies from the south.[29] Their complaints rested on the fall in trade brought on by the uncertainty of the outbreak of the Seven Years War, which resulted in the workers loss of earnings, and the fact that grain prices had risen fifty per cent between 1753 and the summer of 1756.[30] However, things were going to get much worse. In the first months of 1757 prices continued to rise, work was at best sporadic, and in early June the first flashpoint arrived, in the form of a riot, mainly of women and boys, over the cost of potatoes.[31] According to the *Manchester Mercury*, "On Tuesday-last [June 7th], two Women cheapening some Potatoes in the Market, and the Seller asking what they thought an unreasonable Price, they, without further Ceremony, overturned their Sacks, and scatter'd the Potatoes abroad, which the Boys and Women near, seized and carried away."[32] The report goes on to suggest that the tensions built up in the previous eighteenth months caused the women to expand their protest.

> Encouraged by this, and joined by more Rabble, they directed their Way to the Meal-House, which they entered, and began to Plunder, but by the Resistance of the Owners of the Meal, and the Magistrates of the Town, assisted by the principal Inhabitants, they were drove away, except a few who were made Prisoners in the Meal-House, the Doors whereof were secured. A Part of the dispersed Rioters, joined by some others near Ardwick-Green, stopped a Cart coming to Market, and plundered it of eight Loads of Meal.[33]

At this point, the two women who had started the riot were arrested but only as a warning: "The Magistrates discharged their Prisoners out of the Meal-House, after two Hours Confinement, with Admonitions to retire peaceably to their respective Homes." However, instead of observing the advice they re-assembled and

> grew more numerous and insolent, broke the Windows and into the Shop of one Bramhall, a Corn-factor and Corn-Chandler at Hide's-Cross, carried off his Bread, &c. and abused his Wife, who was forced to fly to avoid worse Usage. The Officers of the Town seized two Women, who they had but just before discharged from the Meal-House, and imprisoned them in the Dungeon, on Salford-Bridge. The Rioters continued together and meeting with no Opposition, they marched to the Dungeon and with large Forging Hammers, broke down Part of the Wall, threw the Door into the River, and carried off the two Women in Triumph. Flushed with their Success, and having tasted the Sweets of

---

29 PRO, *Privy Council Registers*, PC2 Vol. 101, ff 408, (1/12/1756).
30 Prices quoted weekly in the *Manchester Mercury* and *Whitworth's Manchester Advertiser*, this figure refers to the price of oatmeal, but there were similar rises for beans, barley and wheat, see the dates 16/6/1753 and June 14 and 21, 1756 in *Manchester Mercury*.
31 F. Nicholson, and E. Axon, 'The Hatfield Family, of Manchester and the Food Riots of 1757 and 1812' *The Transactions of the Lancashire and Cheshire Antiquarian Society*, Vol. 28, (1910-1911) pp. 81-114. P. 83.
32 *Manchester Mercury*, 14 June, 1757.
33 Ibid.

Plunder, they directed their Course to the Warehouse of the same Bramhall, situate in Toad-lane, broke it open, and began to carry away Grain, Flower [sic]. Meal, Cheese, and here continued plundering.[34]

It was alleged that Messrs. Bramall and Hatfield, millers, whose shops had been broken into, had been deceiving the public by mixing beans and whiting with their flour. This they indignantly denied in a long statement addressed to the High Sheriff, James Bayley, Esq., of Withington, printed again in the *Manchester Mercury* of June 21st, 1757. The basis of their statement[35] was that they were innocent of all charges but simply responding to the high market prices nationally.[36] But these two millers in particular appeared to the crowd to be the villains of the ensuing developments both in the June riots and the more serious disturbances later in November. Yet on both occasions the authorities appeared to have been prepared for some kind of demonstration, as the High Sheriff organised a small citizen's militia and sent word to London for some form of military presence.[37]

What is also revealing in this episode of the actual application of the crowd to assert their right to protest via an understanding of the operation of the moral economy is that, in this instance, the main protagonists were women. This, however, should not be especially surprising given the direct role women had. On the one hand, being in direct contact with the ramifications of high food prices on their ability to feed their families, and, on the other, being the one group who were regularly gauging the nature of price fluctuation, due to their familiarity with the market processes. These were imperatives that, given the often precarious nature of surviving within a subsistence economic framework, women would have experienced first-hand. In fact, this topic of women being involved in protests over the range of issues surrounding provisioning – from the pricing and availability to problems associated with adulteration – is worthy of further, albeit brief, consideration.

Amongst the emerging working class in the proto-industrial outworker system women were obviously directly involved in the production matrix, but they were equally involved in seeing to the needs of their children, as well as the wider family and their allotted regular household work. Price rises and the shady dealings of corn merchants, millers, bakers and general 'badgers' could produce extreme anger amongst women attempting to manage a range of vitally important domestic functions. Indeed they were habituated from an early age to the fact that, as females, their role was crucial, indeed indispensable, to the stability of the family network in all its consequences. Edward Thompson reiterated these points when he reminded us that in usual circumstances women were very often "those most involved in face-to-face marketing, most sensitive to price significances, most experienced in detecting short-weight or inferior quality".[38] Nor was Manchester alone in disturbances initiated by women in

---

34 Ibid.
35 See Appendix Two below.
36 *Manchester Mercury* of June 21st, 1757.
37 Ibid, 22 November, 1757.
38 E. P. Thompson, 'The Moral Economy of the English Crowd in the Eighteenth Century', *Past & Present* 50 (1) (Feb. 1971), pp. 115-16, and section three of 'The Moral Economy Reviewed', in *Customs in Common*, (London: Merlin, 1991, pp. 305-336. . See also J. Bohstedt, 'Gender, Household and Community Politics: Women in English Riots 1790-1810', *Past & Present*, 120 (1) (Aug., 1988), pp. 88-122. Of a later period John and Barbara Hammond wrote of the famine year of 1795 and the riots that accompanied it as the "revolt of the housewives". J. L. and B. Hammond, *The Village Labourer*, (1911); reprint, (Stroud: Sutton Publishing, 1978 edn.) p. 116.

1757, they were also they main protagonists in market riots at Salisbury, Bewdley, Newcastle-under-Lyme, Taunton and Worcester.[39] In the cotton textile districts of the North-West women were regarded as equals in the productive process and this provided them, in the performing their various roles, says Thompson, with

> authority and self-confidence. But this was not because gender roles were almost indistinguishable. The female sphere of authority probably took in most marketing for provisions, and within the household women had the responsibility for baking, brewing, and seeing that the household was fed. They were therefore especially sensitive to price and quality, and were the first to have to work out economies and strategies of survival when dearth threatened. This role made them as much guardians of the household's survival as were the men, who might earn the greater part of the family income. They would discuss their problems, anger or anxieties with other women, not only on market day but daily on their neighbourhood occasions.[40]

What this suggests is that regardless of the presupposed historiographic assumption of women as the 'weaker sex' they could, if times and occasions necessitated, be as assertive as men in a crisis which affected themselves or their families directly. Thus women were predominant in the first series of riots in Manchester in 1757, but they appear to have maintained their presence throughout the rest of the eighteenth century, as Alan Booth tells us of the riots affecting Lancashire in the 1790s:

> Men appeared as often as women in the assize statistics, but in most riots where sexual composition was recorded women appear to have been both more numerous and particularly active: "an assemblage of wrongheaded women", "several women", "a large body of poor women", "chiefly women and boys", "a large number of women and boys", "a gang of tumultuous women", "a number of raggedly women", "a great number of raggedly women", "women ... to the number of two hundred", "a number of women". At Liverpool the women bit the local constable and pulled his hair. At Ashton they urged on the rioters and took hold of the local vicar when he tried to prevent the mob from pursuing its business. More subtle weapons might be employed. Colonel Entwistle of the Rochdale Volunteers lamented that "the Devil in the shape of women is using all his influence to induce the privates to brake [sic] their attachment to their officers, and I am sorry to add has already debouched three from their duty, by delivering up their arms and accoutrements..."[41]

---

39 See R. W. Malcomson, *Life and Labour in England, 1700-1780*, (London: Hutchinson, 1981) pp. 117-118.
40 Thompson, *Customs in Common* op cit, pp. 321-322.
41 A. Booth, 'Food Riots in the North-West of England 1790-1801' in *Past & Present*, 77 (1) (Nov., 1977), pp. 84-107, pp. 98-99, citations used in the quoted text; *Chester Courant*, 8 Oct. 1795 (Holywell). This is discussed in Thompson, 'Moral Economy of the English Crowd in the Eighteenth Century', pp. 115-16. 81 *Chester Courant*, 10 Nov. 1795 (Congleton). *Chester Chronicle*, 22 May 1795 (Chester). "Rowbottom Diary", 30 July 1795, Oldham Local Studies Library; *Manchester Mercury*, 4 Aug. 1795 (Manchester). "Rowbottom Diary", 30 July 1795 (Oldham Local Studies Library). Ibid., 28 July 1795 (Delph). "Diary of Timothy Cragg", Aug. 1795 (Lancaster). Cragg also stressed their role in the 1800 riot at Lancaster: ibid., Jan. 1800. Ibid., I6 Jan. 1796 (Lancaster). Examination of James Web, 13 Oct. 1795: P.R.O., Ches. 24/179 (Northwich). *Manchester Mercury*, 17 June 1800. In almost all the cases where the sexual composition of the mob was recorded, women were numerically pre-dominant. Several of the above sources also stressed the "active" role of women in the disturbances. Information of James Holland, Sept. 1795: P.R.O., P.L. 27/7; Various Informations on the Ashton Riot, Feb. 1800:

Clearly working women throughout the eighteenth century were willing and formidable participants in contesting authority and exhibiting blatant examples of un-deferential conduct when it came to the defence of their families. However, to continue the situation in and around Manchester in 1757, the potato riot was followed the next day by the arrival in Manchester of the Duke of Bridgewater's colliers from nearby Clifton. This further bears out Thompson's claim that on such occasions "women were often leaders of community opinion, and the initiators of actions; sometimes they were the sole executors of actions, and the men joined in in solidarity with them as often as they joined the men."[42] Now the fear of the authorities was that the colliers from the surrounding districts of Oldham would join them. At this point the crowd attacked the premises of George Bramwell, a baker, miller and dealer in corn and succeeded in committing £200 worth of damage. However, before the situation could escalate, the High Sheriff made his presence felt and proceeded through the centre of Manchester in front of "three or four hundred [men] armed with stout Sticks, immediately followed by sixty Gentlemen armed with Muskets and Swords, and in the Rear by eleven or twelve hundred, armed promiscuously with Guns, Swords and Clubs."[43] The High Sheriff stopped at various places in the town centre and explained to the crowds the "Inconveniences that would necessarily arise to the Poor through Tumults, with proper Observations on the Dangers consequent."[44] This armed presence was kept up for three days with all entrances to the town guarded until they were relieved by a troop of dragoons. From this display of civil power the June riots were contained and the crowd were subdued, but the harvest was again poor and by the end of October and the beginning of November riots were spreading throughout Britain. In Staffordshire four were killed when the military opened fire, and at Stockport the *Gentleman's Magazine* reported a classic example of the moral economy when the crowd "sold the farmer's grain at their own prices, and honestly accounted for the money afterwards."[45] However, at Manchester events were to turn more serious.

The popular suspicion of the crowd was that the merchants were holding back supplies to make even more profit. The rights of milling grain in Manchester had, since 1515, been held by the Grammar School. In 1732 the Lord of the Manor of Manchester, Sir Oswald Mosley, had attempted to set up a malt mill in the first stage of ending the monopoly, but failed when the rights of the Grammar School were upheld in court. The next stage was a move by the merchants of Manchester to petition Parliament for an act to allow the monopoly to be broken, but this would not be successful until 1759.[46] In the meantime, the belief was growing that many of the merchants, whether they were operating in the textiles sectors or in food marketing, processing and distribution, were attempting to manipulate the (worsening) situation to their own advantage and to the material and physical disadvantage of working people. In some ways, this was indicative of the growth in class divide and heightening incidences of conflict between the growing and increasingly powerful middle class – becoming

---

P.R.O., P.L. 27/7. John Entwistle to Wyndham, 5 Aug. 1795: P.R.O., W.O. I/1086/25.
42 Thompson, *Customs in Common*, op cit, p. 322.
43 *Manchester Mercury* of June 21st, 1757.
44 Ibid.
45 *Gentleman's Magazine*, November, 1757, p. 562.
46 32 Geo. II. Cap. 61 September, 1759. "Act for the discharging the inhabitants of Manchester from the custom of grinding their corn and grain, except malt, at certain water corn mills in the said town called the School Mills, and for making proper recompense to the feoffees of such mills.

ever more devoted to and influenced by early manifestations of capitalism – and those groups below them who envisaged what little power they possessed was being systematically eroded. Still they demonstrably protested against the egregious actions of the merchant elites, and they did so openly with no attempt to disguise themselves or prevent their identification. This in itself suggests that they believed they were justified in their actions and that the authorities would understand the root causes of their anger. Yet at Manchester it would appear the root causes of these protests were being ignored by those in control of civil authority. According to one contemporary, the schoolteacher, John Collier, writing under the pseudonym of "Tim Bobbin", there was a concerted attempt by the merchants of Manchester to conspire together at this moment of acute shortage. Collier tells us in quasi-Old Testament allegory: "there arose certain Men the Sons of *Belial;* and they took Council together, and said, There is corn in the land of *Chester;* go to, let us buy all the corn in the land of *Chester*, for it will come to pass that the Lord will continue the Famine for yet three years."[47] Collier goes on to make some serious accusations against the leading masters and merchants of Manchester. One of the most serious was that this conspiracy by the masters was a concerted effort to get more work out of the labourers, in sentiments that echoed those of Tucker and Temple in the West of England. "You know how that the Time of Plenty maketh the People to be idle, and that you can have no more Work done for Two-pence in Times of Plenty, than ye can have done for One Penny in Times of Dearth and Famine."[48] The other was that there was a fund set up by the leading men of trade in Manchester to organize the buying of grain, but not for the widespread distribution as in Liverpool or Bristol, but to exploit the situation and make large profits.

> Now the Men of the City did hearken to words of the Sons of Belial, and did make a Covenant between themselves and the Sons of Belial; and delivered unto the Sons of Belial sixteen hundred Talents of Gold, and twelve thousand Talents of Silver; and the Sons of Belial did therewith buy all the corn that the merchants of the Cities of the Sea had brought into the Land: and they did cause that the Famine did increase … even to the Time of Harvest; for it was until the Time of Harvest found any corn in the Hands of any Man; but [only] in the Hands of the Sons of Belial was there Corn found.[49]

In his account Collier tells us that once alerted to the acute shortages the authorities in London and the King, in his Address to Parliament, made sure that grain found its way to areas of most severe dearth, thus it appeared that the plans of the merchants had been thwarted. At this point one of the leading millers and corn dealers in Manchester, George Bramall, whose mill had been a target in June, suggested that they go even further, pool their resources, indeed borrow more money and acquire grain from any source.[50] If true, this was both engrossing and regrating, which were still, at this time, offences in common law. Collier was making (and doing so publically) a serious accusation and had no reason to do so unless there was some substantiation of proof. He also suggests,

---

47 J. Collier, "Tim Bobbin" *The Truth in a Mask, or the Shude-hill Fight, being A short Manchester Chronicle on the present Times,* (Amsterdam, 1757), p. 6. A point needs to be made at this stage over the writing style of Collier. It is in a form of Biblical allegory and one that was fairly typical of the period, done primarily to give gravitas to what was being offered as testimony.
48 Ibid. p. 7.
49 Ibid. pp. 8-9.
50 Ibid pp. 10-11.

somewhat intriguingly, that already there was developing in Manchester the resentment against the privileged landed gentry who, no matter how desperate the straits of the labouring and merchant classes, still managed to see themselves comfortably provided for. "Truth thou Fool, knowest thou not that they are a lazy Generation reaping where they have no sown, and gathering where they have strawed."[51] Thus for these commercial men it appeared obvious that by getting provisions into Manchester at their own expense and then making a profit was justified. This was, however, clearly contrary to the motivations of, for example, the commercial elites of Bristol or Liverpool who sought to import grain to sell to the public at cost price to alleviate shortages, and this key difference was understood by the crowd. This was clearly the operation of greed at a moment in time when the populous was most vulnerable. Yet the people who were apparently guilty of this were also some of the men who were seeking to alter the customary work practices of the country weaver. Thus the point is that there was a mix of motivations in the actions of the crowd and this is reiterated by Collier when noting the effects the shortages were having on the workers of the towns surrounding Manchester, but, crucially, also offering evidence of a conjoining of the actions of the crowd of a conventional provision crisis accompanied in this instance with that of an industrial moral economy:

> So the Famine increased in the Land, for the grinding of the Millstone was low, and the Poor waxed faint for Want of Bread: for as the Price of Bread grew great the Wages of the Poor decreased: for the Merchants who confederated with the Sons of Belial refused the pay the Workmen their accustomed Wages for their Work.[52]

Collier tells us that the leader of the Manchester civil authority (the Tetrarch) called an assembly of the leading merchants and told them of the workers' anxieties, but those involved in the original conspiracy laid the blame at the landed gentry who would not sell their grain at the old prices.[53]

The upshot was the most serious disturbance associated with the advance of market capitalism in Manchester and it involved some measure of organization with groups from the surrounding townships. This outbreak of rioting began on Saturday 12 November 1757, when groups of workers were found to be entering the town from various directions. The contingent from Saddleworth, Ashton under Lyne and from the out-townships of Oldham appeared to be the most vocal. Collier tells us in classical language of the 'Norman Yoke' that a Manchester working man, 'Kenuriel' told the men from Saddleworth and Ashton:

> Will ye bow down your Necks to the Yoke of Oppression? Will you lay down yourselves at the Feet of those who would make you and your Wives and you're Children their Bondsmen; yea their Slaves as long as any of them endure! You see the Harvest is past, and the Summer is ended; yet we are not saved from the Famine: and this is because the Men of the City of Men have bought (with the money they have gained by the Labour of you and your brethren) and heaped in their Store-houses all the Corn of the Land, and will not suffer you to have thereof for the Support of your Lives and the Lives of your little Ones. But will you submit to this? Or can you be content to be their Bond-slaves forever?[54]

---

51 Ibid. p. 11.
52 Ibid. p. 14.
53 Ibid. pp. 15-16.
54 Ibid. pp. 17-18.

The above passage is revealing. It clearly shows a distinction between the money obtained by the merchant middle-men by the labour of the workers, but it is making clear the difference of a class relationship between the labourers and the capitalist middle classes who were seeking to exploit them for their own gain. This may be an early example, albeit one that is somewhat cryptic, of the language of class that was to take on ever more resonance as we move through to the rest of the eighteenth century.

At this point the Saddleworth and Ashton contingent advanced to the Mealhouse at the top of Market Street Lane, which they attacked. The High Sheriff, this time with a battalion of Invalids[55] and some of the town's merchants waited for the order to march on the Mealhouse where, after some confrontation, a number of the rioters were taken into custody, before being released having found sureties for their appearance at the next Quarter Sessions.[56] That evening the crowd re-assembled and went for Bramall's Travis Mill. This time, however, Bramall had armed his defenders and after some shots were fired in the direction of the crowd, and after receiving the promise that they would be sold grain at the old prices, they dispersed.[57] The situation in Manchester remained tense throughout the weekend. The authorities during the first signs of disturbance sent word to the War Office requesting more troops.[58] The Saddleworth, Oldham and Ashton members were dealing with local hucksters in their own districts on Monday, 14 November, but on the Tuesday we find them once again in Manchester this time attacking Clayton Mill owned by Joseph Hawthorn, or 'Hothornia' in Collier's depiction. They discovered elements that were believed to be adulterants, including partially ground up human and animal bones; after this they effectively destroyed the Mill smashing the millstones and breaking the weir. They were now armed with pickaxes, sticks, clubs and other 'dangerous weapons' and moved into central Manchester.[59] When there they were stopped by the High Sheriff and other gentlemen of the town. The crowd put forward a series of demands, including the fixing of the prices of potatoes, oatmeal and flour for the next twelve months. When the Sheriff pointed out it was impossible for him to make such a promise, one of the crowd attempted to strike him with a scythe fastened to a pole. The High Sheriff now took up a position at Shudehill where more armed men and troops were positioned. They were closely followed by the crowd who tore up road cobbles and threw them at the troops, killing one of them. The order was now given for the troops to open fire.

> This Retreat of the Gentlemen was imputed to their Fear of the Rioters, and they received many Insults as they returned, from Numbers of the Inhabitants of Manchester, who attended in Crowds to observe what pass'd. Some Gentlemen of the Town, and one in Particular, continued their Applications and Intreaties to the Rioters for an Accommodation, and to prevent the impending unhappy Consequences, till they advanced very near to the Invalids, and even to the Points of their Bayonets, and

---

55 'Invalids' were men that had fighting experience at some stage in the British army but had since retired but under the terms of their pension could be, when necessity arose be asked by the local authorities to support the keeping of the peace. It was reported in the *Manchester Mercury* and *Whitworth's Manchester Advertiser and Weekly Magazine* that these 'Invalids' came predominantly from Liverpool.
56 *Whitworth's Manchester Advertiser and Weekly Magazine*, November 15 and 22, 1757.
57 Collier, op. cit. p. 19, see also *Whitworth's Manchester Advertiser and Weekly Magazine*, November 15.
58 Ibid, 22 November, 1757.
59 Ibid.

> had stay'd longer than was consistent with their own Safety, but for the great Calmness and Temper of the commanding Officer, who was personally struck at, saw great Numbers of Stones and Brickbats flung amongst his Men; his Corporal kill'd, and several of his men bruis'd, and wounded, and one of the Mob got into his Ranks, before he gave the Command to his Men to fire...The commanding Officer, having an Order sign'd by the Civil Magistrate, to justify him in repelling Force by Force, finding that no other Means could be of any avail, order'd his Men to fire, which was obey'd ; by which two of the Rioters were kill'd on the Spot; and also one innocent Person, the Son of a reputable and substantial Farmer, whom a fatal Curiosity had brought thither, and who stood in a Tree near the Place where the Fray happen'd.[60]

The troops managed to take some of the crowd into custody the rest now retreated. Joined by great numbers of local Mancunians, they re-assembled and once more attacked Bramall's Mill. This time they overran it, took down the roof, destroyed millstones and completely demolished the nearby house of Bramall's partner, Thomas Hatfield. More troops now arrived and the crowd once again dispelled. An armed guard was placed near the bridge over the Irwell at the Bull's Head tavern, but that night the crowd once again re-grouped and attempted a rescue of the prisoners taken earlier in the day. The large number of troops were a barrier to the attempts of the crowd, but when they promised to disarm themselves if the prisoners were released this was agreed to by the commander, "upon which the Prisoner was releas'd, and accordingly the Mob dispers'd and went off."[61] The High Sheriff however, was not persuaded that the actions of the crowd were over, thus:

> An Express was sent away by the Gentlemen of the Town on Tuesday Night to the Secretary at War, with a Representation of what had happen'd, and to desire an additional military Force, which He was pleas'd to order; and in Consequence thereof a Troop of Sir Robert Rich's Dragoons are expected to arrive in Town Tomorrow [Nov. 22nd], who have Orders not only to protect the Town of Manchester, but also to suppress any Riots or Disturbances in the Neighbourhood, and to repel Force with Force whenever it may be found necessary.[62]

Placards were now placed around Manchester to the effect that the authorities were ready to uphold all the laws against forestalling, regrating and engrossing.

> The Gentlemen of Manchester are determined to put the Laws in Execution as far as they can, against all Forestallers, Ingrossers, and Regraters of their Markets, and have publish'd an Advertisement to encourage Informations against Offenders of this kind, and will be very glad if any lawful Means they can make use of, will tend to reduce the Price of Corn, Meal, and other Provisions, and thereby afford the Poor all the Assistance in their Power...[63]

---

60 Ibid.
61 Ibid.
62 Ibid and *Manchester Mercury,* 29 November 1757; "on Wednesday last [Nov. 23rd] a Troop of Sir Robert Rich's Regiment of Dragoons from York; and on Friday [Nov. 25th] two Companies of the Earl of Hume's Regiment of Foot from Derby, arrived here in order to preserve the Peace and Quiet of the Town &c. The same Day the Invalids quartered here marched from hence to Liverpool." See also J. P. Earwaker, (ed.), *The Constable's Accounts for the Manor of Manchester,* (Manchester, 1887). Vol. 3,12 December. 1757, p. 93 and 19 January, 1758, p. 94.
63 *Manchester Mercury,* 29 November, 1757.

A member of leading aristocrats of the region, the Earl of Warrington from his seat at Dunham Massey issued the following statement to his tenants.

> Whereas the necessities of the poor are now very great, as well through the scarcity of work, as the high price of corn, which has been, and still is, artificially kept up, by the policy of the farmers and dealers in corn, flour and meal, to the great oppression of the public, and more especially the lower ranks of people, who are obliged to buy all their bread, or bread corn, at the shops on the worst terms. Therefore I recommend it to all my farmers and tenants, who have any corn, or other eatables, to dispose of, that they gradually thresh up their corn, supply the wants of their poor neighbours, and afterwards bring what they have to spare, to be sold in the public markets on reasonable terms; which I hope will be a means to silence and put a stop to all future riots and disturbance. And such of my farmers and tenants as shall disoblige me of this reasonable request, are not to expect any more favour from me.[64]

But the Manchester authorities were also concerned to keep the peace. So concerned, in fact, that another company of the dragoons, under Colonel Stewart, were barracked in the town until 16 February 1758 and the other, under Colonel Sir Robert Rich, until 13 April and there is evidence that soldiers were still billeted in the town, until at least 20 August, all of which is suggestive that the authorities regarded keeping the peace in Manchester to be a matter of serious alarm and due diligence.[65]

The riot was now effectively over, yet the haste with which the authorities issued assurances to the labouring population of their commitment to maintaining the customary statute and common laws against forestalling, regrating and engrossing suggests that, in their view, this was a primary reason for the anger of the crowd. This is further suggestive that there was some basis for the indignation of the crowd and it is supported by what Collier says about the adulterants that were found at the mills of Hawthorn and again at Bramall and Hatfield.[66] In the case of the latter, the rioters went back on three occasions to wreak damage on those specific targets whom they believed were attempting to make profits at the expense of the hunger of the masses. The presence of so many troops to control this escalating situation at the moment when the Seven Years War was not going well is also suggestive of the seriousness which the authorities believed the position in and around Manchester to be. There is also the matter of the organisation of the rioters. They came from out-townships encircling Manchester and were joined by the local inhabitants in great numbers and, to reiterate, they appeared very clearly to know the merchants who were

---

64 *Gentleman's Magazine*, (December, 1757) p. 598.
65 J. P. Earwaker, (ed.), *The Constable's Accounts for the Manor of Manchester*, (Manchester, 1887). Vol. 3, (16 February, 1758), p. 95 and (13 April, 1758), p. 96, and (20 August 1758), p. 98.
66 According to Collier "...behold on the fifteenth day of the ninth month, they assembled themselves together, and sent unto the *Oldhamites* and the *Ashtonians*, and others, to meet them on the plain of *Newton*, and the met together about the third hour of the day; and the *Newtonians* told them how that a son of *Belial* had possession of a mill in the country of *Clayton*, and did there grind things hurtful, and sold it to the poor for bread-corn. And when they heard this they chose unto themselves as captain of the host, whose name was *Jamah*, an *Oldhamite*; and Adamah led them to *Clayton* mill: and finding in therein wheat, mixed with acorns, with pease, and with beans, and with chopped straw, and with French-whiting, together with dried men's bones, and horse dung died; some thereof ground for bread, some grinding on the mill, and some to grind; he showed the mixture to the people; and when they saw it, they were wroth, and burnt the bolsters, the sieves, broke the wheels and stones, and destroyed the mill; so that the ruins thereof remain even unto this day." *The Truth in a Mask*, chapter two, numbers 8 and 9.

perpetrating the acts of perceived mass injustice. The crowd, in a very real sense, were demonstrating their collective strength at the precise time when not only was their access to reasonably priced provisions in serious jeopardy, but when many of them felt their customary work practices were under threat. In the eyes of the crowd none of the key figures in authority came out of the provision crisis with any credit and the crowd did not appear in a mood of any forgiveness. From the *Manchester Constable's Accounts* for 1759 we discover that two years after the events, on the 15 November, £1 7s 6d was spent on an "especial Watch (of) twelve nights (on the property of) Justice Bayley complaining of being abused in the Night time." James Bayley, of Withington, was High Sheriff at the time of the disturbances, and the 'abuse' he was suffering was likely to be a form of 'Rough Music' whereby a crowd would have shown their displeasure by gathering under his window and making a loud constant noise all night and every night.[67] In his original and seminal article, 'The Moral Economy of the English Crowd in the Eighteenth Century' Edward Thompson described the parameters of what the motivations for the actions of the crowd; "a highly-complex form of direct popular action, disciplined and with clear objectives." He goes on to add,

> But these grievances operated within a popular consensus as to what were legitimate and what were illegitimate practices...This in turn was grounded upon a consistent traditional view of the social norms and obligations, of the proper economic functions of several parties within the community, which, taken together, can be said to constitute the moral economy of the poor. An outrage to these moral assumptions, quite as much as actual deprivation, was the usual occasion for direct action.[68]

What has been described in this chapter fits this model. However, when these events are coupled with the next set of developments on the industrial front, this significantly adds to the power of the moral economy as an explanatory concept. In terms of its use in the specific example of provision protests it was even more powerfully expressed in the events of the Autumn of 1766 as we shall see in due course, but attitudes were changing, with those of political economy gaining the ascendency and, in fact, the old laws against forestalling, regrating and engrossing were repealed in 1772.[69] This is not to say that this ended the popular perceptions of the moral economy nor were traditional attitudes and, indeed, the actions of the local authorities superseded by this repeal, there are many examples of this not being the case well into the early 1800s.[70] It was rather the

---

67 J. P. Earwaker, (ed.), *The Constable's Accounts for the Manor of Manchester*, (Manchester, 1887). Vol. 3, (15 November, 1759), p. 105.
68 E. P. Thompson, 'The Moral Economy of the English Crowd in the Eighteenth Century' *Past & Present*, 50 (1) (Feb., 1971) pp. 78-79.
69 For more on how the sentiments of the moral economy were maintained after the repeal of the old statutes in 1772 see D. Hay, 'Moral economy, Political Economy and Law', in A. J. Randall and A. Charlesworth, *Moral Economy and Popular Protest*, (London: Macmillan, 2000), pp. 93-121.
70 That many, particularly of a paternalistic persuasion still held notions of a moral economy see the 'Address to the Grand Jury of Shropshire' by Lord Chief Justice Kenyon saying the forestalling was still an offence and indictable. *Annals of Agriculture*, (1795). See Thompson, *Customs in Common*, (London: Merlin, 1991) pp. 197-224. Also see for example R. Wells, *Wretched Faces: Famine in Wartime England*, (London: Breviary Stuff, 2011), *passim*; and A. Booth, 'Food Riots in the North-West of England 1790-1801' in *Past & Present*, 77 (1) (Nov., 1977), pp. 84-107. Between 1800 and 1801 for example there were food riots in Stockport, (January, 1800) and in the same month riots at Lancaster and Manchester. In February of the same year there were riots at Macclesfield, Oldham, Ashton-under-Lyne and Ulverston. In May 1800 there were disturbances over provisions in Oldham and Bolton, and in June another riot in Manchester. In

terms of the perceptions of those whose primary concerns were trade, commerce, and especially industry which had changed, and they now believed their positions had been greatly strengthened. In order to achieve success these masters knew that they must change the traditional customary practices and attitudes of working people. One way to achieve this was to firstly see that the old paternalist attitudes enshrined in the gentry-magistracy be confronted in order to put a halt to the workers' recourse to arbitration in a dispute they deemed unjust or unfair. Then they had to gain acceptance in law that they had a right to change these practices enshrined in the belief system of their workers who, in turn, had to understand that the law allowed this magisterial arbitration. It is how these ends were achieved in the case of the weavers of the North-West to which we now turn our attention.

September, 1800 there were food riots at Lancaster, Blackburn, Wigan and Bunbury. In January, 1801 there were food riots at Chorley, Whitehaven and Bury.

9

The Legal Death of the Industrial Moral Economy

We have seen in chapter seven how the cotton weavers of the North-West had organised protective 'box' clubs as a means of fending off the attempts by the masters to encroach on their customary work practices. This was operational from 1747, but in 1756 it became better organised with a set of rules governing the actions of the members and the institution itself. The smallware weavers and the broadcloth weavers had both now printed these rules in the form of their respective 'Apologies' for having felt the need to confront the masters. Yet against this backdrop of rising provision prices, the evident contrary dealings of provision merchants, and the lack of work due to the uncertainty surrounding the Seven Years War, tensions were raised even further when some cotton masters attempted to implement their new terms. Across the region this tension was palpable not only in the cotton textiles but in a range of trades. As early as 1754 we see from the Manchester constable's accounts that a weaver from Royton, near Oldham, was taken into custody and charged with "entering into a weaver's combination."[1] At Liverpool, in 1757, the shoemakers and tailors had struck for improved wages, and the following year the potters were agitating for better conditions.[2] It would appear that the cotton masters had been tinkering with not only the customary work practices, (for example over apprenticeship regulations from the 1740s), but also changing the lengths of pieces to their advantage and altering the piece-rate payments downwards. What the weavers of the North-West essentially wanted, given the escalation in the prices of provisions and the fact that the masters had changed the lengths and payments per finished piece, was that the piece lengths and piece rates should be returned to their values of the 1730s. This demand, the masters argued, was in fact declaring for a wage increase. On 16 September 1757, the smallware weavers struck for improved piece rates initially in Manchester but soon after in the outlying townships.[3] Other weavers, such as the broadcloth and check weavers, were, by the end of 1757 and early 1758, contributing to their boxes for the need of short-term support when they took the decision to strike. The South-East Manchester silk weavers were also active, limiting the number of apprentices taken on, and the textile bleach workers were also agitating.[4] At this point the masters mounted their major offensive.

However, before highlighting how these developments unfolded and evaluating their significance, there is another point regarding the policy of mercantilism as a set of attitudes and how the concept of the moral economy fitted neatly into this view. Implicit in trade, commerce, and industry within the British mercantile system was the notion of trust. Often deals and the viability of enterprises rested on the mutual trust and respect of the various parties involved. There was of course the existence of legal contracts to counter the possibility of fraud on either side, but sometimes even these rested on the implicit understanding of what was expected of the various parties to the agreement. It

---

1 J. P. Earwaker, (ed.), *The Constable's Accounts for the Manor of Manchester*, (Manchester, 1887). Vol. 3, (15 February. 1754), P. 65.
2 *Williamson's Liverpool Advertiser*, 22 July and 4 November 1757.
3 National Archives, Kew, *Palatinate Papers,* (P. L. 26. 39/1).
4 *Whitworth's Manchester Advertiser and Weekly Magazine*, 11 April, and 25 April 1758.

was a logical corollary of the whole manner of operation that the parties concerned would undertake their part of whatever the enterprise involved and perform their duties to the best of their abilities, or at least get the exercise completed to everyone's reasonable satisfaction. Deals were done, for example, concerning loans or buying stock with a simple handshake. Here we see another example that the fair price, (the decent rate of return in terms of profits, the proper quality of work on the basis that not doing so inveighed against the moral imperatives of honesty and fairness that developed over several generations), had been shown to function adequately. In the case of provisioning, the *Book of Orders* maintained that certain weights and quality should be ensured and the assize of bread, which local Court Leets or Borough Councils oversaw, were also designed for the same purpose. Similarly, employers as well as normal customers expected decent quality, but so too did those performing the work. This also depended on the understanding that the employer would allow the worker to perform the work independently on his or her terms, without undue interference, and, importantly, the payments would be made as promised in the proper amount. In the North-West the re-organisation of the weaver's box clubs, from that of a trade-wide mutual assurance fund into a means of collective defence, were seen as a necessary imperative against what these working people saw as threats to their position as an independent group of workers in defence of their customary work practices, which were now threatened by the cotton merchants. Certainly, in the early to mid-1750s, times had been hard and onset of the Seven Years War in 1756 compounded these problems. In short, on both sides the necessary trust in the fair operation of the labourer/employer nexus (what could termed the industrial moral economy) had been broken. Workers no longer trusted their masters and vice-versa.

With regard to the immediate developments and the dramatic deterioration of the relationship between the cotton weavers of the North-West and their masters, on 16 April 1758 the check and broadcloth weavers notified their members that collections were due for the box. This was a signal for their impending actions against the masters to refuse work. On 21 April the masters placed an advertisement in *Whitworth's Manchester Advertiser and Weekly Magazine*.

> Whereas several Weavers employed in the Manufactures carried on in Manchester, and the neighbouring Towns, have lately formed themselves into unlawful Clubs and Societies, and have presumed contrary to Law, to enter into Combinations and Subscriptions, and to make By-Laws or Orders by which they pretend to regulate Trade, of which there is already some Evidence discovered. *This is to give Notice* that such Person or Persons as have not, nor will enter into such Combinations and Subscriptions...may be assured of being protected and employed; and such Person or Persons as shall continue such Combinations and Subscriptions, are hereby to take Notice that they are liable to, and will be prosecuted as the Law directs.[5]

By May the weavers strike had commenced, with thousands of weavers' involved and its geographical range was from not only Manchester itself but Bury, Radcliffe and Whitefield in the north, through Salford and Eccles in the west, Ashton in the south east, and Oldham and Royton in the east. For an indicator of how advanced a sense of 'class' feeling had developed among the

---

5 *Whitworth's Manchester Advertiser and Weekly Magazine*, (25 April, 1758).

workers of the North-West by the later 1750s we can determine from Edward Thompson's statement, again taken from his first essay on the 'Moral Economy'. Here Thompson reiterates that if "Economic class-conflict in nineteenth-century England found its characteristic expression in the matter of wages; in eighteenth-century England the working people were most quickly inflamed to action by rising prices."[6] What is being discussed here was a dispute about worker's perceived rights to their customary work practices, but it was crucially also about their rights to combine to maintain or even raise their wages, and in the eyes of the workers what the masters were attempting to do constituted an infringement of the law. On the other hand, for the masters this was their best chance lay of bringing these upstart weavers down to earth and at same time place themselves in the overall dominant position. Yet all this was occurring at the same time as tensions were rising due to widespread suspicions that some merchants were manipulating the marketing of essential provisions. Hence, in this situation we can observe both the effects of falling wages (which was one consequence of the masters' assault) and the increase in the price of provisions, which is suggestive of the emergence of an identity of interests in a class sense. Thus this corresponds to both elements laid out by Thompson.

The weavers' demands were fivefold. Firstly, they wanted the old standard payment per piece to be guaranteed, also the standard length of check cotton pieces was to be eighty yards, and they would be paid more by the yard if they were above this figure and less if below. Secondly, for finer cotton mixes the length was to be sixty yards and the same rules as above for less or greater lengths. Thirdly, and very importantly, the weavers demanded that the masters should employ no workers that the weavers' combination deemed 'unfit weavers'. This meant that those workers who were not members of their combination and by extension had not served the requisite appropriate apprenticeship. Fourth, they explained in some detail why they called them 'unfit' and unfair weavers, but, importantly, they reiterated their sense of collective will and solidarity when they said such people were unwilling to contribute to the charity stock of the box to "assist and relieve the poor distressed sick weavers, and prosecute those who are proved offenders, which ... would be of great benefit to all the townships where the trade is carried on."[7] All the above signify the weavers understanding of what the masters were intending the new work practices to be and the fifth point hammered this home, but with the caveat that they simply wished to protect themselves and the trade:

> Fifthly, the reflection cast upon us, that we intend to oversee or judge bad work, or new inventions, or fixing wages for such, is entirely false and groundless, having no other view, but to support and maintain this beautiful branch with experienced and honest work-men, and to bring into a trade, under the statute of 5th Eliz. C.4.[8]

If these proposals seem innocuous it is primarily because they were the articles the weavers chose to be published just prior to their putting them forward to placate and conciliate with the masters, as we shall discover shortly, on the suggestion of a local magistrate.

---

6 Thompson, 'Moral Economy' op cit, p. 79.
7 T. Percival, *A Letter to a Friend: Occasioned by the late Disputes betwixt the Check-Makers of Manchester and their Weavers; and the Check-Makers Ill-Usage of the Author*, (Halifax: J. Buckland, 1758), Appendix One, p. 29.
8 Ibid.

By the early summer the masters, consisting of the leadership of Thomas Tutchet, Robert Ayreton, William Starkey, Marsden Kenyon and John Markland, began to initiate their first moves. As noted earlier, in any dispute regarding workers and employers it would fall to the magistracy in the first instance to arbitrate. At this point these masters accused Thomas Percival, a magistrate of Royton Hall near Oldham, of being not only a friend to the weavers' but also of being the author 'Tim Bobbin' who had just published an account of the confrontation in Manchester the previous November entitled *Truth in a Mask or the Shude-hill Fight*. The implication was that just such paternalistic minded 'country' justices as Percival were always likely to favour the workers in a dispute invoking their opposition to oppression and that these masters in particular were being accused by the weavers' combination clubs as being especially oppressive. Also the Manchester masters suspected that country magistrates and small landed gentry, such as Percival, saw themselves as elevated in status and perceived business and manufacturing as beneath their social station, hence were naturally biased against the no-nonsense Manchester men of commerce and trade. These men, by their actions, were upsetting the balance of the organic basis of mid-eighteenth century society as it was understood by the country gentlemen and thus were engaging in highly dangerous actions simply to make greater profits. In fact Percival's background was that in the seventeenth century his family had been involved in the textile trades, but the family had done well, sold their assets, and moved into gentry status by purchasing Royton Hall. Percival himself had been raised and become accustomed to his place in the Whig county gentry; he was well educated and was a member of the Royal Society, as well as being a leading member of the county magistracy,[9] but there is also evidence that he had a deep contempt for the 'badger' masters of Manchester.[10] In a classic example of extolling the moral economy, it was these Manchester merchants that Percival blamed for the provision rioting of 1757 when he said "... those who were concerned in engrossing the corn, and those who took undue advantage of the high price of corn to sink wages, are only to be blamed for provoking the check-weavers to this measure, is it to be expected that inferior people are to be honest, when the rich scorn to be so"?[11] Yet, during the June provision riots in 1757, Percival had been singled out for praise by the *Manchester Mercury* for preventing the Oldham colliers from joining the disputants in Manchester.[12]

The reason why the Manchester manufacturers wished to nullify the role of magistrates such as Percival was due to the enormous power they possessed in the localities in eighteenth century society. The highest level was the Quarter Sessions, which comprised of all the magistrates in the county and which possessed the power from 1689 to pass sentence of death on certain offenders, meaning it operated in a similar function to that of the Assizes. The Quarter

---

9 *The Concise Dictionary of National Bibliography*, vol. 3, p. 2353 (Oxford, 1992), "Percival, Thomas (1719-1762, antiquary; a Lancashire country gentleman, contributed to papers on the antiquity of Northern England to the Royal Society and the Society of Antiquaries."
10 T. Percival, *A Letter to a Friend: Occasioned by the late Disputes betwixt the Check-Makers of Manchester and their Weavers; and the Check-Makers Ill-Usage of the Author*, (Halifax: J. Buckland, 1758), pp. 4-8.
11 Ibid, p. 27.
12 *Manchester Mercury*, June 14, 1757. "Apprehensive least these escaping (rioters) should Influence the Oldham Colliers, Persons on Horseback were dispatched, who soon returned, with an Account, that by the prudent Conduct of Thomas Percival, and Edward Gregge, Esq. "all Danger from that Quarter was prevented."

Sessions of the magistracy also possessed significant administrative functions. Again, after the reforms of 1689, it carried out most of the civil administration of the county. According to the Webbs their functions included:

> The repairing of bridges, the maintenance of the King's gaols, the building and management of the newer Houses of Correction, the fixing of wages, prices and rates of land carriage, the licensing of various kinds of traders, the suppression of disorderly houses, the sanctioning of special levies for various parish needs, the confirmation or disallowance of the orders of individual Justices or pairs of Justices on every conceivable subject, were among the multifarious civil functions of Quarter Sessions.[13]

It fell to these men to administrate and effectively govern the county, in divisional or petty session one, two or more of them meeting in a local inn or tavern, or indeed in their own parlour, could appoint Surveyors to the Highway to make sure the local transport system operated. They were responsible for the appointment of parish constables, Overseers to the Poor, and to inspect and allow their accounts, ensure that paupers were returned to their places of settlement, order the maintenance of illegitimate children by the alleged father, confine to the Houses of Correction parents who neglected their children, or parish officials who neglected or embezzled their accounts, as well as to hear, try and convict the cases of those accused of petty crimes or refer those of more serious offences to the Quarter Session or the Assizes. Added to these multifarious administrative and legal functions, at the local level there were other binding yet vaguely defined operation which involved the individual justices acting 'on their own view'.[14] This term carried with it certain obligations on the part of the magistrate and gave him significant powers of social control in his given locality. These empowered the justice with the same authority and weight as 'if made by a Jury of twelve sworn men.'[15] In fact, "the strength of the magistracy was still greater than the growth of their formal powers suggests because they were simultaneously developing a range of informal powers which do not appear in any Statute. Their extensive discretionary powers and the absence of any effective control from above enabled them to become a *de facto* legislature."[16] According to the Webbs:

> The same power of themselves deciding the cases, coupled with the power to give commands to all officers of townships or parishes, enabled the Justices, in practically any detail of local administration, to convert their own opinions into mandatory enactments.[17]

Thus, initially it was the weavers' who appealed to Percival, as was the accepted convention, to arbitrate the question of not only the legitimacy of their dispute but also the existence of their boxes, and, by extension, their combination and its aims.[18] To these entreaties he said, "I told them that all combinations were

---

13 B. and S. Webb, *English Local Government: The Parish and the County*, (London: Longmans, 1906) pp. 296-297.
14 Ibid, p. 301.
15 Ibid.
16 See the introduction by B. Keith-Lucas to B. and S. Webb, *English Local Government: The Parish and the County*, (London: Longmans, 1906) p. x.
17 Ibid p. 539.
18 T. Percival, *A Letter to a Friend: Occasioned by the late Disputes betwixt the Check-Makers of Manchester and their Weavers; and the Check-Makers Ill-Usage of the Author*, (Halifax: J. Buckland, 1758), p. 10.

against the good of trade, and contrary to an express Act of Parliament, and advised them not to meddle."[19] A couple of days later the weavers returned and asked to see the Act and to borrow it, but instead Percival wrote out the relevant passage. For some months he heard little about the weavers or their masters, being confined, he said, to his house with an illness. He then heard the weavers were to go on strike against the masters, but also revealed that the masters had formed their own combination of interests, thus there existed an equal 'association' of the leading manufacturers. In June of 1758 Percival met with a delegate from Ashton, on behalf of the striking weavers in that district, to ask if he felt they were doing the right thing. He advised them they were not and that they should seek an 'opportunity of making it up with the masters'. He advised them that the length of piece question should be forwarded by a petition to parliament for an act to be passed, much in the same way the woollen disputes of the West of England were in the mid-1750s.[20] The weavers' delegate then contacted the local weaver's box steward to convey Percival's sentiments on conciliation towards the masters when the weavers were to hold their next region-wide Manchester meeting of all the branches. Percival, in turn, promised the local worker he would forward their five proposals to the masters. On 1 July the old local delegate weaver returned and told Percival they had followed his advice, but that it appeared the masters had refused the proposals. Percival told him to tell his fellow weavers that he was sure that the masters would let the matter be arbitrated by some of the county magistracy, who would act honestly without prejudice to any side in the dispute, and further that he believed the masters were men of honour.

> ... the old man shaked his head and said "I knew little of them, their honour was *severity*, their mercy was *oppression*." And as I will always acknowledge my errors, when they are known to me, so I will do by this, and I do therefore own, that I had then a very good opinion of the check-makers (the masters) in general, which I am convinced was a mistake in me, as to many of them. The old man and I parted, and he promised to desire the weavers to re-consider the message from the masters; another party of weavers came on the same errand, and a deal of discourse passed to the like purpose; but these people having heads about the pitch of the Manchester check-makers, they left me, I think more obstinate in their opinions than they were when they came; a natural consequence to those who have proud spirits and weak heads.[21]

A third set of weavers met with Percival and promised to consider his reasoning with the masters. Ten days after these meetings another set of weavers proposals were shown to Percival. He did not believe the masters would accept them and accordingly drew up a new set to which Percival added that no money could be removed from the box without the consent of a least two masters and that an act of parliament be applied for in order to set the piece rates and lengths.[22] The next day the weavers returned (July 12) saying that they thought that Percival's draft proposals were hard on the weavers, particularly regarding having to gain the masters consent for the disposal of their box funds. He then outlined his reasoning. The main reason was that the masters suspected that the box funds were to support combinations, and if the real reason was that they

---

19 Ibid.
20 Ibid, p. 10.
21 Ibid p. 13.
22 Ibid Appendix Three, pp. 30-31.

would be used to support the poor, what objections could they have? Not only this, but this solution appeared the only way of reconciling the contending parties. The weavers in turn suspected, with just cause, that the masters would block the uses of the box simply as a means to disband all the boxes. Later in the day another group of weavers appeared before Percival, this time concerned with whether the apprenticeship clauses in 5th Eliz., allowed for seven years apprenticeships in the cotton sector. He said he doubted it, but it did mention linen workers. On the face of it this apprenticeship condition appeared to be the least of the weavers immediate concerns, given the nature of the new work practices, piece-lengths and payments, and the rising cost of living, but it actually went to the heart of their case. This is because if the masters won on this point they could determine who worked for them and on what terms. In such a situation the weavers could not claim the high piece-work rates as time-served artisans, thus losing their own control of the trade entry stipulations which they had organised for centuries. This further went to the crux of the masters' assault on the traditional work practices, for with the lack of formal guild status the Lancashire weavers' grounds for applying their own apprenticeship regulations were on shaky legal foundations, save that of the precedence of custom for at least the previous two hundred years.

Thus far Percival was acting in strict accordance with the law as he understood it. What lay behind his strategy of letting the matter be decided by impartial county justices of the peace, was that the magistrates and especially the country justices should remain a pivotal bulwark against underhand practices on both sides and be seen to be just and fair arbitrators. However, the masters apparently had no intention of allowing the matter to be settled by the country gentry magistrates. In fact they did not want any interference with how they dealt with their labour from anyone.[23] Percival, on July 22, got word from the Manchester merchants' envoy, a Mr Styth, that they wished him to involve himself no more in the matter. Meanwhile Percival heard that one of the leaders of the Manchester masters, John Markland, had let it be widely known that Percival was the weavers' principal advisor and "that they do nothing without my advice, and that Mr *Markland* said, I was greatly to blame."[24] This was a shock to Percival, primarily because it was Markland who had suggested to him in a personal request to attempt to arbitrate the matter in the first place.

Thus the situation was that not only were the masters disavowing any knowledge of asking Percival to intervene in the dispute, also they were placing blame on him for the actions of the weavers. But things were going to get much worse for Percival and the weavers. The summer assizes at Lancaster were due to be held at the end of July. First of all the Manchester merchants wrote to the court of the Kings Bench to have Percival struck off the list of Justices of the Peace, stating that the main reason for doing so was that it was he who was principally responsible for the deteriorating situation and increasing the tensions between masters and workers, and, further, that his actions went directly against the interests of trade, not only for Manchester and the North-West region but, importantly, for the whole nation at this time of war crisis. They argued that if such a precedent as that being pursued by Percival was allowed to stand it sent an awful message at such a moment when the whole country should be acting

---

23 T. Percival, *A Letter to a Friend: Occasioned by the late Disputes betwixt the Check-Makers of Manchester and their Weavers; and the Check-Makers Ill-Usage of the Author*, (Halifax: J. Buckland, 1758), pp 14-15.
24 Ibid. pp 15-16.

together. This was a clever tactic on the part of the masters for they had sowed the seed of doubt in the practical benefit of supposed impartiality and posed the question of whether the country magistracy could be trusted when dealing in matters of trade and industry, especially at a time desperate national crisis. It therefore began the process of limited interference or, indeed, non-interference in terms of the conducting of local industrial practices, which was exactly what the Manchester merchants wanted. They went yet further when a message was sent to the presiding judge at the Lancaster assizes which was the same as the indictment against Percival sent the Court of the Kings Bench. Their timing could not have been more perfect because the presiding judge at these assize sessions was the Lord Chief Justice, Lord Mansfield, a man whose advanced beliefs in the need for political economy could not have been more pronounced.[25] Whether the Manchester merchants knew of Mansfield's strong position on free trade is not known but, if not, they were incredibly fortunate, as it was on the public record that his rulings when dealing with disgruntled workers was one of uncompromising harshness. On the matter of his views on the need to be rid of the protectionism embedded in the mercantile system, according to Lord John Campbell, Mansfield was besotted with his "ultra-free trade principles, that indeed, he would furnish a defence of the Dutch doctrine, that a besieged city should sell gun powder and balls to the besieging army."[26] According to Mansfield's legal biographer, the Lord Chief Justice was a fervent advocate of the need for a flourishing national trade and commercial system, but crucially he was also usually favourable to the legality of established customary practices, the protection of which was a vital reason why the weavers had formed their combination in the first place.

---

25 A brief biographical note on William Murray, the first Earl of Mansfield. He was educated at Perth, Westminster School, Christ Church, Oxford, his family had been Jacobite. Thomas Foley, (Baron Foley of Gloucestershire) a contemporary of Mansfield's at Westminster believed that Mansfield was regarded as an avowed free trader from 1747 when he attacked Lord Sandwich's prohibition of the insuring of French ships and made this the scene of an indictment of the policy of commercial restriction which had been Whig policy for the previous thirty years. In 1752-3 he was accused of toasting the health of the Pretender in his younger days at the house of a known Jacobite in Ludgate. The affair was dropped without a division in the Lords. Mansfield was made Solicitor General in 1742 and became Lord Chief Justice in 1756 (8/11/1756). He was Chancellor of the Exchequer between 5/4/1757 and 30/6/1757, and was a supporter of Bute throughout his tenure of office. Mansfield's purported opposition to the actions of the Ministers during the crisis of 1766 was on a point of law, but one cannot but help but conjecture whether his ideological leanings also played a part. Briefly what happened was that Mansfield attacked Chatham's Ministry in 1766 for the technical breach of the Constitution involved in the prohibition of grain exports by the Order in Council, essentially on the point that Parliament had not been consulted. The fact was that at the height of the crisis Parliament was in recess but Mansfield argued that it should have been recalled, for its sanction was necessary for such an important matter. In strict legal terms Mansfield was correct, but in practical terms this delay would undoubtedly escalated an already very dangerous and alarming situation, and the Ministers knew this. Mansfield again held the office of Chancellor of the Exchequer between September and October 1767 under the same Ministers he had attacked the previous year. In June 1780 he was so stunned by the ferocity of the attack on him by the Gordon Rioters that he took no part in quelling the riots and was not consulted as to the legality of firing on the crowd. *The Directory of National Biography* adds that Mansfield was trained at the Guildhall and attached himself to a select body of special jurors who were regularly empanelled in the cause of commerce, and taught him the usages of trade; 'and he began moulding the law into accordance with the needs of a rapidly expanding commerce and manufacture'.

26 J. Campbell, *The Lives of the Chief Justices of England*, 3 vols., (London: John Murray, 1849-1857), vol. 2, p 365. See also J. Oldham, *The Mansfield Manuscripts and the Growth of English Law in the Eighteenth Century*, (Chapel Hill and London: University of North Carolina Press, 1992) vol., 2. 'Labor and Employment'.

Both in war and peace, Mansfield wanted to see that the channels of international commerce remained open. His support for free trade was consistently grounded in a conviction that unrestrained commerce would ultimately prove more beneficial to England than artificial barriers imposed by Parliament, municipalities, or the courts... he was usually of the view that legitimate, progressive commercial practices should shape commercial law, rather than the reverse... Mansfield was usually willing to support customs clearly established by ancient usage, but municipal impediments to trade were undesirable, and in the case of Mansfield's trial notes, the merchants prevailed.[27]

The Manchester merchants also forwarded to Mansfield the names of approximately half of the delegates to the weavers' box clubs who attended the regional meetings at Manchester, along with notes on their activities and their attempts at a combination, and the reasons why, which they said was to raise wages and not to defend the precedent of the retention of their customary practices. Thus, in their appeal to the Lord Chief Justice, the Manchester masters were being deliberately disingenuous to a judge who was known to be decidedly hostile to any group of workers who take it upon themselves to conspire together to raise their wages.

At this stage it is important to get an understanding of Mansfield's methods of administering the law to the lower orders. In the West Midlands in August 1756, as in other parts of the country, there was widespread food rioting. Riots had taken place at Walsall, Wednesbury, Atherstone, Polesworth, Tamworth, Baugley and Heartsfall, but at Nuneaton one of the rioters had been shot dead. Several of the rioters had been arrested and taken before Mansfield, then sitting in session at the Warwick assizes. Four of those arrested were capitally convicted and two were due to be executed the following Wednesday, with four more ordered to be held until the next assizes. At this point Mansfield adjourned the assizes until the following Monday, presumably to allow the emotions of the crowd to be pacified. Yet if this was the case, he had a somewhat brutal way of displaying his concerns, because when he adjourned that week's assizes he said that he would reconvene the following Monday morning, and then he declared:

> ... that he will hold assizes every Monday till the rioters are dispersed, [he] has been pleased to say, that if they will return to their homes, and promise to remain quiet, the two whose execution is respited, shall be pardoned, and ordered to be released, with the other four that are in gaol; but that if the riot is continued, every person who shall be taken up and committed, shall be executed the day after he is found guilty.[28]

Needless to say, the riots ceased, but only because Mansfield had indulged in legal blackmail by frightening the lower orders into submission, and he was about to use the same tactic again with the weavers of the North-West, but this time the consequences would be much more long-lasting and significantly more influential. Before 'waiting' on Lord Mansfield at the assizes, the Manchester merchants had prepared their ground well. First of all they discredited one of the leading county magistrates, and one with especial links to the Manchester region, forwarded their complaints to the Court of the Kings Bench and supplied Mansfield with the same information, that it was Percival who was encouraging the weavers. They also informed Mansfield that 10,000 weavers had re-organised

---

27 Oldham op cit, p 695.
28 *Gentleman's Magazine*, (August, 1756) pp 408-409.

their box clubs to form a means of collective aggression expressly for the purpose of forming illegal combinations to raise wages by force.[29] The weavers, they said, had formed committees to conduct their work stoppage, their leaders had travelled to personally approach all the weavers in the large towns and also their country namesakes, they had appointed stewards in every township in the region, and ordered weavers to leave their masters and use their box money collected specifically for the purpose of the supporting the weavers in dispute. Additionally they also supplied Mansfield with nineteen names of the principal leaders. Then they strategically placed reports that there was widespread rioting and disturbance by the rioters and, further, that they were engaged in intimidation not only of those weavers who refused to enter their boxes but also by writing threatening letters to masters who "opposed their Designs."[30] They furnished Mansfield with their manipulated evidence against Percival,[31] and stressed to the Lord Chief Justice the need for urgency and, if this situation was allowed to continue unchecked, the enormous damage it would have on the trade at this critical time, and also on future prospects not only of Manchester, but the whole of the North-West region.[32]

During the assizes Mansfield did nothing except conduct the business before the court, but at its conclusion in his Charge to the Grand Jury the Manchester merchants got exactly what they wanted. First of all Mansfield instructed the Grand Jury to prefer bills of indictment against the nineteen box club leaders whose names had been forwarded by the masters, he then signed arrest warrants for their immediate apprehension, even though they had not been brought before him and the ink was barely dry on the indictments he had instructed of the jury. Of the nineteen men whose arrests warrants were signed, thirteen were from Manchester, four from Salford, one from Eccles and one from Rusholme.[33] He then said that he would be recommending that all those who had contributed to the boxes were as liable to prosecution as the stewards.[34] Mansfield then discharged the Grand Jury, but the foreman asked him, probably at the instigation of the Manchester merchants, for this vitally important Charge the Lord Chief Justice had delivered orally to be formally written out in order to "convince and amend [rather] than punish this ignorant and much deluded Multitude."[35] The activities of the box clubs were not immediately ended however, and the weavers continued their dispute until the middle of October, although there were some arrests and one man from Salford was sent to prison for assaulting a weaver who had taken work from the Manchester merchants. Yet Mansfield's ruling had effectively ended the weavers struggle and given the Manchester masters a free hand to control the cotton industry on precisely their terms.[36]

The question remains, why did Mansfield not formally write his Charge to Grand Jury down for the record, given the vital importance of his interpretation of the law and with the full knowledge of its consequences? Also, on the face of it, he had nothing to lose as he views on the need for free trade were well known. We get some indication of Mansfield's reluctance to write his Charge out and,

---

29 Ibid, (August, 1758) p 391.
30 *Whitworth's Manchester Advertiser and Weekly Magazine*, 29 August, 1758.
31 Percival op cit, p 5.
32 *Whitworth's Manchester Advertiser and Weekly Magazine*, 29 August, 1758.
33 National Archives, Kew, Palatinate Papers, Lancashire, Indictments, P.L. 26. 39/1.
34 *Whitworth's Manchester Advertiser and Weekly Magazine*, 5 September, 1758.
35 Ibid.
36 Ibid.

indeed, have it published first of all from the response of the masters. They were desperate for Mansfield to make an official written statement of his decision and his actions. They needed this as a matter of law in case of any future problems. In their original advertisement against the weavers and their combination they ended by saying that, if they did not disband their organisation the weavers "will be prosecuted as the Law directs". This is interesting phraseology. They do not say as the 'statute' directs but in terms of the much more vague 'Law' directs. Yet what law were they attempting to enforce? They probably knew (or at least the person who drew up the wording for the advertisement knew) that the statute law covering the textile trades and worker combinations did not cover the cotton branch of the trade but only the woollen sector. According to established common law it was perfectly legal for an individual worker to challenge the terms of his employment by a master or, indeed, his rates of pay, but when this was done in combination with other workers it was illegal, as it represented a conspiracy.[37] But Mansfield's legal biographer also tells us that in the absence of exact references or precedents in statute law, Mansfield presumed to prosecute under common law.[38] The framer(s) of the Manchester merchants' advertisement certainly knew precisely who they were intending to hear their claims and this judge would undoubtedly be favourable to their pleas. However, the main reason that Mansfield did not want to formally write down his Charge or be seen to create a legal precedent was that if he formally brought a charge of criminal conspiracy against the weavers and their conviction were ratified, then there was nothing to stop the weavers from bringing the same charges against the Manchester merchants, because they had been as much involved in a conspiracy as the weavers. Firstly, by collecting together as a group and then initiating the changes to piece lengths and prices, apprenticeship rules, and by their combining to put a stop to the weavers' box clubs; some of them were also accused of being involved in the scheme to engross grain and force up prices during 1757. This spirit of co-operation, or, indeed, conspiracy, was not unknown to these new men of industry, we saw, for example, in chapter two above that when it came to raising capital and organising the import of raw materials and the export of finished goods they had experience of combining together with others of their class to achieve their ends, and they had been doing so since the 1730s.

Yet Mansfield's ruling was, in one important sense, inconsistent with his purported concern for upholding the primacy of customary practices. The weavers could have easily proved that the operation of the Elizabethan Statutes as being a keystone of the way their trade had operated for over two hundred years – and apparently operated quite efficiently. Mansfield, however, let his economic doctrines govern his implicit belief in the practical and historical benefits of custom and precedence and to further ignore the old apprenticeship regulations in this sector of industry. But, as noted above, once the apprenticeship rules were abandoned, which they were sure that was the intention of the masters, then anyone could be employed in the cotton textile sector at the whim of the Manchester merchants for prices now solely determined by them. The remarkable equality of the sexes in this textile sector, with women receiving exactly the same terms as the men, serving and training apprentices just like the men, would also be gone. The Manchester merchants knew full well that the cheapest of all available labour were women and children and it was these sections of the population who were the easiest to discipline and

---

37 Oldham, op cit pp 1317-1318.
38 Ibid.

make accustomed the new processes which they were now free to apply.

The weavers strike lasted four and half months and it was as close to a demonstration of the actions of a 'class' as any of the disputes involving the working class in early nineteenth century. So bitter was this conflict and so complete was the defeat of the workers that, effectively, by 1760 the former position of the artisan weavers had been destroyed, and the position of the masters dramatically enhanced. This is why the events of the later 1750s are so important. In some ways these box clubs were an easy target, but one that in the past had been tentatively accepted by the employers and the authorities as long as they kept their box for the relief of poor weavers and not as combinations in their own protection against the actions of the seemingly avaricious masters. Yet the climate of war and the urgent need for international trading expansion, in addition to the dramatic enhancement of alternative perceptions of the overall functioning of the economy meant that the position of the textile workers of the North-West was now precarious. They were about to lose many – if not all – of their customary practices that were encapsulated in the Elizabethan Statutes. Their self-help organisation had been effectively outlawed and with it their only means of an adequate defence against the masters. This was an important first stage of the onset of capitalism and the industrial capitalists, as represented by the new masters, were now free to control as they pleased the only factor of production they had the effective means of controlling: the cost, organisation, productive efficiency and discipline of labour. If an industrial moral economy existed at all – and it the contention of this book that it did – then for the cotton workers of the North-West it was about to be significantly curtailed from August 1758. There could be no doubt the masters had won, but if anyone harboured any doubts then these were going to be scotched during the very next assize after Mansfield's manipulation of the law.

At the Lancaster assizes of March 1759 the indicted weavers appeared before a close colleague of Mansfield's and one who, like the Lord Chief Justice, shared his beliefs in the necessity of moves towards free trade and the primacy of capital over custom. Sir Michael Foster initially imposed on those indicted a token fine of one shilling, but he also gave them a salutary lesson in political economy. He told them in no uncertain terms what the indictments represented, but he did so in an interesting and subtle reinterpretation of the role of custom, by effectively turning it against the weavers who, in reality, were attempting to protect it; he forcefully reiterated Mansfield's judgement against the weavers, but the choice of words was interesting. They had been charged, he said, with "an unlawful Combination to raise the wages of your labour to a Pitch above what hath heretofore been *usual* and *accustomed*, [my emphasis] and more than the several Articles of Manufactory can possibly bear."[39] He went on to tell them that the offence with which they were charged and their actions, if left unchecked, would have resulted in "the most dreadful Consequences: It would have ruined that Branch of Manufacturing in particular in which you are concerned, and, by the iniquitous Schemes set on Foot, compelled the Traders therein to have removed their Capitals to a more happy Climate."[40] He then proceeded to pile on the guilt of the recalcitrant weavers by noting the war and "this Time of Distress", saying that their actions could have meant that "some foreign Nation rob us of the Jewel..." of trade and manufacturing. He eventually moved on to question the utility of the old Elizabethan Statutes in this now

---

39 *Manchester Mercury,* 3 April, 1759.
40 Ibid.

modern age, but not before he had reinforced the need for the reassertion of the social order, which he suggested was really the most damning aspect of the weavers' social insubordination in having the effrontery of effectively confronting the masters as a *class* to oppose to their actions.

> And there seems the greater Reason to have feared their [the weavers] Success, in such Attempt, as such Confederacies would have occasioned the greatest Confusion betwixt the lower Class of People and their Superiors, in all Trades and Occupations, in every Manufactory, and in every Employ. If Inferiors are to prescribe to their Superiors, if the Foot aspire to be the Head ... without Restraint or Control, to what End are Laws enacted? And how plainly Appears the Subversion of the most happy Constitution the known World can boast of? And yet I wish I could say that there was no strange Infatuation amongst the lower Class of People to imbibe these Notions. In the present Case, if a Company of Weavers must lay down the Rules to be observed by their Employers, under pain of their not working at all; their Demands (as it appears) will be too great and extravagant for the Trade to support, and consequently destroy it.[41]

He then specifically dealt with the apprenticeship question, with words that must have sounded like angels singing in heaven to the masters. He said that if the apprenticeship rules were continued, then eventually "particular Trades will be lodged in a few Hands, to the damage of the Publick; and that Liberty of setting up Trades, (the Foundation of the present flourishing Condition of Manchester) destroyed."[42] Foster continued:

> In the Infancy of Trade, the Acts of Queen Elizabeth might be well calculated for the publick Weal; but now, when it is grown to that Perfection we see it, it might perhaps be of Utility to have those Laws repealed, as tending to cramp and tye down that Knowledge it was at first necessary to obtain by Rule... Therefore all Combinations of this Kind and Nature, are to be guarded against as much as possible; and it is the indispensable Duty of everyone, as a Friend to the Community to endeavour to suppress them in their Beginnings...[43]

The indicted weavers were ultimately fined one shilling and severely warned as to their future conduct, with the judge giving them the parting message they should count themselves fortunate, as the punishment for their offences could have been very much greater.

The masters had won a comprehensive and decisive victory. They were now clear to suppress the weavers' attempts at organisation, to employ who they liked without any apprentice regulations, and to decide on the methods of payment without the weavers' recourse to arbitration by magistrates. However, although the check-weavers had been decisively defeated in January 1759, the smallware weavers embarked on a strike and the masters flexed their now powerful muscles. They issued a proclamation saying that all those involved would be given no work in the future and they would be prosecuted.[44] The masters were true to their word and twelve smallware worsted weavers were arrested and indicted for combining.[45] They were held at Lancaster for over fourteen months

---

41 Ibid.
42 Ibid.
43 Ibid.
44 *Manchester Mercury,* 9 January, 1759.
45 Manchester Constables Accounts, Vol. III, pp 106-107.

before the case came before the assizes in March 1760 and they were then encouraged to make a submission of contrition whereby the court would show leniency. They promised they would, in the future, work for the wages already agreed on by the masters, that they would never organise a combination, and that they would destroy their box.[46] They were then released. There were some weavers at Wigan and Kendall later in 1760 who attempted combinations to improve conditions and shorten the hours of work, but these too were soon repressed.[47]

Yet it was not merely the cotton workers who were in dispute during the crucial period from the mid-1750s into the 1760s. In July 1753 the building workers of Manchester were in dispute with their employers regarding changes in wages, and on this occasion the magistrates stepped in to conciliate and mollify the two sides in the classic style of the moral economy. As the *Gentleman's Magazine* reported:

> July 6 Manchester. The journeymen carpenters here have left their work, and obstinately persist not to return except their master augment their wages; and this morning the bricklayers and their labourers followed their example. A great number of them were this afternoon before justice Birch, who earnestly urged them to return to work till the next quarter-sessions, for the common wages, and then the bench of justices would take that affair under consideration; but they were not in the least satisfied with what the justice said; so that building is at present entirely suspended in this place.[48]

As well as a series of serious disturbances in and around Manchester there were also severe episodes of popular protest in Liverpool. In June, 1756, the tailors were defending their rights to the old apprenticeship laws and the establishment of their box clubs.[49] At the same time the city's shoemakers went on strike against their masters over a reduction in their wages and they alleged the masters had formed a combination to act in concert to force wages down, which the journeymen then accused them of acting illegally, which again harks back to why Mansfield in the case of the check-weavers of the North-West did not bring charges of illegal conspiracy against them as they likewise could have turned this charge back onto the masters.[50] Working people clearly understood exactly what their rights were and knew exactly when they were being infringed. Later in 1756 the shoemakers of Chester struck work, claiming the same wage rates as those paid in Liverpool and Manchester.[51] Back at Liverpool and again in 1756 the coppersmiths and pewterers struck over the training of new workers who were not apprentices.[52]

The disputes of 1757 to 1760 had resulted in a complete victory for the Manchester merchants. They were now totally free to conduct and organise their branch of the cotton textile trade as they saw fit and, as such, they could begin the process of dismantling the old customary practices of the workers. Probably the most important element in their victory was that the masters had effectively

---

46 *Whitworth's Manchester Advertiser and Weekly Magazine,* 25 March, 1760.
47 *Williamson's Liverpool Advertiser,* 29 August, 1760, see also PRO Palatinate Papers, P. L. 26. 39/2, 39/3.
48 *Gentleman's Magazine, pp. 342-343.*
49 *Williamson's Liverpool Advertiser,* 25 June, 1756, and 2 and 23 July, 1756.
50 Ibid, 25 June, 2 July, 9 July, 16 July, 1756.
51 Ibid 19 November, 1756.
52 Ibid 20 August, 1756.

removed the barrier of the seven years apprenticeship. This de-skilled the workers in the cotton sector, their status as artisans was devalued, the equality of the working relationship between males and females, which had been such a unique feature of this branch of textiles, could now be dismantled. Probably only marginally less important as the loss of the apprenticeship provision which guaranteed their craft status and their control of the entry to the trade was the diminishing of the role of the country magistracy which, to a significant extent, had maintained the industrial moral economy for so long. As noted above, this had been seriously undermined by Mansfield's ruling and the master's tactics at discrediting Thomas Percival. His name was removed from the Lancashire Commission of the Peace, not by the Court of the Kings Bench but by his death at the age of forty three in 1762. One final thing of significance came out of this for the weavers and, indeed, others of labouring population, without recourse to the magistracy to offer impartial judgement, working people knew they would have to act for themselves, which moved them significantly further along to becoming, in a meaningful sense, a viable class.

The cotton merchants could now begin to introduce new innovations that would enhance production and put into effect the preparations that would soon lead to the conducting of their businesses along lines more akin to modern capitalism. But the memories of those workers involved in the disputes remained and lasted long in the collective consciousness of the working class. The *Manchester Guardian* of December, 1876, recounted the story of a doctor from Clifton, near Salford, who, in 1826, recalled what he had been told about the strike of 1758. He said one worker "old Tom Boardman was hung up in a wisket (a wicker basket) in a great oak tree for fetching work out to weave, contrary to the weavers' agreement with one another."[53]

The famous or infamous upshot in the struggle to maintain the essential ethos of the moral economy in legal terms came in 1800-01 with the Waddington and Rusby cases. As Douglas Hay tells us, in these cases brought by prosecution in the Court of the King's Bench was effectively the trial of Adam Smith and, more specifically, what he had to say regarding food shortages and famine in *Wealth of Nations*. Waddington, a Jacobin brewer, and Rusby, a London corn merchant, became a *cause célèbre* and the pivotal moment in the defence of the moral economy in legal terms under common law. The guiding legal driving force behind these cases was the new Lord Chief Justice Kenyon, who believed implicitly in the most "practical usefulness of prosecutions for forestalling, regrating and engrossing". Like country gentlemen for centuries past, he knew that the promise of such prosecutions was often enough to stop a riot.[54] He reacted with Burke's (in his view) blasphemous sentence, that 'the laws of commerce, which are the laws of nature, and consequently the laws of God' made in his 'Thoughts on the Present Discontent...' As Kenyon put it, the essence of morality was not in making money by exploiting the starving, but in upholding 'Our (common) law [which], thank God, is the same with the divine.'[55] Yet this turned out to be only a slight and not very long-lasting victory and in the sphere of industrial relations the old views of the nature of the equitable operation of the employer/worker relationship was effectively dead. Yet

---

53 *Manchester Guardian*, 26 December, 1876.
54 D. Hay, 'Moral Economy, Political Economy and the Law', in A. Randall, and A. Charlesworth, (eds.), *The Moral Economy and Popular Protest: Crowds, Conflict and Authority*, (London: Macmillan, 2000) p. 109 and pp. 107-112.
55 Ibid, p. 109.

the values entrenched in the traditional practices of the moral economy did not go down without a fight and if there was one decade in which this battle was most severe it was during the 1760s.

10

Mass Protest in the 1760s: The Provisioning Sector

With the growth of ideas and the initial implementation of new microeconomic practices surrounding, especially, cotton manufacturing but also generally encompassing trade and commerce, there came the concomitant conflict between masters and men which, in turn, was associated with the general status of working people and the perceived loss of their intrinsic rights. This was the position at the death of the old king in October 1760 and the accession to the throne of a young man with an apparent openness and the outward absence of many of the disagreeable encumbrances of the previous two Hanoverians. This was coupled with the very real possibility that an end to the Seven Years War might actually be in sight. It thus appeared to contemporaries that this was a bright new chapter in British social, political and economic development, because here for the first time in almost a hundred years was a monarch who gloried in being born and, indeed, simply being English.[1] Yet despite this promising beginning the actuality was that in the decade of the 1760s the incidence of popular protest, for a variety of grievances, was arguably the most numerous and occasionally intense of any time within the entire eighteenth century. During the 1760s, as well as the on-going disputes regarding work practices in the North-West, there were a range of issues which found the crowd mobilising across the nation. Thus, in order to convey an impression of the pressures facing ordinary men and women as the features of industrial and commercial modernity encroached more and more on their lives, we will widen our discussion at this point to evaluate not only the nature of the situation developing in and around Lancashire and the cotton sector but also to briefly discuss conditions nationally. This is necessary in order to convey the nature of the issues that prompted many law abiding, ordinary people to protest in order to get the attention of the elites and highlight their complaints regarding their occupational status, the old problem of provision shortages and, at this stage, the changing nature of politics. Although, as we shall see, there were serious protests surrounding politics and elections, the actions of magistrates and the mustering of the militia, by far the most numerous disturbances were those associated with provisioning, land use and, once again, industrial disputes.

Food riots predominated the incidents of disputes during the 1760s as they had in the previous decade, but it should be noted that those involved in the production of food were themselves undergoing momentous changes to their customary work practices which would have an impact on their lives just as dramatically as it did the weavers of North-West. To set in context just how fundamental these changes were to agricultural workers in relation to those in the industrial sectors it is worth digressing momentarily to discuss the pressures they were facing at the same time as the changes affecting the industrial out-workers. This will give credence to the argument that considerable sections of the British workforce were undergoing processes of major change which significantly informed their class position in terms of the perceived need to visibly and demonstrably protest. In fact, the whole productive process from start to finish, from tilling the land in preparation for planting the crops to the marketing of the

---

1 Thomas Somerville, *My Own Life and Times, 1741-1814*, (Edinburgh, 1861) p. 52.

grain and the milling of the flour through to it being sold in markets across the country was open to corruption and malpractice. Yet Britain, as we approach the 1760s, was still effectively an agrarian country with the majority of its population living in a rural or semi-rural setting and the vast majority of its working population reliant on the land for their subsistence, at least for some part of the year. As more and more of this agricultural land began to be enclosed and the old practices discarded in favour of more labour efficient methods of the production of food at all levels a significant number of workers were facing a very precarious future. The right to maintain and allow customary practices and common rights to be upheld in this sector was, in the final analysis, always with those who owned or controlled the land, thus once again this was about power. As one historian who examined the changing nature of eighteenth century customary practices in Westmorland explained, it was about class and it was about conflict:

> Custom, then, was not something fixed and immutable, carrying the same body of meaning for both social classes. On the contrary, its definition was highly variable in relation to class position, and accordingly it became a vehicle for conflict not consensus. A final observation that needs to be made about the conjunctural pressures sustaining the structurally antipathetic relations binding lord to peasant in Cumbria is that they were not peculiar to this region alone. In other parts of the country where the customary economy of small farmers and cottagers still survived, the enlargement of its antithesis, the market economy, gave rise to a revolutionary and destructive attitude towards custom among the aristocratic and gentry landowning class.[2]

In terms of those workers involved in the production of food, the enclosure of common land has been a source of intense historiographic debate, which could in itself be another book but it is worthy of a brief summation, as it offers a relevant contrast to the nature of change in the industrial sector. The traditional argument ran that it was in the seventeenth century that the pace of agricultural change became initially meaningful with the adoption of new methods of fertilisation, land use, productive techniques and the deployment of crops, yet this was accelerated during the eighteenth century.[3] At the start of the twentieth century John and Barbara Hammond produced the argument that as a direct result of the efforts of Commissions of Enclosure agricultural labourers were effectively stripped of their customary rights to common land and, in strict legal terms, this was affected quite easily when no titled legal rights could be found. This allowed rationalization of land use in order to deny access to ordinary labourers and effectively permitted quite large tracts of land that had formerly been held in common for all to use to be placed in the possession of private landowners and landlords. The key point to note is that the vast majority of these labourers depended on the use of this land for their very survival. Once again, as with the out-workers of the cotton sector in Lancashire, these agricultural

---

2 C. E. Searle, 'Custom, Class Conflict and Agrarian Capitalism: The Cumbrian Customary Economy in the Eighteenth Century', *Past & Present*, 110 (1) (Feb., 1986) pp. 106-133, pp. 120-121. See also R. W. Bushaway, *By Rite: Custom. Ceremony and Community in England, 1700-1880* (London: Breviary Stuff, 2011), pp. 10.

3 The literature on this subject is huge, but to gauge the essence see, J. Thirsk (ed.), *The Agrarian History of England and Wales*, (Cambridge: Cambridge University Press, 1967), E. L. Jones (ed.), *Agriculture and Economic Growth in England, 1650-1815*, (London: Methuen, 1967), J. D. Chambers and G. E. Mingay, *The Agricultural Revolution, 1750-1880* (London: B. T. Batsford Ltd., 1966).

labourers lost a significant source of their independence in terms of their access to common land for grazing their livestock and growing their own produce and made them utterly dependent on an increasingly capitalist oriented land-owning class.[4] This traditional view was subsequently challenged with the argument that the traditional and customary use of the commons was economically inefficient in the effective productive capacity of such land.[5] The assertion was made that when enclosures took place it made the land more productive and was thus of benefit to consumers and the nation generally. The implication being that the old system was too regulated at all levels from initial productive inefficiency right through to regulatory marketing which allowed privileges to individual communities at the expense of the many who required more food and cheaper food. That, in effect, economic rationalisation along lines of greater economic freedom associated with the dictates of political economy would, via the ubiquitous 'invisible hand', assure greater benefit to all at the expense of the unfortunate but economically backward few who were deemed expendable. As one early nineteenth century supporter of a free trade in provisioning, Thomas Malthus, and himself not only an Anglican cleric but also political economist from the University of Oxford, put it:

> Why are the cattle on a common so puny and stunted? Why is the common itself so bareworn and cropped so differently from the adjoining enclosures? If a person puts more cattle into his own field, the amount of the subsistence which they consume is all deducted from that which was at the command of his original stock; and if, before, there was no more than a sufficiency of pasture, he reaps no benefit from the additional cattle, what is gained one way, being lost in another. But if he puts more cattle on a common, the food which they consume forms a deduction which is shared between all the cattle, as well that of others as his own, and only a small part of it is taken from his own cattle.[6]

Yet the fact was, and Malthus conveniently omits to mention, that those who benefited most from enclosures were already substantially wealthy landed elites, and they used this newly acquired land as forms of rental income. This was a process which served to 'prolentarianise' agricultural labourers, within which they exploited in exactly the same ruthless way as the Manchester merchants were proletarianising the North-West weavers.[7] Just as capital encroached on the

---

4 J. L. and Barbara Hammond, *The Village Labourer, 1760-1832* (London, 1911, Reprinted 1995), pp. 26-42, 97-105; J. D. Chambers and G. E. Mingay, *The Agricultural Revolution, 1750-1880* (London: B. T. Batsford Ltd., 1966), pp. 88-104; J. D. Chambers, 'Enclosure and the Labour Supply in the Industrial Revolution', *Economic History Review*, 2nd ser., v (1953), J. H. Porter, 'The Development of Rural Society', in G. E. Mingay (ed.), *The Agrarian History of England and Wales*, vi, *1750-1850* (Cambridge: Cambridge University Press, 1989), pp. 848-55, 860-6, also his *Parliamentary Enclosure in England. An Introduction to its Causes, Incidence and Impact, 1750-1850* (London: Routledge, 1997), pp. 148-58; E. C. K Gonner, *Common Land and Inclosure* (London: Cass, 1966), 259-79; J. A. Yelling, *Common Field and Enclosure in England, 1450-1850* (London: Palgrave, 1977), 94-119.
5 For example see M. Overton, *Agricultural Revolution in England: The Transformation of the Agrarian Economy 1500-1850*, (Cambridge, Cambridge University Press, 1996) re-asserts the case for revolution after 1750.
6 William, F. Lloyd, *Two Lectures in the Checks to Population*, (Oxford: Oxford University Press, 1833). Lecture One, p. 30.
7 Between 1750 and 1790 Professor Mingay found that rents increased from between 40% and 50% and that between 1790 and 1815 from between 80% and 90% increases on the previous rises. G. A. Mingay, 'The Course of Rents in the Age of Malthus' in M. Turner, (ed.) *Malthus in his Time*, (Basingstoke: Palgrave Macmillan, 1986) pp. 90-91.

customary work practices prompted resistance by the Lancashire weavers so the agricultural labourers and small farmers similarly attempted to construct a defence mechanism based on protest and community action. Such features were the concern of an influential and in some way controversial article by Robert Brenner in 1976, 'Agrarian Class Structure and Economic Development in Pre-Industrial Europe'.[8] Here Brenner plotted how the development of the broad sweep of change affected the agrarian systems across Europe from the medieval period to that of the eighteenth century. At which point, and specifically in the case of England, he tells us, "in my view, it was the emergence of the classical landlord-capitalist-tenant-wage labour structure which made possible the transformation of agricultural production in England, and this, in turn, was the key to England's uniquely successful overall economic development."[9] After the manumission of serfdom in England and over a period of several centuries ordinary agricultural workers were unable to gain the necessary rights of freehold to determine their own futures. Over these centuries the nature of property rights were increasingly controlled by the landlords and the possession of land were seen as a necessary pre-condition to access into the gentry class, as well as the aristocracy. The system developed whereby the landlords, in order to 'improve' their holdings and make them more intrinsically valuable, would engross, consolidate and enclose the land. Then they would lease increasingly larger parcels of their land to substantial capitalist tenants, the so-called yeoman famers, who in turn, with the security of long or copyhold leases, would continue the capitalisation process through further investments. According to Brenner:

> This was the indispensable precondition for significant agrarian advance, since agricultural development was predicated upon significant inputs of capital, involving the introduction of new technologies and a larger scale of operation. Such higher levels of agricultural investment were made feasible through the development of a variety of different lease holding arrangements, which embodied a novel form of landlord-tenant relationship. By virtue of these arrangements the capitalist tenants entered into essential partnership with landlords. They were assured that they could take a reasonable share of the increased revenue resulting from their capital investments and not have them confiscated by the landlords' rent increases. They were therefore set free to bring in those key technological innovations, most especially convertible husbandry systems ... as well as to make sizeable investments in farm facilities, which were generally far less practicable on small unenclosed farms operated by peasants.[10]

Increasingly the small holdings were swallowed up or enclosed, as were the commons, and small-holders became effectively waged labourers. In fact and in law the industrial workers were in a stronger position than those in the agricultural sector because their customary work practices were sanctioned in the guild system or statute law – even though the argument by the mid-eighteenth century was that such statutes were out-dated – whereas the agricultural worker possessed little actual law to back up their customary, or probably more accurately described as manorial, rights. Instead, although arguably the process

---

8 R. Brenner, 'Agrarian Class Structure and Economic Development in Pre-Industrial Europe', *Past & Present*, 70 (1) (Feb., 1976), pp. 30-75.
9 Ibid, p. 63.
10 Brenner, op cit. pp. 63-64. See also E. Kerridge, *Agrarian Problems of the Sixteenth Century and After*, (London: Routledge, reprint, 2013), and E. L. Jones. 'Agriculture and Economic Growth in England, 1660-1750: Agricultural Change', *Journal. Of Economic History.*, xxv (1965).

of proletarianisation began earlier for agricultural workers, the nature of custom and the manner in which landlords (up to 1815 at least) required access to a fairly substantial labour force, (which, at some levels they were required to protect), meant that the relationship between the two was often less fraught than that in the industrial sectors.

Yet working people in both the agricultural and industrial sectors were suspicious of the 'rationalisation' changes which informed the decisions being made by those commissioning enclosures. This was also true regarding the repealing of the statutes on regrating, engrossing and forestalling or changing customary industrial practices affecting apprenticeships, workers independence, the introduction of labour saving innovations and factories. All such 'innovations' threatened the very essence of the work done by working people, their communities and, indeed, their lives. It is one of the most enduring and self-sustaining myths that the introduction of the body of theory and practices associated with political economy from Smith's time onwards resulted eventually in greater freedom and improved living standards for working people. This is certainly not the case for the working class in the industrial North-West during the seventy years after the publication of *Wealth of Nations*. As the factory system gathered pace, enhanced technological innovation, such as the application of steam power, meant that more and more workers were forced out of the setting of domestic production into the urban environment. Here they lived in cheap jerry-built housing, cheek by jowl, with little or no clean water or sanitation, often all the family (including young children) working long hours in the factories with no guards on dangerous machinery. Unsurprisingly the life expectancy of working people plummeted.[11] To give another example, if one takes the price of bread and the campaign to remove the state interference of the Corn Laws which epitomised the so-called 'Manchester School' and the Anti-Corn-Law League, one can see that the overwhelming majority of working people did not believe the promises of these advocates. From the outset working people were suspicious that if cheaper food prices did result in the removal of these laws, the likely result would be that their wages would be in turn reduced to enable the capitalists to realise even more profit. Likewise, it made more sense for traditionalistic tory sentiments held by some working people that the maintenance of the Corn Laws, even though they benefitted the rich landowners, meant that Britain was not reliant on a potential enemy for the supply of her grain. And the fact was that the price of bread was not as significantly reduced when the Corn Laws were repealed in 1846 so much as when the Great Plains of the United States began to export grain that could potentially feed the entire world at reasonable prices.

The defence of customary practices was a significant part of Edward Thompson's argument and in the agricultural sector, particularly in the work of

---

11 See for example P. Gaskell, *The Manufacturing Population of England*. (London, 1833), pp.161-162, 202-203 "Factory labour is a species of work, in some respects singularly unfitted for children. Cooped up in a heated atmosphere, debarred the necessary exercise, remaining in one position for a series of hours, one set or system of muscles alone called into activity, it cannot be wondered at–that its effects are injurious to the physical growth of a child. Where the bony system is still imperfect, the vertical position it is compelled to retain, influences its direction; the spinal column bends beneath the weight of the head, bulges out laterally, or is dragged forward by the weight of the parts composing the chest, the pelvis yields beneath the opposing pressure downwards, and the resistance given by the thigh-bones; its capacity is lessened, sometimes more and sometimes less; the legs curve, and the whole body loses height, in consequence of this general yielding and bending of its parts."

Jeanette Neeson.[12] Here the use of custom over centuries meant that it became part of the very fabric of existence of rural workers operating on the very cusp of subsistence. The fact that those bringing commissions of enclosure could use the body of existing law to force their claims was pure expediency, and they were often perceived as a self-serving interest over long-held custom which served the benefit of all the community, regardless of the arguments that they would bring enhanced efficiency of land-use. Yet again it was an example of the dominant class using the law to overcome the perceived rights of the powerless. One recent writer has questioned Thompson and Neeson's interpretation of their use of custom.[13] Sara Birtles argued that their "writing elevated custom, which they construe to be an actual practice, to the level of peasant law, which they use to rival statute and common law deployed by property owners in justifying drastic economic and social change."[14] She continues:

> Custom, they imply, is morally superior because it evolved slowly and organically over the centuries and because it informed the traditions and relationships that lay at the very heart of rural society. Although the same claims could be made for the common law, the new orthodoxy maintains that the established legal framework was fundamentally unjust – the tool chosen by the powerful to deny the rights of the powerless. This interpretation, however, presupposes that the use-rights exercised by the poor were of ancient origin and that they developed slowly within a manorial context. A close examination of enclosure documents, local poor relief and charity records, however, shows that many of the rights exercised by the landless were in fact extra-manorial and of comparatively recent origin: the result of the practical implementation of statutory poor relief.[15]

This use of custom by labourers in the sphere of obtaining poor relief in times when agricultural work was always, at best, seasonal by its very nature and was not an especially novel feature of the eighteenth century, indeed a good case can be made that the inception of the Tudor and Stuart statutes regarding the Old Poor Law were put in place to offset this regular seasonal anomaly. As for the extra-manorial nature of some customary practices, Birtles is correct, but rather more in specific examples than in terms of a general rule. Also in such places custom often took on an even more radically independent outlook than in parish or manorial districts. Take, for example, the Forest of Dean in Gloucestershire. This was a royal demesne and extra-manorial, but the nature of its much needed natural resources in timber and iron deposits meant it attracted settlers. Like the Kingswood district around Bristol, residents of the Forest of Dean gained a reputation of being lawless and ungovernable. Under the Protectorate the Forest was administered more efficiently, and after the Restoration, Charles II's

---

12 E. P. Thompson, *Customs in Common* (London: Merlin, 1991), 97-184; also his *Whigs and Hunters* (London: Breviary Stuff, 2013 edn.), pp. 202-210; also his 'The Grid of Inheritance: A Comment', in Jack Goody, Joan Thirsk and E. P. Thompson (eds.), *Family and Inheritance Rural Society in Western Europe, 1200-1800* (Cambridge: Cambridge University Press, 1976); J. M. Neeson, *Commoners: Common Right, Enclosure and Social Change m England, 1700-1820*, (Cambridge: Cambridge University Press, 1993), 55-80, 158-84, and her 'The Opponents of Enclosure in Eighteenth Century Northamptonshire', *Past & Present*, 105 (1) (Nov., 1984) pp. 114-139. See also R. W. Bushaway, *By Rite: Custom, Ceremony and Community in England, 1700-1880* (London: Breviary Stuff, 2011 edn.), pp. 1-6, 17-19.
13 S. Birtles, 'Common Land, Poor Relief and Enclosure: The Use of Manorial Resources in Fulfilling Parish Obligations 1601-1834' in *Past & Present*, 165 (1) (Nov., 1999), pp. 74-106.
14 Ibid. p. 74.
15 Ibid. pp. 74-75.

government, committing itself to a policy of cultivation as a source of ship timber, half the demesne was enclosed under an Act of 1668, the ironworks and illegal squatters removed and evicted, and much more effective administrative developed. During the 18th century, however, governmental controls lapsed and the lack of local administration allowed encroachment, the stealing of wood and poaching to again become pre-eminent. Once again the squatters established hamlets on the edges of the demesne and it was estimated there were almost 600 dwellings by 1787. These settlers lived in undeveloped conditions even by eighteenth century standards, in scantily-built cottages, and the nonconformist preachers and evangelical clergy, who attempted to minister to them around 1800, equated the missions with that of bringing Christianity to the heathens.[16] These so-called 'free miners' were as notorious in their dealings with the authorities as their counterparts in Kingswood, on the outskirts of Bristol. In the West of England in the especially bad shortage year of 1740 the inhabitants of Dean scoured the district for corn factors and millers, coupled with attacks on the properties of millers seemingly with impunity.[17] Likewise, in 1756 the colliers of Dean joined other locals in stopping a barge laden with grain and carried away 600 bushels before the arrival of the military.[18] During the disputes surrounding the Cider Tax in 1763, as with the Kingswood colliers ten years previously, they also took a prisoner, on this occasion an excise officer, and held him captive in one of the mines.[19] Importantly, it appears that it was not their perceived rights at defensive actions, derived in some way from the Poor Laws, that drove these people to act, but rather their inherent belief that their very survival justified their actions in common law, and they further believed that such actions would receive the empathy of the authorities sitting on the magisterial bench.[20] Rather more importantly, regarding such specific cases as that of the Forest of Dean, it was highly likely that the majority of the inhabitants in such areas that bordered on, but were not actually part of, established parish districts would not have rights of settlement and thus very often would not be entitled to claim poor relief, which meant again that their exploiting of resistance based on custom was their only recourse to their survival.[21]

Thompson, in fact, never asserted that these agrarian customary practices were something historically fixed and rigid over time, unlike, say, the perception the industrial workers of the North-West, who believed their customary practices had been determined for centuries in both statute and common law. The

---

16 *A History of the County of Gloucester: Volume 5, Bledisloe Hundred, St. Briavels Hundred, the Forest of Dean*. A. P. Baggs and A. R. J. Jurica, 'Forest of Dean: Introduction', in C. R. J. Currie and N. M. Herbert (eds.), *A History of the County of Gloucester: Volume 5, Bledisloe Hundred, St. Briavels Hundred, the Forest of Dean*, (London: Victoria County History, 1996), pp. 285-294.
17 *Gloucester Journal,* 5 and 12 February, 1740.
18 *Bath Journal*, 20 December, 1756 and National Archives, *War Office Papers*, WO/4.52, Mayor of Bristol to War Office.
19 *Bath Journal*, 25 July, 1763, see also A. Randall, *Riotous Assemblies*, op cit. pp. 62, 108, 154.
20 The token fines of £5 to those guilty of the most flagrant violations against the property of millers in 1740 suggests that the authorities had sympathy with the actions of the inhabitants of the Forest of Dean,
21 See for example, Anon, *The Laws and Customs of the Miners in the Forest of Dean in the County of Gloucestershire*, (London: William Cooper, 1687), or Sir Robert Atkynes, *The Ancient and Present State of Gloucestershire*, Second Edition, (London: W. Herbert, 1768), and looking specifically at the lack of poor law provision, Gloucestershire County Archive, The Correspondence of the Reverend John Foley and Charles B. Bathurst, regarding the relief of the extra-parochial poor in the Forest of Dean, (1801), D421. X/5.

situation for agrarian workers was indeed much more tenuous in legal terms, as Thompson himself explained:

> Agrarian custom was never fact. It was ambience. It may best be understood with the aid of Bourdieu's concept of "habitus" – a lived environment comprised of practices, inherited expectations, rules which both determined limits to usages and disclosed possibilities, norms and sanctions both of law and neighbourhood pressures. The profile of common right usages will vary from parish to parish according to innumerable variables... Within this habitus all parties strove to maximise their own advantages. Each encroached on the usages of others. The rich employed their riches, and all the institutions of awe and local authority. The middling farmers or yeoman sort, influenced local courts and sought to write stricter by-laws as hedges against both large and petty encroachments; they could also employ the discipline of the poor laws against those beneath them ... the peasantry and the poor employed stealth, a knowledge of every bush and by-way and the force of numbers.[22]

Yet all too often enclosures hit the poor and the semi and unskilled agrarian workers the hardest as the denial or removal of custom and common rights were all that kept them from sliding under the level of bare subsistence, which to many of them was a very real possibility. As a process this was of course just as radical a change towards economic rational progress as those being implemented by the manufacturers of the North-West in their spheres of control and, similarly, it occasioned disturbances and the belief amongst those it affected that this process of change was about the need to exact greater profits and, at its most extreme, the pure greed of the exponents of such changes. Certainly the pace of change was increasing in the agrarian sector as it was in the industrial. Between 1730 and 1740 there were thirty nine Enclosure Acts passed in parliament, between 1740 and 1750 the figure was slightly less at thirty six acts, but between 1750 and 1760 the figure rises substantially to one hundred and thirty seven, and another significant increase between 1760 and 1770 of three hundred and eighty five acts and between 1770 and 1780 there were six hundred and sixty acts of enclosure passed in the House of Commons.[23] However, enclosure riots *per se* were less frequent than this increased pace presumes because, as Thompson and Neeson tell us, they were often accompanied by the use of other tactics, including petitioning, the lobbying of interested and possibly contending parties, (sometimes threatening) letter writing, the destruction of records and then onto to the guerrilla tactics of attacking surveyors *en masse*, pulling down fences, and riots which often did not involve the use of troops.[24] Yet Birtles does make a valid point that in these rural settings where face-to-face contact was part of the fabric of the community of high or low birth, the recourse to the use of the poor law (when it was available) could be used as a device to quieten and subdue a disgruntled local workforce or, indeed, be an intimidatory factor in achieving their quiescence.[25] However, the fact was that enclosure protests were, by their very nature, local and involved groups who were often numerically small and scattered. Thus, given that the numerical strength of crowd in demonstrating that

---

22 E. P. Thompson, 'Custom, Law and Common Right' in *Customs in Common*, (London: Merlin, 1991) pp. 102-103.
23 *Eighteenth-century Sessional Papers, The Harper Collection of Private Bills*, (1695-1814) Parliamentary Papers, House of Commons Papers.
24 Thompson, op cit pp. 120-121.
25 Birtles, op cit, pp. 74-75.

their grievances be addressed was a critical factor in the tactics of popular protest, the success of remonstrations against the effects of enclosure by a usually numerically small and localised groups were less successful than other types of crowd actions. A factor which is heightened when it is remembered that they were opposing some of the most powerful interests not only locally and regionally but also nationally, who now had the benefit of recently enacted statute law on their side. In the end these semi- and unskilled agricultural workers, probably the least powerful of all the eighteenth lower orders, were doomed to failure and to scratch out a living as best they could existing often as they did on the very edge of survival. Yet the battle for enclosure in the second half of the eighteenth century was another example of the march of market forces and as such was a class battle, as Edward Thompson once again reminded us:

> Custom was a place in which many interests contested for advantage in the eighteenth century. Ultimately, when the commons were enclosed, it was a place of unqualified class conflict. The law was employed as an instrument of agrarian capitalism, furthering the "reasons" of improvement. If it is pretended that the law was impartial, deriving its rules from its own self-extrapolating logic, then we must reply that this pretence was a class fraud.[26]

At the other end of the provisioning process, that concerning food distribution and marketing as opposed to its production, we know that the incidences of riot were much more frequent and the 1760s marked some of the most serious in terms of the sheer number of people involved and the apparent increasing desperation of such groups. Also, in terms of legality in this area, the protesters were on much surer ground than the defence of common rights and customary practices for agricultural labourers, as forestalling, regrating and engrossing were, until 1772 at least, prohibited by statute law and there were also a plethora of by-laws forbidding the adulteration of foodstuffs afforded by the *Book of Orders*. In the 1750s and for most of the 1760s the price of all grains used to make some form of bread, rye, oats, wheat, were rising, as was the preference for wheaten, preferably white, bread. Wages, as we have seen, were under stress in a range of occupations of working people. At Manchester the problems associated with the food riots and violent skirmishes of 1757 had not disappeared. In 1760 George Bramall, one of the corn dealers and a miller, who had been the principle object of the wrath of the Shudehill crowd in November 1757, suffered another attack by the crowd.[27] In July 1762 the crowd were back again, coming from Oldham, Saddleworth, and Ashton "and other Places adjacent". On Monday, 12 July, "a great number of disorderly persons entered this town, under pretence of regulating the prices of grain, flower [sic] and oatmeal, which had lately been very much advanced."[28] Yet the report tells us that they did not apply to local town leaders or magistrates to report their grievances but once again resolved to act as their own agents of change and redress. On this occasion their anger was such that they declared not only to set the fair price and to attack the suspected speculator in grain, but to kill him. The report continued that they were…

> … avowed their Intentions to murder a considerable Dealer in Corn. He

---

26 Thompson, op cit, pp. 175-176.
27 J. Higson, *The Gorton Historical Recorder* (Drolylsdon, 1852) p. 102.
28 *Manchester Mercury,* 17 July, 1762.

escaped their Fury, but they instantly set to Work, and plundered his Shop and Warehouse of all the Grain, Flower (sic) Beans and Oatmeal... They robbed his house entirely of all the furniture, and with Pick Axes, and other Instruments, which they brought in a Cart for that Purpose, destroyed the Window Frames, the Body of the House, and Part of the Front Wall, in the Course of which a Person lost his Life, by the Fall of Part of the Warehouse Furniture. Now being joined by a considerable Number of Women and Children, and a very few Townsmen, they attacked and plundered the Shop, Warehouse and House of another Dealer in Corn, and destroyed the Window Frames there likewise. From the last place they proceeded to Houses and Shops of other Dealers in, and Retailers of Corn, broke into them, drank all their Liquors, and carried off what Eatables they thought proper.[29]

As in 1757, the leading town authorities immediately got in touch with the Secretary of War in London and the commanders of the groups of militia nearest to Manchester, and as a result troops of the Flintshire and Cheshire militia arrived the following day. Several arrests were made and warrants issued for the apprehension of other suspects. According to the report in the *Manchester Mercury*, this was "one of the most daring Insults upon the power of well-ordered government that has been remembered," and in order to enforce the law over thirty special constables were enlisted. Once again the authorities responded in a similar manner to the aftermath of the 1757 Shudehill episode by making and widely publishing a commitment to punish any merchant who flaunted the statutes when on the Thursday following the riot the leaders of local government wrote:

> WHEREAS several reports have been brought to us of *George Bramall*, of *Manchester*, having long made a practice of buying Corn growing, and ingrossing Corn in an illegal Manner, This is to give Notice, that any Person or Persons will appear before us, and give such Evidence as shall enable us to convict the said *George Bramall*, of the said Practices, we will put the Laws strictly in Execution against him. JOHN BRADSHAW, JAMES BAYLEY, GEORGE LLOYD.[30]

Two days later Bramall responded to the pressure being brought upon him by the crowd and by his erstwhile friends in high local office by inserting an advertisement in the *Manchester Mercury* which said that it had 'industriously' been reported that he had frequently and unlawfully bought corn growing in the field before there was a chance for its open sale in the market:

> Whereby I have undeservedly sustained great Damages. Therefore to satisfy the Publick whether I have or not been guilty of the above Practices, and to do myself Justice, I hereby offer a Reward of Five Pounds to any Person who can and will prove the same against me.[31]

Unlike the immediate aftermath of the Shudehill incident, the efforts of both the local authorities and Bramall's pleas of innocence did not appease the working people of Manchester and its out-townships. By late August and September 1762 it was being reported that the crowd intended to return and "burn and destroy the said Town of Manchester."[32] On this occasion they targeted James Bayley, the

---

29 Ibid.
30 *Manchester Mercury*, 24 July, 1762.
31 Ibid.
32 *Manchester Mercury*, 21 September, 1762.

boroughreeeve of Manchester during the November, 1757 Shudehill incident. On 1 September he received a threatening letter and it tells us a great deal about the sentiments, desperation and utter fury of the crowd at this time. The letter is worth quoting in full with vernacular spelling intact:

> This is to acquaint you that We poor of Rossendale, Rochdale, Oldham, Saddleworth, Ashton have all mutually and firmly agreed by Word and Covinent and Oath to Fight and Stand by Each Other as Life doth last for We may as well all be hanged as starved to Death and to see ower Children weep for Bread and none to give them nor any likeness in ever mending wile You all take Part with Brammul and markits drops at all the princable markits elcewhere but take this for shure Maxon, That if You dont put those good Laws in Execution against all those Canables and Men Starvers That have the Curse of God and all honest Men both by Gods Laws and Mens Laws so take notice Bradshaw, Bailey and Lloyd the biggest Rogue of all Three I know You all have the Power to stop such vilonas Proceedings if your please and if You dont imaidatley put a stop and let us feel it by next Saturday We will murder You and all we have down in Ower Lifs and We will bring a Faggot and burn down all your Houses and Ware Houses and make Your Wifes Widdows and Your Children Fatherless for the Blood of Shul ede hill lyes cloose to Ower Harts and Blood for Blood we Require.[33]

Manchester in the early 1760s was once again rocked by the actions of the crowd, which appeared to many in positions of authority as exceeding the normal parameters of social protest.[34] According to the *Gentleman's Magazine*, writing some months later, "The licentiousness of the lower class of people was never more notorious than at present; in Ireland they are *levellers*,[35] in England they are *masters*. (Writer's emphasis)[36] This letter elicited a response from George Grenville, Home Secretary (North), to the effect that they would offer a pardon to any two of the July rioters and anyone associated with the threatening letter (but not the actual writer), and this was coupled with reward of fifty pounds offered by John Tipping and Henry Fielden, the two constables of Manchester, to "each of the Persons making such discovery or discoveries ... to be paid by them upon the Conviction of the offender or offenders."[37] At the end of September, 1762 a letter appeared in the *Manchester Mercury* extolling the virtues of political economy and free trade in a manner which would have been totally in tune with sentiments of the 'Manchester School' one hundred years later. The aim was to present the logic of the situation to the papers' readers in a way that offered ineluctable reasons why, in the topographic and economic sense,

---

33 Ibid.
34 *Gentleman's Magazine*, 15 July, 1763.
35 In Ireland in the 1760s, the 'Levellers' referred to by the *Gentleman's Magazine* were also known as the "Whiteboys". These were large groups of men, sometimes numbering in their thousands, wearing white smocks over their clothes who rode the countryside initially of Munster during the night burning barns, tearing down fences, and ham-stringing cattle. They also sought out the stewards the retainers of the landlord's and the tithe collectors. When they were caught, the groups remaining dispensed a form of people's justice sometimes in terrible acts of revenge. They further rode up to manor houses shooting through the windows and destroying property. At this time, many landlords barricaded their houses and had them guarded by teams of sentries. See for example S. Connolly, 'Jacobites, Whiteboys and Republicans: Varieties of Disaffection in Eighteenth-Century Ireland', *Eighteenth-Century Ireland*, Vol. 18, 2003, (Belfast: Queens University), p. 63-79.
36 *Gentleman's Magazine*, 15 July, 1763.
37 *Manchester Mercury*, 21 September, 1762.

Manchester, by its very geographic and situational sense, had to resort to measures such as engrossing and regrating. This piece of self-justifying propaganda went by the typically verbose eighteenth-century title of *Considerations relating to the Provision of Corn for the Consumption of Manchester, and the Country's lying North, West and East of it, 10 or 15 Miles Distance from it, referred to all well Wishers of their Country*.[38] The letter began by stating the obvious fact that the district around Manchester could not grow sufficient grain for the needs of this rapidly growing urban area. Thus corn merchants had to travel to areas of other counties to purchase the necessary and cheapest stocks of grain for consumption in Manchester, and, importantly, this had essentially always been the case. The writer continued:

> What remedy have we in this Case, but to fetch it in due Time, by Land or Water, from the Markets most advantageous to us, but this is call'd Ingrossing by the Mob, and those who join them in their groundless Complaints; groundless they are from them, because they themselves are the Cause of their Grievances: Let such alter their Conduct, and give no Obstruction to Grain coming to our Markets, and we shall always be supplied, on terms agreeable to the Plenty or Scarcity of the Year; but the way we have been Mobbing, is so far from any relief to us, that it has a direct Tendency to Distress; it will intimidate all Dealers from bringing Grain to our Market, as they cannot deal in it in Safety of their Lives and Fortunes: Every one of us therefore ought to give due Encouragement to all legal dealers in it, the more there are the more us brought to us, and the cheaper it will be, it is so in all Things, as speculative only they are certain Effects necessarily arising from the above premises: The Metropolis of this Kingdom has always been well supplied this way; France, Spain and Portugal, (when they are at Peace with us) are very frequently supplied with Grain from this Nation, and must we when we are in so much want of it have no Resource for our Relief.[39]

There was of course an element of truth in the central argument of the piece in that in non-corn-growing areas where large amounts of grain was brought in, purchased in bulk, often direct from the producer, was in strict terms contrary to the statutes against engrossing.[40] Yet when the price was rising, as was the case for much of the 1750s and 1760s, the tensions of ordinary consumers were heightened, especially, as in the case of Manchester, when there had been recent examples of shady dealings by corn merchants, dealers and millers. What principally concerned the crowd who were the subject of high prices was that in periods when such bulk buying was taking place the ordinary small-scale consumers were being held in a monopoly by these large merchants. Their reasoning was simple: in times of high prices over half a worker's wages were

---

38 *Manchester Mercury*, 28 September, 1762.
39 Ibid.
40 For more on the marketing of food, especially grain and the operation of the Corn Laws in the eighteenth century see, D. Barker, 'The Marketing of Corn in the First Half of the Eighteenth Century: North-East Kent', *The Agricultural History Review* Vol. 18, No. 2 (1970), pp. 126-150 A. Randall and A. Charlesworth, (eds.), *Markets, Market Culture and Popular Protest in Eighteenth-Century Britain and Ireland*, (Liverpool: Liverpool University Press, 1996) pp. 69-91, G. E. Fussell and C. Goodman, 'Traffic in Farm Produce in Eighteenth Century England', *Agricultural History*, Vol. 7, Number 2, (1938), J. Blackman, 'The Food Supply of an Industrial Town', *Business History*, Vol. 5, (1963), R. B. Westerfield, *Middlemen in English Business*, 1660-1760, (1915), N. S. B. Gras, *The Evolution of the English Corn Laws from the Twelfth to the Eighteenth Century*, (Cambridge, Mass., 1915), Barnes, D. G., *A History of the English Corn Market*, (London, 1930), C. R. Fay, *The Corn Laws and Social England*, (Cambridge, 1932).

spent purely on bread and this was occurring at a time when wage rates were at best static or being reduced.[41] Clearly, what the writer missed entirely were the grievances which the crowd were bringing to light by their protests. Popular protest over the price of essential foodstuffs or, as they were termed at the time, the 'necessaries of life', were not simply whether the corn dealer made a profit or whether that corn was being transported from a plentiful growing area to one where corn was not grown. These were seen as part of the process of food distribution and marketing. What the crowd were concerned with went back to the original basis of why the statutes, the *Book or Orders* and the Assize of Bread, were enacted in the first place. This was to ensure that in the corn growing regions the ordinary local population had reasonable access to affordable grain and other foodstuffs, and in the non-arable regions that, in times of dearth and high prices, the great mass of consumers were not held to ransom by unscrupulous profiteers deliberately exploiting the situation for pure greed and at the expense of the possibility of widespread starvation. Once again we are back to the nature and the prevailing historical attitudes surrounding the 'common weal'. What these attitudes signify were popular attitudes relating to the nature of mercantile protectionism, the prevailing and historic views of the paternalistic hierarchy of the duties of privilege, just and fair government at national and local levels, age-old legal positions based on statute and common law, and, once again, customary practices. The fact was (and still is) that the economic system based on principles of capitalism gives very little credence to any, if not all, of the above positions. The basic position of classical capitalist economics from Smith onwards was that if one allows markets to operate unfettered then the high prices (and profits) occasioned by periods of dearth or shortages will incentivise those producing such commodities to devise means by which such supplies can be produced more efficiently; thus alleviating the original situation. However, in the production of food, such considerations enter a different sphere of concerns. If the production of basic essential foodstuffs is allowed to be governed by pure market forces in times of shortage its sale and consumption will always gravitate towards those most able to pay the higher prices, thus denying the opportunity of those sections of the community to purchase such products at prices they can afford. Such a situation does not produce a free and open market as the classical economists believed would ensue but, in essence, a 'black market' whereby all such goods are transferred according to those best able to pay the inflated prices, thus by-passing normative 'rules' of supply and demand and, of course, if allowed to flourish, evading any legislative or other forms of regulatory controls. This argument lay at the heart of why the crowd in and around Manchester were demonstrating their anger, in that they, as the most financially vulnerable, were unable to cope with violent price fluctuations and actual availability of essential foodstuffs, and were constantly under threat of very real starvation and had been for some years.

    The troops drafted in, comprising of two sets of militia and a company of Sir Robert Rich's dragoons, did not leave Manchester until the end of March 1763. On 23 July, 1763, one man and four women were charged for activities surrounding the riots of the previous year, one woman was sentenced to be whipped and the other four to be transported for seven years. Yet clearly the

---

41 See the estimates found in D. Davies, *The Case of the Labourers in Husbandry*, (Bath, 1795), Sir F. Eden, *The State of the Poor*, (London, 1795) and for specific examples see, D. J. V. Jones, 'The Corn Riots in Wales, 1793-1801', *Welsh Historical Review,* Vol. 2, Number 4, (1965), Appendix 1, p. 347.

mood of the local working population in and around Manchester was volatile and the authorities had to be on their guard to ensure that the supply and, importantly, the price of essential foodstuffs remained affordable to the great mass of its population, at least in the short term, whilst the immediate shortages remained. Evidence that the crowd were dissatisfied with the way in which the authorities of Manchester dealt with these periods of pressure on the cost of food can be seen in the allegation of conspiracy of the leading merchants of the town and those in its administration in John Collier's *Truth in a Mask*, dating back to the 1757 disputes. Aitkin's *A Description of the Country from thirty to forty Miles round Manchester* as well the Earwaker's *The Court Leet Records of the Manor of Manchester* and his *Constable's Accounts for the Manor of Manchester* all confirm that up until the 1750s the local authorities were quite conscientious in their supervising of all the markets of Manchester and all the products sold in them. However, unless prompted by some crisis, such as the actions of ordinary local people, they were less diligent until the mid-1790s.[42] This would explain the propensity to protest by ordinary working people in and around Manchester as a means of nudging the authorities into action on their behalf, as they had first-hand experience that if left to themselves the local forces of government would do little because, in fact, the widespread belief was that the self-same forces of local authority were part of the profit mongering operation in the first place.

However, nationally, by far the most extensive riots concerning the marketing of food occurred in 1766. To a significant extent the discretion for the maintenance of civil order had been placed by the national state in the hands of those best placed to know and understand the situation prevailing in their part of the country, thus the role of the local institutions of maintaining order and upholding statute and common law was crucial. At the top were the Lord Lieutenants of the County, along with the High Sheriffs, down to the local magistracy, and, in towns and cities, the Court Leets and local councils, whose role was to ensure that normality prevailed in terms of the peaceful pursuance of commerce and trade in which each particular national region specialised. In times of disturbance these bodies had the power of arrest and to read the Riot Act; only as a last resort would there have been contact with the authorities in London for the deployment of troops. The chief reason for this was that it did not reflect well on aspiring local politicians or, indeed, any of those assuming the status of local leader to be seen as unable to manage a difficult situation. Hence the calling for troops signified very serious breakdown of local control and indicated, for example, that in the region around Manchester in the later 1750s and into the early 1760s the situation could indeed be regarded as serious. Thus it was at the discretion of the local forces of authority to bring the laws against forestalling, regrating and engrossing into effect during troubled times, and in normal times ensure that the Assize of bread be operational and all manner of foodstuffs be brought to market and generally offered for sale in an unadulterated form with the proper weights and measures assured. Undoubtedly, this was not an easy task for the local authorities given the nature and tendency of unscrupulous traders to seize every opportunity to enhance their profits, but at Manchester they had signally failed year upon year and this is why the crowd

---

42 John Collier (Tim Bobbin), *The Truth in a Mask or the Shudehill Fight*, (Manchester, 1758) pp. 1-3, J. P. Earwaker, *The Court Leet Records of the Manor of Manchester* (Manchester, 1888-1889) Vols., 7, 8, and 9, and by the same author, *Constable's Accounts for the Manor of Manchester*, (Manchester, 1892), pp. 212, and Vol. 2, p. 94.

were so volatile. But normally national government would only interfere in the most extreme and dangerous of circumstances. As we have seen, the principles of the British version of mercantilism were concerned first and foremost with the maritime nature of an island state, hence the maintenance of the Royal Navy for domestic and imperial security and to ensure trading routes, and a merchant fleet to bring in the primary products which Britain lacked and to convey the finished products all over the world. Trading practices, to a significant extent, started and finished with national policy formulated at Westminster. The primary aim was to extract duties, levies and customs through trade. Thus potentially any commodity was fair game for this model of ensuring the liquidity of the national coffers, including the export of grain, and as encouragement this government would pay a bounty to any dealer or merchant who could successfully trade in commodities which the state felt would stimulate its production and thus an overall increase of national wealth. However, in circumstances where a national shortage was likely, parliament could place an embargo on the export of crucial commodities, such as grain, and the point is that everyone knew this to be the case, including ordinary men and women. Such was the fluid nature of a trading situation, which in the case of the production of cereals, could often depend on conditions not under human control, such as the weather and the harvest, yet when shortages seemed likely – and this could be gauged by the monthly price indexes published in all the leading newspapers of the day – importantly the parliamentary installation of an embargo on grain was not put on a permanent footing. It was argued that the situation had to be monitored constantly, thus parliament initiated an annual standing order for, first of all, the importation of grain free of all duties and, secondly, (and of paramount importance to the crowd) the enactment of a grain export embargo to be initiated as soon as the circumstances – such as information on the projected harvest and the levels of prices – demanded action. However, parliament needed to be sitting to allow the standing order to come into effect; if it was not then the standing order lapsed and any sort of grain was available for export. This was precisely the situation which prevailed in the late summer of 1766. It is clear that the situation which developed was due in large part to the complete mismanagement at the highest level of government, which appeared to take no notice of a mounting, potentially widespread and very dangerous set of domestic disturbances.

In fact, the same problem had been seen in August 1765 when the ministry headed by the Marquis of Rockingham, whether by design or oversight, allowed the standing order to lapse. This meant a bonanza for corn merchants who had been importing grain from the continent duty free and could now export the same grain, and more besides, if they could find it, and be paid the government bounty of five shillings per quarter of corn exported. This situation triggered some disturbances in January and February 1766 in the coastal area of Lyme in Dorset and again at Winchester in Hampshire.[43] By the end of January, 1766 the government had acted to restore the *status quo,* but as it maintained the same practice of a standing order, this again was due to expire on 16 August, 1766. Throughout the spring and early summer adverse weather conditions presaged future problems over the potential harvest yields in grain, yet once again the government allowed the standing order to lapse. In the northern counties and in Scotland the yields were good but in the usually prodigious midland and

---

43 D.E. Williams, English hunger riots in 1766. Ph.D. Thesis, Wales (Aberystwyth), and by the same author, 'Morals, Markets and the English Crowd in 1766', *Past & Present*, 104 (1) (Aug., 1984), p. 62.

southern counties and across continental Europe the yields were drastically reduced and in many cases the grain proved, once harvested, to be so badly diseased as to be effectively unusable. Yet, relatively speaking, by far the largest aggregate yields for wheat were in the midlands and south of England, but the fact the yields were reasonable in the north does explain why there were so few reports of disturbances in those regions. The chief reason for the poor crops of the traditionally prodigious areas was the unusual weather patterns. From spring through the summer the northern areas were subject to lengthy periods of high pressure systems whilst in the midlands, the south of England and, effectively, the whole of continental Europe there was a succession of low pressure fronts that retarded the quality and the yields of the crops.[44] As soon as these features became clear substantial orders, regardless of what the cost would be, began to be received from Europe and corn dealers in the South of England were primed to, once again, make a fortune. By this time the leader of the government was William Pitt who now gloried in his new title of the Earl of Chatham, but throughout that summer he was busy 'politicking' to maintain his ministry and prevent its imminent collapse. By the end of that current parliamentary session it was too late and Chatham appeared to have recognised this as on the 10th September, when an awkwardly worded and clearly rushed proclamation was issued reiterating the old statutes against forestalling engrossing and regrating, knowing full well that he could not reinstate the standing order without parliament's approval. Yet on the same day as the proclamation was issued it was also made public that parliament would be prorogued six days later, which effectively meant that no restating of the standing order would be forthcoming for at least the next seven weeks, as the majority of members were leaving for their constituencies or their country residences. But still it remains a mystery why Chatham did not attempt to re-enact the standing order in the six days remaining. One reason could be that he believed philosophically or as a matter of policy that the incentive of the bounty, of using an open trade option in grain would stimulate growth in that sector; yet this was an impossibility in a mere six days. As a Whig whose platform had always been to expand the British empire for the benefit this would give the nation as a whole and indeed stimulate trade and commerce, this view of a more open trading system, now being supported by the early political economists such as Charles Smith, does have some credence.[45] Alternatively, and more realistically, it could have been that Chatham believed, now that he had accepted a peerage and moved up to the House of Lords, (which in itself lost him a massive amount of popular support), his support in the House of Commons was so weak that the members who remained would have thrown out the standing order as a means of throwing him out of office, his mantle having fallen so much in popular opinion.[46] Thus parliament rose on 16 September until 11 November and the embargo lapsed once again as the dealers began to rub their hands and looked forward to counting their enormous profits which they understood would be theirs in the intervening seven

---

44 D. E. Williams, 'Morals, Markets and the English Crowd in 1766', *Past & Present*, 104 (1) (Aug., 1984), pp. 62-64.
45 British Library, Newcastle Papers, (Ad Ms 32977), ff. 135, Smith to Townsend, (copied by Newcastle) 23 September, 1766. "I esteem the bounty on corn, the amendment of roads, among the great blessings our law procures for us, and beg what goes before, not be understood in the least to undervalue them. All that I mean, is to point out some effects they appear to me to have had; and which I do not remember to have seem remarked by others."
46 See, F. O'Gorman, *The Long Eighteenth Century, British Political and Social History, 1688-1832*, (London: Bloomsbury, 1997), p. 206.

weeks that parliament had risen. They now made preparations to export not only the old stocks of grain – which, once again, many of them had imported duty free and were laying in their warehouses – but the new stocks as well, and also they believed that the inaction of the government had given them *carte blanche* to do so. Yet the proclamation of 10 September, which was widely publicised, was a clear spur to the ordinary consumers of grain to be on their guard against forestallers, regraters and engrossers, especially those existing just above the levels of subsistence, which was the vast bulk of the labouring population.[47] What is amazing is that all the facts and the implications of what was happening and the seriousness of the worsening situation appeared too well known to all the major political figures (as well as the general public), which makes Chatham's action (or rather inaction) all the more inexplicable. It is also clear that the politicians of the mid-1760s were aware of the power of the crowd in such conditions of widespread distress and they further understood that it was imperative that remedial actions be taken as quickly as possible. The day after parliament had been prorogued the Duke of Newcastle wrote to the Marquis of Rockingham and said, "I hear the ministers are, and with reason, puzzled about the exportation of corn. If some method cannot be found to prevent it, before the Parliament meets, the consequences may be very bad." He went on to say that his nephew, the Chancellor of the Exchequer [Charles Townsend] and Dowdeswell [the previous Chancellor of the Exchequer] are "...out of humour; and even my Lord Shelburne [Home Secretary, South] is said to be not so well with the Minister [Chatham] as he was."[48] Four days later Newcastle received a letter from the Home Secretary (North), Henry Seymour Conway:

> My Lord as I think it is possible Your Grace may have received a summons a Committee of [the Privy] Council, the order being for all Lords in or in the neighbourhood of London. I think I owe Your Grace to inform you that the object of the Council is the great and repeated complaints and apprehensions from many different quarters on account of the excessive prices of corn and flower [*sic*] which under the licence of the late Corn Act in regard to any powers for a farther prohibition becomes a subject of the greatest difficulty and worthy of the utmost attention in all who are in a situation to give their advice or opinion in a matter of this high nature.[49]

Newcastle replied that he "looked upon this affair to be [of] such national concern, that tho' it may be inconvenient for me to go to London tomorrow, I shall not fail to attend the Council."[50] The same day as he received Conway's letter Newcastle wrote to Lord Winchelsea, informing him of the deteriorating circumstances and the urgency of this special meeting of the Privy Council: "this affair is of such national concern, that every part of the kingdom is so much affected by it, and that the City of London are making the strongest instances

---

47 For example one corn dealer commented that the proclamation initiated the distribution and wide publicity of the old statutes which were: "published in every newspaper, and stuck up in every corner, by order of the justices, to intimidate the engrossers, against whom many murmurings are propagated. The common people are taught to entertain a very high opinion and reverence for these laws..." Anon. *Reflections on the present High Price of Provisions, and the Complaints and Disturbances arsing therefrom*. (1766) Also cited in Thompson, *Customs in Common*, op cit, p. 209.
48 British Library, *Newcastle Papers*, (Ad Ms 32977) ff. 93-94, Newcastle to Rockingham, 17 September, 1766.
49 Ibid, Conway to Newcastle, ff. 120, 21 September, 1766.
50 Ibid, Newcastle to Conway, ff. 139, 23 September, 1766.

everywhere upon it, I am determined to go, and shall be very glad if Your Lordship agrees with me in opinion..."[51] Later that same day Newcastle received a letter from Lord Winchelsea, who told him he had not been summoned to the special Privy Council meeting, but that the continued embargo "will, in a short time rather increase the mischief than be as a remedy to it. I believe all embargo's upon... provisions have done more harm than good and been a job."[52] In this assessment that the mischief would increase Winchelsea was absolutely correct.

Hence it was clear from 10 September that parliament was not going to place an embargo on the export of corn and that the vast majority of the ordinary population were aware of the rising prices and were also conscious of who they believed were responsible for this state of affairs. This was coupled with the fact that every corn dealer from southern sea ports, London, and all the market towns south of line from Hull to North Wales, could read accounts of the high prices that corn was fetching on the continent which meant that from 10 September farmers were driven to get as much corn threshed out as soon as they could in order to get onto the export bandwagon, or, alternatively, just gather it in and wait until the prices reached record proportions and they could make fortunes. Although, of course, the marketing of grain was to be of paramount importance, the circumstances of widespread provision shortage had a knock-on effect to other alternative foodstuffs, thus making the prices of potatoes, cheese and all meats more expensive.[53] It further raised the spectre of the increased likelihood of adulteration particularly of grain or flour. Thus, if this date of 10 September was the starting gun for massive profits for farmers, millers, corn dealers and middle men it was also a signal to the crowds to be ready and mobilised in their need to gain access to food. Yet also, although this proclamation had given all these interested parties a licence to act, it also served to enlighten those local authorities in charge of maintaining civil order to be on their watch for illegal practices in the marketing of all foodstuffs at this difficult time, and it is not beyond the realms of possibility that they too had sympathy for the plight of ordinary working people and the actions which they were prompted to take as a result of mismanagement at the highest level of government. Indeed, even as Chatham was vacillating on what to do, the pressure on the need for decisive action was mounting and indeed some local authorities were pre-empting the government and acting in their own interests, and, further, the crowd was already becoming uneasy at the relentless rise in food prices, as the reports from Bristol make clear. On 16 August it was reported in the local Bristol press that the inhabitants of Sherborne (Dorset) bought wheat by "a contribution, and sold it out to the poor at 7 shillings per bushel, which is about 3 shillings under price. And it is proposed to continue it every market day till the harvest."[54] Yet, although such measures would placate the crowd, the rumblings of unrest were

---

51 Ibid Newcastle to Winchelsea, ff. 141, 23 September, 1766.
52 Ibid Winchelsea to Newcastle, ff. 143, 23 September, 1766. It was again rather odd that Daniel Finch (1689-1769), 8th Earl of Winchelsea, 3rd Earl of Nottingham, was not called upon to attend this special meeting of the Privy Council give that in the previous administration headed by the Marquis of Rockingham he had been Lord President of the (Privy) Council. It could well have been that knowing Winchilsea's 'advanced' views on free trade his voice would have one of opposition to the Council's eventual enacting of the suspension of the Embargo.
53 *Gentleman's Magazine*, 18 September, 1766. "At Stourbridge, cheese sold dearer than has been known; Cheshire from 38 to 40 shillings; Gloucester, from 38 to 42; Warwickshire from 30 to 34. Hops sold reasonable, horses and cattle sold dear.
54 *Felix Farley's Bristol Journal*, 16 August, 1766.

becoming manifest. "The poor we hear have pulled down Bunting Mills at Cullumpton, Bradnich, Tiverton, Silverton etc. In most places they behave remarkably well, taking only corn, and leaving the value of it in money, at a moderate price."[55] There is also evidence that just a week before Chatham was to make his momentous non-decision regarding the bounty it was taken as expected that the standing orders forbidding the export of grain would be re-established. "We are told that one farmer, between this place (Bristol) and Tewkesbury, has thirteen old wheat ricks standing, but if the late fine weather continues, and the Bounty of Exportations should be suspended he will find to his cost that he has missed a price he will never see again."[56] Maybe this farmer knew rather more than the editor of *Felix Farley's Bristol Journal.* As news began to filter through that the bounty had not been suspended, a series of questions were published in this newspaper:

> Should anyone assert that the Exportation of Corn is for the Good of the Country, I would ask him two or three plain questions.
>
> 1. How is the Poor Man benefitted from My Lords raising the Rents of his Farms?
>
> 2. How is the Poor Man benefitted by the Destruction of Villages, by six or eight farms being thrown into one, and by the Establishment of so many Tyrants, as our monopolising Farmers are?
>
> 3. How is a Poor Man benefitted by paying 4d or 5d a pound for meat, instead of one halfpenny, and 2d, and obliged to give 6d out of every shilling he lays out to his rich neighbour?
>
> 4. How is the Poor Man benefitted by being taxed to make up for the loss by the Corn Bounty?[57]

The serious riots began from the start of the second week in September and reports began to feed back to London as to the sheer geographic scale of the disturbances; from Norfolk, Suffolk into Cambridgeshire and Buckinghamshire, all around the home counties surrounding London into Oxfordshire, Worcestershire, Warwickshire, Nottinghamshire, Leicestershire, onto Gloucestershire, Wiltshire, Somerset, Devon and Dorset. From this second week in September until the final trial sentences were passed took over three months, or just before Christmas day. It would be an entire book in itself to relate all these riots but, safe to say, there were hundreds of thousands of people seeking redress for high prices and calling for the export embargo to be immediately re-enacted. Clearly there was a wellspring of frustration building up; amongst ordinary working people and, indeed, amongst the landed gentry generally, as this letter from a Wiltshire landowner to the Earl of Hardwicke makes clear. It is worthy of lengthy quotation.

> ...and for the riots the best account I can give is as follows. On a market day a fortnight since a mob assembled of about four or five hundred people, at least as many women as men. These attacked first the wheat that stood for sale, and paid for 5 shillings and 5s 6d a bushel, which bushel of ours is one eighth larger than the statute bushel...But little of what wheat could be found, for the farmers had brought thither, the

---
55 Ibid.
56 Ibid, 6 September, 1766.
57 Ibid, 13 September, 1766.

rumour of a rising having spread some days before. After this exploit they attacked the butter sellers, whose butter they took for 6d per pound – they then proceeded to our mills, and here the matter became more serious, for they began to pull down the Baulting Post, as it is called, the Post by which the wheat when ground is dressed. The Mayor was now called in an attended, after much persuasion to desist; the Proclamation was read – the military assisted, and one offender, a woman was seized and committed. By these events we have all been sufferers, there being no farmers willing to sell corn, nor millers to grind it. The farmers however have been persuaded to bring it in at a moderate price for the use of the poor, under assurance of protection from the magistrate, whom the military on this occasion have received orders to obey, and things have since continued quiet. This is the state of things in my own immediate neighbourhood, but near Westbury and Trowbridge, two manufacturing towns, we hear of more mischief done to houses and some lives lost. That dreaded monster, the military is now courted by everyone, to save his person and his property. The regiment we have here has sent off two detachments to Devizes and Westbury at the request of the inhabitants, and our people have petitioned that no man may go, lest they should be left defenceless. The magistrates are generally backward to exert themselves, fearing the malice of the mob at a future day, when the soldiers are gone. As for the proclamation about putting the laws in force against forestalling, I don't find the magistrates can do much more in that... *Temporary* [writer's emphasis] expedients relative to the present distress (which I think very great) are undoubtedly necessary. But if we are to make a general change in our Corn system on account of this distress, I wish we do not put a stop to that plenty, which we have for so many years enjoyed, and induce that scarcity, that we seek to prevent... I most sincerely commiserate [with] the hardships of the poor; wish them to be alleviated; I am ready to lend my assistance, but care not to have the poor demolish my estate, or the merchants sink it to what value they please, and comfort me by saying how much I am indebted to trade.[58]

From Worcestershire, Hardwicke received a much shorter letter but one that conveyed a similar sense of desperation of the state of the country. On the troubles, a W. H. Lyttleton of Stowe wrote: "We have had our share in Worcestershire of the disorders of the time; [and] I fear with your Lordship that the root of them is deep."[59] Reports of the worsening situation in the country began to filter to the national press and, needless to say, these mass disturbances caused considerable concern in London and especially for those charged with conducting national affairs. On September 23 at the Guildhall in London "letters were laid before the court, from the country, setting forth the great difficulties of the poor, on which the court came to the resolution to send the sheriffs, to lay the affair before his majesty; which they did accordingly the next day, and were desired to attend the Privy Council. This special meeting of the Privy Council [but interestingly not Chatham] met on 24 September where a range of witnesses were questioned including London corn merchants who told them of the near famine conditions prevailing across continental Europe where their merchants had large commissions. One merchant (a Mr Prescott) was told "to buy up all the corn that can be got at any price," and he said under oath that if the exportation curtailed, the price would not fall: "but will prevent a very considerable rise. If

---

58 British Library, Hardwicke Papers, (Ad Ms 35607) ff. 312-314, James Harris (of Salisbury) to Hardwicke, 3 October, 1766.
59 Ibid. ff. 315, Lyttleton to Hardwicke, 12 October, 1766.

the exportation continues certainly prices would rise."⁶⁰ Another merchant (a Mr Farrer) gave evidence to the effect that the "chief use of prohibition [of exports of corn] to quiet the minds of the people. If exportation continues, all wheat will be sent abroad immediately, if the ports were left open [the price of] wheat would continue rising, orders would be executed as fast as possible."⁶¹ Conway, (Home Secretary North), read out letters which he had received from High Sheriffs and Lord Lieutenants of the various counties. One was from William Dallaway, the High Sheriff of Gloucestershire, in which he detailed his efforts to placate the crowd in various places, but also ominously warning of the dangers of a general armed insurrection by the lower orders:

> Were I to enumerate all that had been done by the different bodies of rioters, it would be too much for me to write, or you to attend to. It would consist in general of many acts of violence, some of wantonness and excess, and in other instances acts of courage, prudence and Justice, and consistency [to] that which they profess to obtain.⁶²

Dallaway then spoke of his own personal position in the light of the present crisis:

> ...this riot has already driven us to great distress. The Destruction and Prevention of the Mob will occasion us in a few days to want bread. I know not how [the bakers being obliged to stop baking] at present, to supply my own family with sufficient for three days to come, unless I send a great distance for it, and steal home without observation. Then what must be the distress of the poor!⁶³

He then advised the Home Secretary of an even greater threat unless the embargo was immediately reinstated.

> I must absence to your lordship that there are many of the militia in the mob, and many more that have been militia men, and consequently understand the use of fire-arms. That these threaten that if the military are called in, they will seize the militia arms, in order to oppose them, [and] they have sergeants and corporals already amongst them, and can easily make captains.⁶⁴

Lord Shelburne (Home Secretary South) received similar information from Charles Garth and James Sutton from Devizes in Wiltshire, writing at 10 pm in the evening, saying they had just received intelligence that the crowd intended to "come to this place in order to possess themselves of the Militia Arms of this county, which are deposited in this borough, with which the threats they have declared against the inhabitants fill them with the greatest terrors."⁶⁵ Thus the Privy Council had a great deal of evidence of the very dangerous state of the country. There were already ongoing major political problems surrounding the significant fall in the levels of trade and commerce which resulted in the sharp rises in indirect taxation, disillusionment with the once popular but now apparently apostate Chatham, the nature of the peace settlement surrounding the Seven Years War, the increasing tensions in the Colonies of North America, the

---
60 National Archive, Privy Council Papers, PC/1/8 Number 41. Ff. 1, 24 September, 1766.
61 Ibid.
62 Ibid. ff. 17, Dallaway to Conway, 20 September, 1766.
63 Ibid.
64 Ibid.
65 Ibid, ff 21, Garth and Sutton to Shelburne, 20 September, 1766

whole fracas over John Wilkes and the rising unpopularity of George III. Then came the debacle over the gross mismanagement of the existing government to place the corn embargo in due time. The sinister escalation of some of the crowd to obtain arms with which they could confront the already depleted and stretched armed forces – the vast majority of which had been disbanded at the end of the Seven Years War – meant that this situation could have exploded into some form of armed rebellion. By the end of the first session on 24 September the sixteen members of the council had unanimously decided that the embargo on all export of grain would be immediately re-introduced. The following day Conway wrote to Dallaway of the decision of the council:

> Sir, I had last night the favour of your third letter of the 22 instant, giving a further account of the progress of the rioters in your county; and after assuring you Sir, that the activity and attention you have shown upon this occasion, does you the greatest honour here. I lose no time in acquainting you that it was yesterday in a full and respectable council, that the exportation of corn should be immediately prohibited; this resolution must be reported to His Majesty, so that by the necessary forms it will be yet two [or] three days before you receive the actual Order in Council. As I have not the smallest doubt of its passing, I give you this early intelligence, which in the present unfortunate state of your county, I imagine may be of consequence of you to receive. I hope at the same time, the troops ordered into your county, of which I apprized in my last, will be sufficient if any part of the same mutinous spirit should remain in your county.[66]

Upon the news that the exportation of corn was to be re-enacted the riots began to subside.[67] What remained was for the state to display its ability to punish whom it deemed to be the worst offenders and those it considered the ring-leaders. This it did with the use of a Special Commission of Oyer and Terminer, a special panel of assize judges sent to 'hear and determine' the evidence and to pass sentences with the benefit of a Grand Jury. This was used in only the most serious of civil disturbance and once before it those charged would find themselves in very grave trouble. Within the normal parameters of the eighteenth century 'bloody code' of judicial terror, those brought up on charges which in normal circumstances carried a capital sentence, (which effectively any attack on property carried with it) and especially when a special commission assembled, the hangman would have been busy. Although a response to give out a warning about the consequences of ungovernable disorder was considered by the national authorities,[68] it does not appear to have been

---

66 *Annual Register*, (14 September, 1766) Conway to Dallaway, p. 135. See also National Archives, State Papers Domestic, SP 37/5 and SP 37/6 (1766-1767) passim.
67 In June, 1767 the Court of Common Council of the City of London presented Charles Townsend (Chancellor of the Exchequer at the time of the 1766 riots) with a gold box in thanks of his efforts "for his spirit and resolution in advising the late extraordinary, but necessary exertion of power, in savour of the poor, under the alarming prospect of famine, without attempting to endanger the liberties of his country, by exalting the royal prerogative above the law."
Gentleman's Magazine, 23 June, 1767, pp. 328-329. Also a year later the same mistake as had beset the authorities in the previous two years and initiated the riots of the previous year was not be allowed again when on 5 September, 1767 an order in council allowed the duty free importation of corn and extended the ban on all export of grain. Ibid. 5 September, 1767, p. 475. The act for the continued importation of all grains was renewed in December, 1767, Ibid. 7 December, 1767, p. 606.
68 Although a memorandum was written by the Treasury Solicitor and circulated to ministers but the belief was that there were just too many cases where the evidence was so scant that in all

followed through in the aftermath of the riots of September/October 1766.[69] On this occasion the state appeared to have been more placatory than in most cases of serious disturbances.[70] When pressed by worried magistrates as to how they should proceed, Conway was decidedly uncommittal.[71] By the middle of December 1766 Dallaway was writing to Conway, calling for demonstrations of mercy on those rioters of Gloucestershire who may be convicted, in order to encourage the great majority of working people return to their peaceful occupations. To which Conway replied:

> The Secretary of State will not fail at the proper time to mention to the rest of His Majesty's servants the application he [Dallaway] proposes, after the [Special] Commission is ended, for His Majesty's Act of Grace or general pardon, which for reasons given, will probably have good effect in encouraging persons to return to their several callings.[72]

However, in spite of this occasion of mass rioting in support of the customary practices regarding the marketing of grain and general foodstuffs deemed 'necessaries of life', and the relative success at gaining the objective to re-instating the embargo on the export of corn, the days of the old protective statutes prohibiting forestalling, regrating and engrossing were numbered. Just what role the demonstrations of resistance expressed by the crowd in the autumn of 1766 had in this is debatable. It probably convinced those who were calling for the wholesale removal of 'impediments' and for the more fluid movement of trade that such widespread disruption was indicative of the backward and ignorant nature of the lower orders generally. The view that it was their addiction to outdated customs and protectionist practices served merely their own selfish purposes, whilst holding back the inherent trading potential of the nation. Plus it was clear that the national finances needed a sharp increase, which it was believed would inevitably follow once the rising potential commercial wealth of the country was realised. Clearly this was the way forward and highlighted the need not to cling on to the old methods which did not fit with the modern times of global competition. If Britain did not secure its trading supremacy by dint of its now greatly enhanced empire then some other country would. The commercial future of the country, argued the proponents of the emerging political economy, must not be held hostage by the actions of the deluded masses of working people, nor should those gentry of a paternalist persuasion be encouraged to do so either. In the classic telling of the history of Britain's rise to a global trading superpower, one of the key battles was the freeing of the corn trade from all the traditional impediments in the period from the conclusion of the Seven Years War to the eventual repeal of the Corn Laws in 1846. It may

---

likelihood would not have brought convictions. See National Archives, State Papers Domestic, 44/41, November, 1766 see also Shelburne Papers, Vol. 132, William L. Clements Library, University of Michigan, Ann Arbor.

69 For lists of indictments, offences and verdicts, also lists of members of the Grand Jury and judges see National Archives, Treasury Solicitors Papers, (Kings Bench), TS11/55, KB8/75; KB8/76; KB8/77.

70 See for example the manner in which the state mobilised to punish the Kingswood colliers after the Bristol riots of 1753, see National Archives, State Papers Domestic, SP36/152/3; SP36/153 ff. 30, Newcastle to Attorney General, Dudley Ryder, 3 June, 1753. Also SP44, ff. 200-213 and Ryder to Newcastle, SP 35/14 ff. 203, and British Library, Newcastle Papers, Ad Ms, 32732, ff. 43-63. Or the Gordon Riots of June, 1780, SP37/21, ff. 11-140.

71 British Library, *Calendar of Home Office Papers, 1766-1769*, (2073/153), Domestic Entry Books, (273-410).

72 Ibid. 424, Conway to Dallaway. 8 February, 1767.

have to be a painful process, but it was for the good of the nation as a whole in the long run. The fact was that at the intellectual level and at the level of commercial and trading practice these arguments won the day in the years after the disturbances of 1766. This they did in quite rapid fashion, as the old statutes were repealed in 1772. Thus in a mere six years the 'victory' of the crowd was gone and the provision sector, as in the cotton industrial sector, was succumbing to the progress of modern capitalism.

The positions adopted in support of the necessity of change were more clear and direct in the industrial sphere than in the provision sector, but the effects were the same in both areas. Those merchants and industrialists who argued for the need to abandon the old customary work practices and the protective apparatus that surrounded them did so purely on the pragmatic basis that the process of manufacturing had to change to meet future competition and thus get rid of the moralising claptrap of ancient rights and customary practices. Similarly, the attitudes of those who supported the old ways with their constant accusations of greed and avarice on the part of the new, thrusting and uncompromising men of industry had to be silenced by demonstrating that the former practices were backward and retarding the industrial development of the North-West and, ultimately, the nation. For the political economists who advocated the need to open up the corn trade the arguments were more subtle and nuanced. Thus if the new masters in the industrial sector focused on the practical need for change in relation to the needs of the rationalisation and reorganisation of labour as a factor of production, and of the effectiveness and necessity of the virtues of new microeconomic practices and ideas, then those advocating changes in provisioning – especially in the corn trade – did so in the manner of the theoretical need for change. According to these advocates for change the best regulation was no regulations at all. Let the free and open market determine prices. Their argument ran along these lines. In the immediate post-harvest period corn was freely available to all, thus up until the Christmas period prices would be relatively low. For the smaller farmers this was their time to make their most significant profits, for those next up in size and yields, they sell some but would hold some grain back until the following spring to cash in at that time, and for the largest farms they would hold grain back even longer until the prices naturally rose due to the relative scarcity between May and August. This was a natural and rational process linked to the differing size of the producers and the organic growing process of the product itself and the fact that prices fluctuated owing to these differing levels of the availability of the commodity during the year. In fact, according to this theory, the corn dealers actually provided a service to the public by distributing the grain to those places which did not have naturally growing local supplies. They also knew where to import grain from abroad in times of shortage and in times in plenty where to find the most lucrative export markets for the wider benefit to the nation's trading surplus. Not only this but also when there was a possibility of a shortage, the fact that the prices would rise would ensure that not all the grain was consumed in a few short months but evenly spread throughout the year to maintain supplies. Thus even in such times the law of supply and demand knew best because, due to high initial prices, this ensured an even distribution not only in geographical terms but it also promoted an evening-out of supplies through the year to prevent acute shortages from mid-summer. The things that interfered with this process were, once again, the ignorance of the actions of the lower orders whose actual knowledge of the way that markets functioned was only narrowly perceived through their own immediate blinkered and selfish needs. Or, alternatively, by those of a paternalistic persuasion in local and national government who buckled – as they invariably did – under the storms of protest initiated by the ignorant mobs and reinforced the old and outdated ancient statutes forbidding engrossing, forestalling and regrating. If famines did occur, ran this argument, it was due to interference and not the lack of it, because in altering the natural balance the interference would result in the grain markets being unduly localised in nature when, in fact, there was no need for this to be the case if the natural flows according to demand had their way. If farmers were always interfered with when there was a rumour of shortage or the actions of corn merchant raised local suspicions, then their natural proclivity would be to remain at the same size and produce the same amounts because their excess demand, if they embarked on improvements, would incur the wrath of the local mob and involve the paternalist interferers. In fact, Adam Smith and his followers argued, when a producer of grain was forced to sell to ease a local shortage due to a temporary rise in prices, this often resulted in wastage because it produced a brief glut, forcing an inevitable shortage later in the year.

However, what the self-justifying logic of the political economy model overlooks is the precarious reality of those hundreds of thousands of ordinary working people whose existence was always wavering on the edge of subsistence. For them bread was the staff of life in a very real sense, without it there was precious little else to eat and keep their families alive. As the writer of the anonymous threatening letter wrote in September, 1762, "We may as well all be hanged as starved to Death and to see ower Children weep for Bread and none to give them."[73] The fact was, as it was to prove in the industrial sphere, that the largest producers determined the demand for a given commodity at key moments in the process of serving the market needs. Yet in the provision sector this was even more open to the vagaries of forces which ordinary mortals had little control, such as the weather or blight or unusually high levels of demand at any given time in any given place. Thus those in positions of sustaining their own large supplies or holding back supplies, such as the largest farmers, corn merchants and millers, to a significant extent controlled the given price at any given time. And the fact was that the crowd knew this only too well, which explains why they came out in such huge numbers to redress the imbalance of marketing created by the lapsing of the standing order. They were, in Thompson's phrase, acting in relation to "the reciprocal obligations and duties of the governors and the governed in times of dearth, and of paternalistic social control."[74] Yet this massive display ultimately operated against the subliminal understanding of the crowd that they had a 'right' to demonstrate in such situations to force the hand of the authorities. For those in positions of national government, and indeed some in charge of the local state, these kinds of displays of wanton disruption to the free movement of products had to be put a stop to; they were seen as damaging to the local and national trading position of the country, and thus the pressure to remove the old statutes built up quickly in the aftermath of 1766, towards their eventual repeal in 1772.[75] It should not appear

---

73 *Manchester Mercury*, op cit.
74 Thompson, *Customs in Common*, op cit, p. 269.
75 There were some further provision riots in 1767, and in London in April and May 1768 (*Westminster Journal*, 30 April, 14 May, 1768) but from 1766 up to1769 the harvests were good then from 1770 to 1774 the harvests were once again poor and there were a succession of further provision riots once again in the home counties, East Anglia and the West of England. See

strange to the modern reader or to someone of advanced economic thinking, such as Smith and his acolytes, that in the second half of the eighteenth century this was the case; it was a natural flashpoint; that someone who had the power to provide sustenance to many was manipulating the market to their own end for purely personal financial motives. As we move out of our period of enquiry and toward the later eighteenth century, when the views of the political economists became much more pervasive, their solution to the wartime famines of the 1790s was for even more enclosures, to make larger units of agricultural production and to make its distribution under the control of an even smaller set of large dealers, millers and middlemen. As a long-term solution this was in keeping with notions of the ultimate 'progressiveness' of political economy, but in the short term it produced a real famine.[76]

The correlation between Smith's abstractions on the general social and economic utility of political economy, the rationalisation of the corn trade, its marketing and the necessity to improve the productive efficiency of labour as the only factor of production under the total control of the capitalist, did overlap and did, of course, have important long-term consequences, particularly for the nature of working class communities in both the agrarian and industrial sectors. For example, the enclosures and the enhanced capitalisation of grain production impacted significantly on the rise of under and unemployment in the agricultural sector in those regions which were overwhelmingly agrarian in nature. This resulted in a major strain being placed on the old poor law as the only remaining rural welfare safety net. This situation, in turn, prompted polemicists, such as the Reverend Thomas Malthus, to issue forth with doom-laden prognostications on the limited ability of the Corn Laws to ensure adequate wheat provision for a labouring population spiralling out of control due to the beneficence of the existing poor law.[77] This led eventually to the Poor Law Amendment Act of

---

Charlesworth, *An Atlas of Rural Protest*, op cit, pp. 92-94. For food disturbances in 1767 see *Gentleman's Magazine*, 24 April, 1767, p. 190, for veal being sold by the crowd for 2d per pound in Sudbury in Suffolk. There was the seizing of corn by Cornish tinners from a farmer near Turo, which the crowd paid for, but one of their number stole a set of spoons, whereupon his comrades searched him found the spoons and returned them to the farmer, the offender was then "scourged to such a degree that he took to his bed, and it was thought he would hardly recover." 25 April, 1767, p. 275. In November at Kidderminster in Worcestershire "a great" crowd assembled and demanded that the famers sell their wheat at 5s a bushel (2s cheaper than the going rate) and butter for 6d per pound when previously it was 8d per pound. Ibid, 14 November, 1767, pp. 559-560. At Bristol in December 1767 the corporation and the society of merchants sent commission to Danzig for "several thousand quarters of wheat to be imported there, which these bodies intend to sell to the poor at a low price." Ibid. 7 December, 1767, pp. 606-607.

76 For more on the 'famine' years of the 1790s see, R. Wells, *Wretched Faces; Famine in Wartime England 1793-1801*. (London: Breviary Stuff, 2011).

77 T. Malthus, *An Essay on the Principle of Population*. (1st ed. London, 1798). It is somewhat ironic that this committed priest of classical economics although never taking a stipend in his own Anglican church became the first professor of political economy at the East India Company College at Hertford Heath, known now as Haileybury in Hertfordshire, where he taught political economy and the virtues of free trade to future employees of the East India College given that at the time it was probably the biggest monopoly in the world.

Malthus wrote that while food production increases according to arithmetic principles, population increases naturally at a much quicker rate proportionally. Thus he argued that it was not a surprise that people could reduce the rate of population growth. Food production, he believed, can only be increased by slow, difficult methods such as by intensive farming or reclaiming unused land; they can however, reduce population growth by marrying late, using contraceptives, emigrating, or, in more extreme circumstances, resorting to reduced funds allocated to the care of health, enduring ferocious social diseases or living in impoverished living conditions, the effects of warfare, and even resorting to infanticide. Which, warfare apart was

1834 and the dramatic realisation on the part of some (most notably those adherents to so-called 'Manchester School' economic theory) in the possibility that Britain might lose the momentum began by the Industrial Revolution in the eighteenth century, as was the case in large parts of continental Europe where industrialisation had only been partial and limited to certain sections of their economies. This was because under the terms of the Poor Law Amendment Act those agricultural labourers in the predominantly agrarian regions of the country simply to avoid being driven into the workhouses or the alternative of starving to death would be to force them to move to where employment was plentiful in the industrial areas. This meant that labour would be abundant, and thus cheap and so maintaining the elasticity of labour with what was hoped would be a relatively subdued and cowed workforce. However, to return to the 1760s we must now return developments on the industrial front in relation to the cleavages of the traditional communities, the responses of protest and the impact of change.

---

pretty much the situation in many northern industrial towns in the 1830s, 1840s and beyond. Malthus was convinced not only with the inevitability of human demise, but with why more humans did not die off in even greater number given that such overwhelming odds are stacked particularly against the working class. As an economist, he studied responses to what he termed 'incentives', such as making the poor law only available in the most extreme need .

11

Mass Protest in the 1760s: The Industrial Sector

Although in the short term the enhanced trading potential of the final years of the Seven Year War did result in a temporary respite in the manufacturers' advance into the customary practices of the working class and, indeed, improved earning power for some sectors, this situation for cotton workers was by no means a permanent one.[1] In fact nationally levels of overall trade did fall at the conclusion of the Seven Years War, yet the embryonic capitalists of the North-West found the period between the end of the Seven Years War in 1763 and the outbreak of serious hostilities in the Thirteen Colonies in 1778 was a period of steady growth in the cotton sector of trade. They consolidated their now ascendant position in a variety of ways, all of which to a greater or lesser extent conformed to the now established economic practices which they had initiated. However, for the North-West region this era of commercial and manufacturing growth – although one in which the working class of the North-West undoubtedly benefited through increased work and income – did not diminish the manufacturers' desire for greater advance and control of as many and as much of all the factors of production as possible. In such a situation, when orders are plentiful, employers will grant concessions to workers primarily because the orders needed completion, profits were assured and cut-throat competition was, momentarily at least, less intense. Yet when this phase began to curtail the need to get an advantage over a competitor became, once again, imperative – as the manufacturers realised only too well – then the establishment of new forms of enhancing production became paramount, and this would impact on the working class. In fact, even during this boom period there were examples of the manufacturers attempting to impose more rigid control over labour and improve methods of production. Moreover, in direct response to this there were vigorous demonstrations of worker unrest from the outset of the 1760s across the North-West. In 1760 the cabinet-makers of both Liverpool and Manchester were in dispute with their masters over wages and hours of work, and at Liverpool, after the dispute had been running three weeks, the magistrates arrested three of the leaders of the strike.[2] While at Manchester, later in 1760, the *Manchester Mercury* was complaining of "a spirit of combination among the journeymen" of the town including the wig-makers, shoemakers, tailors and cabinet-makers, and that this "is a growing evil and wants to be remedied."[3] As well as disputes surrounding trading practices associated with provisions and the on-going industrial disputes there were also problems connected with the raising of local militias across the country. In the North Pennines, at Hexham in 1761, when the deputy-lieutenants of the county were meeting to ballot for the militia the local miners rioted and attacked a band of the local enrollees from Yorkshire. The militia opened fire and killed 42 miners and wounded 48, while three militia men were killed.[4]

---

1 In 1759 regarding the check-weavers Thomas Percival wrote that "they were never in better humour in their lives, their pieces are shortened, their wages raised, and this by the masters' consent, provisions are plenty, and work enough to be had." Op cit p. 20.
2 Ibid, 13 June, 20 June, 1760.
3 *Manchester Mercury,* 17 November, 1760, also the *London Chronicle,* 12 December, 1761.
4 *Gentleman's Magazine,* p. 137-138, March 9, 1761.

Again at Liverpool, as the Seven Years War was coming to a conclusion in November 1762, the sailors marched through the town asserting that they would not go to sea for less than 40*s* per month and, further, that if any other seamen did so they would kill them. Three were arrested, charged with a "dangerous riot and conspiracy in order to raise their wages", but with the aid of the crowd they managed to escape on their way to the assizes at Lancaster.[5] Again later in 1763, the sawyers of Liverpool were in dispute with their employers, and a series of prosecutions were begun for conspiracy to raise wages, but subscriptions were organised for them among the other workers of Liverpool during the winter of 1763.[6] Throughout 1763 and into 1764 the cost of living continued to rise and in the latter year the coopers of Liverpool went out on strike, of which nine were indicted at the Lancaster assize.[7] The first signs of this dispute began in July, 1763, when the journeymen coopers forced an employer onto a pole "and in an infamous manner carried him through the streets, under pretence that he hurt their trade."[8] This was potentially a very serious dispute as all perishable products to be shipped out of Liverpool by sea or inland had to be cargoed in barrels. In 1765 the journeymen tailors of Liverpool were in dispute because the masters were employing non-time-served workers and by this time the authorities were becoming thoroughly sick of the operations of the various trade 'clubs'. Yet what is interesting in this strike was that the magistrates decided to indict four of the suspected leaders. They did so not on the basis of any of the recent statutes against illegal combinations, but went back to the old customary acts of the Elizabethan era, specifically the acts of 1548-1549 and 1563 which enabled prosecutions against workers for not finishing work properly.[9] This again reveals double standards being in play here as it was fine for the authorities to resort to 'ancient' statues to suit their case but when the workers did the same it

---

5 *Manchester Chronicle*, 7 December, 1762; *Williamson's Liverpool Advertiser*, 17 December, 1762, *Gentleman's Magazine*, "...a concourse of people assembled on the road to Lancaster gaol, assembled under the pretence of a bull baiting, surrounded the officers, and suffered the prisoners to escape." 30 November, 1762, p.596. 20 seamen were later arrested for conspiracy. In the next decade the sailors of Liverpool were even more dangerously motivated, as the dispute with the American colonies reduced the ships sailing on the 'slave triangle' to Africa and America many sailors numbering about 3000 were unemployed, when the ship owners announce they were reducing wages, 2000 sailors moved on their houses, sacking some, carrying a 'bloody flag', bringing cannon of a harboured ship and firing on the Liverpool Exchange. According to one source this episode: "with the exception of the alarming disturbances in the Metropolis, in 1780, called Lord George Gordon's riots, it seems impossible to mention any popular outbreak in England, which took place during the last century, of so formidable and extraordinary a description, as the riots which occurred in Liverpool. They were the more dangerous, because the town then had a very inefficient civil force, and there was not a soldier in the place when they broke out; and it is an extraordinary fact, for which no precedent can be found in any other riot in England, that the Liverpool rioters' made use of both cannon and other fire-arms, as well cutlasses and other kinds of weapons, on that occasion. As the then Mayor and the local authorities were not considered to have displayed either courage or judgment, it is not extraordinary that an account of the riots seems to have been suppressed, as far as practicable, on the spot; but they could not prevent some accounts of them being published in the London and the provincial newspapers, as well as in the magazines of that period." See *The London Gazetteer and New Daily Advertiser*, (4 and 5 September, 1775); and R. Brooke, *Liverpool as it was during the last quarter of the Eighteenth Century, 1775-1800*, (Liverpool, 1853) pp. 326-347.
6 *Williamson's Liverpool Advertiser*, 21 January; 28 January; 4 February, 1762.
7 For the rising cost of living see *Williamson's Liverpool Advertiser*, 26 October, 1764, for the indictments of the nine coopers for assault and riotous assembly see, National Archives, *Palatinate Papers*, P.L. 26. 40/3; 40/2).
8 *Gentleman's Magazine*, 15 July, 1763, p. 361.
9 *Williamson's Liverpool Advertiser*, 10 May; 31 May; 14 June and 21 June, 1765.

was deemed pointless to refer to statutes from a bygone age which did not fit the modern circumstances according to Lord Chief Justice Mansfield and his crony Sir Michael Foster.[10] The Liverpool magistrates also gave warning to alehouse keepers who allowed such conspiracies and unlawful assemblies on their premises that if this continued their licences would not be renewed.[11]

Thus, from the degree of disturbance across a range of trades and occupations it would indeed appear that working people were becoming increasingly discontented in their relations with their employers. In the King's Speech to Parliament in 1766 it was stated that "I must with concern take notice that, notwithstanding my cares for my people, a spirit of the most daring insurrection had in divers parts brought forth in violence of the most criminal nature."[12] This speech came, of course, as a backdrop to the series of provision riots in the autumn of that year, but also from the reports we have seen in such organs as the *Annual Register* and the *Gentleman's Magazine* as well as local sources such as *Williamson's Liverpool Advertiser* and the *Manchester Mercury* that the usual disposition of the 'lower orders' was not as it should be. With regard to the weavers the masters had won the day in the disputes which traversed the period between 1747 and 1760. They had got legal backing with the rulings of Mansfield and Foster, they had apparently broken the weavers' organisational basis and they had seemingly got the majority of the magistrates onside. Yet this new breed of masters were not respected either by those groups below them, (as noted one old weaver told Percival "their honour was *severity*, their mercy was *oppression*"),[13] nor by those groups – the 'country gentlemen' – above them, as this quote from Percival reminds us:

> Another objection against me, in common with other gentlemen, is that we envy these check-makers; really sir, I wonder what any country gentleman can be supposed to envy them for! Is it for their houses? What country gentleman has reason to envy the possessor of a house of four, five or six rooms of a floor, with a ware-house under, and warping rooms over... Is it their furniture? See one dressed out like a baby-house. Is it their equipages? Surely no, when one sees their chariots, or post-chaises, with a pair of calendar tits, and a calendar lad for a coachman, it must set any spectator laughing at the grotesque, did not the honest horses, by hanging down their heads, show that they were ashamed of their employment. Is it for their cookery, here I am almost at a stand to find a reason... The last objection against the country gentlemen, and against me in particular, is that we despise them... I can't say what kind of an answer the country gentlemen may give to this accusation, but I believe that if fully pursued, they will obliged to do as I am determined to do, to plead guilty to the indictment.[14]

Yet it is doubtful if the masters were especially bothered by the stinging assessment of Percival, nor indeed anyone else. Their overwhelming concern was to be able to build on their victories and turn these into even greater control over the trade and into profits.

The merchants and manufacturing masters of the North-West were also busy in expanding their interests, not only in the crucial area of the practical operation

---

10 See pp. 138-9 above.
11 *Williamson's Liverpool Advertiser*, 14 June and 21 June, 1765.
12 *Gentleman's Magazine*, 11 November, 1766, pp. 547-548.
13 Percival op cit, p. 13, see above p. 132.
14 Percival op cit, pp. 10-11.

of their individual enterprises but also in wider trading prospects. In the turbulent year of 1766, for example, the masters took advantage of the government's confusion and in its desire to open up the colonies, and, by extension, allow British manufacturers great access to, and more generally the freer movement of, primary products. The priority was of course to facilitate access to grain, but in a series of three Importation Acts raw cotton was allowed entry into the country free of duties.[15] The primary concern now of the cotton masters of the North-West became their ability to speed up the process of spinning the thread and getting it to the weavers more quickly, as this would mean once again improving the speed and overall quantity of finished cloth. Also, with regard to the potential in overseas trade in February 1768, a new scheme was announced to open up international trade in centres other than London, primarily with the aim of curbing the monopolistic privileges of the East India Company. The proposal was to set up offices in London and the sea ports of Liverpool, Bristol, Hull and Glasgow for the benefit of not only the capital but also other maritime centres. The sweetener was to be a series of loans to the government, payable at two percent interest, amounting to eight million pounds.[16] The initial meeting was held in Liverpool, again underscoring that city's rising status as a principal centre of trade, not only to the North-West but to the whole country. Clearly the economic influence of the North-West region was growing in significance, but the need to build on the potential for cheaper cotton as a primary product served to quicken the desire of the masters to speed up the manufacturing process which in fact had been a priority for some time.

As we noted in chapter two above, the first concentration of labour on a factory model was initially confined to the poor in workhouses involving women and children. However, the potential advantage of this precedent was not lost on those seeking to utilise economies of labour. It appeared a logical corollary to embrace the principle of concentrating labour and utilise a similar approach to the next stage in the introduction of both mechanised innovation and the division of the productive processes in the cotton sector. The introduction and adoption of the spinning jenny coincided with a brief spurt in trade in the final months of the Seven Year War and the first months of 1763. The speed at which the advances in the spinning of cotton warp in particular could be improved meant the impetus for even more perfect carding to make the thread smooth and strong, and the need to expand market share both domestically and overseas appeared to offer boundless opportunities for expansion. Thus, although work availability and incomes in the weaving process may have become less fraught than in the 1740s and 1750s, still in the decades following the defeat of the weavers of the North-West in the later 1750s their conditions became increasingly challenged as the realisation for potential profits meant it was imperative for employers to maintain labour discipline and to enhance methods of production. The masters knew only too well that if they relaxed their hold

---

15 *Gentleman's Magazine*, "An act to amend an act for repealing certain duties in the British colonies and plantations...and for further encouraging, regulating and securing several branches of the trade of this Kingdom and the British dominions in America, as relates to the exportation of non-enumerated goods from British colonies in America. 12 December, 1766, p. 598. See also pp. 102, 196, 243, 245, 291. See also T. Bentley, *Letters on the Utility and Policy of Employing Machines to Shorten Labour*, (London, 1780), "In the year 1766, your cotton manufactory was in a declining condition; and you applied to Parliament for relief; which you expected from a free port in the West Indies, and for the free importation of cotton from all parts of the world. Your complaints were attended to; and your desires, in a great measure complied with." p. 9.
16 *Gentleman's Magazine*, 4 February, 1768, p. 91.

over the new spirit of discipline which they had imposed the workers would relapse into the former comfortable customary practices. Also the employers were still in direct competition with other masters, even in the relatively good times, but they knew well enough that once this phase began to ebb the competition would become more concentrated, thus they had to keep the productive capacity of labour as high as possible and its cost as low as possible. The next logical stage was to attempt to reduce the labour intensive process itself by utilising innovations that would make the various processes of the production of cotton fabrics even more amenable to their control and supervision and at the same time enhance its productive capacity. It was recognised by the Society of Arts in the 1760s that at certain key times, such as when the order books being full coincided with the harvest period, that there was always a shortage of spinners to provide adequate yarn.[17] Thus, the availability of labour in such periods could present problems. In the 1730s Lewis Paul began his experiments and development of his early prototypes of spinning machines based on a system of rollers. Indeed we know that he was demonstrating one of his machines to a group of Manchester manufactures in 1739. However, the difficulties that Paul encountered did not lead to a take up of his innovations by the Manchester men.[18] Yet it appears that the need for significant advances in the technological breakthrough on the spinning side was recognised by the manufacturers of the North-West, and the need to achieve such a development was underscored when they successfully lobbied the government to relax its stance on import duties by getting raw cotton admitted free of duty in 1766.

Yet in order to fulfil these objectives the manufacturers would still require a plentiful supply of labour, and it was clear from previous developments that on the one hand this labour was intensely protective of its perceived rights and on the other that, even though Manchester as a centre of industry was growing between 1758 and 1773-74, it was not growing as quickly as it had in the recent past and it became clear that the amount of labour in the North-West was finite.[19] This potentially presented the masters with a real problem because, although the trading prospects in cotton was enormous both domestically and especially overseas, if the supply of labour became limited or belligerently intransigent it would mean that this potential growth would be curtailed or at least severely limited. Clearly for the manufactures the whole process of labour involved in the cotton sector had to be transformed in terms of determining which type of labour was needed for specific processes and how these processes could be improved in terms of productivity: in short, the division of labour. Thus the obvious place to start was in the spinning process which was the one in which both the most serious blockages occurred and the earliest attempts at innovation were to be found. That this was achieved is attested not only by the cotemporary numerous reports of the impact of innovation in the growth of the cotton trade but also by the figures of real productive output. Between 1739 and 1760 cotton production represented 2.8% of overall British output, compared to 32.0% for wool, and then between 1761 and 1770 this figure for cotton had risen to 6.7%,

---

17 See for example Wadsworth and Mann, op cit p. 415.
18 Ibid, p. 429.
19 According to the Duchy of Lancaster Papers between 1700 and 1750 the population of Manchester had doubled in size. However, between 1758 and 1773-74 it was still growing but less quickly as the population was said to have grown only by one third. Duchy of Lancaster Papers, National Archive, Kew, D. L. 4.147, and Dr. Thomas, Edward Percival, *Observations on the State of Population of Manchester and Other Adjacent Places*, (Manchester, 1773) p. 1.

compared to 31.9% for wool. Within the cotton industry itself there was steady growth from 1700, but this increased significantly to 4.59% between 1760 and 1770, and then there was a real surge between 1780 and 1790 of 12.76%, and the cotton sector's overall contribution to the national output had risen from 2.8% in 1760 to 35.4% in 1801.[20] Yet the question remains, what effect did this have on the communities involved and how did they react?

The initial breakthrough came with the introduction and widespread deployment of the spinning jenny, developed by James Hargreaves, from 1764, and this again provoked a response from those workers fearful of what this would mean for them. The original machine developed by Hargreaves operated eight spindles which were operated by one large handle capable of being operated by a woman. Yet Hargreaves did not patent his invention until 1770, which meant that in the meantime others could copy and refine it. This was the essential problem, for whilst eight spindles could be seen as a labour saving device, when the machine was adapted, (principally by Richard Arkwright's water frame), to sixteen, twenty four or thirty two spindles, which were now capable of being driven by horses or waterpower, this constituted a major advance for the manufactures and the likelihood of a confrontation with workers, who saw these advances less as a means of easing their workload while retaining their customary practices, but more one which was, ostensibly, another way in which the masters could impose even more 'rationalisation' upon them. The fact was that this transformation occurred remarkably quickly. By 1767 and 1768 there were rumblings of disaffection on the part of the working class. The key factor was that at this time, although refinements were taking place, the first machines designed by Hargreaves only produced coarse and brittle thread useful only as filling for weft. The point of dispute was not initially that the widespread introduction of the jennys would disrupt traditional work practices, (although this was probably suspected), but rather when. With these improvements the masters would expect finer thread to be spun at the old prices, despite the fact that this involved significantly more work, as Ogden confirms:

> The plenty of weft produced by this means gave uneasiness to the country people, and the weavers were afraid lest the manufacturers should demand finer weft woven at the former prices, which occasioned some risings, and the jennies were opposed, and some being demolished before those who used them could be protected, or convince others of their general utility, till Dorning Rasbotham, Esq.; a worthy magistrate who

---

20 See M. Berg, *The Age of Manufacturers, 1700-1820*, (London and New York: Routledge, 1994) p. 15; S. L. Engerman, 'Mercantilism and Overseas Trade, 1700-1800', in R. Floud and D. McCloskey, (eds.), *The Economic History of Britain since 1700*, Vol. 1, 2nd edition, (Cambridge: Cambridge University Press, 1994) p. 190; P. Deane and W. A. Cole, *British Economic Growth, 1688-1959: Trends and Structure,* (Cambridge: Cambridge University Press, 2nd edn., 1967); N. F. R. Crafts, *British Economic Growth During the Industrial Revolution*, (Oxford: Oxford University Press, 1985); N. F. R. Crafts, 'British Economic Growth, 1700-1850: Some Difficulties of Interpretation', *Explorations in Economic History*, (Vol. 24, 1987): N. F. R. Crafts, 'British Industrialisation in the International Context', *Journal of Interdisciplinary History,* (Vol. 19, Winter, 1989); N. F. R. Crafts, 'Industrial Revolution in Britain and France: Some Thoughts on the Question "Why England First?"', *Economic History Review* (Vol. 30, 1977); N. F. R. Crafts, 'The Industrial Revolution', in R. Floud and D. McCloskey, (eds.), *The Economic History of Britain since 1700*, Vol. 1, (Cambridge: Cambridge University Press, 2nd edn, 1994); N. F. R. Crafts and C. K. Harley, 'Output Growth and the British Industrial Revolution: A Re-Statement of the Crafts-Harley View, *Economic History Review*, Vol. 65 (1992); N. F. R., Crafts, S. J. Leybourne and T. C. Mills, 'Trends and Cycles in British Industrial Production, 1700-1913', *Journal of the Royal Statistical Society, Series A,* Vol. 152, (1989).

lived in that part of the country, towards Bolton, where they were used, convinced the weavers, in a sensible printed address, that it was their true interest to encourage jennies, urging the former insolence of spinners, and the happiness of such as had already relieved themselves, and procured employment for their children; and appealed to their own experience of the fly shuttle, against which the like clamour had been raised, and the inventor driven to France, where he found encouragement, while his shuttles are yet in such estimation here, as to be used generally even on narrow goods, to the benefit of trade in general, without any bad consequence in the experience of several years, but they are rather of particular benefit to the weavers.[21]

A similar refrain was offered by the *Manchester Mercury* when faced yet again in 1779 with these early outbreaks of Luddism. At the Quarter Sessions held in Manchester to try the rioters before a Grand Jury the newspaper compared the present situation with that of ten years previous, when, "in our own time, the invention of the Wheel Shuttle and the Spinning Jennies, all of which have been found of great utility."[22] The fact was that the majority of working people involved in the cotton sector in the North-West do not appear to have had a problem with the utilisation of the Jennies *per se*, but rather when they were expanded into machinery that required specialised buildings to house and operate them; in other words, early factories. In the early phase of their introduction it was expanded from eight spindles to sixteen and thirty two, which seemed to take the machinery to another level and to again place pressure on those using the simpler methods to be out-produced and out-priced in terms of their earning potential. It is almost as if these workers were expecting another element of their customary way of working to be under threat by masters with greater resources to deploy.

In the twenty years from the defeat of both the check and smallware weavers in 1758 and 1760, the advance of both mechanised innovation and the building of the first factories was swift. Indeed, by 1780, at a factory at Heaton Norris, between Manchester and Stockport, a newly equipped factory was offered for sale. Its operational power was not specified, but the location was situated near a confluence of the rivers Tame, Goyt and Mersey and it contained,

> ...an iron pot (for washing the cotton) a stove and 48 flakes to dry cotton on, a large willey for cleaning and opening it, three carding machines and another unfinished, three slubbing jennies of 46, 36 and 26 spindles, twenty slubbers wheels, thirteen spinning jennies; three of 120 spindles each (new with all the late improvements), three of 100 hundred spindles, one of 84; one of 80; two of 60, one of 59 and two of 50. A jack and feeders (for twisting); three Dutch wheels, a warping mill and bobbins, and seven looms. Also included were skips, weigh-beams, joiners benches and tools, tins to slub on, bobbins; a cotton press, reeds and gears, heald yarn, 45 pairs of 12-inch cards, raw cotton, cotton and linen warps, linen yarn, single and double twist for calico, velveret warps.[23]

Just to underscore the growing power and influence of the Manchester cotton masters and the fact that they were willing to cooperate together for the advancement of their industry and their position, in February, 1774 the

---

21 J. Ogden, *Manchester A Hundred Years Ago*, (Manchester, 1887), pp. 88-89.
22 *Manchester Mercury*, 26 October, 1779.
23 *Manchester Mercury*, 23 July, 1780.

Manchester Committee for the Protection of Trade was formed,[24] arguably the forerunner of the formidable sectional interest pressure group in economic, manufacturing and commercial sectors which culminated in the formation of the Anti-Corn-Law League from the mid-1830s. From its inception and in terms of its membership, this was a formidable body consisting of all the main merchants involved in the textile trade in and about Manchester. It was made up of 28 committee members and 127 non-committee members, including one woman, a Mrs Norton. However, its early activities had not yet developed into a vehicle for the promotion and establishment of *laissez-faire*, but rather to warn all those with an interest in the textile trade of strangers spotted in Manchester whose objectives may have been to steal secrets of the trade, and also increasingly to fight off those – such as Richard Arkwright – who wanted to preserve their patent rights, or Samuel Crompton, the inventor of the water-frame or 'mule', who they prevented gaining a patent in the first place. The aim of the Committee was to facilitate the spread and usage of all mechanical improvements that could potentially increase profits without the bothersome payment of fees to the patent holders. Also to be a means of lobbying parliament in matters of direct relevance to the cotton trade in the North-West. In the 1780s, for example, they lobbied to oppose a proposed fustian tax and to oppose Pitt's attempts to promote Irish trade, this, however, is taking us out from the immediate time period under discussion.[25] Yet clearly, by the 1770s the now not-so-new merchants were making their presence felt not only purely in economic and industrial areas, but also socially and, importantly, politically, and it is to the latter area that this study will focus in the final chapters.

Just to return momentarily to Thompson's key point, that it was the widespread understanding and dissemination of the political aspect of working class resistance and the aspirations of an amelioration of their circumstances that imbued them with a sense of class consciousness, which, he suggests, in a truly national sense can only be detected from the 1790s, and it was this that made them discernibly working class. Crucially important for the Thompson thesis is that this was not occurring in one branch of industry, rather it was a phenomenon that was being experienced by all working people whether in factories or not. It was also the fact that they were coming to these realisations themselves and that they were prepared to act in their own interests, which gave them the vitally important aspect of 'agency'. I would suggest that for the workers of Lancashire a case can be made that these facets were developing from at least the 1740s and were becoming more engrained as we move into the 1770s; if one wished to be so bold, an argument could be put forward that the process of class formation in the working class industrial environment began in its embryonic form in the North-West region. If one takes a definition of 'politics' as the holding of power and the ability to make decisions due to that possession of power, which is then manifested in changes to the way people live their lives, their payment of some form of taxation, or otherwise affecting their communities, then, from at least 1747, the working class were beginning to question the economic power that the new generation of manufacturers were using in their attempts to alter working class customary practices, communities and, indeed, their lives. They were, secondly, affectively organising themselves to

---

24 *Manchester Mercury*, 8 March, 1774.
25 *Manchester Mercury*, 26 Jul., 31 Aug. 1784. *Manchester Mercury*, 22 and 29 Mar. 1785. See also R. J. Bennett, 'Alignments, Interests and Tensions over "Reform" in Eighteenth-Century Britain: The Manchester Committee of Trade 1774-86', *Northern History*, Vol. L1 (1), 2014.

resist these efforts and to affect a change in the outcome. Thirdly, they were also making appeals to magistrates in defence of their actions against the impositions of the masters in the time-honoured manner. However, as more and more of the traditional magistracy were replaced by either those with a direct link to commerce and trade, or were sympathetic to the aims and objectives of industrial 'improvements', working people increasingly found little means of redress here compared to the previous periods. Thus, in the way they organised their resistance they reveal that even at this early stage they were willing to act in their own agency and also were becoming aware and indeed frustrated at the disparities relating to power and, by extension, began to articulate a political understanding of their predicament. If they were to support any of the existing political parties or, more accurately, the various factions, it would appear on the surface that it was far more likely to be for those expressing the Tory values of the pre-eminence of customary values than the commercially orientated Whig groupings. Yet in certain locations (as we shall see in subsequent chapters below) such as at Preston where the Tories practiced exclusivity even in matters of local trading practices, which could preclude certain weavers from working, those omitted – who were the great majority of weavers in the country districts surrounding Preston – would not be supportive of this dominant group. However, it was also likely that anyone, be they Whig or Tory, who professed a concern for the prevailing conditions in the industrial regions of the North-West could gain the support of working men and women, which again tallies with the situation at Preston, as we shall see in due course. What would have been the starkest realisation was that in their recent experience of those in positions of authority and possessing the power of decision making in matters impinging directly on these communities of working people, there appeared to be gross inconsistently in their attitudes and actions. For example, the anomaly in the actions and positions taken by, firstly, Lord Mansfield in his dealing with the Lancashire workers and others was that on the one hand these actions were guided by a conviction in the necessity for changes towards free trade, but on the other hand this went diametrically opposite to Mansfield's legal belief that customary practices should be maintained. Likewise, Edmund Burke, in extolling the economic virtues of political economy in his *Thoughts on the Details of Scarcity* in 1795, was allowing his commitment to free trade to override his political beliefs, as noted in his classic critique of the French Revolution where again he placed the priority as relating to a balanced constitution based on custom and the precedent that the institutions had shown in their inherent worth over centuries, and thus should not be given over to rash or untried innovations.

Yet there was an important fourth element of relevance to the emerging working class of the North-West in the period under discussion. This feature acted as a bridge between the actual developments which directly informed working class actions and the changing nature of contemporary political ideology, again seen through the eyes of working people, especially those in relation to the old protective devices built into the mercantilist system. Given the effects of the profound changes affecting the related aspects of a new economic order in both the provision and industrial sectors, to many working people it seemed that the authorities and those making political policy had a general unconcern about the worsening conditions of the working class. As one working class diarist put it in the early 1790s:

> The relentless cruelty exercised by the fustian masters upon the poor weavers is such that it is unparalleled in the annals of cruelty, tyranny and oppression for it is a near impossibility for weavers to earn the common necessaries for life...[26]

As we have seen above, these sentiments of frustration had been growing from at least the end of the 1740s, and the argument here is that this, as a process, directly contributed to a developing sense of an identification of interests among working people drawn from a range of trades across the North-West. This equates to a sense of class and, with the growing political awareness, to class consciousness and a serious and measured curtailing of their liberties.

One of the great rallying cries of the Whig party, as they emerged from the revolutionary period of the mid-seventeenth century, was the paramount importance of English liberty. Concepts of English liberty could be taken into several contexts and in relation to differing sections of the social structure. Probably the most salient and enduring was the historical context in which freedom was obtained over several centuries from the initial imposition of the 'Norman Yoke' through the legal reforms of Henry II in the twelfth century, the baronial limits imposed on King John in 1215, and the signing of the Magna Carta, the manumission forced by the Black Death from the 1350s, the religious reformation which stunted the power of Catholicism from the 1530s, through to the momentous upheavals of the seventeenth century. Yet in respect to working people there were the safeguards written in to notions of liberty and the protection of the potentially vulnerable by the poor laws, the Elizabethan and Stuart statutes regarding food provisioning, the *Book of Orders* and the imposition of contracts regarding employment practices. But taken from the perspective of the working class all these were perceived as being under serious threat by the mid-eighteenth century. Common notions of labour, for example, meant that from the impact of the Black Death and the subsequent manumission of serfs, a worker was free to labour for anyone he or she chose, and thus competition was open to get the best terms in relation to pay and conditions. Yet when, as in the cotton sector for example, all the major employers were changing the terms of employment so that they controlled the whole labour market according to their wishes and needs, it mattered little who the worker laboured for, they were becoming imbued with the same aims; they all strived to gain the most productive labour for the least cost. The balance was now skewed firmly in terms of the employer. Thus the question to be asked of many working people was exactly just how 'free' they were and more saliently what did English liberty mean for them? By the 1760s the answer would most likely have been that 'liberty' for them was illusory and a matter of the least priority for those in charge of the national and local state. As noted in the North-West the appeal to an arbitrating magistrate was now largely futile and in reality the only means which the working class had to bring their grievances into the public domain was through active displays of protest. They were living witnesses to the change of attitudes of those in positions of economic, social and political power. Taking for a moment the most extreme examples of attitudes towards free and unfree labour at a moment towards the end of the eighteenth century, when the issue of slavery was becoming more salient and controversial, here below are two notices of runaways:

---

26 *The Diary of William Rowbottom*, 11 August 1793, p. 27, Oldham Local Studies Library, (Reference, D-M 54).

> June 20, 1780. Run away from Lisworney Estate in the parish of Trelawney, in October last. TWO NEGRO MEN of the Congo country, each about 20 years of age, marked on the right shoulders ID with a diamond on top. Whoever shall give information where the said Negroes may be found, or will lodge them in any of the gaols in this Island, shall receive a reward of TWO PISTOLS for each Negro, and all reasonable expenses, by applying to MR NEWMAN CURTIN, attorney at law.[27]

And this notice from twelve years earlier, but on this occasion from Lancashire:

> RUN AWAY from Huttock Top, Bacup, in Rossendale, on the 14th August, 1768. JOHN HEAP, Woollen Weaver or Comber, seventeen Years of Age, round Face, fresh coloured, has a cut across his Nose, which turns up, and his Lip somewhat down, and brown Hair; had on when he went away a blue Coat, with broad Horn Buttons, with a Knob raised in the Middle, a red double Piece Waistcoat, with red Buttons, white Leather Breeches, grey Woollen Stockings. Whoever employs or harbours the said Apprentice, will be prosecuted according to Law, and any person who will bring him to his Master, *James Lord*, shall receive Half a Guinea Reward.[28]

Whilst appreciating that these two cases are not comparable in terms of the circumstances of labour bondage, the similarities could be associated in the minds of many working people who may have questioned accepted ideas of the degree of liberty encapsulated in their deteriorating situation. Indeed, the contrasting and at times contradicting conceptualisations of liberty appear to have been at the forefront of the political discourse as we approach the end of the 1760s. The Whigs, as we have seen, bore the mantle of the historic defenders of English liberties of the grand seventeenth century revolutionary tradition, be this its violent manifestation of the Cromwellian variety, or the exclusion of James II in 1688, and whilst in both these versions there was never any possibility of the popular formal participation by the lower orders in electoral politics, yet the symbolic presence of the necessity of the preservation of liberty for all British citizens remained at the forefront of the thinking of many people drawn from all ranks of social status. And in many cases they were not backward in making their feelings known at election contests where they did not possess the actual vote. In their eyes their physical presence and their significant numbers were enough to let the authorities know where their feelings lay. Yet for the emerging industrial and commercial middle classes notions of liberty meant something else. This widespread assumption that the Whigs would not only protect liberty but indeed promote a set of policies that ensured greater freedom of economic, industrial and commercial activities was seen as crucial to these new men of trade. They were almost at the stage where they were demanding that the Whigs would usher-in a new set of economic imperatives in their and the nations interest. Hence there was emerging an inherent contradiction between conceptions of what liberty meant in class terms; in fact the term itself became a contested area between the core set of self-interests of classes of business, industry and trade on the one hand, and the needs of the county gentlemen and their interests on the other, and at the lowest, but no less extreme, the demands of the working class that their inherent prescriptive rights be preserved. We will return to this theme of basic liberties in due course, but in

---

27 *The Royal Gazette*, Kingston Jamaica, 20 June, 1780.
28 *Manchester Mercury*, 30 August, 1768.

once sense this is why the general election of 1768 was so important at these differing levels of interpretation, and why the one truly open constituency in the North-West at Preston became such a focal point and indicated the first tentative signs that a form of popular plebeian politics was emerging. As Paul Langford tells us about another more famous election of that year, when John Wilkes emerged at the top of the poll at Middlesex:

> It was perhaps the most famous single election result in the history of British parliaments, and the Middlesex freeholders who brought it about did so in a spirit of plebeian libertarianism which confounded respectable opinion.[29]

It is to a discussion of the existing wider political characteristics as well as how this informed the actions and emerging consciousness of the middle and working class which will be the focus of the next two chapters.

---

29 P. Langford, *A Polite and Commercial People, England, 1727-1783*, (Oxford: Oxford University Press, 1992) p. 377.

12
The Political Dimension: The Heightened State of Politics in the 1760s

It is interesting that as we approach the end of the 1760s and the eve of the imposition of the first factories that working people do appear to have been energised into resistance, but there were also occasions when hints can be seen of them displaying political discontent as well as demonstrations of protest centred largely on social and economic issues. The background and basis of this important dimension requires some consideration both in terms of those who were striving to affect change and those on the receiving end of such changes. Also the interaction of national and local political developments cannot be ignored. The 1760s were a time of great political unrest in a national sense, with numerous administrations called into office and not least the impact of the new monarch, who at this point appeared to be determined in asserting his political will. This in itself was controversial and provoked a good deal of opprobrium in several quarters, from the highest of high politics to those of all sections of society expressing opinions privately in coffee houses, taverns and the like. In local terms there was also a good deal at stake, particularly for the commercial and manufacturing interests and of course the working class who, as we have seen, were witnessing first-hand the rapid transformations in their communities across the North-West. In the main, the manufacturers and men of trade in the two largest centres, Liverpool and Manchester, especially those with a background of nonconformist religious beliefs, would have naturally gravitated towards the Whigs, but throughout the 1760s they were, as a party, in a minority when compared to the number of Tories returned to Parliament for the region. As for the working class, they would have been fairly evenly split in their affiliations, with some seeing the preservationist proclivities of the Tories attractive inasmuch as they were the group, theoretically at least, who would be supportive of traditional customary practices and, as we saw from the vitriol exacted both towards and coming from Thomas Percival, the country gentry, whether Whig or Tory, were not enamoured with the new thrusting Manchester-based manufacturing class. Yet some of the skilled working class particularly may have seen the Whigs as the group who, on the surface at least, were in the long term acting for the best interests of the region in terms of its ability to create wealth and employment opportunities and hence an improved standard of living for the labouring population. For a time these members of the working class may well have believed that the country Whigs could use their influence to rein-in the excesses of the urban-based new masters. It has to be remembered, for example, that Percival himself was a Whig. In fact the working class of north and west Lancashire did in one place have some limited opportunity of not only voicing and demonstrating their support for a favoured candidate at an election, but actually voting, and it is more than coincidental that the test to assert this right came at the moment when the first serious jenny riots were beginning in 1768.

On the face of it the election at Preston in 1768 took on the classic contest between the Whig and Tory factions, transformed in this instance to the supporters of the interests of Lord Derby in the case of the former and the corporation of Preston in the latter. We have noted that the 1760s were a time of heated political feelings, and this was to have an impact in the Preston election of 1768. In a wider sense political support in the eighteenth century during elections and in the intervening period could be drawn from a range of factors, few or indeed none of which can be equated to modern party political support. It could be for perceived loyalist sympathies for both Whig and Tory, in that, historically, the tradition was that the Whigs were in favour of the exclusion of James II in 1688 whilst even some high ranking Tories were less enthusiastic. According to this logic both groups could claim to be loyalist, the one in its support for the rights of parliament so fiercely fought over during the revolutionary period, and the other for the rights of the 'true' royal line of succession and the strengthening of monarchical powers from a 'dictatorial' parliament dominated by a Whig faction. This albeit historically distant yet still relevant division was given added spice when George III began to bring back the Tories into political prominence, meaning that they were indeed once again perceived as being the party of the King. It has to be remembered that it was only fifteen years previous that the Young Pretender had marched as far as Derby in support of the Stuart (and some would say Tory) cause. But on the other side there could also be support for a specific faction within those broad party coalitions in the sense that the candidate would pledge his support for Pitt or for Rockingham or some other national faction leader within the Whig party. Or support was offered due to localism in terms of the paternalistic dominance of local families or it could be down to patronage in the sense that voting for and electing a given candidate would ensure the advance of some local business or that other favours could be expected. This localised element is particularly interesting in the North-West with candidates associated with promoting specific issues, such as cotton or coal or the commercial and industrial interest of the particular parts of the Lancashire that could affect the region and especially the working class, the majority of whom were excluded from the electoral franchise and the political contract. Yet they still had a demonstrable stake in the direction a particular candidate may take if elected. The same could also be said of the commercial and industrial middle classes, many of whom could vote and wanted to see their favoured candidate returned due to the perceived benefits this could bring to their emerging enterprises and interests. The interesting thing about this group was that, although they possessed the property to be allowed official entry into the political contract, they recognised only too well that in the minds of the 'gentry' situated in status above them it should really only be those with the natural lineage and estates who should be in control of the ship of state, yet what those holding this set of elite attitudes did not yet realise that it was the men of commerce and industry who were steadily buying the entire ship. The key point was that for this group of emerging middle classes their influence, in terms of social, political and, of course, economic importance was growing and increasingly could not be ignored. They, like the working class below them, were beginning to combine together for their own specific objectives as they perceived the state becoming demonstrably more interfering not less, and they were gravitating to their own leaders and not blindly following those of the established political elites; they were in reality throwing off the old system of politics, growing increasingly frustrated with the conventional system of political representation.[1] This was hammered home to them by the fact that in the larger

---

1   J. Brewer, 'English Radicalism in the Age of George III,' in J. G. A. Pocock, (ed.) *Three British Revolutions*, (New Jersey: Princeton University Press, 2014 ed.) , pp. 334-36, and by the same author 'Clubs, Commercialization and Politics,' in *The Birth of a Consumer Society,* Brewer, J., N.

manufacturing towns such as Bolton, Blackburn, Oldham, Rochdale, Bury, Stockport and especially Manchester, they did not have parliamentary or even borough electoral franchises. Thus the only opportunity these men of industry in these areas had to vote was in the county elections and these again were dominated by country gentry, men who loathed the men of new wealth and in reciprocation the urban-based manufacturing class detested. In short, for both the working class and the increasingly influential middle class the nature of the political debate was becoming wider and, accordingly, the ideological nexus was no longer fixed but beginning to be more fluid with the specific nature of class interests becoming much more prevalent and important. Both these groups were somewhat paradoxically looking backwards and forwards in the visions that informed their developing ideological positions. The working class were being increasingly drawn to the Levelling virtues of Winstanley and the middle class to the merits of the mushrooming of trade and commerce after the Restoration of 1660, restricting the actions of King and parliament in arbitrarily levying taxes and the philosophical justification for such beliefs dating back to John Hampden, Algernon Sydney and John Locke.[2] There was also the religious dimension of political allegiance with nonconformists or dissenters tending towards the Whigs and Anglicans and the Jacobite remnants supporting the Tories. Then there was the debate surrounding which definition of loyalty one subscribed to; the Tory view that British history and the rights of true succession had been violated or the Whig view that a balanced constitution required the separation of powers but with parliament being the final arbitrator of what was best for the country at large. Or it could be down to plain and simple corruption and the literal buying of a seat in a constituency. The interesting thing about Preston was that it was the only constituency, along with Middlesex, in the entire country which technically speaking was a truly open franchise within which all the residents who paid local rates could vote. This was a right that had been bestowed on the town at the time of the restoration in 1661, but it had rarely if ever been exercised. The usual practice was that the (Tory) borough corporation allowed only free burgess's to vote at parliamentary elections. Yet the question of loyalism, as distinct from patriotism in the first half of the eighteenth century is interesting in itself. To a significant extent this depended on where one stood on the question of the Hanoverian Succession of 1714. The perception was that up until the accession of George III in 1760, and indeed beyond, the Tories were not to be trusted on the succession question given their lukewarm acceptance of the first two Hanoverians, the apparent recognition by many of their rank and file to maintain support for James II (and his successors 'across the water') and, it has to be said, the propaganda and deliberate exclusion tactics of the ruling Whig faction since the time of Walpole from 1721. In the eighteenth century 'patriotism' was, until the advent of the French wars of the 1790s, distinct and different to modern distinctions of loyalist association with one's nation, and

---

McKendrick, and J. H. Plumb, (eds.), (London: Europa, 1982), pp. 197-262; and K. Wilson, 'Urban Culture and Political Activism in England: The Example of Voluntary Hospitals,' in A. Birke and E. Hellmuth, (eds.), *The Transformation of Political Culture in Late Eighteenth Century England and Germany*, (Oxford: Oxford University Press, 1990) p. 377.

2 However, one writer in the *Political Register*, (1768) wrote a letter entitled, 'Cautions to English Electors, against such persons as they ought NOT to represent them in the ensuing parliament'. Here he warned as to the activities of merchants. "The sole object of a merchant in all his undertakings is private gain... But this useful propensity gives bias to his mind, till gain, by degrees, becomes the sole object of his thoughts; and when that is the case, extraordinary opportunities for making it may prove very dangerous baits". p. 41.

given its significance in the eighteenth century context it is worthy of brief consideration.

Before its modern connotations, closely associated with the advent (or many would argue 'invention') of nationalism, there were three distinct interpretations of patriotism, linked to oppositional legitimation, the libertarian tradition, and Britons as a 'chosen' people. Within the accepted language of politics the term 'patriotism' was firstly linked closely to an oppositional stance in politics. It was the legitimation of opposition. Traditionally a formed opposition to the King and his ministers was considered at best political suicide and at worst treasonable. Thus the assertion that opposition was motivated by patriotism was a means of legitimating views different to those of the ruling clique: that one could oppose the government of the state on the grounds of one's deep and honest belief that their actions were not for the betterment of all, the 'common weal'. By extension this meant that providing opposition of this kind to the policies pursued by the existing government was being done for the benefit of the nation as a whole. The term increasingly began to be used as being opposed to the widespread corruption found at all levels of government, found especially, it was alleged, by the Walpolian Whigs, and the desperate need to restore balance to a rotten constitution. The ideal balance as laid down by thinkers such as Machiavelli was that between Monarchy, Aristocracy and Democracy, which in Britain translated into the balance between, King, the House of Lords and the House of Commons. Corruption of the constitution occurred if any of one these institutions were under the undue influence of another. This was the oppositional stance of such figures as Bolingbroke, the first Pitt, and John Wilkes in the 1760s. But there was a second thread to the English patriotic tradition. This view held that in ancient times that before the imposition of the Norman Yoke the constitution was pure, and it was an important strand of this Anglo Saxon view of the libertarian tradition of patriotism which had led the opposition against Stuart tyranny. This was effectively an argument for reform based on the need to return to past practices based on liberty, fairness, justice and the needs of the whole community; the popular view of the common weal. A third derivation of the use of patriotism was closely linked to the historical interpretation was that the English were a chosen nation. That God was English; which effectively translated into the belief that God had bestowed on the English the precious, peculiar values and privileges not available to other nations. If anyone threatened this view of liberty then the freeborn Englishman would be justified in rising up in opposition, inspired by the example of the patriotic martyrs who, in radical eyes, Sydney and Hampden of the seventeenth century were supreme examples. What then was this version of liberty and freedom which the English assumed to be their birthright? It meant freedom from foreign domination. It was further believed that liberty bred prosperity; the freedom to do business with whom one pleased often on the basis of who could offer the best deal.

One of the distinguishing features of an Englishman was his clothes, no wooden shoes, and his food, no thin soup, but the roast beef of old England and good honest English beer. The term of patriot of course was also used by the government, especially in times of war, but in general throughout most of the eighteenth century the patriot was one who stood out against the corruption and the many anomalies of the government, who, in short, sought some version of the liberties we have just noted. Even during the first phase of Tom Paine and the French Revolution in the early 1790s patriotism was claimed as a cloak of righteousness by the radicals. In Sheffield in 1792, for example, Joseph Gales even changed the name of his radical newspaper *The Sheffield Register* to *The Sheffield Patriot* and called for 'liberty, a reform of abuses, and an equal representation of the people to resist the gigantic strides towards despotism and arbitrary power.'[3] Some members of the first national radical political institution, the London Correspondence Society, wanted it to be called the 'The Patriotic Club'. It was the invasion threats of 1794-95 and 1803-1805, which turned the language of patriotism around. What happened was that some of the traditional uses of the term were taken over by popular war propagandists. This was especially so in the way that England was presented as God's country, that she was fighting a foe hell bent on depriving Britons of their birthright and liberty. Thus in the 1790s the connections between 'liberty' and 'patriotism' became even stronger, but on this occasion in the hands of government supporters not their opponents. They played both on the connections between liberty and patriotism and at the same time reclaimed from radicalism the language of patriotism for the loyalists. No longer was the British government seen as the tyrant, but it was Napoleon who was portrayed as the great despot, the madman who wanted to take over the world and only plucky little Britain stood in his way. This is familiar stuff to anyone who had heard the Second World War speeches of Winston Churchill for example, but in the 1790s and 1800s this was quite original. The memories invoked were not only the great national struggles of the past, such as Crecy and Agincourt, but, again stealing from the radicals, the examples of Hampden and Sydney who stood out against Stuart tyranny and despotism. This is not to say that the radicals did not try to win back their use of the term. The fact was that in the 1790s there were different versions of patriotism. The love of the country could still be the radical need to rid of the flagrant abuses of a corrupt state. This can be seen in the way patriotism as a political prize was fought over during the war years. Now there was the loyalist version set against the radical version. But increasingly what we see here is the use of a term which along with other more tangible forms, such as the National Anthem, the Union flag, the newly found reverence of George III that Linda Colley notes became symbolic of national unity.[4] Although the government undoubtedly resorted to repression, official harassment, and judicial persecution, it would seem that there were distinct objectives in mind. The first was undoubtedly to nullify the threat posed by the various types of radicals. Through the government's playing up of the threat posed by French invasion, and what that would mean to Britain's traditions and culture, coupled with the use of patriotism as a stick with which to beat the radicals with their own ideological tools, attitudes of patriotism underwent a subtle but distinct change of meaning. But there appeared to be a second, if not clearly defined, objective, one which the state was happy to see develop. And this related to a second long-term effect of what the British political establishment did, which was to foster an attitude of inherent conservatism, of seeing rash or wholesale change as dangerous and, it could be argued, such an attitude also engendered notions of splendid isolation, a separateness allied closely to a form embryonic nationalism. In effect, what this equated to was an enjoining of this new wider view of patriotism with the comforting notion that we, the British, were the most superior nation not only in Europe but on Earth. In fact this was an inherent trait that had been developing

---

3   H. F. Mahan, 'Joseph Gales, the National intelligencer and the War of 1812' PhD. Thesis, Columbia University, New York, (1958).
4   L. Colley, *Britons: Forging the Nation State, 1707-1837,* (New Haven: Yale University Press, 1992).

throughout the eighteenth century but came to the fore, and became the predominant definition of patriotism, with the need to galvanise nationalism and the nation state during the crisis years of the American and, especially, the Napoleonic Wars.

From 1721 until 1741 Walpole was the consummate Whig politician, utilising the benefits of his office of First Lord of the Treasury or 'prime' minister to offer patronage to the 'friends' of the Whigs, such as the Pelham's and Fox's, to maintain those of the Whig party who were the 'Ins' and keeping rival Whigs (who were the 'outs') at bay, as well as, of course, the hated and untrustworthy Tories.[5] Walpole's success lay it his policy – some may call it an ideology – of keeping Britain out of costly European conflicts whilst allowing the first two George's licence (and a moderate allowance) to pursue their limited European adventures without directly embroiling Britain. At the risk of over-simplification, his policy was to give some latitude to the foreign ambitions of the King so long as he knew full well that His Majesty was not to interfere in domestic politics which were effectively the sole domain of Walpole. This did not sit well with the so-called Patriotic Whigs such as Bolingbroke and later, particularly, William Pitt, who demanded more forthright and aggressive British overseas policies, primarily to build on Britain's huge imperial potential at the expense of rivals such as Spain, Portugal, Holland and especially France. Above all, Walpole knew how to keep both the urban and landed Whigs happy, by maintaining low levels of land taxation and direct taxation and raising revenues by increasing excise duties and various levies on imports and exports. London, and to a lesser extent Bristol and Liverpool, was the supreme *entrepôt*'s and the economic system of mercantilism – for all the increased criticism it was receiving as being too state-centred – reached its zenith under Walpole. His fall was to a significant extent due to his unyielding pursuit of these policies when it was clear that the French, and to a lesser extent the Spanish, were taking advantage of Britain's reluctance to engage in building on her overseas assets. Walpole also suffered from becoming, by the late 1730s, widely unpopular 'out of doors' with those middling sorts and working people for raising costs of essentials, particularly foodstuffs but also items such as beer. Yet his fall in early 1742 did not at first alter the political *status quo* too severely, his protégé Henry Pelham was soon to take control of the ministry and largely the same policies were pursued, but he began to make overtures to bring the widely popular William Pitt and some of his supporters into the political (i.e. ministerial) fold. This remained the political *status quo* until George II died in October 1760 and his grandson acceded to the throne.

George III, however, came to the throne determined to break up the old ruling Whig cliques and, even more shocking, to bring back the Tories into positions of national government prominence. As noted, the Walpolian Whigs had dominated domestic politics and, it has to be said, in this sphere had firm control over first two Georgian kings. George III was the son of Frederick, George II's eldest son, and to say the two did not get along would a major understatement. Frederick had been the darling of the opposition Whigs (i.e. those who were not 'considered' by Walpole) and he entrusted his son's political education to those who following a similar line. Yet also, and importantly, George had been tutored by some eminent Tories, not least the Earl of Bute and when he ascended the throne he brought some of his 'favourites' into government

---

5 For the nature of this usage of these terms see L. B. Namier, *The Structure of Politics at the Accession of George III*, (London: Macmillan; 2nd edn., Reprinted edition 1960).

and what made matters worse, if they ever could be, was that Bute was a Scot who as a race, in the popular mind at least, were mistrusted after the four failed 'risings' of 1708, 1715, 1719 and 1745. The end of the Seven Years War brought with it huge debts and considerable political pressure. Pitt was removed and brought back; Newcastle was removed and brought back, Bute was made Prime Minister but proved to be a disaster, although he remained a favourite of the King and was ever willing to proffer his advice, he was not brought back. As for 'popular' politics, for the established politicians at Westminster, both Whig and Tory, this remained to a significant extent tangential to how the popular will could be manipulated and used by politicians at Westminster. Or indeed by the increasingly influential press, both the independent press and those controlled by politicians, in the form of early pressure groups. Such groups and the spokesmen for issues which they favoured were, to a significant extent, not allowed direct access to Parliament, but rather dropped hints in less formal surroundings such as the gentlemen's clubs, the sitting rooms of major political leaders or in their attempts to set the agenda via specially commissioned articles. Yet this is not to say that ordinary men and women from all classes did not have or express political opinions. One of the most blatant issues that tended to exasperate 'ordinary' people was the seemingly never ending and (regarded by many as) excessive increases in taxation, particularly on those items that affected the day to day lives of the masses. From 1762 indirect taxation in the form of excise duties began to impact ordinary people in day to day commodities whilst those 'luxuries' such as fine wines and liquor enjoyed by the elites appeared to be untouched. The two most reviled items subject to these new taxes were, in the first instance, beer and then, particularly irksome to those parts of the county where it was consumed in quantity, cider. This created a significant outbreak of popular protest and rage against the King's ministers.[6] Indeed, this protest began to take on an almost sacred aspect in the sense that the popular perception was that it was the 'supreme power' or rights of the 'people' to oppose a tyrannical King or his legislature.[7] Yet there was a further element in the nature of the eighteenth century political system which leant itself towards a more populist perception. This was that although the lower orders had to be excluded in the political contact *per se* in accordance with the Lockean view that their lack of property lessened their real stake in conducting good political judgement at elections, there was still the perception that the responsibility rested for those who were elected to tend dutifully to the interests of all their constituents regardless of whether they possessed the vote or not. Hence this theory of 'virtual representation' gave some limited legitimacy to the political views of the masses, indeed the theory was defended by the great jurist William Blackstone as it was defined by Sir William Yonge on the floor of the House of Commons

---

6 See D. Walsh, 'The Cider Tax, Popular Symbolism and Opposition in Mid-Hanoverian England', in A. Randall and A. Charlesworth, (eds.), *Markets, Market Culture and Popular Protest in Eighteenth-Century Britain and Ireland*, (Liverpool: Liverpool University Press, 1996) pp. 69-91. See also, P. T. M. Woodland, 'The Cider Excise, 1763-1766.' (Unpublished D.Phil., University of Oxford, 1982), and by the same author, 'Extra-Parliamentary Political Organization in the Making: Benjamin Heath and the Opposition to the 1763 Cider Excise., *Parliamentary History*, Vol.4, 1985, and 'Political Atomization and Regional Interests in the 1761 Parliament: The Impact of the Cider Debates 1763-1766. *Parliamentary History*, Vol.8, 1989, and 'The House of Lords, the City of London and Political Controversy in the Mid-1760s: The Opposition to the Cider tax Further Considered. *Parliamentary History*, Vol.11, 1992.
7 See the *Salisbury Journal*, 12 March, 1764, the 'supreme power' to oppose the legislative tyranny of the cider tax.

during the troubled days of 1745. This was underscored when in the mid-1760s the Prime Minister George Grenville, anticipating a very real and potent argument which would subsequently come from America regarding parliament's legitimate right to levy duties, said in Parliament in February 1765 that, "The Parliament of Great Britain virtually represents the whole Kingdom", although the theory of virtual representation gained a much wider and historically more defined position due to the stance taken by Edmund Burke from 1774.[8] Yet in the same speech Grenville admitted unequivocally, but almost as an afterthought, yet one that was to have significant implications not only in the Thirteen Colonies but in Britain itself "that not one twentieth of the people are actually represented, which gave added significance and tangible credence to the operation of virtual representation".[9] Given this licence to bring forward their concerns directly into the political arena, for example at the occasion of an election, it was not surprising, given the heightened state of awareness and visibility of politics of the 1760s, that wide sections of the population drawn from a range of social groups began to make their views known. At the centre of politics the storm and increased tension created by John Wilkes from the time of the Middlesex election of 1757, when he defended the free rights of electors to choose their Member of Parliament without interference from Parliament, was now accentuated by his consistent attacks on the ministries of the new King in the 1760s. His unashamed oppositional stance opened up a new phase in British politics in that agitation 'outside' Parliament – for so long deemed impermissible – became increasingly established, ushering in the very real potency of interest or pressure groups attempting to influence decision making in Westminster. Yet this highly populist persona cultivated by Wilkes had another effect. The bringing back of the Tories into the mainstream of politics did not, as one would imagine, make the profile of parties more defined and more oppositional in nature but, in fact, made their leaders realise that for the functioning and, especially, the orderly nature of the system to be preserved on *their* terms, both Whigs and Tories had to present a united front as the legitimate ruling class regardless of factional or party differences. Hence, both parties became more attuned to a conservative approach to political governance, primarily to keep out unwanted radical and reformist interlopers representing their class interests. In effect, although the pressure 'out-of-doors' became stronger and louder, this situation of a broad coalition prevailed among the political elites, (apart from self-promoting 'radical' anomalies like Charles James Fox or Sir Francis Burdett), until it began to be broken down with the pressure for and the eventual passing of the Reform Act of 1832. This was the case regardless of party differences; the patrician state had to be preserved. This need was reaffirmed, and indeed apparently justified, by the scenes of wanton destruction occasioned

---

8   For Grenville speech see P. D. G. Thomas, (ed.), *Parliamentary Diaries of Nathaniel Ryder, 1764-1767*, (Camden Miscellany, Vol. XXIII, Camden, Fourth Series, Vol. 7, Royal Historical Society, 1969) p. 254. See also J. A. Cannon, *Parliamentary Reform 1640-1832*. (Cambridge: Cambridge University Press, 1972) p. 32. P. Langford, 'Property and 'Virtual Representation 'in Eighteenth-Century England.' *Historical Journal* (1988) Vol. 31 number 1 pp. 83-115. M. W. McCahill, *The House of Lords in the Age of George III (1760-1811)* (2009) chapter 16 reprinted in *Parliamentary History* (Oct 2009) Supplement 1, Vol. 28, pp 363-385. W. Blackstone, *Commentaries on the Laws of England* 11th edition, (London, 1791), Vol. I, Book I. Yonge's statement can be found in E. Porritt and A. G. Porritt, *The Unreformed House of Commons*, (Cambridge, 1903) p. 271. E. Burke, *The Works of Edmund Burke*, Seven Volumes, Vo. 2, 'Speeches on arrival at Bristol and at the conclusion of the poll', October 13 and November 3, 1774' (London: Macmillan, 1907). p. 12.

9   Thomas op cit, ibid.

by the Gordon Riots of June 1780s, and then nine years later by events in Paris when the most powerful and rigidly policed state of *ancien regime* was crushed in a matter of days by the revolutionary 'mob'. It mattered little that the increasingly vociferous opponents of the existing system accused those running it of corruption and by their actions holding back the merits of the new middle classes and indeed the national interest. Or that the most numerous group in the country did most of the actual work but got scant reward and, believing that their rights were being systematically eroded, had to be excluded; the prevailing system above all had to be preserved, lest it be destroyed by a 'democratic' mob. Yet although this new informal and unofficial coalition of Whigs and Tories from the mid-1760s, forced as they were to defend the *status quo* and their positions of the control of the central state, (developing quite literally a 'conservative' approach), may have been settled in Westminster and the great houses of the grandee families this was certainly not the case for the masses 'out-of-doors'. The King's support of the Tories and their historic ties with the Jacobites, and, importantly, their role in recent administrations and the issues associated with them (the botched peace with France, the deteriorating situation in the Thirteen Colonies, the continuing high prices of provisions and the raising of excise duties on a range of non-luxury products) made them a popular target of scorn.

Although to a significant extent the factions still vied for the power of office at the centre of the political stage and both the Whig and Tory factions formed a private compact to maintain the influence of the patrician elites, this was not the state of affairs in the constituencies. Here both sides needed to reinforce their positions. The Whigs by recovering what they saw as lost ground now that the Tories were officially back in genuine contention for office and the Tories in attempting to consolidate what they saw as potentially a very bright future under the new King. But it was in the constituencies where the real action was located in terms of some bitter fights for votes and to re-assert the control of the core interests of the respective parties. The Tories still placed a huge significance on what they believed was an anchor of popular support for their loyalty to the established state religion of the Church of England and to their devotion to their monarch, even more so now that George III had seemingly allowed them a potential seat at the high table of cabinet government, unlike his immediate forebears. They were also for limiting the growing power of the merchant, trading and industrial nabobs who were vying for attention and had their own reasons for wanting power at, or at least to send representatives to, Westminster to support their key interests. For many old fashioned Tories these people were playing a dangerous game; not only upsetting the status quo in their efforts for social equality, but upsetting an organic balance in removing, or at best diluting, the customary practices that had served the nation so well historically. The question they asked themselves was, why did these men wish to surge forward with untried and potentially damaging practices, primarily to serve their own selfish interests, when they did not know what the outcome of the effect of these changes would have on wider society? For the Whigs and their supporters in the predominantly urban commercial constituencies it was the reverse set of policies that were now required through the pursuit of policies which promoted Britain's huge imperial trading potential. Britain now more than at any other time needed to give the men of commerce, business, trade and industry their rightful place in putting these new interests to the fore which in their view were the only way Britain would be able to recover and build on the hard won gains of the Seven Year War, and crucially, they argued, reduce the national debt which appeared to be spiralling out of control. What was required was a national economic policy which allowed the men of commerce, trade and manufacturing to be able to influence by central (or indeed local) government in order to pursue their interests not only for their own personal gain but for the overall benefit of the nation at large, or, even more agreeably, to be left unfettered by government. For those persuaded by the need for a drastic rethink the system of mercantilism altogether, or indeed dumping it completely, the need was to limit government spending on the servicing of such huge national deficits in order to further reduce the levels of indirect taxation which could then be redeployed as working capital to the benefit of the entire nation. This would, they argued, be best achieved by focusing the economy on the export of commodities to markets either under the direct control of Britain or at least to those parts of Europe and the globe where such products could be reached by Britain's maritime fleet, which everyone assumed to be biggest and best in the world. Typical of these sentiments were the letters supporting Sir George Warren in his candidature for Lancaster in the 1768 election, especially in relation to the growing importance of commerce, industry and trade in the region. One endorsement from 'A Freeman' ran:

> When I look upon the Letter of Thanks addressed to Sir *George Warren* by so many merchants and traders "with hearts full of gratitude and respect" returning him Thanks for "close attention to the commercial interests of Great Britain and her Colonies, and especially for his Care and Assistance in these Matters, which more particularly appertained to this Part of the Country. When I enquire into the Reason for Sir *George Warren* publishing this Letter of Thanks, and find this warranted every respect; when I see Merchants of the Port of *Liverpool* offering their Thanks to Sir *George Warren* (tho' no representative for that Borough) for his strenuous and distinguished Endeavours in Parliament, and this Honour followed *with the most respectable Compliment* of his Freedom by the Mayor and the rest of the Common Council of the Corporation of *Liverpool*, by a unanimous vote, for his great Attention shewn, and services done in Parliament for establishing the Free Ports. When to this is added the obliging Thanks of that great and opulent Town of *Manchester* signifying their Approbation of his Attention to the commercial Interest of his Country, and approving his integrity in Parliament...[10]

This writer then goes on to attack the Tories, displaying again the high levels of partisanship emerging at this time, suggesting that their tactics reveal an "... extraordinary Performance [to] convince the World, that a Party in Opposition to the present Members, have neither the Legs to stand upon, nor a Prop to lend support to their expiring Faction, and their sinking Cause?"[11] This endorsement was all the more relevant in the sense of propelling an essentially local or at best regional election into one concerned with national and, indeed, ideological questions and issues. Again typically, if also somewhat tendentiously, the Whigs in the localities presented a stance of direct opposition to the calls for factional Jacobitism and High Church Tory values and hence there was the appeal to nonconformist values and to religious dissent and, above all, to

---

10 *Manchester Mercury*, 5 January, 1768. It is not particularly unusual that the Whig dominated, commercial orientated Corporation of Liverpool would back Warren, a staunch supporter of Pitt and the necessity of widening Britain's commercial orbit in the wake of the Seven Years War, yet the endorsement from Manchester also suggests that this party was also gaining ground and influence at this time.

11 Ibid.

restoring the constitutional balance in which the King should know his place and leave off interfering in matters of which he had only strictly limited rights. These men of industry and commerce, like the 'Great Patriot' Pitt, saw Britain's global expansion based on the power of the military and merchant fleet as pivotal to their own commercial success, and the nation must not get distracted in interceding in the mess that was Europe. If the old traditional ways had been shown to be an impediment to potential commercial advance and industrial progress then they had to go. In the immediate run-up to the general election of 1768 the Tories in the constituencies pointed to the mess that the Whigs had got the country into since the Rockingham ministry had taken over in 1765; in America with the Stamp Act, the threatened embargo by the Americans to British trade which had brought a massive slump in exports to that part of the world. The Whigs in contrast pointed to the Grenville ministry that had preceded Rockingham and the damage that increased indirect taxes were having on both domestic consumption through rising prices, and that it was this administration, hand-picked, they argued by the interfering George III that had started the chaos in the first place.[12]

The King's apparent association with the Tories and his close ties with Bute, the so-called Scottish 'foreigner', at the start of his reign had alienated him from the masses and vitriol rained down on him in the London and provincial press. In one sense the resolve of George III to begin his reign by sweeping away the remnants of Walpole's Whig 'junta' and begin to bring in politicians who were not tainted by the endemic corruption associated with the old regime was commendable. It was rather that often the people he chose for high office (such as Bute and the incompetent Chancellor of the Exchequer, Sir Francis Dashwood) were clearly unfit for their roles and the policies pursued, more often than not, had the effect of satisfying few and turning popular opinion against the King.[13] Some of this criticism was downright threatening in tone, thus he had better be careful, warned Junius, lest "he profit by the fate of the Stuarts".[14] However, the case of Wilkes became notorious not only because of his direct assault on the King and his ministers in the *North Briton*, but similar oppositional lampoons began to appear more often in the more respectable journals. These scurrilous and often defaming satires appeared widely in the national press, the two below can be considered quite mild in relation to the mood of the time. The first is a typical early example of an exchange in an alehouse from 1762, taken from the *Gentleman's Magazine* reprinted from *The St. James Chronicle*, not long into the new King's reign.

SCENE in an Alehouse
A. This is good tobacco
B. Where did you buy it?
A. Of *Jemmy Gordon*
B. At the Highlander?

---

12 For a more detailed look at national political questions at this time see P. Langford, *A Polite and Commercial People*, (Oxford: Oxford University Press, 1992) pp. 360-370.
13 It was said of Dashwood's knowledge of finance and his first speech as Chancellor that: "Of financial knowledge he did not possess the rudiments, and his ignorance was all the more conspicuous from the great financial ability of his predecessor Legge. His budget speech was so confused and incapable that it was received with shouts of laughter." W. E. H. Lecky, *A History of England in the Eighteenth Century* (London, 1892 edn.) Vol. iii, p. 224.
14 *Public Advertiser*, 19 December, 1769, also quoted in K. Wilson, 'Inventing Revolution: 1688 and Eighteenth-Century Popular Politics', in the *Journal of British Studies,* Vol. 28, No. 4 (October, 1989), p. 380.

A. Yes
B. Damn all *Scotchmen* say I
A. (*After three whiffs*) This is good tobacco
B. (*After three whiffs*) Hem, hem, hem.
A. Have you heard any news?
B. No
A. (*Laying down his pipe*) We shall have a peace.
B. No! (*Whiffing*)
A. Yes
B. No! (*Whiffing still*)
A. We shall.
B. (*Laying down his pipe*) It can't, it can't be, my Lord Bute will lose his head if he makes one. What of Newfoundland and Guadalupe, and Senegal, and Goree, and Martinico? It can't be.
A. *Jones*, bring us another tankard, but don't let it be too stale. (*Beer brought*)
B. (*Drinking*) Here's confusion to all *Scotchmen*.
A. With all my heart. We have nothing but *Scotchmen* in all places. Who do you think was made *tide-waiter* t'other day in room of *Tom Grant*?
B. Who?
A. A damned *Scotchman* son of a bitch, *Mac* something, I don't know what. Could they ne'er find an Englishman to give it to?
B. Hang all the *Macs* and *Murrays* say I, a parcel of beggarly, lousy, scabby rascals. 'Tis a pity they were not all sent back to their own country to starve with my Lord Bute at the head of them. Pox on them, I am so mad with them, I have broke my pipe, just as I was got to the marrow of it.
A. Fill another, here's my box at your service.
B. No, thank you, I must be going. Here boy, what's to pay? Two tankards– three pence halfpenny apiece. If *Mr Pitt* had continued in, the beer would never been raised. I wish you a good night *Mr Jenkinson*.
A. A good night to you *Mr Tomkins*.[15]

The second example coming again in 1762 is taken from a new satirical political dictionary published in *The Auditor,* below are a selection of the definitions.

> *Germany*. About six years ago we were taught by the *grand pensioner* (Pitt) to understand by this word, the *grave of* Englishmen, *the ruin of the* British *treasury, a millstone around the neck of* England etc. But that *great philologer* has now changed his mind, and it means at present, the place where *America* was conquered.
>
> *Ally*. Some power in Germany that takes £700,000 for fighting his own battles. *Viz. Grand pensioner's treaty with the King of* Prussia.
>
> *The King*. One who ought to enjoy the painful pre-eminence of being a mere cipher in this kingdom, without prerogative, without opinion, without affection etc. at least during the *Demagogue's* (Bute's) life.
>
> *The Mob*. The supreme executive power, who ought to govern their superiors, and rule this nation, at least during the *pensioners* life.
>
> *Oeconomy*. A vice of a very dangerous nature, which should never be practiced in a court, because if cooks, confectioners, wine merchants,

---

15 *Gentleman's Magazine*, September 1762, p. 413.

pages, etc. are not permitted to waste at least £200,000 of the civil list, the king may gain such a kind of independency, as will place him above all ministerial jobs and applications to parliament, and further burthens on the subject to make good the deficiencies.[16]

Hence from the early 1760s there was a decided sharpening of political opinions in terms of their forthright nature and a certain desire, certainly among the Whigs, to rectify what was apparently an ineluctable slide away from the perceived benefits of the settlement of 1688 when the powers of the monarch were balanced alongside that of the legislature and the judiciary. It further seemed that this raising of political awareness was not confined to the polite society of London or the larger provincial centres. For example, John Collier of Milnshaw, near Rochdale, the author of the *Truth in a Mask or the Shude-hill Fight*, was not averse to giving his views, albeit mostly once again in the form of satire or allegory which was the convention at least in the first two-thirds of the eighteenth century. Yet here we find overt sentiments of republicanism as in one of his notebooks he wrote:

> I hate all the kings and those who attend 'em
> And wish that the Gibbets or Ropes may amend 'em."[17]

There was a sense of discontent at all levels of society and the pressure on politicians was not helped by the deteriorating situation in the Thirteen Colonies of North America or, indeed, the generally worsening situation in Europe or India. On top of this was a further rise in the cost of provisions across the country, coupled with outbreaks of industrial disputes. In the early part of 1768 there were serious disputes among the Spitalfields weavers in London, also at Wapping the coal heavers went on strike over wages, which was only settled by the arbitration of the aldermen of the City of London. At Newcastle, North Shields and Sunderland the sailors and keelmen went out on a very violent and acrimonious strike.[18] According to one report "they have carried their cause to such a height that everyone there is obliged to comply with their demands as soon as asked."[19] According to another report, the cry here was for "Wilkes and liberty is said to be as loud among the sailors as at London."[20] In the King's address to Parliament he noted the distress of the people and stressed to improve the trade and commerce of the country whilst at the same time issuing a proclamation by an Order in Council for the "suppressing of riots, tumults and unlawful assemblies." At virtually the same time the whole body of sailors in London were still on strike, unrigging ships in the Thames, and two thousand of them marched to Wimbledon Common to present a petition to the King[21]

This division was further enflamed by a hardening of the attitudes of the elites and employers. One such 'Medius' wrote a damning letter to the

---

16 Ibid. pp. 411-413.
17 Chethams Library, Manchester, (*Bobbin, Tim, 1708-1786*), *Miscellaneous autograph works including 'Subscribers to Human passions delineated', sketch book, accounts with booksellers: manuscript, 1763-1783*, Undated, but likely to be circa, 1765, (Mun Collection, Mun, A.4.40, p. 49). See also, *Sketch book. Pencil, pen and ink, crayon and coloured sketches of people and places, draft lectures and notes, accounts: manuscript, 1763-1783*. Mun Collection Mun.A.4.41
18 *Annual Register*, January, February, March and April, 1768, pp. 68-92. *Gentleman's Magazine*, 22 April and 29, 1768, pp. 198-199. See also National Archive, Kew, State Papers Domestic, SP 37, 2, ff. 189-92; ff. 259.
19 *Annual Register*, 8 April, 1768, p. 92.
20 *Gentleman's Magazine*, May, 1768, p. 241.
21 *Annual Register*, 3 May, 1768 and 10 May, 1768, p. 84 and pp. 105-106.

Gentleman's Magazine on the amount of public money given over to the labouring poor, their general workshy demeanour, the need for free trade and for the state to have a more balanced approach to allow domestic trade and industry to flourish. Indeed, it was expressed in such terms as could have been written as part of the propaganda of the Anti-Corn Law League or the Poor Law Commissioners seventy years later:

> ...all the laws made to discourage foreign manufactures, by levying heavy duties upon them, or totally prohibiting them, whereby the rich are obliged to pay much higher prices for what they wear and consume, than if the trade were open. There are so many laws for the support of our labouring poor, made by the rich, and continued at their expense; all the difference in price between our and foreign commodities, being so much given by our rich to our poor; who would indeed be enabled by it to get by degrees above poverty, if they did not, as generally they do, consider every increase in wages as something that enables them to drink more and work less...St Monday is generally as duly kept by our working people as Sunday; the only difference is, that, instead of employing their time, cheaply, at church, they are wasting it expensively at the alehouse.[22]

This was the divisive political environment which the Preston election of 1768 was contested. Indeed it was being argued by some, even at this early stage in the history of Parliamentary reform, that the working class, if they owned some moderate form of property, should be given the right to elect representatives to Parliament. As one writer of the period suggested universal suffrage was a facet of natural government as it should be and indeed once was.

> A universal representation therefore of such men is no innovation in the constitution; it is merely a restoration of its original purity; from which indeed we have so long and so much deviated, that many seem almost entirely to have lost sight of it, and some are ready to deny that it ever existed.[23]

Or again:

> The design is, that every man whose property of whatever kind, is sufficient to make him independent should vote for a representative: It will hardly be alleged that such a scheme is likely to meet with much opposition without doors. Tis' ridiculous to suppose, that ninety nine parts out of one hundred people, would object to an enlargement of their privileges; or that the clamours of the remainder, who would fancy themselves aggrieved, because the preference they enjoy at present is not part of the constitution, but a corruption of it; it must be remembered, that such of them as are really men of property, would be left in a situation little inferior to what they are in at present.[24]

This discussion of heightening political conflict is relevant for this study because it offers the only significant opportunity in the period under discussion whereupon the working class (of the borough of Preston and its surrounding area at least) could express their political will and actually partake in *bona fide* elections of significance, and it was something which came at a just the moment when the cotton masters were stepping up their efforts to utilise the larger jennies on an industrial scale and once again provoking their workers. The

---

22 *Gentleman's Magazine,* April, 1768, pp. 156-157.
23 J. Burgh, *Reflexions on the Representation in Parliament,* (London, 1766) p. 7.
24 Ibid, pp. 15-16.

workers in the immediate vicinity of East and North Lancashire, where the disturbances associated with the election riots of 1768 occurred, included a mixture of journeymen of a variety of trades, cotton outworkers, agricultural labourers and colliers. The great majority would have witnessed or at least heard of the dispute of the smallware and check-weavers ten years before and the range of other worker disputes taking place in the years leading up to 1768 across the region. The overarching complaint of the working class was that the elites appeared to be abrogating their responsibilities towards these apparent grievances in favour of the new thrusting middle class industrialists. The frustration of the working class, effectively across the entire country, but especially salient in the North-West given the recent bitter disputes, centred on their perceived loss of their customary practices, which to them appeared to have a disruptive and pernicious effect on their community value system. A further important issue touching working people personally was the inflationary nature of prices, especially of provisions, which they had endured for at least the past twelve years, and the apparent insensitivity of a succession of ministries – and the King because he chose them – in imposing a range of swinging new excise duties seemingly aimed directly at them. They understood the reality which was that they were powerless, both politically and now apparently legally, but to them they still possessed the right to demonstrate their exasperation at their worsening situation during and since the conclusion of the Seven Years War. This ability to demonstrate their grievances was a display of their liberties as free people and thus it was part of their inherent constitutional rights. This election, then, gave them an opportunity to bring their anger directly to the notice of the elites. Indeed, this confrontational type of political resistance was encouraged, even by reputable writers such as James Burgh:

> ...remember, liberty is of such importance, that it is no matter what restraints be laid on the power of the few, you can secure the *freedom* of the many. Look into the lamentable histories of enslaved nations; of your own country, when enslaved; then trifle with your liberties, if you dare.[25]

The election contest at Preston came at this unique moment when a convergence of circumstances resulted in an unprecedented and exceptional result. These circumstances were, firstly, the general state of antagonism felt by a significant section of the working class throughout the region, but in this instance and in this locality they were offered an opportunity to give support and make a genuine political statement of what they saw were the inherent wrongs of the moment. Secondly, there was also the widespread feeling of libertarian political activism in the wake of the Wilkes controversy which was by now not just confined to London but had spread to be a national phenomenon.[26] This became the key question of the legitimacy of the English political constitution coupled with notions surrounding the freedom of the press and the invocation of what was popularly understood by the Bill of Rights, enshrined in the so-called

---

25 J. Burgh, *Crito, or Essays on Various Subjects*, Vol. 2, (London, 1767), p. 41.
26 For example in the Isle of Wight there was formed the Revolution Society of Newport and issued the statement of its intent to be that "every true Englishman cherishes the doctrine of resistance, as his palladium." Anon, *A Charge to Englishmen*, (London, 1768), p. 12. Whilst the *Gentleman's Magazine* of May, 1768 reported: "At Newcastle, the cry for Wilkes and Liberty is said to be as to be as loud among the sailors as at London, and attended with the same violences. The women interest themselves in his favour, and are as zealous as the men, but not so *outrageous*." p. 241. See also K. Wilson, 'Inventing Revolution: 1688 and Eighteenth-Century Popular Politics' *Journal of British Studies*, Vol. 28, No. 4 (Oct., 1989), pp. 374-385.

Glorious Revolution of 1688, which had forced the removal of James II. To these features were joined the widespread unpopularity of the King and his apparent unconstitutional interference, and the actions of his seemingly incompetent ministers, the continuing decline in Britain's trading prospects coupled with rising prices on a range of essential provisions and the likelihood of further shortages of grain. Added to these highly volatile set of conditions was the rising frustration on the part of the increasingly important and self-confident middle class, who were coming to the belief that it was they who were the new driving force for the economic betterment of the nation, and that their views should be given due political as well as economic weight. In their view in both these vitally important areas the established political elites and indeed the system itself appeared to be ignoring them. The upshot of what happened in Preston was all the more remarkable because it gave the majority of ordinary working people – males at least – the only platform (along with Middlesex) of an authentic and valid political voice in an industrial constituency, which was a situation that neither of the actual contending parties in the original dispute really wanted. It is clear that the wider society of Preston and its immediate vicinity were politically articulate and understood the balance between questions of national importance and/or local issues which affected not simply their regional situation but also their social position. Also it is clear that the political articulacy of the population of Preston had been present for some time. In the Preston election of 1734, for example, at the nomination of the Tory, Nicholas Fazakerly, it was reported in the newspapers of London that "the general cry among the People (was) liberty and Property, Triennial Parliaments and no Excise."[27] This has led one scholar of the period to suggest, "That this programme should be given such a full airing at Preston is indicative of the involvement of the population both in electoral politics generally and more specifically in the national political issues that were being debated at the time."[28] A point reiterated with the tactical combining of opposition Whigs and Tory interests against what was now being seen as Walpole's biased and, for the region, harmful policies regarding the excise.

> In his study of the Excise crisis and the elections of 1734, Professor Langford has noted that in areas where political rivalries between Whigs and Tories had been fierce, co-operation between opposition Tories and opposition Whigs was not prevalent, but in Preston despite the history of Whig-Tory conflict in the reigns of both Anne and George I, opposition Whigs such as Derby were able to act in concert with an obviously Tory candidate against a ministerial candidate associated with the Excise. This demonstrates a high level of political awareness on the part of the managers of the differing interests in the borough and the population of the town who had expressed their opinions on national issues so explicitly… The Preston electorate and the borough politics were therefore still partisan and participatory, responding to national issues and local rivalries in the same way they had in the 1700s and 1710s.[29]

As we shall discover, at Preston the existence of such widespread and relatively

---

27 *London Evening Post,* 9 March and 12 March, 1734, see also N. Rogers, *Whigs and Cities: Popular Politics in the Age of Walpole and Pitt,* (Oxford: Clarendon Press, 1989) p. 229.
28 R. D. Harrison, 'Parliamentary elections and the political development of Newton, Preston and Wigan, 1689-1768' , PhD thesis, University of Lancaster, 1996. p. 130.
29 Harrison ibid pp. 130-131, citing P. Langford, *The Excise Crisis: Society and Politics in the Age of Walpole,* (Oxford: Oxford University Press, 1975) pp. 114-115.

expressive understanding of politics, especially for the emerging working class, was to have profound and highly significant overtones with respect to the nature of the electoral franchise of the borough at the end of our period of discussion and indeed far beyond the 1770s. However, in order to discover the origins of this inimitable situation we have to go back over a hundred years before 1768 to the Convention Parliament of 1660 which was convened for the restoration of Charles II to the throne.

13
The Political Dimension: The Preston Election of 1768

The town of Preston became historically significant not only due to its role in the famous battle in August 1648 which effectively witnessed the final defeat of the Royalist cause in the Revolutionary Wars, but also because after the Restoration it gradually replaced Lancaster as the premier county town of the region. Most of the officials and, indeed, offices of the Duchy of Lancaster were centred in Preston, making it a relatively rich and salubrious locality as the eighteenth century approached. One should not underestimate the importance of the office of the Duchy in the first three centuries of its existence; from 1265 the Duchy Council included a Chancellor, Chamberlain, two Chief Stewards, a Receiver General, an Attorney General, two Auditors and a Clerk of the Council, all with their attendant officials. The Duchy was a key office not only of national political importance, but also as the administrator of all Royal revenues in the county palatine of Lancaster. It was further expected, and largely adhered to, that the Duchy reserved the right to return one of the town's two members of parliament with the other being allotted to the borough Corporation. As we shall discover it was this assumption of corporate superiority which was to be the key area of contention, but also it was the dispute regarding this circumstance and its ultimate resolution which meant that Preston was offered a truly unique position as one of only two genuinely popular constituencies in the nation. Suffice to say that by the time we get to the eighteenth century Preston was a centre of some importance for the whole of the region. Liverpool was growing as a hugely significant mercantile centre, Manchester as an industrial base and, although Lancaster retained its position as being nominally the county town and in holding the assizes, Preston can be viewed as an administrative centre. Yet it too was developing an industrial core, once again largely associated with the cotton trade and also with all the other service and artisanal trading features associated with such a centre. The key factor was that all grades of Lancashire society would have recognised the town's practical and symbolic importance.

At the time of Restoration Parliament the Corporation of Preston believed it retained the exclusive right to return at least one and possibly two members to the House of Commons, but on this occasion this right was challenged on the basis that the Mayor had not called for a poll, and this was referred to the Commons Committee on Privileges and Elections by some of opposition electors who found evidence of a 'double return', suggesting that some form of unofficial poll had taken place and at least one of the Corporation candidates had lost against a 'popular' candidate.[1] The key issue was whether only the mayor and

---

1 According to Dobson, W. *History of the Parliamentary History of the Representation of Preston during the Last Hundred Years*, (Preston, 1856) for the election of 1660 "there were three candidates for the representation of Preston-Edward Rigby, Dr. Jeoffery Rishton, and Dr. Fife. At this period the Corporation claimed the privilege of being alone allowed to return the members; the in-burgesses insisted upon sharing it with them. The Mayor and Corporation sent up a return that Rigby and Fife had been elected by them. The in-burgesses sent up a return containing the names of Rigby and Rishton; and on the 31st of May, 1661, it was reported to the House of Commons, "by Serjeant Charleton, from the Committee of Privileges and Elections, touching the return for the borough of Preston, that Edward Rigby, Esquire, and Jeoffery Rishton, Esquire, were returned in one indenture, and the said Mr. Rigby and Mr. Fife in another indenture, and the opinion of the committee that the said Mr. Rishton be the proper officer who shall sit till the

twenty-four burgesses had the exclusive right to return Members of Parliament or all the residential inhabitants of the borough had that right, and the Committee came to the verdict that indeed: "Resolved, upon the question, that this house do agree with the said committee, that all the inhabitants of the said borough of Preston have voices in the election; and that the majority of such voices is with Dr. Rishton; and that the said Dr. Rishton is duly elected a burgess for the said borough, and ought to sit in this house."[2] However, up until 1768 this was the only occasion where a popular vote was allowed by the Tory controlled Corporation who in the intervening hundred years had gotten around the problem by calling for polls of only the freemen of the town, the numbers of which only they controlled. They did, however, in deference to the Earl of Derby and the Duchy interest, in normal circumstances allow an opposition Whig take one of the seats.[3]

The situation which had prevailed in Preston of an electoral union of those Whig opponents of Walpole (of which the Derby interest tended to be) and the Tories during the final decade of his tenure not did remain the same after the Walpole had left office in 1742. In fact the death of the tenth earl of Derby in 1736 and the subsequent elevation of his son to the House of Lords meant that one of the county seats for Lancashire had fallen vacant and this was rapidly snapped up by another local Tory, Peter Bold, the former member for Wigan. The concern, then, for the Derby interest in the elections of 1741 was to regain one of the prestigious county seats and to do this it was necessary to take their interest and energies away from Preston which in turn meant that the Tory Corporation would have a clear run at securing two members for the borough, which duly occurred in a contest which once again witnessed significant violence and intimidation.[4] This Tory grip on the electoral fortunes of Preston by the Corporation continued and may even have been assisted by the flaring up of Jacobitism in 1745 which appeared to underscore the inherent anti-George II sentiments and those of his leading Whig ministers in the popular mind. In the elections during the 1740s, 1750s and that of 1761 the Whigs believed putting forward a serious candidate to oppose this interest would be a futile and expensive failure. In fact, in terms of serious policy considerations in the North-West the Excise Crisis of 1733, over which serious opposition had been growing from the previous year, meant that Walpole and his ministry were deeply unpopular throughout the region across the range of social strata. This would again serve to add credence to the views of the new men of business, industry and commerce, and others who were harbouring serious misgivings about the old mercantile economic system and the political means afforded to its maintenance.[5] What they wanted was the opening up of international trade and

---

    merits of the cause shall be determined, and the house passed, a resolution accordingly. On the 18th of December, 1661, the committee reported, and their report was adopted by the house. The words of this report became a century afterwards the electoral charter of the borough, and by an ingenious rendering of the term "inhabitants," gave to Preston the distinction of being the only town in England where universal, or at least man hood, suffrage prevailed to an extent equal to the aspirations of the most ardent democrat." pp. 21-22. Yet Rishton's success was short lived as he died in 1667 and was replaced as MP for Preston by John Otway in the Duchy interest.
2 Ibid. p. 22.
3 8 Feb. 1715 Henry Fleetwood, Jacobite Tory.
4 Harrison, PhD op cit, pp. 132-133. In fact the Stanley interest did gain back one of the County seats at the election of 1741 with James Smith Stanley (Lord Strange) elected.
5 In his endeavour to serve the interests of landed proprietors – the country gentlemen who held the fate of ministries in their hands – Walpole was concerned to reduce the burden of the land tax and shift government revenues to other sources. "The excise scheme of 1733 promised revenues

the ability to utilise Britain's huge navel advantage in safety, which meant in policy terms following the line of Walpole's Whig opponents, most notably, as we have seen, the more aggressive position adopted by William Pitt. Whilst, for their part, the working class, although work and wages were generally good throughout the 1730s, were in fact becoming utterly demoralised by the rising prices of necessities which Walpole's excise increases was producing. Hence, the situation prevailed until we get to the momentous election of 1768 was that the Tory Corporation felt safe and secure in their ability to manage the constituency and control popular opinion. However, in 1768 the leading Whigs of the region felt the situation needed to be remedied, and the Tory Corporation came up against the powerful family interests of the eleventh Earl of Derby (whose nominee was his son-in-law Colonel Burgoyne) and his Whig supporter Sir Henry Hoghton, who ran against the Corporation nominees, Sir Frank Standish and Sir Peter Leicester. The Stanley (Derby) family had links to the town dating back centuries and latterly Derby's son, Lord Strange, had an estate near Preston and was also at this time Chancellor of the Duchy of Lancaster. Similarly the Hoghton family had close ties to the area with their seat at Hoghton Towers. Leicester came from Cheshire but Standish had substantial land holdings in the nearby Chorley and Bolton areas.

It would appear from the numbers involved and the geographic range from which the supporters on both sides were drawn that this election was a focus of the contemporary feelings of heightened partisanship between Whigs and Tories

---

which would permit a permanent reduction of the land tax (which stood at 4 shillings in 1727) to one shilling in the pound" (Langford, op cit p. 28). The measure involved converting the customs duties on tobacco and wine into inland duties. It followed on other fiscal measures that moved in this direction – Walpole had already introduced excise duties on tea, chocolate, and coffee in 1724 and in 1732 he had revived the salt duty (a more sensitive issue, for which he was accused of "grinding the faces of the poor," but the measure nonetheless passed easily enough through the House of Commons (Langford op cit p. 29). So, one can see how Walpole was misled into the idea that the excise bill would not pose any great difficulties. As it turned out, the opposition marshalled an intense and effective campaign against the measure. Opponents revived longstanding criticisms of such measures: "Excise duties involved giving extensive powers of search to revenue officers, and a wide jurisdiction to magistrates and excise commissioners. The Englishman's right to privacy on his own property, and also to trial by jury, were put at risk. An entire genre of horror stories retailed in the press and depicted in broadsheets and prints, exploited such fears." Moreover, merchants and traders--both those engaged in circumventing the existing customs duties and those who paid them--disliked the prospect of dealing with "officious excisemen": "The shopkeepers and tradesmen of England were immensely powerful as a class, scarcely less so in electoral terms than those country gentlemen whom Walpole sought to gratify. Whig or Tory, there was no doubt what they thought of more excises. In the spring of 1733 petitions to Parliament and instructions to MPs flooded in from the provinces in support of a vociferous campaign in London itself. ... In the Commons, when the City (of London) formally presented its petition against the excise on 10 April (1733), Walpole's majority fell to seventeen. In the Lords there seemed an equally damaging aristocratic revolt. ... On the following day (Walpole) announced the withdrawal of the excise scheme in the Commons" (Langford op cit pp. 30.) This announcement was met with exuberant enthusiasm by the public: "On the streets of London Walpole was burnt in effigy, along with Queen Caroline (his supporter). The violence of the populace caused something of a reaction on the back-benches" (Langford 1989: 31). More crucially, George II stood by Walpole. As a result, he was able to recover from this debacle, despite the damage it caused. Walpole engineered the dismissal of his rivals and opponents at court: "The King felt compelled to remove Lord Chesterfield and Lord Clinton from their posts in the royal household forthwith. There followed further dismissals, the Dukes of Montrose and Bolton, the Earls of Stair and Marchmont, Lord Cobham and his followers. In the upper house the ministry survived with its majority barely intact; it took peerage creations as well as dismissals to restore it to health. In the Commons, recovery was swifter and more complete" (Langford op cit pp. 31).

across Lancashire. It was also of the concerns of the various social groups who made up the demographic mix of the population of the North-West and, importantly, it became a vehicle with which to give vent to their principal concerns. What is not known is how the wider population of the North-West were made aware of the particularistic nature of Preston's open franchise, but it would appear that the majority of the large numbers involved were aware that this was indeed an opportunity to make a statement. The nature of the violence apparent for over five months in the run-up to this election bears witness to the inflamed state of public opinion at this time and to the willingness of both sides to inflict as much harm on their opponents as possible, both physical and in terms of their principles. The main reason why these disturbances lasted so long was that everyone knew that under the terms of the Septennial Act a general election had to be called sometime in the spring of 1768 and one witness, who gave a deposition as to the events, suggested that the trouble may have started as early as September, 1767 and was instigated on the Tory side.[6] Thus the Tory Corporation were given ample time to get their plans in place to return two of their candidates to represent the town. Although the representation for Lancashire comprised of only six boroughs and twelve Members of Parliament, the county seat for Lancashire (which also returned two members) was, in terms of the number of voters eligible for the franchise, the second largest in the country with 8,000 names registered.[7] In political terms and in organisational ability, the Tories were the dominant force in Lancashire. At the previous general election in 1761 out of the fourteen seats available they returned ten members to the Whigs four. This is not particularly unusual given the core of Jacobite sympathy there was in Lancashire at both of the 'risings' of 1715 and 1745.[8] It was comprised of the usual mixture of traditional Catholic support and High Church Toryism for those who were loathe to accept the Hanoverian settlement and made worse by their continued enforced ostracisation under the first two George's. Indeed, the families of at least two of the regions Tory Members of Parliament were known to be Jacobite supporters. It was reported that the family of Peter Legh, the member for Newton Le Willows in 1761 and 1768, held meetings in their house at Lyme, near Stockport, to discuss whether they should join the Pretender, which they wisely decided against.[9] Whilst another, Edmund Starkie, the member for Preston between 1754 and 1768,

---

6 "And the deponent John Forgey for himself saith that he resided in Preston aforesaid from or about the month of September in the year of our Lord 1767 until the latter end of the month of April the following (year). And that he hath frequently seen a large mob or riotous assembly of people in the said Borough of Preston headed by Sir Frank Standish baronet of Duxbury in the said county of Lancaster, William Hulton of Hulton in the said county of Lancaster Esq., and Alexander Howell of Preston aforesaid and several other gentlemen in the interest of the said Sir Peter Leicester and Sir Frank Standish and that during the coalescences of the said Sir Frank Standish, William Hulton and Alex Howell (were) among the said mob or riotous assembly divers violences and attacks were committed to the persons and property of several of the said inhabitants of the said Borough who were in the interest of the said John Burgoyne and that they then said Sir Frank Standish, William Hulton and Alex Howell greatly incited and encouraged the said mob so they commit of such outrages and violences and as well by their public appearances amongst them and their approbation and thanks each they all frequently did in the presence of this deponent." Lancashire County Archive, Preston, Deposition 2. DDX 113/6, (taken 20/6/1768, Sergeants Inn, London).
7 *History of Parliament: The House of Commons, 1754-1790*, 3 Vols. L. Namier and J. J. Brooke, (eds.), (Yeovil: Haynes, 1985 edn.) Vol. 1. Yorkshire was the largest electorate in the country.
8 See F. McLynne, 'The Regional Distribution of Jacobite Support in England before 1745' in *Journal of Regional and Local Studies*, no. 3 (1983-84).
9 William Beaumont, *A History of the House of Lyme*, (Warrington, 1876) pp. 186-186.

allowed the Pretender to be a guest at his house near Preston on his way south.[10] Indeed during the 1768 election there were strong Jacobite overtones which gave the contest an added dimension and one which coloured the proceedings towards bitterness and recrimination.[11] However, as the general election of 1768 approached the Tory Corporation of Preston and their supporters would have been buoyed by the apparent shift in the national political culture given that the Tories were clearly back in favour under George III and their stock appeared to be on the rise. Having worked so assiduously to maintain their hold on Preston and the overall North-West for most of the eighteenth century up to this point, this upturn in their fortunes meant nationally that they could be confident in holding onto control.

Hence, given that in the wider public perception the Tories, at least, were on their way back as a national political force, and when this is coupled with their ascendant position in the North-West, it was not especially surprising that the Whigs would attempt to recapture some hold on the region which had not been especially prone to supporting their cause. Yet the North-West was a region that was becoming, year on year, an increasingly essential and significant national asset in economic terms. It could well have been this rise in the commercial, industrial and general trading patterns of the region which gave the Whigs some hope that their position may have improved and thus at the organisational centre in London it was seen as a fight worth engagement and they gave Derby their full backing.[12] Thus this contest was important for a number of reasons, some complex, some not so. Some were bound by historical and religious tradition, others by more pragmatic and especially commercial factors linked, at least in many of the minds of the rising middle class industrialists, by the need to enhance the rich potential of the region in a national sense; and the best way to achieve this was to send friendly and supportive representatives to Parliament. In the thinking of many such men and also given their inherent Nonconformist predilections, their logic led to the belief that if the necessary changes to the old commercial practices were to be accomplished this would be more likely to come from those Whigs who had recently shown a distinct willingness to affect these changes to the economic *status quo* than the traditionalist Tories. When these factors are put alongside the manifest downturn in the economic performance of the nation since the end of the Seven Years War and, particularly, since the new King's dalliance with Bute and his Tory cohorts; then these relatively new men of industry and trade would be supportive of the Whigs. Those Tories of old county gentry stock were persuaded that the actions of the

---

10 J. Byrom, *The private journal and literary remains of John Byrom,* Vol. II, Part 1, (Chetham Society, Old Series, OS 40, 1856) p. 388.
11 Dobson reports that: "Judging from some of the addresses issued it would appear that there was something of a Jacobite feeling involved in the contest, for the Corporation were charged with winking at, if not sanctioning, disloyal cries, such as "Down with the Rump," "No King George," "Prince Charles," "King James," "White Cockades," &c." Op cit pp. 9-10. In 1715 Preston was described as being "one of the greatest T(ory) or J(acobite) towns in England..." Leicestershire Archive, Leicester, DG7/4969, John Chetwynd to Lord Finch, 15 January, 1715.
12 In the eighteenth century context compared to that of the nineteenth century it was rare for a national co-ordinated campaign orchestrated from the centre. The most likely 'system' prevailing was that support depended to a significant extent to just how well connected a particular leading Whig family was to the existing ministry, then financial support could come in the form or secret service money. Yet Derby was a leading Whig and the fact that his son was significant in the House of Commons and Chancellor of the Duchy of Lancaster is suggestive of that interest gaining national backing. For the manner in which general elections were organised by the Whigs from London, see Namier op cit, pp. 196-211.

new men of commerce were having a dilatory effect on the morale of the working people, a fact made clear by the recent phases of popular protest, the periods of dearth and high food prices, the burst of strikes across a range of trades and the apparent breakdown of the traditional deference to social rank by large sections of the lower orders. But also by the very real possibility that the enforced changes to prescriptive work practices could mean less work for women and children and less family income overall for working people, which would further mean that the poor rates would ineluctably rise. The concerns and grievances of the working class in their political preferences would, of course, in most places and indeed nationally, have been at the bottom of any list of political objectives but they could not be ignored at Preston because of the nature of its (at least potentially) popular and socially wide electoral franchise.

Whilst one leading historian of the period describes the general election of 1768 as 'quiet', it certainly was not in North and East Lancashire.[13] We have noted the deteriorating commercial and trading situation, the desperate need of the Treasury to gain funds to ease the growing national debt, the problems this was causing in North America and, to make matters worse, in the run-in to this election at the end of 1767 there was a stock market bubble associated with the East India Company which further spread the economic gloom. Politically the situation was equally dire with the national Whig leadership in disarray and at this election no fewer than four recent Prime Ministers, in the shape of Newcastle, Bute, Grenville and Rockingham, and also the present one, Grafton, not to mention the actual leader of the government at this time, Chatham, all vying for relevance and power. In the North-West the middle class industrialists and men of commerce wished to gain an advantage by getting some form of representation, preferably similar to that seen at Liverpool. Yet what made this election all the more intense was the focus that singled out Preston as the key constituency where these interests may stand a chance of success, the key reason being that the remaining ten borough seats were more or less settled. Key places such as the emerging centres of local industry at Bolton, Blackburn, Oldham, Bury, and Rochdale, not to mention the most important of them all in Manchester, were all unable to send representatives to Westminster. Hence Preston became symbolic of the need to gain a political foothold, to which were added the latent Jacobitism, the perceived rights and desire of the Corporation to maintain their privileged position to determine the town's representatives, the popular disaffection amongst the working class across the region, and the sense of escalating political crisis which meant this was seen as a vital contest for this variety of reasons. Certainly by the time Parliament was about to be prorogued ready for the general election the respective parties at Preston were already in full operation. Indeed, a presage for what was to follow came from a letter from Mitton in the Ribble Valley, some five miles from Preston, in relation to the similar electoral privileges held by the Corporation at Lancaster and here too there was an attempt to widen the franchise.[14] Thus, unlike any previous elections in living memory the contests, in the north and west of region especially, were fought in a heightened and sharply partisan spirit in which all

---

13 Langford, op cit p. 374.
14 However, this was to be on a much smaller scale than that at Preston with extension of the franchise to the sons of freemen and their apprentices, and here it was the mayoral preference for the Cavendish interest which roused the wrath of 19 Tory alderman and common councilmen out of the 32 total. See *Manchester Mercury*, 19 January, 1768, for the anonymous letter from Mitton.

possible advantage was attempted to be gained by both political factions. By the middle of February the heat of battle was well and truly joined and the extent of the conflict can be judged by a letter sent to the *Gentleman's Magazine* from a resident of Preston:

> A letter from Preston, in Lancashire, dated February 21, says: "The contest here is attended with imminent danger. I have just escaped, with many friends. The country is now up in arms. As the town is now abandoned by our men, the cry is: 'Leave not a freeman alive!' God knows where this will end. I think to-night or to-morrow may be fatal to many. This is shocking work in a civilized country". [15]

By March the whole of north and east Lancashire appeared to be fixated by the elections, as another piece in the *Gentleman's Magazine* bears witness to, but in this case there is also evidence of violence against Catholics:

> By a letter from Lancaster, the violences committed on account of the ensuing election at that town and at Preston exceed belief; murdering, maiming, pulling down the houses, destroying places of public worship, and breaking the furniture and burning the effects of each other, are among the acts of the inflamed mob.[16]

The 'places of public worship' referred to were Catholic chapels in Friargate in Preston, (which was all but destroyed), and another at Cottam, just two miles to the west. Thus it is known that in the two constituencies in North Lancashire the party rivalries were heightened to dangerous levels and that this intimidation and violence were being used for at least three months prior to polling taking place; for the Tories the aim was to gain a foothold in Lancaster but for the Whigs at Preston it was the much more ambitious task of loosening the grip of the Tory Corporation and of opening up the constituency to the wider popular franchise.

The localised context of this contest is bound up in the competing interests of the two main political groupings of Whig and Tory, but also in the nature of what the town represented to the region as a whole. Key to understanding the remarkable events that took place at Preston and even more remarkable outcome of being granted a popular franchise was largely down to the actions of James Smith-Stanley, the self-styled Lord Strange (1716-1771), not only because of the dominant role the Derby/Whig interest in the region but also due to his position as Chancellor of the Duchy of Lancaster which Strange held from 1762 until his death in 1771. Traditionally, even before the case of the faulty returns of the Restoration Parliament that laid out the revision to a parliamentary franchise of the town's inhabitants, one seat was to be given over to the choice of the Chancellor of the Duchy.[17] However, the nature of self-perpetuating composition and the dominance of the Tory Corporation meant that from the turn of the eighteenth century it was they who effectively controlled both the seats. Hence what Strange was doing was three-fold; to gain Preston for the Whig interest, to uphold the Derby political prominence in the region and to ensure once again that the predominant local political role of the Duchy be

---

15 *Gentleman's Magazine*, (March, 1768), p. 92.
16 Ibid (April, 1768) p. 138.
17 Indeed this prerequisite was dominant from at least the mid-fourteenth century and continued through the Tudor period into the seventeenth century. See for example British Library Add. MSS 33061, Memorandum, n. d. c. 1727, or P. W. Hasler, *The House of Commons, 1558-1603*, (three vols. London, 1981) i. Pp. 190-191, or J. K. Gruenfelder, *Influence in Early Stuart Elections, 1604-1640*, (Columbus: Ohio State University Press, 1981) pp. 73-85.

returned to its former status. Yet it is doubtful that Strange began this campaign with the view that Preston would become the only borough in the country with an overwhelming popular franchise. As one leading authority on pre-Reform parliamentary history asserts, the Preston franchise stipulations were so remarkable that:

> ... [it] was thus wider than in the popular boroughs in which no contribution to local taxation was necessary to a vote; for in these boroughs some period of residence was required, and the term residence had not in them the elastic meaning that it had at Preston. Moreover in these popular boroughs, even if a voter did not pay poor rate or church rate, he was usually disqualified if he had received help from the poor rate. Many curious anomalies resulted from the determinations of election committees; but none more curious or more at variance with constitutional usages than resulted from the determination under which Preston was freed from its municipal oligarchy, and the right of election thrown into the possession of "all the inhabitants."[18]

However, the main reason why this came about was the nature – which was noteworthy even by eighteenth-century standards – of one of the most acrimonious and violent election contests ever seen in Britain. Yet although Strange and the Whig candidates threatened to widen the polling to all the inhabitants as they believed the Restoration Parliament's ruling entitled them, they did not use this tactic, even during the eleven days of polling.[19] But the threat alone was enough to incense the Tories and the Corporation, who in turn went against their prescriptive pretext of custom and began to canvass out-burgesses or non-residents, whose names, due to kinship, still appeared on the burgess rolls. They further hit back by courting the Catholics but denying any Protestant who they suspected of supporting the Whigs. The Corporation electoral organisers had persuaded upwards of thirty Catholics to take the oath of allegiance to the king in return for being made freemen of the borough and thus being entitled to vote, but ultimately only one voted for the Whigs.[20] This of course served to confirm not only to the Whigs but also to the wider public that the Tory Corporation was not afraid of being labelled Jacobite, but it further established the clear tactical line to Strange and Burgoyne that if the Corporation were willing to broaden the franchise to include the highly suspect Catholics then why may they not do the same with their supporters? However, in the meantime during the run-in to the election and the process of canvassing voters, the town was subject to almost nightly displays of rioting and violence.

In terms of the instigators of the troubles and riots it would appear that both

---

18 E. Porritt and A. E. Porritt, *The Unreformed House of Commons, Parliamentary Representation before 1832*, Vol. I, (Cambridge: Cambridge University Press, 1903) pp. 49-50.

19 The main reason why this election took so long was because there were so many objections on both sides as to who was entitled to vote and this kept the attorney's again on both sides very busy and quite rich. One notable victim of the wrath of the Tories was Richard Arkwright who was as a freeman of the borough entitled to vote but was struck off by the Corporation on the grounds that although he was born in the town he only occasionally lived there and he was a Whig.

20 Lancashire Archives, Preston, (DDPd 11/51) Pedder Papers, "Register of Voters with examinations as to their validity, 21 Mar.-1 Apr. 1768". In the margins of the poll book is written *Jurat All. S. and Ab/.,* to which is also added the term "papist" votes. *Jurat B.,* is the Latin legal term for the bribery oath. See also Register of Tallies at Preston Election, 1768, {DDPd 11/50); "Register of Voters with Examinations as to their Validity", (DDPd 11/51); "John Nabb's Accounts", (DDPd 11/52-53); "Squibs, etc.", (DDPr 131/6 & 7); "Canvassing Book", (DDPr 131/7a); "Letter from Mr. Dunning to the Corporation of Preston", (copy), (DDPr 131/8a); "Register of Foreign Voters", (DDPr 138/7).

sides were equally culpable. However, it is known that the Tories, with Sir Frank Standish and his chief supporter, William Hulton,[21] were active early in the campaign. Three deponents offering evidence testified that on 7 November 1767 they witnessed Standish and his supporters

> assembled in a riotous manner about the house of the said deponent Jeb Davis which they entered and broke open several doors broke several windows chairs and other furniture and assaulted and abused several persons therein the said house and committed divers other outrages and violence... Sir Frank Standish and William Hulton of Hulton in the said county Esq. were present in the street opposite the same house and appeared very active in inciting and encouraging to the commission of the said outrages aforesaid and particularly the said Sir Frank Standish at that time frequently sung or repeated the following words "May Leicester and Standish for Preston be chose, success to your work boys and a damn for your foes", or words nearly to that effect and this deponent Joseph Turner further saith that after the commission of the outrages and violence of the said Sir Frank Standish and William Hulton and also John Smalley of Preston aforesaid grocer appeared in or about the head of a large mob or concourse of people patrolling the public streets of Preston aforesaid in a riotous manner to the great terror and dismay of several inhabitants of the said borough, and the said Sir Frank Standish carrying a flauebrace in his hand and the said John Smalley repeatedly saying out aloud "if any man calls out Burgoyne knock him down" and these deponents Mary Barnes and Joseph Turner severally say that they have reason to believe that the said Sir Frank Standish and John Smalley at different times incited and encouraged the mob to acts of violence they these deponents have frequently seen the said Sir Frank Standish and John Smalley very active in mobs where great disorders have been committed.[22]

Another deponent said that Standish and his supporters "frequently assembled together in the night time in a riotous and tumultuous manner armed with clubs and bludgeons hooped with iron and iron spikes fixed to the end of them, axes, hammers and other offensive and destructive weapons and committed very great violences and outrages upon the persons and properties of several other inhabitants of the said Borough who were in the interest of John Burgoyne Esq."[23] The local historian Dobson tells us that these weapons were provided by the Mayor and Corporation of Preston out of a stock kept at the Town Hall.[24] What is clear in the election squibs is that both sides appealed to popular opinion. Strange was labelled a 'tyrant' by the Tories in his attempt to overpower the corporate borough and destroy its independence. Whilst on their side the Whigs similarly urged the people of the Preston area to free themselves of the 'tyranny' of the Corporation or, in the words of one election song, 'Don't Liberty Barter Away', suggesting that the Corporation "command and domineer over us

---

21 William Hulton (1739–1773) of Hulton Park, of Deane near Bolton was the son William Hulton and the grandson of Jessop Hulton whose relative again named William was MP for Clitheroe and was a supporter of the return of Charles II to the throne. The estate included coalmining interests dating back to the mid-sixteenth century and had, by the 1760s become substantial. His grandson was the William Hulton of 'Peterloo' infamy.
22 Lancashire County Archives, Preston, Deposition 1. DDX 113/5, depositions of Jeb Davis, John Heaton, Joseph Turner, Court of the Kings Bench, Westminster, (1768)
23 Ibid, Deposition 2. DDX 113/6, deposition of John Forgey made before Mr Justice Yates, 20 June, 1768.
24 Dobson, op cit, p. 11.

ancient freemen in our choice of representatives." In this view Leicester and Standish were mere 'tools' of the Tory Corporation. At one important level Strange, according to some of the popular songs circulating during the long run-up to the election, had endeared himself to ordinary working people in and around Preston due to the fact that one of the key reasons he had lost favour with the Corporation was that a few years prior to the election, not long after he had become Chancellor of the Duchy of Lancaster, he had demanded and seized the poor law accounts and had them delivered to London to be examined. There were found to be serious discrepancies in the accounting of the Corporation and it was fined £1,500.[25]

As noted, it does appear clear that Strange and Burgoyne were aware of the parliamentary ruling of 1661 and quite early in the election proceedings threatened to call for an all-out 'inhabitant's' franchise and poll which had induced the Corporation to re-think its tactics and widen its electoral support. Burgoyne was a Brigadier-General in the Coldstream Guards and was popular with the rank and file under his command; it was thus not unusual that those of the Lancashire Militia, billeted in Preston to keep the peace, should, in terms of their support, side with Burgoyne and Strange. In a sense this is where the germ of their eventual tactics became clear, in that when they began to increase their side with men from outside the borough (the so-called 'country people') in order to combat those of Corporation mobs brought into Preston by Hulton and Standish, it probably occurred to them that under the terms of the 1661 ruling it made no mention of just how long a residency these 'inhabitants' was supposed to have. Yet although it was Strange and Burgoyne who had mooted the possibility that they would counter the Corporation's hold on just who would be allowed to vote quite early in the contest, the fact was that both sides were active in canvassing potential voters from outside of the borough boundaries. For the Whigs this was ultimately to prove to be the secret of their success, not only because of the ruling of 1661, but also by their retaliatory actions it was clear that the Tories were willing to risk their supposed customary privileges on which they had based their traditional legal right to call only in-burgesses or resident freemen. This had been the basis which had maintained their predominance throughout the eighteenth century, but now, fearing the poll may be tighter than expected, they began to resort to a call on non-residents whose names were on the electoral rolls in order to be absolutely sure that they possessed a winning electoral base. This was a monumental blunder by the Corporation because by calling in the out-voters they effectively destroyed their own argument of a long-established legal precedent, since if the old customary practice was so legally watertight as they maintained then why go against it and call up non-residents? Now ordinary working people were brought into the town, some to present a counter to the armed gangs of the Tories, but others for the purpose of claiming residency and at least attempting to register a vote.[26] Although not signalled

---

25 Lancashire Archive, In fact the allegations of the inherent Jacobitism of the Corporation are to be found rather than the term 'Tory', and on the other side how the Whigs were 'placing the Church in danger'. See letters, songs and poems, DDPr/131/6 ff. 2-43; and DDPr/ 131/7, ff. 7-13, 38-39, 40-41, 56-57, 93.

26 There were at least 229 of these strangers surged into the borough, intent on asserting that they were genuine inhabitants. Lancashire Archive; The "Register of Foreign Voters" (L.R.O., DDPr 138/7) based on investigations made both before the election and after, many of these would-be voters divided their time between their real homes and temporary accommodation in Preston. Examples of this are: "Helme Wm. Came to town 5th Jan. 1768 stay'd about a week then returned to Manchester, stay'd about a month, and then came to town again and has stay'd almost

directly as intent by Strange and Burgoyne, this was a tactic which they had at least considered given the latitude offered by the parliamentary ruling of 1661. The legal term used for this procedure was *de bene esse*, meaning loosely 'in anticipation of future needs', and it has to be said that it was, at least in loosening the grip of the Corporation, a master stroke on the part of Strange and Burgoyne.[27] The irony was that its use as a tactic was one which the Tories were willing to condone for their side, thus when the eventual challenge to the election committee of the House of Commons was made they had little room to manoeuvre. In one deposition it was claimed that

> this deponent John Baron for himself severally saith that on Tuesday the 16th day of February 1768 the said John Tomlinson came into the township of Brindle of the said county in order to collect people for the purpose as this deponent believed to mob in Preston and that amongst others he desired this same deponent to go which he did upon being also solicited by James Abbott of Brindle aforesaid innkeeper who promised him this same deponent half a guinea for his so doing and this deponent saith that on Thursday the 17th day of February 1768 he went to Preston aforesaid along with a vast concourse or mob of country people to the amount as he believed of over 2000...[28]

This witness also provided evidence that among those drawn into this contest centred on Preston were weavers from the surrounding districts, being paid to support the Tory side; "and this deponent further saith that on Saturday the 20th day of February in the afternoon he saw Thomas Hatton of Preston aforesaid, watchmaker who was considered and called a captain and one of the planners of the said mob pay D. Whittle of Salmesbury of the same county, weaver and Giles Ainsworth of the same county aforesaid, blacksmith who were both in the said mob 6s for staying each four days in Preston for the purpose of mobbing..."[29] However, for all their efforts to gain a foothold in the constituency, it was clear that by the eighth day of polling the Whigs had lost, and it was at this point that Strange and Burgoyne played their ace. They brought forward to the poll the staunchly Whig vicar of Preston, Randal Andrews, who because of this attachment had been excluded by the Tories. As a resident but a non-freeman he claimed the right to vote precisely under the terms of the 1661 ruling that 'all the inhabitants [were] able to vote'. This presented the Tory mayor Robert Moss and his legal advisors with a real problem because once they had used non-residents for their purposes their legal position was effectively void. If it was good for one side then it was equally good for the other. The mayor in fact, when it came to the final tallies, drew up two sets of results. In one with the non-residents the Whigs had won, but with their exclusion the Tories were the winners and it was initially the second tally that was sent to Westminster along with Leicester and Standish as the town's Members of Parliament. The two Whig candidates immediately filed petitions and brought legal actions against a faulty return on the part of the Mayor. However, as if to compound their blunders the

---

constantly followed no business. Thos. Jackson stays 2 or 3 nights (per week) no imploy. Pedder Jas. Revd. (Vicar of Garstang) has been in town 3 or 4 times." Mr. Pedder was allowed to vote at the election. According to L.R.O. DDPd 11/50; "Both parties at great expense brought into the town from different and remote parts of the kingdom, and even from foreign parts, Inn-Burgesses to reside by way of qualifying them to vote as Inn-Burgesses Inhabitants."

27 *Black's Law Dictionary*, (New York, 5th edn., 1981).
28 Lancashire Archive, ('Legal Papers' DDX/123/14) p. 7.
29 Ibid.

Corporation committed another cardinal error in that the second tally signed by Moss also found its way to the Election Committee in the Commons.[30] With the strict adherence to the Tories resident voters there were 800 electors allowed to vote, but with the 'all inhabitants' ruling this figure was doubled.[31] With both the election tallies in their possession and the legal opinions offered the Commons Committee did indeed find that Moss and the Preston Corporation were guilty of faulty election returns and Hoghton and Burgoyne were formally returned as Members, replacing Leicester and Standish in November 1768.[32] Hence Preston became a borough located in the heart of the massive social and industrial transformations of the North-West with a true manhood suffrage and it was one which could now serve as a focal point in future elections for ordinary working people to give vent to their frustrations and their grievances though a very real and viable political channel. However, although it was widely reported that the Whig candidates had immediately issued petitions contesting the result, it was not clear in the days following that they would be successful, and this brings us to the final episode of the actions of the working class at this crucial stage of industrial and communal change.

We have seen that in the intervening years between the defeat of the small-ware and check weavers in 1758 the consolidation of the process of industrial innovation centring on the spinning sector was gaining much wider use across the region. Initially the small scale improvements of between eight, sixteen or even twenty four spindles on the spinning jenny's were, by and large, accepted by working people from their initial introduction of the eight-spindled jenny in 1764. However, by the time we get to 1768 manufacturers were dramatically increasing the number of spindles and, moreover, beginning the process of consolidating their workforces into water-powered factories. Whether it was because they were already mobilised for the respective sides in the Preston election contest and the populist Whig supporters felt frustrated, or whether it was due to the imminent threat posed by the proposals to widen the use of the jennys remains inconclusive, but on the next day that the polling ceased at Preston a crowd assembled at Blackburn some eight miles to the South East of Preston and began destroying spinning machinery. Those arrested were sent to the Lancaster Assizes and two stated that "that 10,000 men would come and destroy the town [and] they had signed a paper for that purpose."[33] The fact that these men were formally signing documents of intent is suggestive not only of deep-seated willingness to affect change (and damage) but also of their collective commitment. Early the following year a crowd assembled at Oswaldtwistle and directly targeted those using multi-spindled jenny's to the extent of pulling down some houses. Some ten years later a Manchester pro-machinery pamphleteer suggested a reason why working people were suspicious of the use of new innovations.

> What rioting and alarm there was, in this Country, about ten years ago upon the invention of Spinning Jennies? Many people foreboded the most dreadful consequences from them. The common cry was that they would take the bread from the Poor, and throw them out of employment. Upon

---

30 W. A. Abram, *Sketches in Local History: Memorials of Old Lancashire Families Preston, Lancashire*, England, (The Preston Guardian, 1877).
31 historyofparliamentonline.org, Constituencies, 1754-1790.
32 Lancashire Archive, ('Legal Papers' DDX 135/5-12) 'Burgoyne v Moss and others' (Preston Election Return).
33 *Manchester Mercury*, 23 August, 1768, *Williamson's Liverpool Advertiser*, 26 August, 1768.

this a mob arose, burnt what Machines they could discover and carried about their fragments in triumph.³⁴

Certainly the writer here is stating the obvious fact that in recent times whenever working people had been on the receiving end of employer innovation or 'improvement' it had often resulted in their actual earnings being threatened.³⁵ It has be remembered that the 1760s witnessed some of the fiercest food riots of the century and Manchester once again saw food rioters assemble at the end of August 1762.³⁶ Yet there was more to worry those engaged in the cotton industry than even that of the value of their earning power, in that a common perception was that rather than acting as a labour saving device the introduction of the jennys would serve to increase the workload for at best the same wages or possibly less, as Ogden attested.³⁷ James Hargreaves, the inventor of the jenny, was forced to flee his home village of Oswaldtwistle to Nottingham, such was the nature of the bitter feelings of working people against him. Yet the coincidence of the violence occasioned both at the Preston election and the assault against the gradual introduction of employer innovations demonstrate, on the one hand, the determination of working people to attempt to preserve their position and, on the other, their increasing desperation at their inability to achieve these ends.

However, in reality any assessment of the potentially enhanced ability of the working class to assert their grievance through political action via the newly arrived popular franchise at Preston was limited by a number of factors. Firstly there was not, even by the advanced and increasingly vociferous politicisation of the 1760s, any particular relish to reform a corrupt political system or the legislature, it did begin in the next decade but these aims were strictly limited and did not include any further examples of the anomaly at Preston. Hence, at a stroke, the value of any attempts by an overwhelmingly working class electorate at Preston to assert their political will would at best be symbolic and a minor irritation to the political elites at Westminster. This is compounded by the lack of any appetite for parliamentary reform from the emerging middle class radicals at this particular time (although it would become manifest in the next two decades), which to a significant extent deprived the working class of a focus of leadership and a concerted plan of action as to what they advocated to replace the existing political system. Second, without the organisation (and money) of the two political groupings, or indeed an emerging radical faction, there was little opportunity for the geographically wider working class to take advantage of the prospect offered at Preston when their work and general lack of financial muscle would undoubtedly have restricted their time and movement. Third, local political managers would want, as far as possible, to contain and control the

---

34 Anon, *Thoughts on the Use of Machines in Cotton Manufacture*, (Manchester, 1769) p. 10.
35 For example it was alleged in the winter of 1762 that a Manchester weaver and his wife had starved to death due to the failure of employers to pay subsistence wages. *Manchester Mercury*, 18 January, 1763.
36 It was reported that workers once again came from Oldham, Saddleworth and Ashton to Manchester to protest against high prices and the operations of 'badgers', to the extent that the King offered a pardon (and presumably a reward) to anyone who would turn informer. No one did. *Manchester Mercury*, 1 September, 1762.
37 Op cit J. Ogden, *Manchester, A Hundred Years Ago*, "The plenty of weft produced by this means gave uneasiness to the country people, and the weavers were afraid lest the manufacturers should demand finer weft woven at the former prices, which occasioned some risings, and the jennies were opposed, and some being demolished before those who used them could be protected, or convince others of their general utility…" p. 88-89.

situation at Preston during the occasion of elections and in the intervening periods keep wider political feelings as calm as possible. Fourth, and finally, the national and local political elites from both political factions would strictly vet any potential candidate and keep the political agenda as narrow as could be safely managed, which quite obviously did not include opportunities of demonstrations of purely working class grievances and anger. Here again, learning from the growth of radical and indeed reformist sentiments that were conjured up by the Wilkes debacle, the leaders of the two factions would create an informal coalition of conformative interests, the main one of which was to preserve the components of the patrician state intact.

All this said that the existing political situation at Preston was undeniably a totem of popularism which was unique not only for an expanding industrial region but indeed for the whole country. The electorate of Preston was more than doubled as a result of the contest of 1768 and the increasing numerical predomination of the working class as the majority group was to continue until the First Reform Act of 1832. After that, until the Second Reform Act of 1867, the proportion of the middle class vote increased as the old working class voters died off and were not replaced under the terms of the Act of 1832.

The situation present at Preston after 1768 was remarkable for a variety of reasons. First and most obvious was the granting of effectively universal manhood suffrage to all males over the age of twenty one. This came almost one hundred years to the day before the granting of national urban householder suffrage as a result of the Second Reform Act. The situation created as a result of the 1768 election offered at Preston at least the opportunity to working class males to give vent in a very real sense to their political inclinations and to, theoretically at least, exercise a significant element of power during election contests, especially if, that is, there was a candidate who was willing to offer some crumbs of comfort in terms of endearing policies towards the working class. Some of these working class electors, in all likelihood a great many in somewhat straightened circumstances, would inevitably be prone to receiving or indeed demanding the 'treats' offered by rival candidates. Yet there would also undoubtedly be some who would have been conscious of their class identity and power to put forward what they and their neighbouring community of workers believed were important to them and their class at any given time. However, there is scant evidence that candidates of either of the political groups paid more than a token account of the overwhelmingly working class electorate of Preston. Obviously one key reason for this was that as it was the only industrial borough in the entire country to possess such a franchise; why should they take any note? As a single constituency it carried little real political weight. And they would have been confident that, in any event, their ability to deal those voters who demanded 'treats' or bribes would in all likelihood be enough to carry them through to victory. Yet it is plausible to suggest that when members of the Preston working class came into contact with other (so-called country) workers in the region who did not obviously possess their privilege, the Preston men would have been informed as to what the interests of the working class were at any given point, and how it was important for those who had such power to send a message by their votes to the elites. But the question remains why the Derby/Whig faction actively pursued a tactic that would allow the potential floodgates of manhood suffrage to happen in Preston? Clearly they wanted to win both seats and wrest control away from the Tory supporting Corporation, but there are also hints that both Strange and Burgoyne were not averse to viewing the working class or the labouring poor in a more sympathetic light than possibly their opponents. For example, even though a substantial landowner himself, Strange voted in favour of the Land Tax, which in general terms infuriated the landed elites, he was against increasing the Excise in principle but voted in favour of maintaining the Cider Tax on the basis that it would be fair to tax the landowning class who were in positions to afford such a tax which was gathered at source. Such policies would have endeared him to both the working class and the emerging industrial middle classes, especially those in and around Manchester. His seizing of the Preston Corporation's Poor Law records to expose defects in the giving out of relief to those in genuine need would once again have made him popular among the working class. 'Gentleman Johnny' Burgoyne was a co-founder of Brook's Club, an associate of decidedly reformist Charles James Fox, and advocated when a serving military commander that his soldiers allowances be paid in full and that ordinary soldiers should not be treated as simple, unthinking cannon fodder. Hence he too could have been considered a 'populist' candidate.[38]

A final area worth considering is why the disturbances and riots lasted so long in Preston. There were almost four months of trouble on the streets of the town, with both sides deserving of their share of blame. Firstly, as soon as the Corporation learned that Lord Strange was putting his brother in law, Burgoyne, forward as a candidate, they knew they were in for a formidable battle to retain both seats for the Tories. As Chancellor of the Duchy of Lancaster, Strange could bring concerted pressure (and money) to bear and, given his high political profile, it was highly likely he would have the full backing of the party's managers in London. The Tories had been successful in the North-West over the recent general elections and they knew the Whigs and the Derby interest wished to claw back some standing in the region. Strange, for his part, wished to re-establish the Derby interest and to maintain the slight improvement in the fortunes of the Whigs nationally, which had begun to develop since the removal of Bute and his Tory supporters. Yet the Tories were not ostracised to anything like the extent they had been under Walpole and the 'Old' Whig elites, and thus they had a real opportunity to bounce back. The realisation of this meant that for the Whigs their new found opportunity had to be seized and then maintained, which indeed it duly was for the immediate election which followed 1768.[39] For both sides the Preston election was of great importance for it would be a beacon of their respective fortunes. Similarly for key groups in the region this was an event of major significance. Liverpool was already safely under the political control of the key Whig commercial interests and while the county seats remained shared between Whig and Tory, and the Tories were still in control of Newton and Wigan, Clitheroe split and the Whigs taking Lancaster, Preston offered an opportunity to the main Manchester industrial and manufacturing men to give their backing in the light of the full knowledge that the Whigs would look more favourably on their attempts at the economic modernisation of the region than the Tories. Also, often these feelings were complimented by the strong

---

38 Op cit J. Brooke, *History of Parliament: The House of Commons*, online version, historyofparliamentonline.org/volume/1754-1790.
39 The Whigs returned members for both the Preston seat until 1802, when with an electoral pact arranged with the Earl of Derby the power cotton mill-owning Horrocks family took one of the seats for the Tories. See *History of Parliament* op cit. This remained the situation until the onset of the reform of parliament movement began to get underway when in 1830 the radical Henry Hunt took one of the seats.

Nonconformist sentiments which the majority of the Manchester industrialists shared, and by their ability from the mid-1770s to begin to concertedly lobby parliament on behalf of the cotton interests of the region. Yet the effective universal manhood suffrage gained at Preston would have been recognised by the working class, who now had the possibility to make their feelings via their fellow class members at Preston.

What have been discussed in these last two chapters are elements of a political dimension at a key moment of dramatic change in the circumstances of the working class development in the North-West. Ostensibly their position remained unchanged, in that they were still becoming ever more subject to the power of the emerging manufacturing middle class, but we have seen they now had a point of focus in real political terms as true universal manhood suffrage was available at Preston. However, we now have to begin to assess the overall significance of just what the preceding pages of this study suggest to the situation prevailing in the North-West during this crucially important period.

14

Conclusions

This book opened with a discussion on the nature of the existing economic system and how, following the example of the Dutch version of mercantilism allowed the British more flexibility in terms of the re-export of goods and commodities from the colonies and imperial possessions. Importantly it gave more impetus to individual profit orientation than the version followed by the French which was organised ostensibly and more rigidly to support the central state. Although this was a crucial aspect of the operation of mercantilism in Britain it did not involve the entirety of functions which the French model demanded. The so-called intendant system which prevailed in France did not allow for the flexibility of individual control, choice or freedom of action in the economic affairs that prevailed in Britain. Here then was the beginning of an opportunity in the economic process for the operation of a much freer, market-orientated system and, crucially, one which allowed budding entrepreneurs a much greater grasp on the access to the key factors of production, including the raising of capital, access to raw materials, and, of course, the ability to increase their control over their labour force. Overall this emerging system allowed early British entrepreneurs to flourish in an age when increasing consumerism gave the realisation of enhanced profit potential not found anywhere else in Europe, including Holland. Although the safeguards built in to the mercantile system in Britain (even after the repeal of the old statutes against forestalling, regrating and engrossing in 1772) retained the vestiges of protection of access to vital provisions at reasonable prices and the supposed independence of individual workers' rights, regardless of if they were guild members or not. Yet, as we saw in the early chapters, it was this relative freedom which fostered the calls for an even more independent role for individual entrepreneurs unfettered by state interference. At another level there began to emerge views and discussions of how the role of the state in the economic fortunes of the nation could be improved and especially how the various branches of trade, commerce and industry could be more successfully integrated (their interests heard and acted upon) and co-ordinated from the level of parliament and the central government. In a sense the over-reliance of the central state on collecting revenues, customs and duties via the *entrepôt* system resulted in an on-going political conflict, as the need to expand Britain's colonial and imperial influence and access went against an increasingly bellicose opposition to Walpole's established practice of minimising – as far as possible – the nation's involvement in expensive external international conflicts. A key aspect of Walpole's policy was the aim of limiting the amount of national debt which expensive foreign wars would undoubtedly cost, but the opposition argued that the enhanced opportunities of an expanded Empire would offset any of the short-term debts incurred. This, the argument ran, would place Britain as a supreme global power, significantly increasing the wealth of all the nation's citizens, and after the removal of Walpole in 1743 the expansionist policies of William Pitt came to the fore. One of the effects of this re-determining of British colonial and imperialist policy was to highlight the need for enhanced detailed understanding of just how the British economy was working and crucially how this could be improved. What was required (so argued Joseph Massey) was the means, mechanisms and information on the complete nature of economics in its totality and how best this information could relate to practical procedures with which to benefit the nation as a whole. It was also noted at several points in this study how notions of the inherent freedoms enjoyed by the citizens of Britain were something that was unique and precious to the nation.

In a key sense the British historic understanding of freedom underwent a subtle but enormously important change with the circulation of ideas surrounding the Enlightenment. On the one hand there was the view that historically inherited liberties should be protected by the state, hence under the British version of mercantilism the belief prevailed that the rights of the 'freeborn Englishman' should at all times be secured, both in terms of law and customary practices. This protective intrusion by the state was wrapped in a series of views which, to a large extent, were backward-looking and conservative in their operation, and these views impinged on the role of religion as well as aspects of common law and were largely seen as expressing a positive liberty which had developed predominantly in the non-Catholic north-western European countries. To a significant extent as the seventeenth century developed, ideas surrounding scientific rationalism and empiricism became to be seen as guiding principles of 'progress'. Yet developing alongside these views were notions surrounding individualism and, importantly, the individual conscience to worship, for example, in one's own individual manner. Ideas surrounding individualism in turn, as they became more sophisticated and confident in their expression, began to shift the emphasis of the understanding of freedom and especially the role of the state in accomplishing genuine individual freedom. Increasingly 'modern' aspirations began to question the involvement of the state in a range of functions, including crucially economic and trading matters. In this view, which became associated with negative freedom, the role of the state needed to be rolled back to allow for the full unfettered development of the self and to arrive at the empowering of the individual and what that person was involved with, in say their business and economic affairs. Although considerations relating to positive (action by the state) and negative (inaction by the state) freedom have largely been the concern of the discipline of political philosophy it has over time possessed considerable relevance to those interested in economic understanding and, although not necessarily phrased in the same tonology, this was true in the increasingly vociferous debate when approaching the mid-eighteenth century. Although seventeenth century scholars would argue (quite reasonably) that this debate surrounding positive and negative freedom – in the British context – really began during the period leading up to the Civil War, in terms of its economic relevance it took on serious shape in the eighteenth century. In the seventeenth century purely political context the nature of freedom hinged on limiting the powers of the monarch more in favour of the individual via parliament, but it was in the middle of the eighteenth century for the first time that scientific rationalism became allied with the increasing needs of a genuine consumer society within the backdrop of what was, relatively speaking, an open political and civil society. Thus it was at that time that the purpose and direction of political *and* economic understanding became fused together.

In the context of this study there were three key areas which contributed to the momentous changes associated with the coming of the industrial capitalist system. The first, as we saw in the early chapters above, concerned challenges to the existing mercantilist system, not exclusively by the class of emerging industrial manufacturers but certainly by proponents and polemicists on their behalf. Yet what these writers appear to have overlooked was the enormous benefits the protective mercantilist system bestowed on British manufacturing in terms of the cost of primary products from the colonies and Empire territories and, by the same token, ensuring potentially huge global markets for the finished products. Also, rival goods in direct competition to British made products were subject to substantial tariffs extracted by the central state, which again gave British manufacturing an enormous boost. In modern economic parlance the classic 'export led' approach. A second factor was the changing relationship between master and labourer, which will be dealt with shortly. But the third area also needs to be noted at this point, again to be considered in more detail later, and this was the changing political culture within which the economic direction of the nation often took centre stage. All three of these features acted as the *milieu* or petre dish within which the first tentative but increasingly powerful initial strides towards the relatively modern industrial capitalist economy began to take place. However, the core of the case-study of the North-West, which was the central discussion of what has been deliberated above, concerned the changing relationship between the cotton textile masters and the emerging working class.

The basis of the Statute of Artificers, beginning with the initial Act of 1563, was a response to rising levels of inflation, due largely to the debasement of the currency by the central state and pressures of population increase, resulting in Elizabeth I's attempts to curb wages and fix the conditions of all types of workers by giving significant powers of arbitration to the magistracy. By the mid-eighteenth century however, these statutes were seen by the early proponents of economic reform (and negative freedom) as encouraging workers into complacency and, coupled with the Poor Laws, into idleness. Over the ensuing period the aims and functions of the Acts had been corrupted, giving undue powers to the labouring population at the expense of the masters and, the arguments ran, stifling the economic potential of the nation. In short, they were no longer required. Thus from this small acorn of criticism of existing and on-going state action (or more precisely interference) did the massive oak tree of classical economic thought and practice take root and flourish. In this way what became one man's freedom to act without any interference from the state (the industrial entrepreneur or grain merchant) was, at the other end of the scale, the dramatic reduction in the degrees of freedom, security and independence of the working class man (and woman and child). In the twentieth century there were many defenders of negative liberty, both in terms of its desirability in a politico/philosophical context and especially in an economic sense.[1] The

---

1 See, for example, I. Berlin, 'Two Concepts of Liberty', in I. Berlin, *Four Essays on Liberty*, (Oxford: Oxford University Press, 2002 edn.). 'From Hope and Fear Set Free', in I. Berlin, *Concepts and Categories. Philosophical Essays*, ed. H. Hardy, (London: Hogarth Press, 1978). *Liberty*, ed. H. Hardy, (Oxford: Oxford University Press, 2002). F. A. von Hayek, *The Constitution of Liberty*, (London: Routledge and Kegan Paul, 1960), *Law, Legislation and Liberty*, (London: Routledge, 1982). G. C. MacCallum, Jr., 'Negative and Positive Freedom', *Philosophical Review*, 76: 312–34, (1967). A. Sen, 'Well-being, Agency and Freedom', *Journal of Philosophy*, 82: 169-221 (1985), 'Freedom of Choice: Concept and Content', *European Economic Review*, 32: 269-94, (1988), *Inequality Re-examined*, (Oxford: Oxford University Press, 1992). *Rationality and Freedom*, (Cambridge, Mass.: Harvard University Press, 2002). Q. Skinner, *Liberty before Liberalism*, (Cambridge: Cambridge University Press, 1998), 'A Third Concept of Liberty', *Proceedings of the British Academy*, 117 (237): 237-68 (2002), 'Freedom as the Absence of Arbitrary Power', in Laborde and Maynor (eds.), *Republicanism and Political Theory*, (Oxford: Blackwell, 2008). C. Taylor, 'What's Wrong with Negative Liberty', in A. Ryan (*ed.*), *The Idea of Freedom*, (Oxford: Oxford University Press, 1979, reprinted in D. Miller

backward or historical projection of conceptions of freedoms endowed by customary practices and held onto as a form of the necessary needs of security, as seen clearly in the practices and tactics adopted by the working class from the 1740s, were, according to Isiah Berlin,

> harmful and one-sided, because the spread of the fatalistic-deterministic approach entails the suppression and erosion of individual autonomy. The need for security hinders critical thought and a mature behaviour, and facilitates the spread of various forms of faith-healing and mumbo jumbo.[2]

This new environment of thought and practice was encapsulated in chapter nine above with the words of Judge Sir Michael Foster, when he considered what the weavers were doing when they attempted to cling on to their historic liberties by collective action was effectively wrenching power away from the masters which, in Foster's view, was turning the world upside down. "And there seems the greater Reason to have feared their [the weavers'] Success, in such Attempt, as such Confederacies would have occasioned the greatest Confusion betwixt the lower Class of People and their Superiors, in all Trades and Occupations, in every Manufactory, and in every Employ. If Inferiors are to prescribe to their Superiors, if the Foot aspire to be the Head ... without Restraint or Control, to what End are Laws enacted?"[3] And he went on to locate the cause of the problem as being the retention of the old Statutes which may have been useful in the sixteenth century but were of no use in the eighteenth. "In the Infancy of Trade, the Acts of Queen Elizabeth might be well calculated for the publick Weal; but now, when it is grown to that Perfection we see it, it might perhaps be of Utility to have those Laws repealed, as tending to cramp and tye down that Knowledge it was at first necessary to obtain by Rule... Therefore all Combinations of this Kind and Nature, are to guarded against as much as possible; and it is the indispensable Duty of everyone, as a Friend to the Community to endeavour to suppress them in their Beginnings."[4]

Hence it is a reasonable postulation to adduce that if high ranking members of the judiciary were of the belief that the old customary privileges on which working class security and independence rested were no longer relevant or suitable by the end of the 1750s, then firstly that such views were in wide circulation and, secondly, that clearly the moves open to the manufacturers striving to change the terms of the worker/employer relationship were now boundless. Thirdly, this was coming from a high court judge of the Kings Bench. If ever there needed to be a clear message delivered to the emerging working class, that they now no longer could rely on the unbiased arbitration of those in charge of justice (as they could for centuries) and that now they had to act for their own interests; their 'agency', then this statement of Foster's encapsulated the new situation. This may have just been the start of the changes that began the procession towards a modern capitalist system but it was a crucial moment in that process. In relation to the debate surrounding positive and negative freedom which, in contemporary terms, was the clear choice between the maintenance of measures of the interventionist state or the adoption of policies based on non-interventionism. This cleavage of belief systems lay at the foundation of the

---

'Constraints on Freedom', *Ethics*, 94, pp. 66–86, (1983).
2 I. Berlin, *Four Essays on Liberty*, (Oxford: Oxford University Press, 1969) pp. 118-172.
3 *Williamson's Liverpool Advertiser*, 22 July and 4 November 1757.
4 National Archives, Kew, *Palatinate Papers,* (P. L. 26. 39/1).

direction on which the entire economic structure of the new system rested, and it was bound to result in a clash between the two opposing positions. For the emerging working class, as the political scientist Charles Taylor reminds us, "freedom resides at least in part in collective control over the common life", to which Quentin Skinner perceives, "because the exercise of such control is the form of activity in which the essence of our humanity is most fully realised."[5] We saw in chapter four that as far as the prevailing attitudes to labourers and to labour generally three positions can be identified by 1750. The first, which may be termed the traditional view, was that wages need to be set at just above subsistence and taxes high (and hence provisions) to keep workers industrious and to retain a cost advantage for the export of British products in relation to similar products overseas and their labour costs. Any enjoyment of so-called 'luxuries' was to be discouraged amongst the labouring classes by the imposition of high duties. The reasoning behind this view was that workers would attempt at any opportunity to work less once their immediate needs had been reached and that by normal predilection workers were often dissolute and idle in their habits. This was the position adopted by employers such as William Temple of Trowbridge and the redoubtable polemicist Josiah Tucker. In an important historical sense Temple's position appears to possess some credence if we look at the fortunes of the woollen sector in the West of England. In 1700 it was still flourishing in areas around West Wiltshire, North East Somerset and central and southern Gloucestershire. Yet by 1800 it had been completely overtaken in productive efficiency by the West Riding of Yorkshire, and by 1830 it had effectively died out. Whether the cause of this was the abject resistance to any 'rationalisation' of enhanced productive process by the workers of the West of England, or how much was due to changing market fortunes or lack of entrepreneurial incentive on the part of the clothiers is debatable. Yet, as we saw, the danger signs were being witnessed by the Dean of Gloucester, Tucker, and he produced a steady flow of articles and books to point out just how the old system of master/labour relations desperately needed reform, and in his position and status he was significantly influential enough to be widely read.

There was, however, another developing stance emerging in the first half of the eighteenth century, such as that adopted by Daniel Defoe, which was diametrically opposed to this. Defoe's view suggested that the payment of higher wages was to be encouraged wherever possible as an inducement to work harder and improve productive capacity, which would also encourage the advance of the economy in a national sense, in that workers would be able to spend more and become viable consumers, hence stimulating overall economic growth. In fact, what commentators such as Temple and Tucker missed, and the extraordinarily perceptive Defoe realised some forty years previously, was the interaction of incentive and overall economic growth. This runs that if a worker is paid a reasonable wage they may indeed be able to afford 'luxuries' instead of bare subsistence. In such cases they will in fact work harder to gain greater remuneration and be able to purchase greater amounts of goods on offer, hence stimulating economic growth. If, on the other hand, they are paid minimal rates and heavily taxed, the incentive to work harder disappears for the very reason there is no incentive for them to do so, and hence they would take any advantage

---

5 C. Taylor, 'What's Wrong with Negative Liberty', in A. Ryan (ed.), *The Idea of Freedom*, (Oxford: Oxford University Press, 1979, reprinted in D. Miller 'Constraints on Freedom', *Ethics*, 94, p. 175, (1983), Q. Skinner, 'A Third Concept of Liberty', Proceedings of the British Academy, 117(237): p.242, (2002).

– fair or foul – they could. Yet the attitudes expressed by Temple and Tucker are clear evidence of the exasperation felt by some critics of the existing economic system, and the urgent need, as they saw it, to reform the existing master/labourer relationship. Indeed, some views, such as those based on the positions adopted by Bishop Berkeley, David Hume and, even earlier, by Dudley North, advocated that the increase of living standards for all the citizens of Britain should be the ultimate goal of any national economic policy.[6] Yet, as we have seen in this discussion, there was a third stance taking root, which in the industrial sector at least was to become the dominant view, and this was that labour was an essential factor of production and the only one in fact that the capitalist entrepreneur has any real certain control.

To a certain extent this third view took its stance from the first, in that the role of labour needed to be tightly controlled, but in this instance the methods utilised were much more methodical and uniform both in theory and practice. The key factor in the emerging system of manufacturing was to be able to maximise the earning potential of the capital deployed by making labour more productive, which, if effectively managed, would result in greater profits, which in turn would free-up even more capital to be organised and yet made profitable. Adam Smith put this position forward most emphatically when he wrote concerning the division of labour:

> The number of [any nation's] productive labourers, it is evident, can never be much increased, but in consequence of an increase of capital ... The productive powers of the same number of labourers cannot be increased, but in consequence either of some addition and improvement to those machines and instruments which facilitate and abridge labour; or of a more proper division and distribution of employment. In either case an additional capital is almost always required. It is by means of an additional capital only that the undertaker of any work can either provide his workmen with better machinery, or make a more proper distribution of employment among them... When we compare, therefore, the state of nation at two different periods, and find that the annual produce of its land and labour is evidently greater at the latter than at the former, that its lands are better cultivated, its manufacturers more numerous and more flourishing, and its trade more extensive, we may be assured that its capital must have increased during the interval between those two periods.[7]

Yet the key feature of note was that the manufacturers of the Manchester region were, by their actions in changing the existing microeconomic practices, putting into application the strictures of Smith almost thirty years before *Wealth of Nations* was published. Moreover, this third position took little stock of the welfare or, indeed, the value of the worker, apart from their ability to produce to the maximum of their potential the goods apportioned to them at the cheapest possible rate by those controlling the capital in whatever enterprise they may be engaged in. The lacuna of focus in terms of the need for a new economic direction, as we say in chapters two and four, ranged across the various branches of industry, but became especially relevant to the cotton manufacturers in the North-West who believed that existing policies relating to their branches of

---

6 A. A. Luce & T. E. Jessop, (eds.), *The Works of George Berkeley Bishop of Cloyne*, (London: Thomas Nelson & Sons, 1953), D. North, *Discourses Upon Trade: Principally Directed to the Case of the Interest, Coynage, Clipping, Increase of Money*, (London, 1691).
7 A. Smith, (R. H. Campbell, *et al.*, (eds.), *An Inquiry into the Nature and Causes of the Wealth of Nations*, 2 vols. (Indianapolis: Liberty Fund, 1981) Vol. I, p. 343.

industry demanded re-assessment. From the middle of the 1740s there developed a 'community of interests' amongst the emerging masters of manufacturing, and in some cases provisioning in pursuance of a distinctly different programme of economic organisation. This was based on the potential opportunities on offer. Yet certain obstacles had to be overcome before their tentative aspirations had a remote chance of being realised. Clearly the Manchester masters, in particular from the later 1740s, were attempting to bring about changes to their relationship with their workers in terms of their customary work practices. This was revealed in the resistance to these changes made by the workers themselves through their relatively sophisticated use of the box clubs. Yet similarly, as the testimony of John Collier bore witness, the merchants were also active on the supply of essential provisions in the immediate districts of Manchester. On this front as well the working class demonstrated their frustration and anger at the actions of the merchants and the inactions of the local authorities. This two fronted assault on the key interests of the working class was not to be an isolated incident but it began the process of a consolidation of the working class. To a significant extent this was achieved by their will to act collectively in their own interest. This was, in accordance with the Thompson model, by the introduction of their agency in terms of a clear recognition of their vulnerability as they witnessed at first hand, and clearly understood, what the evident failure of the civil authorities meant to them, especially with regard to the local magistracy to arbitrate their grievances in an unbiased manner. As noted, this was evidenced most graphically in the legal ruling of Lord Chief Justice Mansfield and underscored and endorsed by Justice Sir Michael Foster and the manner in which traditional magistrates like Thomas Percival were effectively silenced and rendered powerless.

Yet there were some contemporaries who began to realise what the effects and possible impact would be of judicial attitudes (and actions) by those leading members of the British legal establishment. One such was the indefatigable 'Junius', who targeted Lord Mansfield in particular. In two of his published letters he singled out Mansfield for outright bias and fulfilling his own personal economic and, especially, political agenda. Some twelve years after his legally highly dubious oral (but not written) charge to the Grand Jury at the Lancaster Assizes which effectively ended the concerted resistance by the cotton workers of the North-West, Junius published his first open letter against Mansfield. In this letter Junius accused Mansfield of never actually rejecting his familial and personal advocacy of the Stuart cause and what that meant politically in terms of royal power in relation to the powers of wider society.

> I see through your whole life one uniform plan to enlarge the power of the crown, at the expense of the liberty of the subject. To this object your thoughts, words, and actions, have been constantly directed. In contempt or ignorance of the common law of England, you have made it your study to introduce into the court where you preside, maxims of jurisprudence unknown to Englishmen. The Roman code, the law of nations, and the opinion of foreign civilians, are your perpetual theme; but who ever heard you mention Magna Charta, or the *Bill of Rights*, with approbation or respect? By such treacherous arts the noble simplicity and free spirit of our Saxon laws were first corrupted. The Norman Conquest was not complete, until Norman lawyers had introduced their laws, and reduced slavery to a system. This one leading principle directs your interpretation of the laws, and accounts for your treatment of juries. It is not in political questions only (for there the courtier might be forgiven,) but let the cause

be what it may, your understanding is equally on the rack, either to contract the power of the jury, or to mislead their judgment.[8]

Not content with calling into question Mansfield's political bias, Junius made (in terms of the subject under discussion here) the more serious charge against him, to suggest that his legal rulings were decidedly suspect, perhaps unlawful, certainly at odds with British notions of liberty, and possibly unconstitutional. That in the treatment of juries Mansfield was at best leading them or at worst misleading them.

> Instead of those certain positive rules by which the judgment of a court of law should invariably be determined, you have fondly introduced your own unsettled notions of equity and substantial justice. Decisions given upon such principles do not alarm the public so much as they ought, because the consequence and tendency of each particular instance is not observed or regarded. In the meantime, the practice gains ground; the court of king's bench becomes a court of equity; and the judge, instead of consulting strictly the law of the land, refers only to the wisdom of the court, and to the purity of his own conscience... But I understand your Lordship. If you could succeed in making the trial by jury useless and ridiculous, you might then, with greater safety, introduce a bill into parliament for enlarging the jurisdiction of the court, and extending your favourite trial by interrogatories to every question in which the life or liberty of an Englishman is concerned.[9]

In his second letter directed against Mansfield, published in 1772, Junius once again accused the Lord Chief Justice of legal and personal bias, this time against a wealthy fellow Scot who conclusively appeared guilty of theft. Junius ended his attack:

> I then affirm, that you support injustice by violence, that you are guilty of a heinous aggravation of your offence, and that you contribute your utmost influence to promote, on the part of the highest court of judicature, a positive denial of justice to the nation.[10]

Thus, although the weavers of the North-West may, by the early 1770s at least, have some reason to believe that the actions of this judge at the height of their struggles with their employers was clearly biased in favour of the masters, and there was little they could do. Effectively all the power now lay with the manufacturers. Yet with the nature of this struggle and the increasing erosion of their former customary practices, the argument presented in this study is that these circumstances resulted in the beginning of the formation of a viable and meaningful working class in a class sense. This was so in the lead up to the struggle with the employers, and because of the negative result they now knew that as a distinct class they would have to act for themselves and not rely on other 'agencies'. As we have noted on several occasions in this study, the fact that the working class were capable of agency reveals their growing maturity as a class. Yet to a significant extent this was also true of the middle class manufacturers, as they too were rapidly developing the traits which would make them distinctive in terms of being imbued with middle class values of economic and political self-

---

8 Junius, Letter XLI: To the Right Honourable Lord Mansfield: 14 November 1770. (London: Leopold Classic Library, 2015).
9 Ibid.
10 Junius, Letter LXVIII: To Lord Chief Justice Mansfield; 21 January 1772, (London: Leopold Classic Library, 2015).

interest. They too were developing their 'agency'. The bifurcation of the two classes based on their relationship to economic organisation, access to capital and productive relations, by the end of the 1760s and especially after the events at the Preston election, was given the necessary added element of a political dimension. Crucial to their understanding at this time was the fact they understood that if their economic aims and aspirations were to be realised they had to become more politically active in organising themselves within the existing political system. By its very nature politics is divisive in terms of opinions regarding policy and, in due course, the commercial and industrial middle class elites in Manchester and indeed the North-West would divide over grand issues such as loyalty and emerging radicalism from the later 1780s and especially into the 1790s. Yet in terms of the need to develop a political understanding to enjoin and advance their economic position the great majority were in agreement. In this sense and at this time the middle class were in a more advanced position in terms of their development than the working class, in that the key ingredients of what would become nineteenth century mainstream Liberalism were already taking root. Whereas for the working class the examples of their radical political programme would have to wait for the graphic examples of the outcome of the American Rebellion, and even more so in the events of the French Revolution, to have an impact and their literal codification in the works of Thomas Paine and others. In later 1760s and in terms of the two main political alignments it was clear to these thrusting men of manufacturing that their fortunes would be best served by the Whigs. For the emerging working class there were few at this time who would be willing to champion their cause, not until the growing criticism of existing corrupt political system began to come under serious scrutiny later in the century. Then this growing criticism could be coupled with claims by the working class that their grievances needed to be addressed and redressed by gaining some form of parliamentary representation, which in turn would mean parliamentary reform. To have their claims taken more seriously by a wider audience would take the examples of revolutions noted above, the polemics of Paine, and the exertion of extra-parliamentary pressure by organisations such as the various Correspondence Societies. It would see the emergence of those coming to radical political solutions drawn from their own ranks, such as Samuel Bamford from Middleton or John Knight from Oldham, but this again was some years away. Yet even by the examples cited in this study, beginning from the later 1740s and the commencement of the loss of their customary work practices and the ensuing loss of independence, the nature of their willingness to organise themselves, the growing unreliability of an impartial magistracy in the North-West, the increasingly exploitative relationship with industrial capital, the changing nature of market relations in necessary provisions, all signalled what the nature of a working class future was likely to be. But it would take the institutionalisation of the process and the witnessing of even greater hardships for these working class communities to be truly realised. Yet even for the working class there was a crumb of comfort in what had occurred at Preston in 1768, with the granting of a universal male franchise and it was clearly something on which, in the ensuing decades, an overtly radical political discourse could begin to build an effective critique in favour of greater working class political understanding and action.[11]

---

11 According to Frank O'Gorman's figures the electorate of Preston between 1761 and 1802 amounted to 82% being made up of 'craftsmen, semi and unskilled workers and agricultural workers', with a further 9% made up of those in the retail sector. F. O'Gorman, 'The Unreformed

Although buoyed by recent advances by 1770, especially in terms of the advances they had made in dismantling the traditional work practices of their employees, the manufacturers of Manchester in particular knew only too well that in political terms the old order still held an entrenched and powerful position in the seats of national political power. They needed those Whigs who sympathised with their way of economic thinking to be in positions of strength, not only in the defence of their actions but also in the possibility of advancing the causes of the potential wealth that the cotton sector (and by association their own personal wealth) could generate. Yet they could make their voices and concerns heard in the local political arenas of the North-West. This is again why developments at the Preston election of 1768 were so important. Gradually, but markedly, the essence of the political structure of Britain was undergoing change by the 1770s and it was one within which the manufacturing middle classes would play an increasingly important role. Yet for those groups below them in terms of property and status, the significance of this contest and its outcome and, indeed, for future years until the First Reform Act of 1832, was that even after minor alterations to the rules governing the status of resident 'householders' in 1786, Preston remained a 'popular' franchise and one in which the considerations of 89% of the population of the constituency had to be considered, and these were the working class.[12]

However, the question remains, just how much were the views of working people considered in political terms? This question has even more relevance in the context of the eighteenth century political culture and society, given the overwhelming importance of status, rank, deference and patronage. Yet even in the corrupt environment of eighteenth century electoral contests the sheer numerical size of the working class electorate at Preston would not have been lost on those attempting to control the outcome of future elections, because here the working class possessed a real and tangible political voice, no matter what the existing conventions of deference and patronage were. As O'Gorman tells us, deference, patronage and electoral influence were features that worked both ways for those expecting deferential respect and those giving that respect to patrons of higher social status.

> For electoral influence was not simply a right of property. Contemporaries were keen to point out that it was a moral trust, although not a legal one, involving distinct obligations of service not merely to the voters but to the community as a whole.[13]

Hence there was a degree within which the views of the electorate had to be considered even if this lasted but a short time in the build up to, and the engaging in, the actual election itself. They would not shape the great affairs of

---

Electorate of Hanoverian England: The Mid-Eighteenth Century to the Reform Act of 1832', *Social History*, Vol. 11, No. 1 (Jan., 1986), pp. 33-52, p. 40.

12 O'Gorman, op cit, and 26th Geo. 3rd, c. 100 (*1786*), "to prevent occasional inhabitants from voting in the election of members in Parliament for cities and boroughs," by which no person exercising the franchise as Scot and Lot voters, householders, pot wallers, or inhabitants, should vote unless they had been an inhabitant six months previous to the election.

13 F. O'Gorman, 'Electoral Deference in "Unreformed" England: 1760-1832', *The Journal of Modern History*, Vol. 56, No. 3 (Sep., 1984), pp. 391-429, p. 7. See also by the same author 'The Unreformed Electorate of Hanoverian England: The Mid-Eighteenth Century to the Reform Act of 1832', and *Voters, Patrons, and Parties: The Unreformed Electoral System of Hanoverian England 1734-1832: The Unreformed Electorate of Hanoverian England, 1734-1832*, (Oxford: Oxford University Press, 1989).

state, that would still be conducted by ministries chosen by the King, or be able to form a majority in Parliament, but local considerations would unquestionably feature during these election contests and at that time it would have been clear to all what the concerns of working people would have been. Because they were working class did not mean they were politically inarticulate or overawed by the status of their social superiors, as Pocock tells us:

> But the yeomen must first find and evaluate their superiors. They are presumed capable not only of knowing a fake natural aristocrat when they see one, but also of asking sensible and pertinent questions of the genuine article. Deference precludes them from the capacity for leadership, but not from an intelligently critical attitude toward those who possess that capacity. It is wholly compatible with proportionate quality and public virtue. Indeed, if these things presuppose political relations between individuals of diversified capacity, they depend upon deference, and deference is no more than the recognition of one capacity by another. It might even be shown by the few toward the many.[14]

Thus the inter-relationship between political deference and patronage was complex, and this was especially so within the context of the eighteenth century. Pocock puts forward the position that deference is suggestive of a reciprocal relationship involving obligations – often tacitly expressed – on both sides. O'Gorman puts forward the view that this can be extended into the area of electoral contests with the rituals surrounding reciprocally negotiated support based on patronage. As he tells us:

> It took some political will and determination to exercise electoral influence, especially to the extent of exerting public pressure not merely on tenants and other direct dependents but also on shopkeepers, customers, and even friends. Consequently, the electoral rituals of canvassing and visitation, parades and processions, treatings and entertainments signify the persuasion of equals rather than bullying of subordinates. The landlord or patron would normally make his political wishes and preferences known, and he would advise his dependents on the political line which he would like them to follow but he was reluctant, to make them follow it against their consciences.[15]

In both the examples of Pocock and O'Gorman those involved in the whole process of the performance of an election there were opportunities for ordinary people to give vent to their independence as participants. Indeed, this was often seen as an occasion for the expression of political liberty of the many and not merely of only those in positions of direct political power. On occasions there may be exhibited concerns over national political issues and policy, but often it was the situation in the locality which took centre stage because these were of direct and immediate importance. The key point to note was that it was the instance of a general election where the theatre of political drama was played out and, for a few weeks at least, all those situated in this local area were invited to participate, and that included the working class. The example of Preston then, with its unique franchise, was an opportunity for the working class to express a political will and this also would have been an impetus for their engaging in

---

14 J. G. A. Pocock, 'The Classical Theory of Deference' *The American Historical Review*, Vol. 81, No. 3 (Jun., 1976), pp. 519-520.
15 F. O'Gorman, 'Electoral Deference in "Unreformed" England: 1760-1832', *The Journal of Modern History*, Vol. 56, No. 3 (Sep., 1984), pp. 391-429, pp. 401-402.

questions which were of direct significance to them. This, when this was coupled with their heightened sense of social, communal and economic self-identification as a class, would have ensured the added element of a developing political consciousness.

This study has attempted to place before the reader the nature of the fundamental changes to the communities of working people in a range of crucial areas affecting their daily lives from the 1740s up to 1770. This was done through the examination of their industrial situation and the changes to their customary work practices, through the struggle for normative market relations that ensured they gained access to the 'necessaries of life' at reasonable prices, and the advancement of a political will to act on their own behalf by engaging in social and political protest. The situation was by no means resolved by 1770 for either the emerging working class or the manufacturing middle classes but, as had been attempted here, significant advances towards 'modernity' were being made in terms of the relations between capital and labour and the multitude of consequences this entailed in the communal, social, political and, obviously, the economic inter-relationship between the emerging classes. Yet there were momentous and hugely significant changes to come in the years following 1770. Most obviously in the short term, given by now the massive importance of the cotton industry to the North-West region, was the loss of the American colonies and access to the primary product of raw cotton generated in the southern colonies. Although it may appear, at first sight, incongruous, the loss of the American colonies actually acted as a spur to the promotion of British industry. The primary reason for this was that after 1782 entrepreneurs and men of commerce had to find new markets instead of relying on the relative ease of trading with the Thirteen Colonies. In so doing they increasingly looked to Asia and they found in India a massive market where they could 'dump' British exports and one capable of soaking up all the excess spending within the entire structure of the national debt. It was now that Lancashire cotton textiles began to come into their own in terms of building on the foundations of forming a new series of productive processes and patterns of the organisation of work. This had the effect of the possible realisation of even greater profitability for the manufactures of Lancashire and, by the same token, meant that the changes they had initiated between the 1740 and 1770 were to be used as the establishment upon which to build even greater control over the crucial asset of the labour of the region. How this unfolded in the decades after 1770, however, will have to be reserved for a future volume.

What we have seen in this study and in its analysis of the ramifications involved is the combination of ideas surrounding the need and, indeed, in some quarters, the demand for a change in the economic basis of Britain's commercial and trading position. It was argued that this was required both internally in the production and marketing of commodities and internationally. To this was joined at the microeconomic level, the practical imposition of processes and actions that began to change the manner in which industrial employers envisaged control mechanisms over their workers. The nature of the new master/worker relationship and its effects impacted the attitudes and actions of the emerging working class and began the process of transforming the traditional basis of the communities in which they lived. The argument presented here is that these events had momentous implications for the manner in which the economic and social basis of eighteenth century British society rested. The study focused on the North-West because as a region it was the first to feel the effects of this transformative process. A significant sub-theme explored was that at a significant level this was about power – economic, social and political – that began to ignite the process of transformation and the realisation on both the part of the emerging industrial middle and working classes that their interests were not being served by the existing state of affairs. Both were being wrenched from their traditional positions; their attitudes were undergoing profound changes due to the experiences they were facing and coming to terms with. By no means was this process over at the conclusion of the present study in 1770. It is the events and the developments that occurred in the phase between 1770 and 1800 that will be the focus of the next volume and it is there that we shall see the full impact of the processes began and enjoined in what has been discussed here.

Bibliography

Primary Materials

The British Library

Calendar of Home Office Papers, 1766-1769, (2073/153), Domestic Entry Books, (273-410).
Egmont Papers, Historical Manuscripts Commission, Egmont Diary, vol.1.
Grenville Papers, 42083-8, 57804-37.
Hardwicke Papers, 35349-36278, 45030-45047.
Harley Papers, (for papers relating to Charles Davenant, British Library, Harley MSS, 1223, I, fols. 187-189, (c. 1695)).
Newcastle Papers, Correspondence, Ad Mss 32686-32992.
Petty Papers, 72850-72908F.

The National Archive, Kew

Assize Papers, Western Circuit: Indictment Files, Gaol Delivery, Oyer and Terminer and Nisi Prius, (1740-770) ASSI 24, 25, for Criminal Depositions see ASSI 26.
Custom House Accounts, Records of the Board of Customs and Excise, (Customs 3, 1755).
Duchy of Lancaster Papers, D. L. 4.147.
Palatinate Papers, Lancashire, P. L. 6, 44/52; (1675); P. L. 6, 36/109, (1684-1688); 36/120; *Palatinate Papers*, P. L. 6, 51/93, (1704) P. L. 6.58/6; P. L. 7. 126, (1714); P. L. 7, 130, (1720); P. L. 6.70/25; P. L. 7, 141. (1727-28); P. L. 6.69/21; 71/36; P. L. 7. 142, (1729); P. L. 26. 39/1, (1757); Palatinate Papers, Lancashire, Indictments, P.L. 26. 39/1. 5 September, 1758; P. L. 26. 39/2, 39/3. (1760).
County Palatinate Notebooks, Lancashire, (1645-1646) Book iv.
Journals and Papers of the Board of Trade and Plantations (C.O. 388/22 Q.151 and Q. 159 see also C.O. 388/23 R. 29).
Kings Bench, Special Commissions of Oyer and Terminer, KB 8.74, (1753-1766).
State Papers Domestic, SP 35, /14 ff. 203, (1766); SP36/152/3; SP36/153 ff. 30, 36. SP 36 Vol. 136, ff 84-85 (1757); SP 36, Vol. 136, ff 117, (June, 1757); SP 36, Vol. 136, ff 186, Letters from Wigan, (11/8/1757); SP 36, Vol. 138, ff 48, letters from Wigan (1757), ff 45-47; Riots at York, (2/9/1757); SP 36, Vol. 138, ff 127-129, Riots at Liverpool, (22/11/1757); SP 37/5 and SP 37/6 (1766-1767) *passim*; SP 37, 2, ff. 189-92; ff. 259. (1768); SP37/21, (1780); SP44, ff. 200-213.
Home Office Papers, HO 40, 42 series.
Historic Manuscripts Commission, Kenyon Mss, (1894). Flintshire Records Office.
Privy Council Registers, PC1; PC2.
Treasury Solicitors Papers, TS 1, Conflict, Crime (1740-1770); TS. 11. (1740-1770; TS II. 995 (1766) Riots, Preservation of the Peace, Indictments and Depositions; TS 18.181 Criminal Cases, (1740-1770).
War Office Papers, WO/4.52-53, (1756-1758); WO/4.81-83 (1766-1768).

Birmingham Reference Library

Johnson Letters, undated, 1742 Cave to Paul, (185,462).

Chethams Library, Manchester

Manchester Court Leet Records.
Lancashire and Cheshire Wills, New Series, Vol.28.
Bobbin, Tim' (John Collier) 1708-1786. Miscellaneous autograph works including *'Subscribers to Human passions delineated'*, sketch book, account with

booksellers; manuscript, 1763-1783.
Colliers's Mss. 7 bound as one volume. MUN Collection- Shelf position: Mun.A.4.40.
BYROM, J., *The private journal and literary remains of John Byrom,* Vol. II, Part 1, (Chetham Society, Old Series, OS 40, 1856).
PERCIVAL, T., *A Letter to a Friend: Occasioned by the late Dispute Betwixt the Check-Makers of Manchester and their Weavers; and the Check-Makers Ill-Usage of the Author,* (Halifax: J. Buckland, 1758), Byrom Collection 2.K.5.77 (7).

Gloucester County Archive

The Correspondence of the Reverend John Foley and Charles B. Bathurst, regarding the relief of the extra-parochial poor in the Forest of Dean, (1801), D421.X/5.

House of Commons, Parliamentary Papers

Eighteenth-century Sessional Papers, *The Harper Collection of Private Bills*, (1695-1814).

Lancashire Archives, Preston

Assize Papers, 1740-1770, NRA 19460.
Cragg Family Memorandum,1698-1816: mainly The Diary of Timothy Cragg, (DDX 760).
Election 'letters, songs and poems', (DDPr/131/6) ff. 2-43; and (DDPr/131/7), ff. 7-13, 38-39, 40-41, 56-57, 93, (1768).
Legal Papers Relating to the Preston Election of 1768, (Summary) (DDX/123/14); 'Burgoyne v Moss and others' (Preston Election Return). (DDX 135/5-12).
Pedder Papers, "Register of Voters with examinations as to their validity, 21 Mar.-1 Apr. 1768". (DDPd 11/51); "Register of Tallies at Preston Election, 1768", (DDPd 11/50); "John Nabb's Accounts", (DDPd 11/52-53); "Election Squibs, etc.", (DDPr 131/6 & 7); "Letter from Mr. Dunning to the Corporation of Preston", (copy), (DDPr 131/8a); "Register of Foreign Voters", (DDPr 138/7).
Witness Deposition 1. DDX 113/5, depositions of Jeb Davis, John Heaton, Joseph Turner, Court of the Kings Bench, Westminster, (1768).
Witness Depositions, 2. (DDX 113/6), Unnamed Deponents, (taken before Mr. Justice Yates, 20/6/1768, Sergeants Inn, London).
Deposition of John Forgey made before Mr Justice Yates, Sergeants Inn, London, 20/6/1768. (DDX 113/6).

Leicestershire Archive, Leicester

Finch Papers, *(DG7/4969),* (1715).

Liverpool Reference Library

Port Books, E. 190, 1351/1, (1690).

Manchester Central Reference Library

Burton Manuscript, Vol. vii.
The Worsted Small-Ware Weavers' Apology, Together with all their Articles, which either concern their Society or Trade. To which is added a Farewell Discourse, made by their First Chair-Man. All faithfully collected together, by Timothy Shuttle. (Manchester, 1756).

Oldham Local Studies Library

William Rowbottom's Diary, 1787-1799. (D-M 54).

Wigan Reference Library

The Linen and Cotton Broad-Ware Weavers' Apology: Humbly addressed to the Gentleman Manufacturers of Manchester, And all others whom it may concern. By a Well-Wisher to Trade. (Liverpool, 1758*).*

University of Michigan, Anne Arbor, William L. Clements Library

Shelburne Papers.

'A True Account of Mr. John Daniel's Progress with Prince Charles Edward in the Years 1745 and 1746 Written by Himself.' Walter Biggar Blaikie, 'Origins of the 'forty-Five, and Other Papers Relating to That Rising' *Scottish History Society, Second Series*, Vol II, (March, 1916).

ABRAM, W. A., *Sketches in Local History: Memorials of Old Lancashire Families Preston, Lancashire, England*, (*The Preston Guardian*, 1877).

ANDREWS, T., *The miseries of the miserable: or An Essay laying open the decay of the fine woollen trade, and the unhappy condition of the poor Wiltshire Manufacturers, by a gentleman of Wilts.* (London, 1739).

ANON., *Considerations on the Policy, Commerce, and Circumstances of the Kingdom*, (London, 1771).

_____, *Considerations on a Bill for A General Naturalization,* (London, 1748).

_____, *Propositions for the Improving the Manufactures, Agriculture and Commerce of Great Britain*, (London, 1763).

_____, *Remarks upon the Serious Dissuasive from an Intended Subscription for Continuing the Races*, (London, 1733).

_____, *The Causes of the Dearness of Provisions Assigned*, (London, 1767).

_____, *The Laws and Customs of the Miners in the Forest of Dean in the County of Gloucestershire*, (William Cooper, London, 1687).

_____, *The Occasion of the Dearness of Provisions and the Distress of the Poor*, (London, 1767).

_____, *The Devil drove out the warping-bar; or, The snap-reel snap'd...*, (London, 1727).

_____, *Thoughts on the Use of Machines in Cotton Manufacture*, (Manchester, 1769).

Annual Register, 1758-1770.

ATKYNES, SIR R., *The Ancient and Present State of Gloucestershire*, Second Edition, (London: W. Herbert, 1768).

AXON, W. E. A., *Manchester a Hundred Years Ago* (Manchester, 1887) a reprint of *Ogden's Description of Manchester*, (Manchester, 1787).

BASSET J., *Chronicum Rusticum-Comerciale*, (ed. John Smith), 2 vols. (London, 1747).

BEAUMONT, W., *A History of the House of Lyme*, (Warrington, 1876).

BENTLEY, T., *Letters on the Utility and Policy of Employing Machines to Shorten Labour*, (London, 1780).

BERKELEY, G., *The Querist* (London and Dublin, 1735-1737).

BLACKSTONE, W., *Commentaries on the Laws of England* IIth edition, (London, 1791), Vol.I, Book I.

BROOKE, R., *Liverpool as it was during the last quarter of the Eighteenth Century, 1775-1800*, (Liverpool, 1853).

BURGH, J., *Reflexions on the Representation in Parliament,* (London, 1766).

_____, *Crito, or Essays on Various Subjects*, 2 Vols. (London, 1767).

BURKE, E., *Thoughts and Details on Scarcity. Originally Presented to the Right Hon. William Pitt, in the Month of November, 1795,* (London, 1800).

_____, *The Works of Edmund Burke,* Seven Volumes, (London: Macmillan, 1907).

CAMPBELL, J., *The Lives of the Chief Justices of England,* 3 vols., (London: John Murray, 1849-1857), Vol. 2.

Chester Chronicle, (1795).

Chester Courant, (1795).

CHESTERFIELD, EARL OF, Letter from the Earl of Chesterfield to Solomon Dayrolles, (June, 1756), printed by John Bradshaw, ed. *The Letters of Philip Dormer Stanhope, Fourth Earl of Chesterfield,* (London: Swan, Sonnerschein and Company, 1905).

COLE, ROBERT, in *The Life and Times of Samuel Crompton: Inventor of the Spinning Machine Called the Mule: Being the Substance of Two Papers Read to the Members of the Bolton Mechanics' Institution,* (Manchester, 1859).

COLLIER, JOHN, "Tim Bobbin", *The Truth in a Mask, or the Shude-hill Fight, being A short Manchester Chronicle on the present Times,* (Amsterdam, 1757).

DAVIES, D., *The Case of the Labourers in Husbandry,* (Bath, 1795).

DEFOE, DANIEL, *A tour thro' the whole island of Great Britain, divided into circuits or journies* (London: JM Dent and Co, 1927 Everyman Edition), Vol. ii.

_____, *The Complete English Tradesman I,* (London, 1726) *The Plan of English Commerce,* (London, 1730).

DOBSON, W., *History of the Parliamentary History of the Representation of Preston during the Last Hundred Years,* (Preston, 1856).

EDEN, SIR F., *The State of the Poor,* (London, 1795).

EARWAKER, J. P., (ed.) *The Constables' accounts of the Manor of Manchester: from the year 1612 to the year 1647, and from the year 1743 to the year 1776,* (Cornish, Manchester 1891) 3 Vols.

FORSTER, H., *An Enquiry into the Causes of the Present High Price of Provisions,* (London, 1767).

FAZY, J. J., *Princi es d'organisation industrielle pour le développement des richesses en France* (Paris, 1830).

GASKELL, P., *The Manufacturing Population of England.* (London, 1833).

Gloucester Journal, (1740-1770), *An Essay on Riots* (19 December, 1738).

GUEST, R., *A Compendious History of the Cotton Manufacture,* p.11 (Manchester, 1823).

HIGSON, J., *The Gorton Historical Recorder* (Drolylsdon, 1852).

HUME, D., *Writings on Economics,* ed. J. Rotwein, (London, 1955 ed.).

_____, *The History of England.6 vols.* (London: A. Millar, 1754-62).

_____, *Political Discourses* (Edinburgh, 1752).

Journal of the House of Commons, (1740-1770).

Journal of the House of Commons, Evidence of Robert Livesay, vol. xxii, (1751).

LATIMER, J., *The Annals of Bristol in the Eighteenth Century,* (Bristol, 1893).

LLOYD, WILLIAM F., *Two Lectures in the Checks to Population,* (Oxford: Oxford University Press, 1833).

LOCKE, J., *Two Treatises of Government.* Cambridge Texts in the History of Political Thought. Ed. Peter Laslett. (Cambridge: Cambridge University Press, 1997).

_____, *Political Writings.* Cambridge Texts in the History of Political Thought, ed. Mark Goldie. (Cambridge: Cambridge University Press, 2002).

_____, "Two Tracts on Government" in *Political Writings.* Cambridge Texts in the History of Political Thought, ed. Mark Goldie. (Cambridge: Cambridge University Press, 2002).

_____, "Essay on the Law of Nature" in *Political Writings.* Cambridge Texts in the History of Political Thought, ed. Mark Goldie. (Cambridge: Cambridge University Press, 2002).

McCulloch, R. J., *Essay on ... the Condition of the Labouring Classes,* (Edinburgh, 1826).
Malthus, T., *An Essay on the Principle of Population.* (1st ed. London, 1798).
Manchester Mercury, (1752-1770).
Massie, J., *Representation Concerning the Knowledge of Commerce as a National Concern; Pointing out the Proper Means of Promoting such Knowledge into this Kingdom,* (London: T. Payne, 1760).
Moore, F., *Considerations on the Exorbitant Price of Provisions,* (London, 1773).
Mortimer, T., *The Elements of Commerce, Politics and Finances, in Three Treatises* (London, 1772).
Mun, Thomas, *A Discourse of Trade from England unto the East Indies,* (London, 1621) and *England's Treasure by Foreign Trade.* (London, 1664).
Murray, P., *Thoughts on the Money, Circulation and Paper Currency,* (London, 1758).
North, D., *Discourses Upon Trade: Principally Directed to the Case of the Interest, Coynage, Clipping, Increase of Money,* (London, 1691).
Ogden, J., *Manchester A Hundred Years Ago,* (Manchester, 1887).
Percival, Dr. T. E., *The Works, Literary, Moral and Medical: To which are Prefixed Memoirs of His Life and Writings and a Selection from His Literary Correspondence,* (London: J. Johnson, 1807 edn.) Volume 4.
Philanthes, *Case between the clothiers, weavers and other manufacturers with regard to the late riots in Wilts, 1738,* (London, 1739).
Postlethwayt, M., *Britain's Commercial Interest Explained and Improved,* Two Volumes, (London, 1757).
_____, *Great Britain's True System* (London, 1757).
Preston Pilot, 'Local Sketches' (April, May, 1875; and 12 October, 1889).
Salisbury Journal, 1740-1770.
Somerville, Thomas, *My Own Life and Times, 1741-1814,* (Edinburgh, 1861).
Smith, A., *The Theory of Moral Sentiments,* (London: A. Millar, 1759).
_____, *Wealth of Nations,* (Penguin edition), *(London, 1999).*
Smith, C., *A Short Essay on the Corn Trade, and the Corn Laws,* (London, 1758).
_____, *Three Tracts on the Corn Trade and Corn Laws,* (London: J. Brotherton, 1766).
Smollett, T., *History of England, from the Revolution to the Death of George the Second,* 3 Vols. (London, 1804 edn.).
Steuart, J., *Inquiry into the Principles of Political Economy,* (Edinburgh, 1767).
The Letters of Junius, 1768-1772, (London: Leopold Classic Library, 2015 edn.).
Temple, W., *The Case as stands between the Clothiers, Weavers and other Manufacturers, with regard to the late Riot etc.,* (London: T. Cooper, 1739).
_____, *A Vindication of Commerce and the Arts,* (Bristol, 1758).
_____, *An Essay in Trade and Commerce,* (London, 1770).
The Gentleman's Magazine, Vols. 10-40, (1740-1770).
The London Gazetteer and New Daily Advertiser (1775).
The Spectator, Letter Number 232, (26 November, 1711).
Twiss, Travers, *View of the Progress of Political Economy in Europe since the Sixteenth Century* (London, 1847).
Tucker, J., *Six Sermons,* (Bristol: Felix Farley, 1745)
_____, *Reflections on the Expediency of a Law for the Naturalization of Foreign Protestants in Two Parts: Part Two, Important Queries.* (London: T. Trye, 1752).
_____, *Elements of Commerce,* (Bristol, 1755).
_____, *A Brief Essay on the Advantages and Disadvantages which Respectively Attend France and Great Britain with Regard to Trade with some Proposals for Removing the Principal Disadvantages of Great Britain. In a New Method.* (London: George Faulkner, 1757)

_____, *Instructions for Travellers; A Brief Essay on the Advantages and Disadvantages which respectively attend France and Great Britain with Respect to Trade,* (Dublin, 1758).
_____, *Four Tracts on Political and Commercial Subjects,* (London, 1774, 2nd edn).
URE, ANDREW, 'This Island is pre-eminent among civilized nations for the prodigious development of its factory wealth'. *The Philosophy of Manufactures. An Exposition of the Factory System of Great Britain* (London, 1835).
VANDERLINT, J., *Money Answers All Things,* (London, 1736).
WALKER, T., *Review of some of the Political Events ... in Manchester,* (Manchester, 1794).
WALPOLE, H., *Memoirs of the Reign of King George the Third,* Four Volumes, vol. I, (London, 1894 edn.).
Western Flying Post, 1766.
WHISTON, J., *A Discourse on the Decay of Trade* (London, 1693).
Westminster Journal, 1744-1770.
Whitworth's Manchester Magazine, (1742-1760).
Williamson's Liverpool Advertiser, (1756-1770).
YOUNG, A., *The Expediency of a Free Exportation of Corn,* (London, 1770).

Articles, Journals, and Theses

ALAVI, H., 'India: The Transition to Colonial Capitalism' in H. Alavi *et al.* (eds), *Capitalism and Colonial Production,* (London: Croom Helm, 1982).
ANDERSON, B. L., 'Provincial aspects of the financial revolution of the eighteenth century' in *Business History,* Vol. 11, Issue 1, (1969).
_____, 'The Attorney and the Early Capital Market in Lancashire', in J. R. Harris, (ed.) *Liverpool and Merseyside. Essays in Economic and Social History of the Port and Its Hinterland,* (London: Frank Cass and Co., 1969).
_____ 'Aspects of Capital and Credit in Lancashire during the Eighteenth Century', (University of Liverpool, M.A. Thesis, 1966).
ANDREW, E., 'Class in Itself and Class against Capital: Karl Marx and His Classifiers', *Canadian Journal of Political Science / Revue canadienne de science politique,* Vol.16, No. 3 (Sep., 1983).
ASPROMOURGOS, TONY, 'The life of William Petty in relation to his economics' in *History of Political Economy* 20: 337-356 (1988).
BAGGS, A. P. AND JURICA, A. R. J., *History of the County of Gloucester: Volume 5, Bledisloe Hundred, St. Briavels Hundred, the Forest of Dean.* 'Forest of Dean: Introduction', in C. R. J. Currie and N. M. Herbert (eds.), *A History of the County of Gloucester: Volume 5, Bledisloe Hundred, St. Briavels Hundred, the Forest of Dean,* (London: Victoria County History, 1996).
BARKER, D., 'The Marketing of Corn in the First Half of the Eighteenth Century: North-East Kent', *The Agricultural History Review* Vol. 18, No. 2 (1970).
BENNETT, R. J., 'Alignments, Interests and Tensions over "Reform" in Eighteenth-Century Britain: The Manchester Committee of Trade 1774-86', *Northern History,* Vol. L1 (1), 2014.
BERLIN, I., 'Two Concepts of Liberty', in I. Berlin, *Four Essays on Liberty,* (Oxford: Oxford University Press, 2002 edn.).
_____, 'From Hope and Fear Set Free', in H. Hardy (ed.), *Concepts and Categories. Philosophical Essays,* (London: Hogarth Press, 1978).
BEZANSON, ANNA, 'The Early Use of the Term Industrial Revolution', *Quarterly Journal of Economics,* XXXVI, pp. 343-9, (1922).
BIRTLES, S., 'Common Land, Poor Relief and Enclosure: The Use of Manorial Resources in Fulfilling Parish Obligations 1601-1834' in *Past & Present,* 165 (1) (Nov., 1999).
BLACK, J., 'Newspapers and Politics in the 18th Century', *History Today,* Volume 36,

Issue 10, October 1986.
BLACKMAN, J., 'The Food Supply of an Industrial Town', *Business History*, Vo. 5, (1963).
BOHSTEDT, J., 'Gender, Household and Community Politics: Women in English Riots 1790-1810', *Past & Present*, 120 (1) (Aug., 1988).
BOOTH, A., 'Food Riots in the North-West of England 1790-1801' in *Past & Present*, 77 (1), (Nov., 1977).
BRENNER, R., 'Agrarian Class Structure and Economic Development in Pre-Industrial Europe', *Past & Present*, 70, (1) (Feb., 1976).
BREWER, J., 'English Radicalism in the Age of George III', in J. G. A. Pocock, (ed.) *Three British Revolutions,* (New Jersey: Princeton University Press, 1980).
_____, 'Commercialisation and Politics', in N. McKendrick, J. Brewer, and J. Plumb, (eds.), *The Birth of Consumer Society*, (Bloomington: Indiana University Press, 1982).
BROADBERRY, S. AND GUPTA, B., 'Cotton Textiles and thee Great Divergence: Lancashire, India and Shifting Competitive Advantage', 1600-1850, (Conference Paper at the conference, 'The Rise, Organisation and Institutional Framework of Factor Markets', 23-25 June, 2005, (Department of Economics, University of Warwick, 2005).
BUSH, M., 'The Risings of the Commons in England, 1381-1549', in *Orders and Hierarchies in Late Medieval and Renaissance Europe*, J. Denton, (ed.) (Basingstoke: Palgrave Macmillan, 1999).
CAMPBELL, S., 'The Economic and Social Effect of the Usury Laws in the Eighteenth Century', *Transactions of the Royal Historical Society*, Fourth Series, Vol. 16 (1933).
CAMERON, RONDO, 'A New View of European Industrialization', *The Economic History Review*, Second Series, Vol. 38, No. 1, (1985).
CARUS-WILSON, E. M., 'An industrial revolution of the thirteenth century', *Economic History Review,* 11 (1941).
CHAMBERS, J. D., 'Enclosure and the Labour Supply in the Industrial Revolution', *Economic History Review,* 2nd ser., v (1953).
CHAPMAN, S. D., 'Fixed Capital Formation in the British Cotton Industry 1770-1815', *Economic History Review*, (1970).
_____, 'Fixed Capital Formation in the British Cotton Manufacturing Industry', in J. S. Chaudhury, 'European Companies and the Bengal Textile Industry in the Eighteenth Century: The Pitfalls of Applying Quantitative Techniques', *Modern Asian Studies*, 27 (1993).
COATS, A. W., 'Changing Attitudes to Labour in the Mid-Eighteenth Century', *Economic History Review,* New Series, Vol. 11, No. 1 (1958).
COLE, W. A., 'The measurement of industrial growth', *Economic History Review*, 2nd ser., XI (1958).
COLLEY, L., 'The Politics of Eighteenth-Century British History', *Journal of British Studies*, Vol. 25, No. 4, (Oct., 1986).
CONNOLLY, S., 'Jacobites, Whiteboys and Republicans: Varieties of Disaffection in Eighteenth-Century Ireland'. (*Eighteenth-Century Ireland,* Vol. 18, 2003, Queens University, Belfast).
COPELAND, T. W., 'Edmund Burke and the Book Reviews in Dodsley's Annual Register', *Publications of the Modern Language Association*, Vol. 57, No. 2. (Jun. 1942).
CRAFTS, N. F. R., 'Industrial Revolution in Britain and France: Some Thoughts on the Question "Why England First?"', *Economic History Review* (Vol. 30, 1977).
_____, 'British economic growth, 1700-1831: A review of the evidence', *Economic History Review*. Vol. 36, No 2 (May, 1983).
_____, 'British Economic Growth, 1700-1850: Some Difficulties of Interpretation',

Explorations in Economic History, (Vol. 24, 1987).

———, 'British Industrialisation in the International Context', *Journal of Interdisciplinary History,* (Vol. 19, Winter, 1989).

——— AND KNICK-HARLEY, C., 'Output Growth and the British Industrial Revolution: A Re-Statement of the Crafts-Harley View', *Economic History Review*, Vol. 65 (1992).

———, 'The Industrial Revolution', in R. Floud and D. McCloskey, (eds.), *The Economic History of Britain since 1700*, Vol. 1, 2nd edition, (Cambridge: Cambridge University Press, 1994).

———, 'Economic Growth', in J. Mokyr (ed.), *Oxford Encyclopaedia of Economic History*, vol. 2, (Oxford: Oxford University Press, 2003).

———, LEYBOURNE, S. J., AND MILLS, T. C. , 'Trends and cycles in British industrial production, 1700-1913', *Journal of the Royal Statistical Society,* ser. A, 152 (1989).

——— AND KNICK-HARLEY, C., 'Output growth and the British industrial revolution: a re-statement of the Crafts-Harley view', *Economic History Review*, 45/4 (1992).

DAS, T., Review of *The Economic History of India: 1600-1800, American Historical Review* 51.2 (January, 1946).

DAVIES, R. S. W., AND POLLARD, S., 'The iron industry, 1750-1850', in C. H. Feinstein and S. Pollard, (eds.), *Studies in capital formation in the United Kingdom, 1750-1920,* (Oxford: Clarendon Press, 1988).

DEANE, P., 'The growth of British industry', *Economic Journal,* 46 (1956).

———, 'The output of the British woollen industry in the eighteenth century', *Journal of Economic History*, 17 (1957).

DOS SANTOS, T., 'The Concept of Social Classes', *Science and Society 34* (1970).

DRAPER, H., *Karl Marx's Theory of Revolution: The Politics of Social Classes* (New York: Monthly Review Press, 1978).

ENGERMAN, S. L., 'Mercantilism and Overseas Trade, 1700-1800', in R. Floud and D. McCloskey, (eds.), *The Economic History of Britain since 1700*, Vol. 1, 2nd edition, (Cambridge: Cambridge University Press, 1994).

FEINSTEIN, C. H., 'Capital Formation in Great Britain', in P. Mathias and M. M. Postan, (eds.), *The Cambridge Economic History of Europe, Vol. VII, The Industrial Economies, Part I,* (Cambridge: Cambridge University Press, 1978).

———, 'National Statistics, 1760-1920', in C. H. Feinstein and S. Pollard, (eds.), *Studies in Capital Formation in the United Kingdom, 1750-1920*, (Oxford: Clarendon Press, 1988).

FUSSELL, G. E. AND GOODMAN, C., 'Traffic in Farm Produce in Eighteenth Century England', *Agricultural History*, Vol. 7, Number 2, (1938).

GOLDIE, M., 'The Roots of True Whiggism, 1688- 94', *History of Political Thought* 1 (1980).

HAY, D., 'Moral economy, Political Economy and Law', in A. J. Randall, and A. Charlesworth, (eds.) *The Moral Economy and Popular Protest, Conflict and Authority*, (London: Macmillan, 2000).

HARRISON, R. D., 'Parliamentary elections and the political development of Newton, Preston and Wigan, 1689-1768'. Unpublished PhD. thesis, University of Lancaster, 1996.

HIGGINS, P. P. AND POLLARD, S., *Aspects of Capital Investment in Great Britain, 1750-1850*, (London: Methuen, 1971).

HOBSBAWM, E. J., 'The Tramping Artisan', *Economic History Review,* New Series, Vol. 3, No. 3 (1951), pp. 299-320, New Series, Vol. 3, No. 3 (1951).

HONT, I. AND IGNATIEFF, M., 'Needs and Justice in Wealth of Nations', in I. Hont and M. Ignatieff, (eds.), *Wealth and Virtue*, (Cambridge: Cambridge University Press, 1983).

HOPPIT, J., 'Political Arithmetic in Eighteenth-Century England', in *Economic History*

Review, New Series, Vol. 49, No. 3 (Aug., 1996).

―――, 'Counting the industrial revolution', *Economic History Review,* 2nd ser., XLIII (1990).

―――, 'The Contexts and Contours of British Economic Literature, 1660-1760', *The Historical Journal,* 49, 1 (2006).

HUTCHISON, TERRENCE, 'Petty on Policy, Theory and Method', in *Before Adam Smith: the Emergence of Political Economy 1662-1776.* (Blackwell, Oxford, 1988).

JONES, D. J. V., 'The Corn Riots in Wales, 1793-1801', *Welsh Historical Review,* Vol. 2, Number 4, (1965).

JONES, E. L., 'Agriculture and Economic Growth in England, 1660-1750: Agricultural Change', *Journal. of Economic History,* xxv (1965).

KING, PETER, 'Edward Thompson's Contribution to Eighteenth-Century Studies. The Patriarch-Plebeian Model Re-examined'. *Social History,* xxi (2) (1996).

KNICK HARLEY, C., 'British industrialisation before 1841: evidence of slower growth during the industrial revolution', *Journal of Economic History,* 42/2 (1982).

―――, 'Slavery, the British Atlantic economy and the Industrial Revolution', *University of Oxford, Discussion Papers in Economic and Social History*, No. 113, (April, 2013).

LANGFORD, P., 'Property and 'Virtual Representation' in Eighteenth-Century England', *Historical Journal*, Vol. 31 number 1, (1988).

Lees, R. M., 'Parliament and the Proposal for a Council of Trade, 1695-6', *English Historical Review*, LIV (1939).

LEVINE, D., 'Proto-Nothing: *Customs in Common* by E. P. Thompson', *Social History,* Vol. 18, No. 3, (1993).

Low, J. M., 'An Eighteenth Century Controversy in the Theory of Economic Progress', *The Manchester School*, XX, (1952).

McCAHILL, M. W., *The House of Lords in the Age of George III (1760–1811)* (2009) chapter 16, reprinted in *Parliamentary History*, Supplement 1, Vol. 28 (Oct 2009).

McLYNNE, F., 'The Regional Distribution of Jacobite Support in England before 1745' in *Journal of Regional and Local Studies,* no. 3 (1983-84).

MACCALLUM JR., G. C., 'Negative and Positive Freedom', *Philosophical Review*, 76: 312-34, (1967).

MAHAN, H. F., 'Joseph Gales, the National intelligencer and the War of 1812', Unpublished PhD. Thesis, Columbia University, New York, (1958).

MINGAY, G. A., 'The Course of Rents in the Age of Malthus', in M. Turner, (ed.) *Malthus in his Time*, (Basingstoke: Palgrave Macmillan, 1986).

MOKYR, J., 'The Industrial Revolution and the New Economic History', in J .Mokyr, (ed.) *The Economics of the Industrial Revolution,* (London: Allen and Unwin, 1985).

NEAL, L., 'How it all began: the monetary and financial architecture of Europe during the first global capital markets, 1648-1815', *Financial History Review*, Volume 7 / Issue 02 / October 2000.

NEESON, J. M., 'The Opponents of Enclosure in Eighteenth Century Northamptonshire', *Past & Present*, 105 (1) (Nov., 1984).

NEF, J. U., 'The Progress of Technology and the Growth of Large-Scale Industry in Great Britain, 1540-1640', *Economic History Review*, 5/1 (1934).

NICHOLSON F. AND AXON E., 'The Hatfield Family, of Manchester and the Food Riots of 1757 and 1812' *The Transactions of the Lancashire and Cheshire Antiquarian Society*, Vol. 28, (1910-1911).

O'GORMAN, F., 'Electoral Deference in "Unreformed" England: 1760-1832', *The Journal of Modern History*, Vol. 56, No. 3 (Sep., 1984).

―――, 'The Unreformed Electorate of Hanoverian England: The Mid-Eighteenth Century to the Reform Act of 1832', *Social History,* Vol. 11, No. 1 (Jan., 1986).

PARTHASARATHI, P., 'Rethinking Wages and Competitiveness in the Eighteenth Century: Britain and South India', *Past & Present*, 158 (1) (Feb., 1998).

PERLIN, F., 'Proto-industrialisation and Pre-colonial South Asia', *Past & Present*, 98 (1) (Feb., 1983).

POCOCK, J. G. A., 'The Classical Theory of Deference' *The American Historical Review*, Vol. 81, No. 3 (Jun., 1976).

POLLARD, SIDNEY, 'Investment, consumption and the Industrial Revolution', *Economic History Review*, Second Series, Vol. 11, No. 2, (1958).

_____, 'Fixed Capital and the Industrial Revolution in Britain', *Journal of Economic History*, Vol. 24, Number 3, (1964).

PORTER, J. H., 'The Development of Rural Society', in G. E. Mingay (ed.), *The Agrarian History of England and Wales,* vi, *1750-1850* (Cambridge: Cambridge University Press, 1989).

PRAKASH, O., 'Bullion for Goods: International Trade and the Economy of Early Eighteenth Century Bengal', *Indian Economic and Social History Review*, 13 (1976).

_____, 'On Estimating the Employment Implications of European Trade for the Eighteenth Century Bengal Textile Industry – A Reply', *Modern Asian Studies,* 27 (1993).

PRZEWORSKI, A., 'Proletariat into a Class: The Process of Class Formation from Karl Kautsky's *The Class Struggle to Recent Controversies*', *Politics and Society* 7 (1977).

RANDALL, ADRIAN, 'The Industrial Moral Economy of the Gloucestershire Weavers in the eighteenth century', in J. Rule (ed.) *British Trade Unionism, 1750-1850,* (London: Longmans, 1988).

ROLLISON, D., 'Property, Ideology and Popular Culture in a Gloucestershire Village, 1660-1740', *Past & Present*, 93 (1) (Nov., 1981).

ROSE, R. B., '18th Century Price Riots and Public Policy in England', *International Review of Social History,* VI, 287 (1961).

SEN, A., 'Well-being, Agency and Freedom', *Journal of Philosophy*, 82: 169-221 (1985).

_____, 'Freedom of Choice: Concept and Content', *European Economic Review*, 32: 269-94, (1988).

SEARLE, C. E., 'Custom, Class Conflict and Agrarian Capitalism: The Cumbrian Customary Economy in the Eighteenth Century', *Past & Present*, 110 (1) (Feb., 1986).

SCHWOERER, L. G., 'The Bill of Rights: Epitome of the Revolution of 1688-89', in J. A. G. Pocock, *Three British Revolutions: 1641, 1688, 1776*, (New Jersey: Princeton University Press, 1980).

SKINNER, Q., 'A Third Concept of Liberty', *Proceedings of the British Academy*, 117(237): 237-68 (2002).

_____, 'Freedom as the Absence of Arbitrary Power', in Laborde and Maynor, (eds.), *Republicanism and Political Theory*, (Oxford: Blackwell, 2008).

A. SMITH, (R. H. CAMPBELL, *et al.* eds.), *An Inquiry into the Nature and Causes of the Wealth of Nations*, 2 vols., Vol. I, (Indianapolis: Liberty Fund, 1981).

STIGLER, G. J., 'The Early History of Empirical Studies of Consumer Behavior', *Journal of Political Economy* 62, 2, (1954).

TAYLOR, C., 'What's Wrong with Negative Liberty', in A. Ryan (ed.), *The Idea of Freedom*, (Oxford: Oxford University Press, 1979, reprinted in D. Miller, 'Constraints on Freedom', *Ethics*, 94, pp. 66-86, (1983).

THOMPSON, E. P., 'Class Struggle without Class', *Social History,* Vol. 3, No. 2 (May, 1978).

_____, 'Custom, Law and Common Right', in *Customs in Common,* (London: Merlin, 1991).

_____, 'Time, Work Discipline and Industrial Capitalism', *Past & Present*, 38 (1) (Dec., 1967).
_____, Review of W. J. Shelton, *English Hunger and Industrial Disorders: A study of social conflict during the first decade of George III's reign*, *Economic History Review*, Second Series, Vol. 28, No. 3, August, 1974, pp. 480-484.
_____, 'Patricians and Plebs', in *Customs in Common*, (London: Merlin, 1991).
_____, 'The Moral Economy of the Crowd in the Eighteenth Century', in *Customs in Common*, (London: Merlin, 1991).
_____, 'The Moral Economy Reviewed', in *Customs in Common*, (London: Merlin, 1991).
_____, 'The Grid of Inheritance: A Comment', in Jack Goody, Joan Thirsk and E. P. Thompson, (eds.), *Family and Inheritance Rural Society in Western Europe, 1200-1800* (Cambridge: Cambridge University Press, 1976).
WADDELL, D., 'Charles Davenant (1656-1714) – A Biographical Sketch', *Economic History Review*. New Series 11, 2, (1958).
WALSH, D., 'The Cider Tax, Popular Symbolism and Opposition in Mid-Hanoverian England', in A. Randall and A. Charlesworth, (eds.), *Markets, Market Culture and Popular Protest in Eighteenth-Century Britain and Ireland, (*Liverpool: Liverpool University Press, 1996).
WILLIAMS, D. E., 'English hunger riots in 1766'. Unpublished Ph.D. Thesis, University of Wales (Aberystwyth), 1978.
_____, 'Morals, Markets and the English Crowd in 1766', *Past & Present*, 104 (1) (Aug., 1984).
WILSON, K., 'Inventing Revolution: 1688 and Eighteenth-Century Popular Politics' *Journal of British Studies*, Vol. 28, No. 4 (Oct., 1989).
_____, 'Urban Culture and Political Activism in England: The Example of Voluntary Hospitals', in A. Birke and E. Hellmuth, (eds.), *The Transformation of Political Culture in Late Eighteenth Century England and Germany*, (Oxford: Oxford University Press, 1990).
WOOD, A., 'The Place of Custom in Plebeian Political Culture', *Social History,* 22, 1, (Jan.1997).
_____, 'Subordination, Solidarity and the Limits of Popular Agency in a Yorkshire Valley *c.*1596-1615', *Past & Present*, 193 (1) (Nov., 2006).
WOODLAND, P. T. M., 'The Cider Excise, 1763-1766', (Unpublished D.Phil., University of Oxford, 1982).
_____, 'Extra-Parliamentary Political Organization in the Making: Benjamin Heath and the Opposition to the 1763 Cider Excise', *Parliamentary History,* Vol. 4, (1985).
_____, 'Political Atomization and Regional Interests in the 1761 Parliament: The Impact of the Cider Debates 1763-1766', *Parliamentary History,* Vol. 8, (1989).
_____, 'The House of Lords, the City of London and Political Controversy in the Mid-1760s: The Opposition to the Cider tax Further Considered', *Parliamentary History,* Vol. 11, (1992).
WRIGHT, J. F., 'British Government Borrowing in Wartime, 1750-1815', *The Economic History Review*, New Series, Vol. 52, No. 2 (May, 1999).

Books

ASHTON, T. S., *The Industrial Revolution, 1760-1830* (Oxford: Oxford University Press, 1948).
ADBURGHAM, A., *Shopping in Style: London From the Restoration to Edwardian Elegance*, (London: Thames & Hudson, 1979).
BAIROCH, P., *Victoires et déboires: Histoire économique et sociale du monde du XVIe siècle à nos jours*, (Paris: Gallimard, 1997).

BAUMGARTEN, L., *What Clothes Reveal: The Language of Clothing Colonial and Federal America,* (New Haven: Yale University Press, 2002).
BACKHOUSE, A., *The Worm-Eaten Waistcoat,* (York, 2003).
BARNES, D. G., *A History of the English Corn Laws*, (London, 1930).
BELL, J., *Hugo Grotius: Historian*, (Ann Arbor: Michigan University Microfilms, 1980).
BERG, M., *The Age of Manufacturers, 1700-1820*, (Routledge: London and New York, 1994).
BERLIN, I., *Four Essays on Liberty*, (Oxford: Oxford University Press, 1979).
_____, *Liberty*, ed. H. Hardy, (Oxford: Oxford University Press, 2002).
BISSONNETTE, A., *Fashion on the Ohio Frontier 1790-1840,* (Ohio: Kent State University Museum, 2003).
Black's Law Dictionary, Fifth Edition, (New York: West, 1981).
BLOM, H. W., (ed.) *Property, Piracy and Punishment: Hugo Grotius on War and Booty in De Iure Praedae – Concepts and Contexts*, (Leiden: Brill, 2009).
_____ AND L. C. WINKEL, *Grotius and the Stoa*, (Assen: Van Gorcum Ltd, 2004).
BOHSTEDT, JOHN, *Riots and Community Politics in England and Wales, 1790-1810*, (Cambridge, Mass.: Harvard University Press, 1983).
_____, *The Politics of Provisions: Food Riots, Moral Economy, and Market Transition in England,* c. 1550-1850, (Aldershot: Ashgate, 2010).
BORSCHBERG, P., *Hugo Grotius, the Portuguese and Free Trade in the East Indies*, (Singapore and Leiden: Singapore University Press and KITLV Press, 2011).
BREWER, J., *The Sinews of Power: War, Money and the English State, 1688-1783*, (London: Hutchinson, 1988).
_____ AND STYLES, JOHN A., *An Ungovernable People: The English and their Law in the 17th and 18th Centuries*, (New Jersey: Rutgers University Press, 1980).
BUCK, A., *Dress in Eighteenth Century England*, (London: Holmes & Meier, 1980).
BUCKLE, S., *Natural Law and the Theory of Property: Grotius to Hume.* (New York: Oxford University Press, 1993).
BUSHAWAY, R. W., *By Rite: Custom and Community in England 1700-1880*, (London: Breviary Stuff, 2011 edn).
CANNON, J. A., *Parliamentary Reform 1640-1832.* (Cambridge: Cambridge University Press, 1972).
_____, *Aristocratic Century: the Peerage of Eighteenth-Century England*, (Cambridge: Cambridge University Press, 1984).
CARR, C. L., (ed), *The Political Writings of Samuel Pufendorf* (Oxford: Oxford University Press, 1994).
CHAMBERS, J. D. AND MINGAY, G. E., *The Agricultural Revolution, 1750-1880* (London: B. T. Batsford Ltd., 1966).
CHANDA, N., *Bound Together: How traders, preachers, Adventurers, and Warriors shaped Globalization*, (New Haven: Yale University Press, 2007).
CHARLESWORTH, A., *An Atlas of Rural Protest in Britain, 1548-1900*, (Beckenham: Croom Helm, 1983).
CLAPHAM, J. H., *An Economic History of Modern Britain*, i., (Cambridge: Cambridge University Press, 1926).
CLAIRMONTE, F., *Economic Liberalism and Underdevelopment: Studies in the Disintegration of an Idea*, (New York: Asia Publishing House, 1960).
CLARK, H., (ed.), Commerce, *Culture and Liberty: Readings on Capitalism Before Adam Smith*, (Indianapolis: Liberty Fund, 2003).
COHEN, G. A., *Karl Marx's Theory of History: A Defence* (Oxford: Clarendon Press, 1980).
COLLEY, L., *In Defiance of Oligarchy: The Tory Party, 1714-60* (Cambridge: Cambridge University Press, 1982).
_____, *Britons: Forging the Nation 1707-1837*, (New Haven: Yale University Press,

1994).
CORBETT, J., *England in the Seven Years War*, Vol. 1, (London: Longmans, Green, and Co., 1907).
CROWSTON, C. H., *Fabricating Women: The Seamstresses of Old Regime France, 1675-1791*, (North Carolina: Duke University Press, 2001).
CRAFTS, N. F. R., *British Economic Growth during the Industrial Revolution* (Oxford: Oxford University Press, 1985).
CROUZET, F., *Capital Formation in the Industrial Revolution*, (London: Methuen, 1972).
CUNNINGTON C. WILLET AND CUNNINGTON P., *Handbook of English Costume in the 18th Century*, (London: Faber, 1957).
DANIELS, G. W., *The Early English Cotton Industry*, (Manchester: Manchester University Press 1920).
DEANE, PHYLLIS, *The First Industrial Revolution* (Cambridge: Cambridge University Press, 1967).
_____ AND COLE, W. A., *British Economic Growth, 1688-1959: Trends and Structure* (Cambridge: Cambridge University Press, 1962).
DELPIERRE, M., Dress *in France in the Eighteenth Century*, (New Haven: Yale University Press, 1998).
DICKSON, P. G. M., *The Financial Revolution in England: A Study of the Development of Public Credit*, (London: Macmillan, 1967).
ELTON, G. R., Studies *in Tudor and Stuart Politics and Government*, 3 vols. (Cambridge: Cambridge University Press, 1974-83).
FARNIE, D. A., *The English Cotton Industry and the World Market* (Oxford: Oxford University Press, 1979).
FAY, C. R., *The Corn Laws and Social England*, (Cambridge: Cambridge University Press, 1932).
FEINSTEIN, C. H., AND POLLARD, S., (eds.), *Studies in capital formation in the United Kingdom, 1750-1920*, (Oxford: Clarendon Press, 1988).
FOHLEN, CLAUDE, *Qu'est-ce que la révolution industrielle?* (Paris: Laffont, 1971).
FRANK, A. G., *Re-Orient: Global Economy in the Asian Age*, (Berkeley: University of California Press, 1998).
GILLESPIE, C. C., (ed.), *A Diderot Pictorial Encyclopaedia of Trade and Industry*, (London/New York: Dover Publications, 1959).
GONNER, E. C. K., *Common Land and Inclosure* (London: Cass, 1966).
GRAS, N. S. B., *The Evolution of the English Corn Market from the Twelfth to the Eighteenth Century*, (Cambridge, Mass.: Harvard University Press, 1915).
GRUENFELDER, J. K., *Influence in Early Stuart Elections, 1604-1640*, (Columbus: Ohio State University Press, 1981).
HAMMOND, J. L. AND HAMMOND, BARBARA, *The Skilled Labourer, 1760-1832* (London, 1919).
_____, *The Town Labourer, 1760-1832* (London, 1917).
_____, *The Village Labourer*, (London, 1911; reprinted Stroud: Sutton Publishing, 1978).
HASLER, P. W., *The House of Commons, 1558-1603*, 3 Vols. (London: The Stationery Office, 1981).
HECKSCHER, ELI, *Mercantilism*, (London: Allen & Unwin, 1935).
HERSCH, T. AND HERSCH, C., *Cloth and Costume 1750-1800 Cumberland County Pennsylvania*, (Carlisle: Cumberland County Historical Society, 1995).
HIGGINS, P. P. AND POLLARD, S., *Aspects of Capital Investment in Great Britain, 1750-1850*, (London: Methuen, 1971).
A History of the County of Lancaster: Volume 4, 'Townships: Manchester', (part 2 of 2) (1911).
HOBSBAWM, ERIC, *Industry and Empire, from 1750 to the Present Day*,

(Harmondsworth: Penguin, 1968).
HOFFMANN, W. G., *British Industry, 1700-1950* (Oxford: Blackwell, 1955).
HULL, CHARLES H., (ed.), *The Economic Writings of Sir William Petty* (London: Routledge/Thoemmes, 1899).
HUNDERT, E. G., *The Enlightenment's Fable. Bernard Mandeville and the Discovery of Society*, (Cambridge: Cambridge University Press, 1994).
JOHNSON, E. A. J., *Predecessors of Adam Smith*, (New York: P. S. King, 1937).
JONES, E. L., *Agriculture and Economic Growth in England, 1650-1815*, (London: Methuen, 1967).
KENNEDY, P., *The Rise and Fall of the Great Powers: Economic Change and Military Conflict from 1500 to 2000*, (New York: HarperCollins, 1989).
KERRIDGE, E., *Agrarian Problems of the Sixteenth Century and After*, (London: Routledge, reprint, 2013).
KOWALESKI-WALLACE, E., *Consuming Subjects: Women, Shopping and Business in the Eighteenth Century*, (New York: Columbia University Press, 1997).
LANDAU, NORMA, *The Justices of the Peace*, (Berkeley: University of California Press, 1984).
LANDES, D. S., *The Unbound Prometheus: Technological Change and Industrial Development in Western Europe from 1750 to the Present*, (Cambridge: Cambridge University Press, 1969).
LANGFORD, P., *The Excise Crisis: Society and Politics in the Age of Walpole*, (Oxford: Oxford University Press, 1975).
_____, *A Polite and Commercial People, England 1727-1783*, (Oxford: Oxford University Press, 1992).
LEMIRE, B., *Dress, Culture and Commerce: The English Clothing Trade Before the Factory, 1660-1800* (London: Palgrave Macmillan, 1997).
_____, *Fashion's Favourite: The Cotton Trade and the Consumer in Britain 1660-1800,* (Oxford: Oxford University Press, 1991).
LETWIN, W., *The Origins of Economic Science*, (London: Methuen, 1963).
LUCE, A. A. AND JESSOP, T. E., (eds.), *The Works of George Berkeley Bishop of Cloyne* (London: Thomas Nelson & Sons, 1953).
MCCORMICK, T., *William Petty and the Ambitions of Political Arithmetic*. (Oxford: Oxford University Press, 2009).
MCKENDRICK, N., BREWER, J. AND PLUMB, J. H., *The Birth of Consumer Society*, (Bloomington: Indiana University Press, 1982).
MALCOLMSON, R. W., *A Set of Ungovernable People: The Kingswood Colliers in the Eighteenth Century*, No. 2 in the Kingswood History Series, (Kingswood, 1986).
_____, *Life and Labour in England, 1700-1780*, (London: Hutchinson, 1981).
MARKS, R., *The Origins of the Modern World: A Global and Ecological Narrative*, (Lanham, Maryland: Rowman & Littlefield, 2002).
MATHIAS, P., *The First Industrial Nation: An Economic History of Britain, 1700-1914*, (London: Methuen, 1969).
MARX K., AND ENGELS, F., *Collected Works*, Vol. ii, (New York: International Publishers, 1976).
MIDDLETON, R., *The Bells of Victory: The Pitt-Newcastle Ministry and the Conduct of the Seven Years' War, 1757-1762* (Cambridge: Cambridge University Press, 1985).
MOE, E., *Governance, Growth and Global Leadership: The Role of the State in Technological Progress, 1750–2000*, (Aldershot: Ashgate, 2007).
MOKYR, J., (ed.), *The British Industrial Revolution: An Economic Perspective*, (Oxford: Westview Press, 1999).
MORELAND, W. H., *India at the Death of Akbar* (London, 1920).
MORRILL, J. S., *Cheshire, 1630-1660* (Oxford: Oxford University Press, 1974).
_____, *Reactions to the Civil War, 1642-1649* (London: Palgrave Macmillan, 1982).

MUKERJEE, R., *The Economic History of India: 1600–1800*, (Allahabad: Kitab Mahal, 1967).
MUSSON, A. E., *The Growth of British Industry*, (London: B. T. Batsford Ltd., 1978).
NAMIER, L. B., *The Structure of Politics at the Accession of George III*, (London: Macmillan; 2nd edn., repr. 1960).
_____ AND BROOKE, J. J., (eds.) *History of Parliament: The House of Commons, 1754-1790*, 3 Vols. (Yeovil: Haynes, 1985 edn.).
NEESON, J. M., *Commoners: Common Right, Enclosure and Social Change m England, 1700-1820* (Cambridge: Cambridge University Press, 1993).
NEF, J. U., *The Rise of the British Coal Industry*, (London, 1932).
O'GORMAN, F., *Voters, Patrons, and Parties: The Unreformed Electorate of Hanoverian England, 1734-1832*, (Oxford: Oxford University Press, 1989).
_____, *The Long Eighteenth Century: British political and social history, 1688-1832* (London: Arnold, 1997).
OLDHAM, J., *The Mansfield Manuscripts and the Growth of English Law in the Eighteenth Century,* Vol. 2, (Chapel Hill and London: University of North Carolina Press, 1992).
OVERTON, M, *Agricultural Revolution in England: The Transformation of the Agrarian Economy 1500-1850*, (Cambridge, Cambridge University Press, 1996).
PARTHASARATHI, P., *The Transition to a Colonial Economy: Weavers, Merchants and Kings in South India, 1720-1800*, (Cambridge, Cambridge University Press, 2001).
PLUMB, J. H., *The Growth of Political Stability in England, 1675-1725* (London: The History Book Club, 1967).
POCOCK, J. G. A., (ed.) *Three British Revolutions*, (New Jersey: Princeton University Press, 1980).
POMERANZ, K., *The Great Divergence: Europe, China, and the Making of the Modern World Economy*, (New Jersey: Princeton University Press, 2000).
PORRITT, E. AND PORRITT, A. G., *The Unreformed House of Commons*, (Cambridge, Cambridge University Press, 1903).
PORTER, J. H., *Parliamentary Enclosure in England: An Introduction to its Causes, Incidence and Impact, 1750-1850* (London: Routledge, 1997).
PORTER, R., *English Society in the Eighteenth Century,* (London: Allen Lane, 1982).
PRICE, R., *British Society, 1680-1880: Dynamism, Containment and Change,* (Cambridge, Cambridge University Press, 1999).
POULANTZAS, N., *Political Power and Social Classes* (London: New Left Books, 1973).
RANDALL, A. J., A. *Riotous Assemblies, popular protest in Hanoverian England* (Oxford: Oxford University Press, 2006).
ROSTOW, WALT WHITMAN, *The Stages of Economic Growth: A Non-Communist Manifesto*, (Cambridge, Cambridge University Press, 1960).
ROGERS, N., *Whigs and Cities: Popular Politics in the Age of Walpole and Pitt*, (Oxford: Clarendon Press, 1989).
_____, *Crowds, Culture and Politics in Georgian Britain*, (Oxford: Clarendon Press, 1998).
ROLLISON, D., *The Local Origins of Modern Society: Gloucestershire 1500-1800* (London: Routledge, 1992).
RIBEIRO, A., *A Visual History of Costume: The Eighteenth Century,* (London: B. T. Batsford Ltd., 1983).
_____, *Dress in Eighteenth Century Europe: 1715-1789,* (London: Holmes & Meier, 2002).
_____, *The Art of Dress: Fashion in England and France 1750-1820,* (New Haven: Yale University Press, 1995).
ROCHE, D., *The Culture of Clothing: Dress and Fashion in the Ancien Regime*, (Cambridge: Cambridge University Press, 1996).

ROTHSTEIN, N., *Barbara Johnson's Album of Styles and Fabrics,* (London: Thames & Hudson, 1987).
ROUTH, GUY, *The Origin of Economic Ideas*, (London: Macmillan, 1989).
RUDÉ, GEORGE, *The Crowd in History: A Study of Popular Disturbances in France and England, 1730-1848*, (London: Serif, 2005 edn.).
_____, *Wilkes and Liberty: a social study of 1763 to 1774*. (Oxford: Oxford University Press, 1962).
RULE, JOHN, (ed.) *British Trade Unionism, 1750-1850,* (London: Longman, 1988).
_____, *British Trade Unionism: the formative years*, (London: Longman, 1988).
_____, *The Experience of Labour in Eighteenth-Century Industry,* (London: Croom Helm, 1981).
RUSSELL, C., *Parliaments and English Politics, 1621-1629*, (Oxford: Oxford University Press, 1979).
SANDERSON, E., *Women and Work in Eighteenth-Century Edinburgh*, (London: Palgrave Macmillan, 1996).
SCHUMPETER, JOSEPH A., *Capitalism, Socialism and Democracy*, (New York: Harper & Row, 1942).
_____, *A History of Economic Analysis*, (London: Allen & Unwin, 1954).
SCOTT, J. C., *Domination and the Arts of Resistance: Hidden Transcripts* (New Haven: Yale University Press, 1992 edn.).
_____, *The Moral Economy of the Peasant: rebellion and Subsistence in South-East Asia*, (New Haven: Yale University Press, 1976).
_____, *Weapons of the Weak: Everyday forms of Peasant Resistance,* (New Haven: Yale University Press, 1985).
SEN, A., *Inequality Re-examined*, (Oxford: Oxford University Press, 1992).
_____, *Rationality and Freedom*, (Cambridge, Mass.: Harvard University Press, 2002).
SHARP, B., *In Contempt of all Authority*, (London: Breviary Stuff, 2009).
SHAPIRO, S., *Capital and the Cotton Industry*, (New York, Ithaca: Cornell University Press, 1967).
SHELTON, W. J., *English Hunger and Industrial Disorders: A study of social conflict during the first decade of George III's reign.* (London: Macmillan, 1973).
SKINNER, Q., *Liberty before Liberalism*, (Cambridge: Cambridge University Press, 1998).
SNELL, K. D. M., *Annals of the Labouring Poor,* (Cambridge: Cambridge University Press, 1985).
THOMAS, P. D. G., (ed.), *Parliamentary Diaries of Nathaniel Ryder, 1764-1767*, (Camden Miscellany, Vol. XXIII, Camden, Fourth Series, Vol. 7, Royal Historical Society, 1969).
_____, *John Wilkes: a friend to liberty*. (Oxford: Oxford University Press, 1996).
_____, *George III King and Politicians, 1760-1770*, (Manchester: Manchester University Press, 2002).
THIRSK, J., *The Agrarian History of England and Wales,* ed. Thirsk (Cambridge: Cambridge University Press, 1967).
THOMPSON, E. P., *The Making of the English Working Class* (London: Littlehampton Book Services Ltd., 1963).
_____, *Customs in Common*, (London: Merlin, 1991).
TOYNBEE, ARNOLD, *Lectures on the Industrial Revolution of the Eighteenth Century in England* (London, 1884; reprint. 1920).
TOZER, J. AND LEVITT, S., *The Fabric of Society: A Century of People and Their Clothes 1770-1870,* (Manchester: Laura Ashley, 1983).
TUPLING, J., *Economic History of Rossendale,* (Rossendale, 1927).
VON HAYEK, F. A., *The Constitution of Liberty*, (London: Routledge and Kegan Paul, 1960).

_____, *Law, Legislation and Liberty*, (London: Routledge, 1982 edn.).
WADSWORTH, A. P. AND DE LACY MANN, J., *The Cotton Trade and Industrial Lancashire, 1600-1780*, (Manchester: Manchester University Press, 1965 edn.).
WEBB, S. AND WEBB, B., *English Local Government: The Parish and the County*, (London: Longmans, 1906).
_____, *A History of Trade Unionism,* (London: Longmans, 1894).
WELLS, R., *Wretched Faces; Famine in Wartime England 1793-1801*, (London: Breviary Stuff, 2011).
WESTERFIELD, R. B., *Middlemen in English Business, 1660-1760*, (New Haven, 1915).
WOOD, A., *Riot, Rebellion and Popular Politics in Early Modern England, (Social History in Perspective)*, (Basingstoke and New York: Palgrave Macmillan, 2002).
WRIGHTSON, KEITH, *English Society, 1580-1680*, (London: Routledge, 1982).
_____ AND LEVINE, D., *Poverty and Piety in an English Village, Terling, 1525-1700.* (Oxford: Clarendon Press, 1979).
_____, *Earthly Necessities. Economic Lives in Early Modern Britain, 1470-1750*, (New Haven: Yale University Press, 2000).
YELLING, J. A., *Common Field and Enclosure in England, 1450-1850* (London: Palgrave, 1977),

Appendices

Appendix One

Manchester Constables Accounts APPENDIX No. II

Contributions from the Gentry and Merchants of Manchester and Salford to put down Riots, &c. In 1749.

The following document has a special interest for this volume of Accounts, which contains so many references to food riots and other disturbances in Manchester and the neighbourhood. By it all the principal inhabitants of Manchester and Salford agreed to contribute towards a fund, by means of which those persons who incited and encouraged such riots and disturbances might be punished. The names of the contributors to this fund are appended, and supply a list of the chief inhabitants of the two towns in the middle of the last century. The original document is in my possession, and it has never been printed before.

Whereas great Riots Tumults and disorders have of late arisen and been committed by some evil disposed persons within the Townships of Manchester and Salford to the great disturbance of the peace of the said Townships and to the great terror and danger of the Inhabitants thereof.

And whereas such Offenders are greatly encouraged in their wicked and disorderly practices by the impunity they too often meet with occasioned partly by the poverty and inability of the more immediate Sufferers to prosecute and bring to justice such Offenders and partly by the Connivance if not the encouragement of those whose duty it is to restrain and suppress such disorderly practices

Now Know All men by these presents that for the better and more effectual putting a stop to such Riots Disorders and abuses and for restoring the peace quiet and security of the said Townships and the Inhabitants thereof We whose names are hereunder written being Inhabitants or Landowners of the said Townships of Manchester and Salford do promise and agree to pay upon demand into the hands of Sir Thomas Grey Egerton Baronet Edward Greaves Esquire John Houghton Esquire John Dickenson Robert Livesay Otho Cook Joseph Bancroft Roger Sedgewick and James Massey Gentlemen or some of them tie several and respective sums set over against our names for the better carrying on and supporting such prosecutions as aforesaid in manner hereafter mentioned.

And we do hereby authorize and impower them the said Sir Thomas Grey Egerton Edward Greaves John Houghton John Dickenson Rob' Livesay Otho Cook Joseph Bancroft Roger Sedgewick and James Massey or any five or more of them from time to time as there shall be occasion by with and out of the monys so subscribed or so much thereof as shall be necessary to prosecute criminally as Councel shall advise all such person or persons as they shall from time to time upon enquiry or Information find or have reason to believe have been or hereafter shall be guilty of any Riots Tumults disorders or abuses in prejudice or disturbance of the peace of the said Townships or of the Inhabitants thereof And for that purpose to demand and receive from us the several Subscribers hereto the several sums so respectively subscribed or so much thereof as shall from time to time be necessary for the carrying on and maintaining such prosecutions rateably and proportionally according to the several sums by us respectively subscribed.

In Witness whereof we have hereunto set our hands this third day of May in the year of our Lord one thousand seven hundred and forty nine [1749].
(Signed)

Edward Byrom	15	15	00	John Robinson	10	10	00
John Lees	10	10	00	James Wroe	10	10	00
Rob.Booth	10	10	00	Benj. Makin	10	10	00
Edwd' Greaves	10	10	00	J.Cooke	10	10	00
Rob' Livesey	10	10	00	Henry Hindley	10	10	00
John Dickenson	10	10	00	John Gatliff	10	10	00
James Liptrott	10	10	00	James Chadwick	10	10	00
Otho Cooke	10	10	00	Thomas Taylor	10	10	00
J. Greaves	10	10	00	Edwd Markland	10	10	00
Wm Starkie	10	10	00	Robt Ayrton	10	10	00
Joseph Bancroft	10	10	00	Thos White	10	10	00
Thos Parrott	10	10	00	Richard Hall	10	10	00
Robert Gartside	10	10	00	James Wroe	10	10	00
Jn Fletcher	10	10	00	Saml Goodier	10	10	00
Charles Downes	10	10	00	John Bell	10	10	00
Chas Newdigate	10	10	00	Lawrance Taylor	10	10	00
Edwd Borron & Co	10	10	00	Richard Barton	10	10	00
Tho' Phillips	10	10	00	Joseph Heywood	10	10	00
Ja' Bateman	10	10	00	Sam' Riding	10	10	00
John Broome	10	10	00	Wm Harrison	10	10	00
Jn Hawkswell	10	10	00	James Greatrex	10	10	00
James Blinkhorn	10	10	00	Tho' Barlow	10	10	00
Avery Jebb	10	10	00	Witt Barlow	10	10	00
John Clough	10	10	00	Cha' Bramell Jun	10	10	00
Sam' Edgley	10	10	00	Rob' Barlow	10	10	00
Thos Green	10	10	00	Sam' Hall	10	10	00
Jn Heywood	10	10	00	Rich' Gorton	10	10	00
Thos Boardman	10	10	00	John Upton	10	10	00
Richd Holme	10	10	00	Thos Dunnington	10	10	00
James Clough	10	10	00	Hugh Holt	10	10	00
Thomas Holme	10	10	00	Walker & Taylor	10	10	00
Thos Stott	10	10	00	Jos Boardman	10	10	00
Rand' Woolmer	10	10	00	Richard Assheton	10	10	00
Daniel Woolmer	10	10	00	Adam Bankes	10	10	00
James Edge	10	10	00	Thomas Moss	10	10	00
Goodwin Oates	10	10	00	Wm Shrigley	10	10	00
Jos Bullock	10	10	00	John Clayton	10	10	00
Ra' Woolmer	10	10	00	Tho' Aynscough	10	10	00
Jas Horton	10	10	00	Ashton Lever	10	10	00
John Cotgreave	10	10	00	Wm White	10	10	00
Miles Bower Jun'	10	10	00	William Thackeray	10	10	00
Thos Grey Egerton	10	10	00	John Hardman	10	10	00
Rob' Feilden	10	10	00	Tho' Arrowsmith	10	10	00
R. Sedgwick	10	10	00	Dan' Whittaker & Co	10	10	00
James Marsden	10	10	00	James Massey	10	10	00
Sam' Walker	10	10	00	R. Davenport	10	10	00
Kendrick Price	10	10	00	Jas Berwick	10	10	00

| Josiah Nichols | 10 | 10 | 00 | Jonathan Patten | 10 | 10 | 00 |
| John Wilson | 10 | 10 | 00 | | 10 | 10 | 00 |

Appendix Two

Statement of Messrs. Bramall and Hatfield taken from the *Manchester Mercury* 10/1/1758.

Whereas some persons concerned in the riot on Tuesday the fifteenth day of November last, being the Time the Rioters assembled in *Manchester*, in the county of *Lancaster*, forcibly broke into, pulled down, and demolished the Mills called Travis Mills, near Manchester aforesaid, belonging to us *George Bramall* and *Thomas Hatfield,* and plundering us of the Stock of Grain and Flour therein, it hath been industrially reported, that great Quantities of Acorns, Whiting, Beans dryed, Horse Dung, chopt Straw, Peas and Bones, were found in the said Mills, and several of the said Articles were actually in the Hoppers, in order to have the same ground down with Corn and made into Flour, for the Use and Consumption of the Publick: And several Samples of Whiting or plaister, and chopt Straw, have been handed about the Neighbourhood, with and intent to give Credit to such Reports, and to induce a more favourable Construction of the several Acts of Violence and Felony committed by the said Rioters, during the said Riots. Now in order to prevent the Publick being imposed upon by such Reports, We declare, that they are all utterly false and groundless, and that we never did mix either Whiting, chopt Straw, or any of the Articles before mentioned, with our Corn, at that or any other Time, and Notice, that tho' the like Practices were heretofore publickly laid to our Charge, when our Warehouse in *Manchester* aforesaid, was in the like Manner broke open and plundered, and which we publickly denied by printed advertisements, and called upon the Authors, whoever they might be, to make any Proof that could be brought in Support of such Charges, yet no one single instance ever appeared, or could be made out against us, and as a Charge on this Sort, founded merely on a general Clamour, is not capable of being defended, without some particular Facts being charged upon the persons so generally complained of: We the said George Bramall and Thomas Hatfield protesting out innocency in the premises, do again desire and request, that the Articles wherewith we are generally charged, may be strictly examined into, and that we may be dealt with according to Law. If it shall appear that we have offended in any of the premises aforesaid; and contrary shall upon such Examination appear, we doubt not but Justice will be done to Characters, by a Publick Representation of the Facts, as they shall upon such Examination appear.
BRAMALL AND HATFIELD

Appendix Three

The debate in the local press as to the value of the old statutes against engrossing.

Manchester Mercury 10/1/1758
Notwithstanding our late plentiful Harvest, and what the Parliament has already

done to lower the Price of Grain, by opening up the Ports, and shutting up Distillery: Corn, particularly Wheat, still; continues to advance in our Markets, to the great Hardships, as well as Dissatisfaction of the Poor. Suffer me therefore before the Evil *once again,* becomes intolerable, which, if we do not alter our Way of Thinking, I am of Opinion may be expected; to point out what I take to be the Cause of it.

The Word ENGROSSER is in every Bodies Mouth, and of late has been apply'd to every One that has the least Dealings in Corn, or Meal, from the greatest Merchant, down to the lowest Huckster, it has been apply'd most shamelessly to a Number of Gentlemen in this Town, whom every Body knows, or may know, emply'd many Thousand Pounds last year, in importing Grain from distant Parts of the Kingdom, and who retailed it out to the Poor, with a very great Loss to themselves.

To the ENGROSSERS in this large, wild, and ridiculous Sense, we have attributed hitherto all our Troubles and I Question not, shall do it again, whenever we find the Price of Corn or Meal is advanced: But the Word has been greatly misapply'd, and without some Kinds of Engrossers, as they are call'd, I fear Matters will go from *bad* to worse.

It is extremely well known, by those who know any thing of the Matter, that this county does not in the best of Seasons produce Corn enough to supply its inhabitants. The Town of *Manchester* in particularly, and its Neighbourhood, has always been oblig'd to have a Foreign Supply; by a Foreign Supply, I mean Grain of all Kinds, together with Meal from other Countries, and other parts of the Kingdom; for this we have been oblig'd to the Merchants of *Liverpool* and *Chester*, who have imported it, and to other Dealers who have gone to distant Markets, and have their purchas'd large Quantities, in order to Sell it again at Home.

Upon this Account, if we have had any Time Plentiful Markets, we have been oblig'd to these Gentlemen for them, and if we expect them again, we must be indebted to these Dealers. It cannot be our interests therefore, by fixing an odious Character upon them to deter them from following this, to Us very useful employment.

What must be the Consequence of preventing the Merchants from importing Grain, and these Dealers from fetching it from distant Markets? We must, in such Case, trust entirely our neighbouring Farmers, who at best can but poorly supply Us, and who, it is notorious, always advance the Price of their Commodity, in Proportion to the small Quantity they find at the *Cross,* or the *Meal-House,* where we have one of these Engrossers, therefore I could with we had Ten, since I think it is in their Power alone to remedy the Evil, which we shall soon have too much Cause to complain of.

There is not, that I know of, any large Number of People concern'd in this Business, and few as there are, it seems we are to expect fewer. Since some Merchants have totally declin'd the *Corn-Trade*; and *Dealers* in General (are) now quite discouraged from going to any distant Market, from whence they cannot bring a single Bag of Corn, without the greatest Hazard, as well as *public Odium.*

I am no Friend to Engrossers in the strict legal Sense of the Word; to those who Purchase large Quantities of Grain, and hoard it up, till, having occasion'd a Dearth, they have the fairest Opportunity of Grinding the Face of the Poor, but a Distinction should be made, and those who are mere importers, together with such as have only acquired an honest livelihood, or shall hereafter endeavour to do it, by attending distant Markets, and bringing the Produce to their Town- ought in my Mind to meet with the greatest Encouragement, and not be so Liberally charged with the Character of ENGROSSER as they have been.

One Word more, about the Bakers in Town, and Millers in the Neighbourhood, who must constantly have some kind of a Supply, the One to carry on his Occupation, and the Other to keep his Mill a going, do now most notoriously infest our Markets; and by their Eagerness to purchase, do certainly raise the Price, particularly of Wheat. What is the Reason? Why in Truth they dare not go to any other Market, for fear of having the Character of ENGROSSERS, and consequently they are oblig'd to take up with what little, they can find, at any Rate, in our Own.

The Remedy IS easy, let us moderate our Resentment against Dealers in General; let us not confound the Innocent; with the Guilty; nor be persuaded that no Man can purchase any considerable Cargoes Abroad without being an *Engrosser*. Since this may be done, as I will venture to affirm it was done by the Gentlemen concern'd in the Subscription, with very great Advantage to the Poor, as well as the Town in General; and till some Persons *dare venture* to do it again, I will take the Liberty to pronounce, we can have no reasonable Expectation of seeing *better Times*.

I am, Sirs. Yours,
A BY-STANDER
MANCHESTER
January 4, 1758.
Manchester Mercury 17/1/1758
Sir

A WRITER in your Paper, of January 10, who calls himself a *By-Stander*, having favoured the Public with a Defence of the Dealers in Corn, and learnedly distinguished how far a man may ENGROSS CORN, or at least Attempt to distinguish, and as the *By-Stander* had declared, *He is, No Friend to* Engrossers, *in the strict and legal Sense of the Word*, He will I hope, Pardon me, in saying I am no Friend to them in any Sense of it, and as he has been pleased to shew how far *Engrossers* (as he calls them) are Friends to the Public, that their Virtues may be more fully known, I beg Leave to be indulged with a Corner of your Paper, for me also to *point out I take to be the real cause of it*.

THAT the Hundred of Salford (is) not able to maintain its inhabitants by its own Product is a Truth, and has been equally true for a Hundred Years past.

THAT the Hundred of *Salford* has always been obliged to have a *Foreign* Supply, requires some Explanation. The *By-Stander* by Word *Foreign* Supply, says he means, Grain of all Kinds, *together with Meal from* other Countries, *and other parts of the Kingdom*. Now if by *other Countries*, he means Places out of the Island of Great Britain, it is not true, except in Times of general Scarcity, for in common Years, the neighbouring Hundreds of *Derby, Leyland,* and *Amounderness,* supply *Bolton* Market, which supports the inhabitants of *Bolton, Dean, Bury,* and *Radclysse;* for what little is sent into these Parishes from *Manchester*, I compute is fully answered by what goes from *Bolton* Market to *Rochdale*. The neighbouring Counties of *York* and *Chester*, supply the Markets of Manchester and Rochdale with Grain of all Kinds, and are in moderate Years well able to do so is a known Fact.

THAT the neighbouring Counties are able to support us in moderate Years is proved by this, that within these four Years no Merchant, or Tradesman in Manchester, was concerned in the Corn Trade, yet was the Markets well supply'd, nor was any Dealers in Corn seen in our Markets, but common Farmers, Millers, Sweaters, whose Purses were too shallow for them to become Monopolists, tho' their Hearts were never so well inclin'd.

THAT the Crops have been very bad in the neighbouring Counties of late Years is confessed; that there was a Necessity for us to be supply'd from other parts of the Kingdom is allowed; that the Man who either from distant parts of the Kingdom, or from Foreign Lands, brought Corn into this Market, and Sold with a reasonable Profit only, is a Friend to his Country; is agreed to; but if any Man bought with a View *only to make Gain*, and not sold not his Corn but at the very utmost Farthing People would give, he is entitled to no more Thanks than are due to a Hangman for ridding the World of a Knave. The more there are even this Way concerned in the Corn Trade, will indeed conduce to lower the Price, tho' as it lessens the Profit, it can't be supposed to please such Dealers, whatsoever Pleasure may accrue to the Consumers.

THAT several Mills are now in the Hands of People in this town at Present, is a Fact. But pray are four Years let elapsed since the Mills of *Bury, Travis, Clayton, Heaton, Holm*, &c. were leased to Bakers of this Town, and Tradesmen (as) their Partners, and yet we have neither better nor Bread than we had in former Times, when no Baker had a Mill, nor no Miller a Bake-house. I remember when very little Meal or Flour was sold in the Market; Oats and Wheat were bought by the Consumer, and sent to neighbouring Mills. The *Chester* People, first introduced the selling all Kinds of Corn ground, and the *Yorkshire* Dealers followed their Example. This did not improve our Bread in Wholesomeness, tho' it did in Colour; and what has been said of our worthy Townsmen's Improvement in the Trade may be seen in Messrs. *Bramall* and *Hadfield's* Advertisement in your Paper, tho' with what justice I cannot say.

THAT many of the Gentlemen who subscribed to buy Corn for Use of the Poor, were actuated by Principles of Charity and Generosity, (Principles this Town has been deservedly allow'd to have) is believed. Yet such was either the Wickedness or Stupidity of the Managers, that tho' the *By-Stander* confesses the neighbouring Farmers, calculate the Price by what they see left at the Meal house at the End of the Market, yet did these People buy every *Saturday* all that was left at the Meal house all that was left of the Subscription Money, and by this very Means raised the Market several Shillings a Load, so that the intention of the Charity was defeated, whether intentionally or ignorantly. God Knows.

THAT the Subscribers very properly ordered Grain to be bought in distant Parts and brought to this Market, is with Pleasure acknowledged, and with the warmest Gratitude; yet whatever wisely a design may be formed, it is necessary to have able Managers. I could wish this had been as well managed, as it was wisely designed; but I fear the country has had little Good, and the Subscribers will have great Loss. However, I hope worthy Subscribers will unite their Endeavours to remove our present Sufferings, and not be discouraged.

THAT there has been a general Out-cry against *Engrossers* is certain, but I solemnly believe that there could not be all this Smoke without some Fire at the Bottom, nor the Country so generally believe there were People concerned in Engrossing Corn, if no such thing were done. We have heard of Rooms in this Town unable to support the Weight of Corn without propping; and to what Use keeping it up could be, without it was to hinder it coming to Market I cannot conceive: Perhaps the *By-Stander* can inform us, as he seems better acquainted with the Mysteries of Engrossing than he cares to tell; and indeed to have little Objection to any Part of Engrossment but the Punishment. I must here observe, how unfortunate this Defender of this worthless Race of Man is in his assumed Character that of a By-Stander, thereby saying, he neither sells Corn nor eats it; but if he does either, he is certainly not a mere By-Stander; as he does not chose to rank himself either in the Class of Buyers, or Sellers, I have a right to rank him one, and he must excuse me in believing him to belong to the latter, and I am more confirmed in it, as he says, more are leaving off the Trade. I am apt to believe he is one of the Number, and that Shame has done that, that his Confidence left short, and he is now willing to make as good an Excuse as he can for his Misdeeds: 'Tis never too late to repent', and if he added to his Forbearance of Engrossing, (he must Pardon my using the Word, as he wishes for more Engrossers,) The Forbearance of his Pen, it would not prejudice either the Engrossers or his own Credit. As he has *ventured to affirm the Subscription was carried on with very great Advantage to the Poor, as well as the To*wn in general, the Town will not hesitate at once to pronounce what Degree of Credit this *By-Stander* deserves: And as to his last *Liberty he has taken to pronounce*, that till some Persons *dare-venture* to do it again, there is no reasonable *Expectation of seeing better Times.* If this Gentleman will condescend to give us the Names of these worthy Persons, we will signify to him, whether we rank them in the Number of those who oppress or no, and till we know who they are, 'tis impossible for us to know who he Means'; for I will take it upon me to say, for there is not one Man in Town, that will with Pleasure see his Name in the advertised list of ENGROSSERS; and whether those, whom the *By-Standee* plead? For, ought to come into the List or no, is not to be determined till we know them. The Pubic will neither condemn without a hearing, nor acquit, and why the By-Standers Clients expect to be acquitted on his bare Word, is not readily to be apprehended, and that before Accusation for ought we know.

THE By-Stander says, we have been obliged to some Gentlemen, who are Dealers, for our plentiful Markets. Tis an odd Assertion: For some Time all we have been kept by them is Hand to Mouth: Not ten Loads, at an Average in the Meal-house, or Cross. I hope he will indulge us with a List of these Friends of their Country, who have so plentifully furnished our Markets. For if he goes back some Years when we had plentiful Markets, there was not then a Gentleman in Town concerned in the Trade, (I had almost said not one but would have been ashamed of being concerned in it) and how they come not to be ashamed of it now, let the *By-Stander* tell, and their Conduct in it has been such it resounds not to their Credit, whosoever it may have done to their Profit.

Now give me Leave in Turn to propose a Way to mend the Times. Let all those who have lent these apparent ENGROSSERS Money, call it out of their Hands. That will at once make a plentiful Market; for they must dispose of their Stock to pay their Credit, and their own Purses will never be of Bulk sufficient to raise a Market, or fall it Six-pence a Load.

AND next apply to Parliament for a Law to licence Badgers, &c. in this County, as they are in most others.

AND LASTLY, to apply to the same Authority that no Miller may be a Baker, and no Baker a Miller a Dealer in Corn, and no Dealer in Corn to have more Corn in his Possession than is sufficient for a Month's Sale, the Quantum to be ascertained by his Books, and a Justice of the Peace, on Complaint to have the Power to inspect them. No Corn to be bought out of a public Market, or by Way of Sample, unless to a Neighbour for his own Use who lives nearer the Seller than the next Market Town. With a proper Provision for Importers of Corn to sell not exceeding Bushels to one Man, but Leave to import what

Quantity thy please, but this leave is already taken Care of by the Legislature. And would our Land Owners in the Corn Countries but agree to it, to take away that Ban to Home Manufacturers, the *Bounty* on Exportation of Corn; a Law whose fatal Consequences we now feel, and have severely felt; and this sure is the Time, if it ever will be done, to obtain a Repeal; and (to add still more common Good to the Trading Interest of these Nations, and the Ruin of the *French* Commerce) a Repeal of the Law against Importation of *Irish* Cattle, which GOD in his infinite Mercy grant. I am, Sir, your humble Servant, P. W.

Index

Andrews, Thomas, 54-7
Anglicans, 185
Annual Register, 104, 173
Anti-Corn Law League, 147, 178, 196
apprenticeship, 80, 89, 91, 95-6, 103, 107, 129, 133, 139, 141, 147
Arkwright, Richard, 176, 178
Ashton under Lyne, 120, 121, 132, 151, 153
Assize of Bread, 25, 50, 128, 155, 156
Auditor, 194

Bamford, Samuel, 225
Barns, Elias, 33
Barnstaple, 114
Bayley, James, 124, 152-3
Berlin, Isaiah, 220
Bewdley, 117
Bill of Rights, 197, 223
Birtles, Sara, 148, 150
Black Death, 180
Blackburn, 77, 89, 91, 212
Blackstone, William, 189
Board of Trade, 18
Bohstedt, John, 72
Bolton, 30, 77, 83, 89, 91
Book of Orders, 108, 128, 151, 155
Booth, Alan, 117
Bourn, David, 33
Bourn, Thomas, 34
Bowker, Holden, 34
box clubs, 45, 52, 94, 95, 127, 128, 129, 131, 133, 135-8, 140, 223
Bradford upon Avon, 52, 55
Bradshaw, John, 152, 153
Bramall, George, 116, 119, 121-2, 123, 151
Brenner, Thomas, 146
Brewer, John, 16, 18
Brickdale, John, 111
Bridgwater, 114
Bristol, 110-11, 174
Burdett, Sir Francis, 190
Burgh, James, 197
Burgoyne, John, 208, 209, 210, 211, 212, 214, 215
Burke, Edmond, 67-8, 104, 179, 190
Bushaway, Bob, 75
Bute, Marquess of, 189, 193, 194, 205, 206, 215

Camden, Earl, 28
Cannon, John, 16
capitalism, 12, 29-30, 42, 50, 65, 69, 74, 97-8, 119, 141, 146, 155, 166, 169, 220
  individualism, 19, 21, 65, 218, 224-5
  proto-capitalists, 78, 84
  industrial capitalism, 79, 93, 105, 218, 219, 225
  raising of capital, 30-31, 217
Catholicism, 107, 208
Chester, 140
child labour, 33, 101, 147 n.11
Cider Tax (1763), 149, 215
Church of England, 191
Churchill, Winston, 187

class consciousness, 46, 50, 51, 72, 74, 75, 104, 113, 128, 141, 178, 180, 197, 213, 214, 224
clientage, 79, 89, 93, 103
Clitheroe, 77
Colley, Linda, 187
Collier, John, 119-21, 156, 195, 223
Colloden, Battle of, 58
combinations, 102, 127, 129, 131, 134-6, 137, 140, 171, 220
Committee of Trade, 18
common law, 6, 25, 45, 64, 68-71, 100, 107, 120, 123, 137, 141, 148, 149, 155-6
commonweal, 65, 71, 139, 155, 186, 220
Connecticut, 11
Connway, Henry Seymour, 159, 164
corn trade, 24, 69, 77-85
corruption, 28, 37, 185, 186, 191, 213, 225
cotton trade, 13, 40-1, 76, 79, 88, 101, 127, 176
Crompton, Samuel, 178
Crouzet, François, 29
customary rights/practices, 45, 64, 70, 84, 87, 89, 101-3, 129, 133, 134, 141, 144, 146, 155, 166, 171, 175, 176, 178, 218, 220, 224, 225, 228

Dallaway, William, 163, 164
Dashwood, Sir Francis, 193
Defoe, Daniel, 221
Davenant, Charles, 18
Delaware, 11
Derby, Earl of, 202, 203, 205, 207, 215
Devon, 52, 95
division of labour, 175
domestic industry, 80

East Anglia, 52, 81
East India Company, 28, 33, 39-42, 77, 81, 174, 206
Eccles, 128, 136
election riots, 108
Elizabethan Statutes, 45, 106, 137, 138, 139, 172, 219
embezzlement, 90, 131
employer/worker relationship, 46, 51, 54, 103, 128, 219, 220, 221, 222, 228
enclosure, 144-7, 150-1
enclosure riots, 149-50
engrossing, 25, 65, 68, 108, 120, 122, 123, 124, 130, 141, 147, 151, 154, 156, 158, 165, 167, 217
English Liberty, 180
Enlightenment, 218
entrepôt system, 18, 42, 188, 217

factory system, 32, 33, 147, 177, 183
famine, 168
Felix Farley's Bristol Journal, 161
Freeborn Englishmen, 47, 70, 186
friendly societies, 45, 95
food riots, 108-25, 135, 143, 151-3, 161-2, 165, 173, 191
  women, 116-18

257

Forest of Dean, 148-9
   free miners, 149
forestalling, 14, 25, 65, 68, 108, 122, 123, 124, 141, 147, 151, 156, 158, 162, 165, 167, 217
Foster, Sir Michael, 138-9, 220, 223
Fox, Charles James, 190, 215
France, 11, 12, 17, 25, 26, 217
French Revolution, 46, 179, 186, 225
Frome, 52, 112, 114
fustian masters, 77, 82, 83, 88, 179-80

Gales, Joseph, 186-7
Gentleman's Magazine, 25, 27, 58, 104, 114, 118, 140, 153, 173, 193, 196, 207
George III, 17, 18, 38, 49, 66, 164, 183, 185, 188, 191, 193, 205
Georgia, 11
Germany, 9
Glasgow, 174
Glorious Revolution (1688), 11, 17, 181, 195, 198
Gloucester Journal, 55, 58, 87
gomasthas, 43
Gordon Riots, 191
Granville, Earl, 27
Grenville, George, 190
Grotius, Hugo, 19
Guest, Richard, 88
guild system, 90-1, 146, 217

Hammond, John, 144
Hammond, Barbara, 144
Hampden, John, 185, 186, 187
Hanseatic League, 77
Hardwick, Earl of, 28, 161-2
Hargreaves, James, 176, 213
Harrington, Lord, 13
Hawthorn, Joseph, 121
Hay, Douglas, 141
Hexham, 171
Hont, Isvan, 67, 68
Hull, 174
Hulton, William, 209, 210
Hume, David, 21

Ignatieff, Michael, 67, 68
immigration, 97
imperialism, 35-44
Importation Acts, 174
India, 39, 42-3, 228
Isle of Wight, 114

Jacobitism, 185, 191, 192, 202, 204, 206, 208
James II, 185, 198
journeymen, 95
Junius, 223-4

Kay, John, 33
Kendall, 140
Kenyon, Lord Chief Justice, 141
King, Peter, 72, 73
Kingswood Colliers, 110-11, 148-9

Knight, John, 50-1, 225
Kuhn, T. S., 63

labour, price of, 19, 40
laissez faire, 9, 20, 178
Lancashire, 15, 20
   cotton weavers, 15
Lancaster, 90, 91, 140, 192
   Duchy of, 201, 203, 207, 210, 215
Landau, Norma, 75
Langford, Paul, 38, 182
Levant Company, 77
Levine, David, 73-4
Lewis, Sir Arthur, 28
Liverpool, 90, 91, 113, 140, 171, 172, 174, 183
   Corporation of, 114
Lloyd, George, 152, 153
Locke, John, 21, 185
London, 27, 30
London Correspondence Society, 187
Luddism, 177, 212-13
Lyttleton, W. H., 162

Magna Carta, 180, 223
Malthus, Thomas, 145, 168
Manchester, 13, 16, 91, 113, 140, 153, 156, 171, 183, 185, 206, 213, 226
   cotton merchants, 30, 31, 77, 101, 177, 183, 222, 223
Manchester Act (1736), 83, 85, 88
Manchester Committee for the Protection of Trade, 178
Manchester Committee of Working Men 50
Manchester Grammar School, 88, 118
Manchester Grand Jury, 136, 177
Manchester Guardian, 141
Manchester Mercury, 115, 116, 130, 152, 153, 171, 173, 177
Manchester School, 147, 153, 169
Mandeville, Bernard, 19
manhood suffrage, 214, 216
Mansfield, Lord Chief Justice, 28, 134-8, 140, 141, 173, 179, 223, 224
Marx, Karl, 49, 106
Massie, Joseph, 22-24, 25, 66, 217
Maryland, 11
Massachusetts, 11
Melksham, 52, 53, 55
mercantilism, 9-10, 12, 17, 18, 19, 20, 24, 25, 28, 39-40, 51, 57, 63, 79, 81, 87, 108, 127, 155, 157, 179, 188, 192, 202, 217, 218-19
Merchant Adventurers, 77
middle class, 29, 72, 185, 198, 224, 225
Middlesex, 190
militia, 171-2
monetary policy, 24
moral economy, 21, 46, 56, 61, 63-76, 100, 106, 107, 120, 122-3, 127-42
Mun, Thomas, 10

national debt, 35-6, 39, 60, 88, 191-2, 206
nationalism, 186-7

Navigation Acts, 9, 40
Neesom, Jeanette, 148
New Hampshire, 11
new masters, 94, 96, 101, 102
New York, 11
Newcastle, Duke of, 159-60, 189, 206
Newcastle-under-Lyme, 117
Norman Conquest, 223
Norman Yoke, 120, 180, 186
North Britain, 38, 193
North Carolina, 11
Northampton, 33, 34

O'Brien, Bronterre, 64
O'Gorman, Frank, 105, 226, 227
Ogden, J., 176-7, 213
Old Poor Law, 148, 168
Oldham, 120, 128, 130, 151, 153
Oswaldtwistle, 212, 213
outworker system, 89, 92

Padstow, 114
Paine, Thomas, 186, 225
Palatinate of Chester, 14
Parliament, 14, 16, 183
paternalism, 64, 112
patriotism, 186-8
Paul, Lewis, 33, 175
Percival, Thomas, 130, 131-3, 135, 141, 171 n.1, 173, 183, 223
Pelham, Henry, 188
Pelham-Holles, Thomas, 22
Pennsylvania, 11
Petty, William, 10
  The Treatise on Taxes and Contributions, 10
Pitt, William, 28, 35-6, 37, 158, 159, 160, 163, 178, 185, 188, 193. 194, 203, 206, 217
Pocock, J. G. A., 227
political economy, 63, 71, 74, 168
Pollard, Sidney, 29
poor relief, 26, 58, 72, 75, 102, 150, 206
Poor Law Amendment Act (1834), 168-9, 196
populism, 36, 214, 215
Preston, 90, 91, 179, 182
  election of 1768, 183-5, 196, 197, 198, 201-16, 225, 226
Preston Guild Company, 90
private enterprise, 20
proletarianisation, 145, 147
protectionism, 27, 45, 57, 81, 101, 134
Protestantism, 107, 208
Prowse, Thomas, 112, 114
Pufendorf, Samuel, 19
putting-out system, 32

Randall, Adrian, 71-3, 74, 75
regrating, 25, 65, 68, 108, 120, 122, 123, 124, 141, 147, 151, 154, 156, 158, 165, 167, 217
Reform Act (1832), 190, 214, 226
Reform Act (1867), 214
Reformation, 107

Rhode Island, 11
Ricardo, David, 23
Riot Act, 52, 108, 156
Rochdale, 91, 153
Rockingham, Marquis of, 157, 159, 185, 193, 206
Rogers, Nick, 75
Rollison, David, 75
Rossendale, 153
Rostow, W. W., 29
Rough Hey, 83, 84
rough music, 124
Royal Navy, 10, 11, 157
Royton Hall, 128, 130
Rusholme, 136

Saddleworth, 120, 121, 151, 153
St. Monday, 94, 196
St. James Chronicle, 193
St. Paul, 21
Salford, 128, 136
Salisbury, 117
Scott, James, 47-8, 73
Septennial Act (1715), 204
Seven Years War, 14, 35-44, 60, 66, 89, 115, 127, 128, 143, 171
Sharp, Buchanan, 70
Sheffield, 186-7
Sheffield Register, 187
Sheffield Patriot, 187
Sherborne, 160
shoemakers, 140
Shudehill, 121, 151, 152-3
Skinner, Quentin, 221
slave trade, 84, 180-1
Smith, Adam, 9, 12, 20, 21, 25, 63, 67, 69, 113, 141, 155, 167, 222
  Wealth of Nations, 9, 12, 20, 27, 67, 68, 141, 147, 222
Smith, Charles, 24-25, 69, 158
  Two Tracts on the Corn Trade, 24
Smith-Stanley, James, 207
Snell, Keith, 75
Society of Arts, 175
South Carolina, 11
South Sea Bubble, 28
Spain, 12
Spectator, 19
spinning jenny, 174, 177, 212, 213
Spitalfields, 101, 195
Stamp Act (1765), 193
Standish, Sir Frank, 209, 210, 212
Statute of Artificers (1562), 45
Stockport, 89, 118
Strange, Lord, 203, 207-8, 209, 210, 211, 214-15
Stuart, Charles Edward, 58, 105, 114, 185, 204-5
Stuart Statutes, 106, 148
strikes, 114, 128, 132, 138, 139, 140, 195, 206
sugar trade, 84
Sydney, Algernon, 185, 186, 187

259

system of trade, 18

tariffs, 24, 219
Taunton, 95, 117
Taylor, Charles, 221
Temple, William, 54-7, 58, 119, 221, 222
Thirteen Colonies of North America, 11, 36, 171, 190, 191, 195, 228
Thompson, E. P., 12, 14, 46, 48-9, 50, 51, 65, 67, 71, 73, 109, 113, 116, 118, 124, 128, 147, 149, 167, 178, 223
   Customs in Common, 12-13, 15, 65, 66, 68, 70, 112, 117, 150, 151
   The Making of the English Working Class, 46, 75
Tiverton, 52
Tories, 17, 66, 183, 185, 188, 189, 191, 192, 198, 204, 205, 207, 210, 211, 215
Touchet, Paul. 34
Touchet, Samuel, 34
trade societies, 98-9
tramping, 95
Trowbridge. 52, 53, 55
truck payment system, 14, 55
Tucker, Josiah, 54, 57, 93, 96-8, 103-4, 119, 221, 222

undertakers, 95-6
United States of America, 9
usury, 30

wage labourers, 94
Wahrman, Dror, 75
Walpole, Horatio, 185, 188, 198, 202, 203, 215, 217

Warren, Sir George, 192
weavers' society (North-West), 100
Webb, Beatrice, 131
Webb, Sydney, 131
West Riding, 77, 81
Westmorland, 144
Whalley, 77
wheel shuttle, 177
Whigs, 17, 18, 37, 48, 51, 105, 130, 180, 181, 185, 188, 189, 191, 193, 198, 202, 205, 207, 210, 211, 215, 225, 226
Whiston, James, 18
Whitney, Eli, 85
Whitworth's Manchester Advertiser and Weekly Magazine, 128
Wigan, 89, 90, 140
Wilkes, John, 37-8, 164, 182, 186, 190, 193, 197, 214
Williamson's Liverpool Advertiser, 173
Wimbledon Common, 195
Winstanley, Gerard, 185
Wood, Andy, 46-7, 48, 51, 70
woollen industry, 52, 59, 60, 80-1, 87, 104
Woollen Manufacture Act (1726), 53
Worcester, 117
worker discipline, 98, 175
workhouses, 33
Wrightson, Keith, 70
Wrigley, Henry, 79
Wyatt, John, 33

Virginia, 11

Yonge, Sir William, 189

Also from
BREVIARY STUFF PUBLICATIONS

Ralph Anstis, Warren James and the Dean Forest Riots, *The Disturbances of 1831*
£14.00 • 242pp *paperback* • 191x235mm • ISBN 978-0-9564827-7-8

John E. Archer, 'By a Flash and a Scare', *Arson, Animal Maiming, and Poaching in East Anglia 1815-1870*
£17.00 • 206pp *paperback* • 191x235mm • ISBN 978-0-9564827-1-6

Victor Bailey, Charles Booth's Policemen, *Crime, Police and Community in Jack-the-Ripper's London*
£17.00 • 162pp *paperback* • *2 colour and 8 b/w images* • 140x216mm • ISBN 978-0-9564827-6-1

Victor Bailey, Order and Disorder in Modern Britain, *Essays on Riot, Crime, Policing and Punishment*
£15.00 • 214pp *paperback* • *5 b/w images* • 191x235mm • ISBN 978-0-9570005-5-1

Roger Ball, Dave Beckwith, Steve Hunt, Mike Richardson, Strikers, Hobblers, Conchies & Reds: *A Radical History of Bristol, 1880-1939*
£18.50 • 366pp *paperback* • *101 b/w images* • 156x234mm • ISBN 978-0-9929466-0-9

Alastair Bonnett & Keith Armstrong (eds.), Thomas Spence: The Poor Man's Revolutionary
£15.00 • 214pp *paperback* • 156x234mm • ISBN 978-0-9570005-9-9

John Belchem, 'Orator' Hunt, *Henry Hunt and English Working Class Radicalism*
£17.50 • 248pp *paperback* • 191x235mm • ISBN 978-0-9564827-8-5

Bob Bushaway, By Rite, *Custom, Ceremony and Community in England 1700-1880*
£16.00 • 206pp *paperback* • 191x235mm • ISBN 978-0-9564827-6-1

Malcolm Chase, The People's Farm, *English Radical Agrarianism 1775-1840*
£12.00 • 212pp *paperback* • 152x229mm • ISBN 978-0-9564827-5-4

Malcolm Chase, Early Trade Unionism, *Fraternity, Skill and the Politics of Labour*
£17.00 • 248pp *paperback* • 191x235mm • ISBN 978-0-9570005-2-0

Nigel Costley, West Country Rebels
£20.00 • 220pp *full colour illustrated paperback* • 216x216mm • ISBN 978-0-9570005-4-4

James Epstein, The Lion of Freedom, *Feargus O'Connor and the Chartist Movement, 1832-1842*
£17.00 • 296pp *paperback* • 156x234mm • ISBN 978-0-9929466-1-6

James Epstein, Radical Expression, *Political Language, Ritual, and Symbol in England, 1790-1850*
£15.00 • 220pp *paperback* • 156x234mm • ISBN 978-0-9929466-2-3

Ariel Hessayon (ed.), The Refiner's Fire, *The Collected Works of TheaurauJohn Tany*
£25.00 • 552pp *paperback* • 156x234mm • ISBN 978-0-9570005-7-5

Catherine Howe, Halifax 1842, *A Year of Crisis*
£14.50 • 202pp *paperback* • 156x234mm • ISBN 978-0-9570005-8-2

Barry Reay, The Last Rising of the Agricultural Labourers, *Rural Life and Protest in Nineteenth-Century England*
£15.00 • 192pp *paperback* • 191x235mm • ISBN 978-0-9564827-2-3

Buchanan Sharp, In Contempt of All Authority, *Rural Artisans and Riot in the West of England, 1586-1660*
£15.00 • 204pp *paperback* • 191x235mm • ISBN 978-0-9564827-0-9

Dorothy Thompson, The Chartists, *Popular Politics in the Industrial Revolution*
£17.00 • 280pp *paperback* • 191x235mm • ISBN 978-0-9570005-3-7

Also from
BREVIARY STUFF PUBLICATIONS

E. P. Thompson, Whigs and Hunters, *The Origin of the Black Act*
£16.00 • 278pp *paperback* • 156x234mm • ISBN 978-0-9570005-2-0
£30.00 • 278pp *hardback* • 156x234mm • ISBN 978-0-9929466-6-1

David Walsh, Making Angels in Marble, *The Conservatives, the Early Industrial Working Class and Attempts at Political Incorporation*
£15.00 • 268pp *paperback* • 191x235mm • ISBN 978-0-9570005-0-6

Roger Wells, Insurrection, *The British Experience 1795-1803*
£22.00 • 372pp *paperback* • 191x235mm • ISBN 978-0-9564827-3-0

Roger Wells, Wretched Faces, *Famine in Wartime England 1793-1801*
£23.00 • 412pp *paperback* • 191x235mm • ISBN 978-0-9564827-4-7

www.ingramcontent.com/pod-product-compliance
Lightning Source LLC
Chambersburg PA
CBHW031424150426
43191CB00006B/388